Juvenile Delinquency

WHY DO YOUTHS COMMIT CRIME?

Cliff Roberson
Washburn University

Elena Azaola
Center for Advanced Studies and Research in Social Anthropology

ROWMAN & LITTLEFIELD
Lanham • Boulder • New York • London

Acquisitions Editor: Becca Rohde Beuer
Sales and Marketing Inquiries: textbooks@rowman.com

Credits and acknowledgments for material borrowed from other sources, and reproduced with permission, appear on the appropriate pages within the text.

Published by Rowman & Littlefield
An imprint of The Rowman & Littlefield Publishing Group, Inc.
4501 Forbes Boulevard, Suite 200, Lanham, Maryland 20706
www.rowman.com

6 Tinworth Street, London SE11 5AL, United Kingdom

British Library Cataloguing in Publication Information Available

Library of Congress Control Number: 2020944335

ISBN 978-1-5381-5194-5 (cloth)
ISBN 978-1-5381-3189-3 (pbk.)
ISBN 978-1-5381-3190-9 (electronic)

BRIEF CONTENTS

CONTENTS

TABLES

PREFACE

In developing this text, we have sought to answer one overriding question: Why do juveniles commit crime? Unfortunately, although we present numerous theories on criminal behavior, there isn't a single theory that completely answers the question. Each one, however, has some kernel of truth or in some way explains one or more of the reasons that youths commit crime.

When reading the text, please keep in mind the role of the family, the process of socialization, and how society reacts to criminal misconduct as factors in ascertaining why youths commit crime. Also keep in mind that criminal misconduct is a very broad subject and describes many different types of human actions. To some extent, labeling all violations of criminal law by youths as a single group of actions, i.e., juvenile delinquency, may be part of the problem as we seek to identify causation factors. There is a sea of difference between the young female who shoplifts lipstick and the youth who is involved in a homicide.

We have organized the criminological theories into certain arbitrary groups. Some may disagree with our classifications and argue that certain theories fit better in different categories. We recommend that the reader pay attention to the substance of the theory rather than the category that it has been assigned. We have included material on juvenile justice in the text to help the reader understand the procedures involved in the juvenile justice system, and to understand that in some ways, our system seems to encourage youths to commit secondary deviance rather than preventing future deviant behaviors.

The text is divided into four parts—Part I: Juvenile Delinquency Overview; Part II: Delinquency Causation Theories; Part III: Delinquency Influences; and Part IV: Juvenile Justice System. This structure was designed to make the broad subject more understandable to the reader and not as an absolute division of parts of the text. The reader will note that there are overlaps in certain chapters because of the complexity of the subject matter.

While the authors are listed as the sole developers of the text, many individuals contributed in various ways to this book. We extend special thanks to our managing editor, Kathryn Knigge; copy editor, Melissa Hayes; and production manager, Alden Perkins. Last but not least, a special thanks to the reviewers who provided valuable assistance in the production of this text.

Any suggestions or corrections may be submitted to cliff.roberson@washburn.edu.

Elena Azaola
Cliff Roberson

ABOUT THE AUTHORS

Cliff Roberson is former managing editor of the journal *Police Practice & Research*, an international journal that is distributed in over fifty countries. In addition, he is professor emeritus at Washburn University and a retired professor of criminology at California State University, Fresno. His previous academic experience includes professor of criminology and director of the Justice Center, California State University, Fresno; professor of criminal justice and dean of arts and sciences at the University of Houston, Victoria; associate vice president for academic affairs, Arkansas Tech University; and director of programs for the National College of District Attorneys, University of Houston School of Law. Cliff's nonacademic legal experience includes Chief, Trial and Legal Services Section, Office of State Counsel for Offenders, Texas Board of Criminal Justice; private legal practice; judge pro tem in the California courts; trial and defense counsel and military judge as a marine judge advocate; and director of the Military Law Branch, Headquarters, US Marine Corps. Cliff is admitted to practice before the US Supreme Court, federal courts in California and Texas, the Supreme Court of Texas, and the Supreme Court of California.

Elena Azaola is professor at the Center for Advanced Studies and Research in Social Anthropology located in Mexico City. She received a PhD in anthropology and did postgraduate study on deviant behavior at Columbia University. She is also a psychoanalyst. Dr. Azaola served as an advisor with the National Commission of Human Rights and a council member at the Federal District Commission of Human Rights. She coordinated the European Commission project for street children in Mexico (1999–2003). She has published more than 150 journal articles and numerous books on human behavior, crime, and human rights. Her research on the commercial sexual exploitation of children was sponsored by the United Nations Children Fund. She co-coordinated a National Report on Violence sponsored by the World Health Organization. She was the board chair of the Institute for Security and Democracy, which created the first center for police accreditation in Mexico and won the MacArthur Foundation Award for Creative and Effective Institutions. Presently Dr. Azaola is working on United Nations–funded research on developing "Standards for Mexican Prisons."

PART I

Juvenile Delinquency Overview

CHAPTER 1

Introduction to the Study of Juvenile Delinquency

CHAPTER OBJECTIVES

After studying this chapter, the reader should be able to:

- Understand the early treatment of children.
- Discuss who constitutes a juvenile.
- Explain how crime is measured.
- Explain the types of juvenile misconduct.
- Discuss the goals of the juvenile justice system.
- Explain the factors that influence juvenile delinquency.

Overview of Juvenile Delinquency

The US Constitution does not guarantee a separate court system for juveniles. In fact, the Constitution does not mention juveniles. As noted later in the text, the juvenile justice system in the United States did not develop until many years after the adoption of the US Constitution and the ratification of the Bill of Rights.

While a separate system is not protected by the Constitution, all fifty US states and the US federal jurisdictions, including the District of Columbia, have created separate justice systems for juveniles. The US state juvenile justice systems were created by state constitutions and statutes. The juvenile court system in the federal jurisdictions was established by federal statutes.

A typical juvenile justice system is the one in the District of Columbia. The Superior Court of the District of Columbia's Family Court Social Services Division (FCSSD) is the District's juvenile probation agency. FCSSD is responsible for serving and supervising juveniles involved in the "front end" of the District's juvenile justice system. As noted in the *Family Guide to the District of Columbia Juvenile Justice System*, one of the goals of delinquency cases in the District of

Columbia Family Court is "to place a premium on the rehabilitation of children with the goal of creating productive citizens and to recognize that rehabilitation of children is inextricably connected to the well-being and strength of their families."[1] The guide states:

> This goal recognizes that you (referring to the parent) know your child better than anyone else does. Therefore, you are in the best position to support your child in the juvenile justice system. Your involvement is a critical part of ensuring your child's successful completion of his or her court involvement.[2]

Prior to the twentieth century, juveniles involved in the justice system were treated as miniature and immature adults. The next time you attend an art museum, look at eighteenth- and nineteenth-century paintings by famous artists. The paintings depict children as miniature adults. Prior to the twentieth century it appears that juveniles in the criminal justice system were handled as miniature adults and not as developing humans.

Before the late 1800s, young people who were believed to have committed criminal misconduct were handled in the same criminal courts as adults. During that period, juveniles were considered young criminals and not juvenile delinquents. Even today, being labeled a delinquent can mean the youth committed a variety of misbehavior which varies according to jurisdiction and places.

For criminal law purposes, the definition of *delinquency* refers to criminal misconduct without regard to the age of the offender. The term *juvenile delinquent* refers to a person who has committed a criminal act and who is defined by the jurisdiction as a juvenile. For example, the State of New York Family Code states:[3]

> Juvenile delinquent; a person over seven and less than eighteen years of age, who, having committed an act that would constitute a crime, or a violation, where such violation is alleged to have occurred in the same transaction or occurrence of the alleged criminal act, if committed by an adult, (a) is not criminally responsible for such conduct by reason of infancy, or (b) is the defendant in an action ordered removed from a criminal court to the family court pursuant to article seven hundred twenty-five of the criminal procedure law.

Juvenile delinquency as an educational discipline developed mainly at the beginning of the twentieth century. For an overview of crimes committed by juveniles in one year, see table 1.1.

TABLE 1.1 Excerpts from FBI Crime in the United States Report, 2017

Crimes in U.S. in 2017	Number for all ages	Offenders under 15 years of age	Offenders under 18 years of age
Murder	9,177	58	685
Rape	17,765	1,135	2,989
Robbery	296,387	2,284	14,703
Motor vehicle theft	69,888	2,983	12,486
Drug violations	1,233,598	10,813	72,334
Larceny-theft	728,141	25,846	91,715

Source: FBI, *Uniform Crime Report* (Washington, DC: GPO, 2018), Table 36, available at https://ucr.fbi.gov/crime-in-the-u.s/2017/crime-in-the-u.s.-2017/tables/table-36 (accessed February 8, 2019).

Defining Adolescence and Lack of a Uniform Definition

In the United States there is no uniform definition of who constitutes a juvenile when the issue involves delinquency. The age at which children become criminally responsible for their conduct varies by jurisdiction. Each jurisdiction has statutes that establish when a minor may be held criminally liable for his or her criminal misconduct. For most of recorded history, there was no such status as "child." Prior to the late 1800s, children were considered as property. The life expectancy of children prior to the nineteenth century was short, and the infant mortality rate frequently exceeded 50 percent. Many researchers contend that because of the high mortality rate, as a defense mechanism, parents did not develop a loving and caring attitude toward the young.

The general rule, which was developed under English common law, is that children under the age of seven years are not held criminally responsible for their conduct.[4] This is based on the concept that children under the age of seven years are not mentally capable of forming the necessary intent to commit criminal misconduct. There is in most jurisdictions the presumption that juveniles between the ages of seven and fourteen years old do not have the required mental capacity. In most jurisdictions, evidence may be introduced by the prosecutor to establish that a juvenile between the ages of seven and fourteen is sufficiently mature to be held criminally responsible for his or her actions.[5]

As a rule, children fourteen years and older are presumed to have the mental capacity to commit criminal offenses. In most jurisdictions, they are under the jurisdiction of juvenile or family court rather than adult criminal court. In determining if a delinquent is a juvenile, the courts use the chronological age, not the mental age. For example, a person with a mental capacity of a minor is not considered a juvenile if he or she is above the chronological age limit determined by the jurisdiction.[6] Photo 1.1 depicts an eight-year-old boy and his family discussing the boy's case, where he was accused of stealing a bicycle.

Types of Juvenile Misconduct

The President's Commission on Law Enforcement and Administration of Justice noted that many individuals think of crime (including juvenile delinquency) as a very narrow range of behavior. It is not. The Commission pointed out that an enormous variety of acts make up the "crime problem." Crime is not just a tough teenager snatching a lady's purse. It is a professional thief stealing cars "on order." It is a well-heeled loan shark taking over a previously legitimate business for organized crime. It is a polite young man who suddenly and inexplicably murders his family. It is a corporate executive conspiring with competitors to keep prices high. No single theory, no single generalization can explain the vast range of behavior called crime.[7] While the Commission was referring mostly to adult criminal conduct, that description applies equally to juvenile delinquency.

The two basic types of juvenile misconduct incidents are status offenses and acts that would be considered as a crime regardless of the age of the offender. Status offenses involve misconduct that would generally not be considered as an offense if the offender was an adult. Status offenses include truancy, curfew violations, running away from home, failure to attend school, underage drinking of alcohol beverages, and similar offenses. The second type of juvenile delinquency cases are those that involve the commission of a criminal offense without regard to the age of the offender, e.g., theft, rape, murder, and assaults and battery.[8]

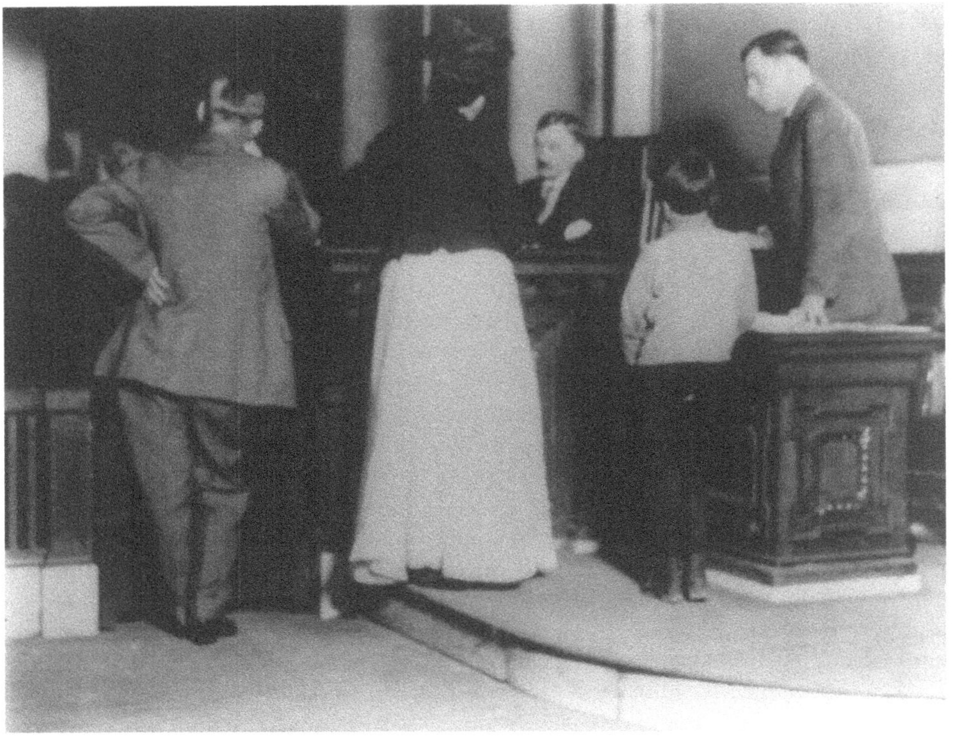

PHOTO 1.1 An eight-year-old boy has been charged with stealing a bicycle. The case is being discussed on Thursday May 5, 1910, in a St. Louis, Missouri, courtroom. (Photo courtesy of US Library of Congress Prints and Photographs Division, Washington, DC, LC-DIG-nclc-04645)

During the 1960s and 1970s, there was a movement toward deinstitutionalizing status offenses. This meant that juveniles who committed status offenses were diverted from the juvenile justice system to public or private agencies outside the juvenile court's jurisdiction. The county or district attorney was given the authority to divert an offender, and this decision was made before a petition was filed.[9]

As noted earlier, prior to the development of juvenile justice systems, juvenile delinquents were treated as miniature criminals. It was not unusual to impose harsh punishments on young delinquents. Box 1.1 discusses the execution of young criminals.

Juvenile Arrests

A 2019 *National Report Series Bulletin* notes that arrests of juveniles in the United States peaked in 1996 at almost 2.7 million juveniles.[10] By 2016, the number of juveniles arrested was 68 percent less than the 1996 peak. The arrests of adults also declined during the same period, but only by 20 percent. The highlights of the report include the following findings:

- Juvenile arrest rates for violent crimes, such as robbery and aggravated assault, have declined in the last decades.
- Conversely, juvenile arrest rates for murder have increased since 2012.
- Juvenile arrest rates for property crimes have declined in recent years.
- By 2016, juvenile arrest rates for larceny-theft, burglary, and arson were at their lowest levels since at least 1980.
- Following six years of decline, the juvenile arrest rate for drug law violations in 2016 was at its lowest level since the early 1990s.

BOX 1.1 **Execution of Children**

Considered to be the youngest person ever executed in Great Britain, Michael Hammond was just seven years old when he and his sister were hanged in 1708. The youngest girl to be executed in the United States is believed to be Hannah Ocuish, a twelve-year-old member of the Pequot tribe who was hanged in 1786 for murdering another child. She was considered to have been mentally impaired.

One of the youngest persons executed in the United States was George Junius Stinney Jr. He was fourteen years old on June 16, 1944, when he was executed. George was an African-American teenager convicted of the murder of two white girls in 1944 in Alcolu, South Carolina. Stinney's trial lasted about three hours. The defense presented no witnesses, no physical evidence, and did not file an appeal. It took a jury of twelve white men just ten minutes to find him guilty. George was so small that he had to be seated on a phone book to be executed by electric chair.

In 2014, a South Carolina circuit court judge vacated George's conviction, holding that he had failed to receive a fair trial. The judge noted that by not putting the State's case to the test—not cross-examining witnesses, not giving a closing argument, in essence, putting up no defense whatsoever—George was never afforded effective counsel, and as a result, his Sixth Amendment rights were violated.

Source: Campbell Robertson, "South Carolina Judge Vacates Conviction of George Stinney in 1944 Execution," *New York Times*, December 18, 2014, B-2.

- Male and female juvenile arrest rates have declined in the last ten years. The relative declines have been greater for males than for females across most offenses.
- Juvenile arrest rates have declined for all racial groups since 2007, and the relative declines have been greater for white youth than for black youth, for all but drug offenses.
- In 2016, law enforcement agencies in the United States made more than 856,000 arrests of persons younger than the age of eighteen.
- Juvenile property crime arrests declined for the eighth straight year.

Box 1.2 displays the changes in arrests for juveniles and adults from 2007 through 2016.

Measuring Delinquency

The science of measuring delinquency is not a precise science. It is at best a guess of the extent of delinquent misconduct that has been, or is, occurring. For the most part, the only delinquent acts that are measured are those that are either reported to law enforcement or reported by victims in surveys. When a juvenile steals a purse and no one reports it, the act is not counted as a delinquent act because no official report has been made. This unreported and unknown criminal activity is often referred to as the "dark side of crime." In juvenile justice it is frequently considered as "unmeasured delinquency."

The US Department of Justice (DOJ) is responsible for the official statistical programs in the United States to measure the magnitude, nature, and impact of crime in the nation. Prior to February 2020, the two major programs were the

BOX 1.2 **Percent Change in Arrests from 2007 to 2016**

Most serious offense	Juvenile	Adult
Violent crime	–48%	–8%
Murder	–36	–10
Robbery	–44	–17
Aggravated assault	–51	–6
Property Crime Index	–56	–2
Burglary	–61	–21
Larceny-theft	–55	5
Motor vehicle theft	–47	–21
Simple assault	–47	–11
Weapons law violations	–55	–5
Drug abuse violations	–50	–10

Source: Charles Puzzanchera, Juvenile Justice Statistics: National Report Series Bulletin, Juvenile Arrest, 2016 (Washington, DC: US Department of Justice, December 2018).

Uniform Crime Reporting (UCR) Program and the National Crime Victimization Survey (NCVS).[11]

National Incident-Based Reporting System

In February 2020, the UCRs were replaced by the National Incident-Based Reporting System (NIBRS) throughout the country. The NIBRS annual reports provide more data than the UCRs. NIBRS is designed to provide detailed information about each criminal incident in twenty-two broad categories of offenses.

NIBRS data show the diversity and complexity of incident-based data and offer more characteristics and associations in crime than has been previously published through the UCR system. Tables included in NIBRS include the following:

- Individual agency data for twenty-four offense categories;
- Victim, offender, and arrestee data;
- Location and time of day of incidents;
- Weapon data for select offenses;
- Drug, alcohol, and gang involvement in offenses;
- Attempted versus completed offenses;
- Clearances by incidents; and
- Relationship of victims to offenders.

National Crime Victimization Survey

The Bureau of Justice Statistics (BJS) is responsible for conducting and maintaining the National Crime Victimization Survey (NCVS) data collection. The NCVS, started in 1973, is designed to provide a detailed picture of crime incidents, victims, and trends. The survey collects detailed information on the frequency and nature of the crimes of rape, sexual assault, personal robbery, aggravated and simple assault, household burglary, theft, and motor vehicle theft. It does not measure homicide or commercial crimes such as burglaries of stores.

Once a year, US Census Bureau personnel interview household members in a nationally representative sample of approximately 87,000 households. Approximately 150,000 interviews of persons age twelve or older are conducted annually. Households stay in the sample for three years. New households are rotated into the sample on an ongoing basis.

The NCVS collects information on crimes suffered by individuals and households, whether or not those crimes were reported to law enforcement. It estimates the proportion of each crime type reported to law enforcement, and summarizes the reasons that victims give for reporting or not reporting the crime to law enforcement.

The survey provides information about victims (age, sex, race, ethnicity, marital status, income, and educational level), offenders (sex, race, approximate age, and victim–offender relationship), and the crimes (time and place of occurrence, use of weapons, nature of injury, and economic consequences). The survey questions include the experiences of victims with the criminal justice system, self-protective measures used by victims, and possible substance abuse by offenders. Supplements are added periodically to the survey to obtain more-detailed information on certain topics, such as school crime.

Goals of the Juvenile Justice System

According to the Juvenile Law Center, the juvenile justice system has grown and changed substantially since 1899. Originally, the court process was informal—often nothing more than a conversation between the youth and the judge—and defendants lacked legal representation. Proceedings were conducted behind closed doors with little public or community awareness of how the juvenile court operated or what happened to the children who appeared before it. Rather than confine young people in jails with adults, the early juvenile courts created a probation system and separate rehabilitation and treatment facilities to provide minors with supervision, guidance, and education.[12]

Present-day juvenile justice systems still maintain rehabilitation as their primary goal. Many law enforcement officials contend that the juvenile justice philosophy should be redirected from saving the youth to protecting the public. As discussed in chapter 3, the current goals take a positivist viewpoint on rehabilitation of the delinquent, whereas the adult criminal justice systems' goals are generally to protect the public. Many professionals believe that goals of the juvenile system should mirror goals of the adult criminal justice system.

Some juvenile justice professionals also contend that the juvenile system should be more punitive in the disposition of youthful offenders. They contend that we are handling the delinquents with "kid gloves." Another issue that has hampered the juvenile system is the concept that juvenile offenders who commit violent crimes should be automatically transferred to the adult criminal courts. Both issues will continue to be debated, both today and tomorrow, and there are no easy answers. Box 1.3 contains excerpts from a national report on juvenile offenders and victims.

Factors that Influence Juvenile Behaviors

What causes juvenile delinquency? This is a question frequently asked researchers who study delinquency. The problem with this question is that there is no single answer. We do not ask a medical doctor what causes illness because we understand that there are many different types of illness and many different causes. A similar situation exists with juvenile delinquency. This section includes a listing and brief

BOX 1.3 **Excerpts from "Juvenile Offenders and Victims: 2014 National Report"**

The juvenile justice system must react to the law-violating behaviors of youth in a manner that not only protects the community and holds youth accountable but also enhances youths' ability to live productively and responsibly in the community. The system must also intervene in the lives of abused and neglected children who lack safe and nurturing environments.

To respond to these complex issues, juvenile justice practitioners, policymakers, and the public must have access to useful and accurate information about the system and the youth the system serves. At times, the information needed is not available, or, when it does exist, it is often too scattered or inaccessible to be useful.

Source: Melissa Sickmund and Charles Puzzanchera, editors, "Juvenile Offenders and Victims: 2014 National Report" (Washington, DC: National Center for Juvenile Justice, December 2014).

discussions on some of the factors involved in the causation process. More-detailed discussion on the major issues and the theories on juvenile crime causation will be covered in later chapters.

The authors believe that it is rare that a juvenile develops into adulthood without being involved at one time or another in acts of criminal misconduct. Think about it; did you ever take a drink of an alcoholic beverage while you were underage? Or, did you pick up and take an item that belonged to someone else? Photo 1.2 is a picture of three young boys who were forced to work long hours by their family as a punishment for their misconduct.

Exposure to Violence

Research indicates that when children are exposed to a traumatic event, their responses vary. Many children suffer from one or more of the following problems: they become fearful, have trouble sleeping, suffer from a lack of appetite, or have trouble concentrating on their school studies. Other reactions include complaints of headaches, stomachaches, and similar symptoms. It is not unusual that some juveniles learn from exposure to violence to resolve their own conflicts in a violent manner. In some cases, the children repeat the violence they have experienced and perpetuate a cycle of violence that may continue for future generations.

Children who are regularly exposed to violence often react like children who are victims of violence. The exposure to violence may even cause post-traumatic stress disorder (PTSD) as it does with children who are victims of violent incidents. The exposed children may suffer from the emotional and physical aftershocks for years after the exposure. A frequent by-product of the exposure is aggressive, violent, or self-destructive behavior. As noted in box 1.4, children are frequently exposed to violence.

Teenaged Brains

Neuroscientists Kristina Caudie and B. J. Casey opine that teens have more trouble controlling their impulses in emotionally charged situations. According to the

PHOTO 1.2 Three young boys, ages seven, ten, and thirteen years old, were discovered selling newspapers after midnight on a street in Washington, DC, in April 1912. (Photo courtesy of US Library of Congress Prints and Photographs Division, Washington, DC, LC-DIG-nclc-03767)

BOX 1.4 Children Exposed to Violence

A 2009 US Department of Justice study indicated that more than 60 percent of the children surveyed were exposed to violence within the past year either directly or indirectly. Children's exposure to violence, whether as victims or witnesses, is often associated with long-term physical, psychological, and emotional harm. Children exposed to violence are also at a higher risk of engaging in criminal behavior later in life and becoming part of a cycle of violence. Additional findings of the study include:

- Children exposed to violence are more likely to abuse drugs and alcohol; suffer from depression, anxiety, and post-traumatic disorders; fail or have difficulty in school; and become delinquent and engage in criminal behavior.
- Sixty percent of American children were exposed to violence, crime, or abuse in their homes, schools, and communities.
- Children are more likely to be exposed to violence and crime than adults.
- Almost one in ten American children saw one family member assault another family member, and more than 25 percent had been exposed to family violence during their life.
- A child's exposure to one type of violence increases the likelihood that the child will be exposed to other types of violence, and exposed multiple times.

Source: David Finkelhor, Heather Turner, Richard Ormrod, Sherry Hamby, and Kristen Kracke, "Children's Exposure to Violence: A Comprehensive National Survey," *Bulletin* (Washington, DC: US Department of Justice, Office of Justice Programs, Office of Juvenile Justice and Delinquency Prevention, October 2009).

researchers, teenagers aren't known for making extraordinarily good decisions, and they have a tendency to do impulsive and risky things. The scientists conclude that many teenagers have difficulty with self-control and react more impulsively in threatening situations.[13]

Abused Children

Researcher Margaret Cutajar states that a study of 2,700 abused children indicates that abused children are five times more likely to commit crimes than children who were not abused.[14] The study conducted in Western Australia noted that up to 30 percent of children experience childhood sexual abuse, and those children are more likely to be victims of crime or to commit crime themselves.

According to researchers Janet Currie and Erdal Tekin, child abuse and child neglect approximately doubles the probability of those juveniles engaging in crime.[15] The researchers noted that boys are at a greater risk than girls in terms of increased propensity to commit crime. They also concluded that the probability of engaging in crime increases with the experience of multiple types of maltreatment.

Poverty–Crime Connection

Millions of children are caught up in the US juvenile justice system, a principal feeder into the criminal courts before they turn eighteen years old. There appears to be no income barrier that a family can cross to eliminate the risk of their child turning into a juvenile delinquent. Many rich families have teens that get involved in crimes and are convicted. But research and numerous studies have strongly indicated that there is a link between juvenile delinquency and poverty. Those studies should be taken with caution. Children from rich families are often treated better and are less likely to be referred to the formal system than children from non-rich families.

Law enforcement officers, based on years of experience, contend that teens immersed in poverty are more likely to turn toward crime. A research study by Cambridge University concluded that children coming from poor families are more than twice as likely to commit criminal behavior when compared to kids from rich or well-to-do families.[16] It should also be noted that law enforcement officers are more likely to turn the rich kid over to his or her parents than they are the poor kid.

As noted by many researchers, poverty is not the sole contributing factor to juvenile delinquency. There are numerous reasons behind juveniles' decisions to commit crime. For example, children who live in poverty are less likely to be involved in hobbies or sports programs than children living in more affluent neighborhoods. In addition, children who live in poverty are less likely to attend good schools and are more likely to drop out of school. Poorer children are also more likely to spend time roaming the streets of their communities, which provides them with more opportunities to commit crime. Poor children who are arrested for committing crimes are more likely to be convicted of and incarcerated for their criminal misconduct.[17]

Family Structure

In most households, the parents are the most important role models in the juvenile's life. The views and behaviors of the parents may have either good or bad influences on the juvenile. The role of the family is discussed in more depth in chapter 6.

Generally, it is accepted that juveniles are less likely to commit delinquent behaviors if they have a good relationship with their parents and can talk openly with them. The families that have established clear and sensible rules and have encouraged the juveniles to follow the rules should reduce the probability that the juveniles will engage in criminal misconduct. Research appears to establish that juveniles are less likely to offend if their parents have an interest in the juveniles' school progress and encourage them to be successful in school.

Juveniles from broken homes or homes where only one parent is present have a higher probability of being involved in the criminal justice system. A similar probability exists when the juveniles are in a family where both parents are involved in other activities and do not have the time to provide guidance to the juveniles.

Social Norms

A lack of appropriate social norms is frequently used to explain delinquent behavior. Norms are rules that govern our behavior in a given situation and at a given time. Norms may also be defined as socially accepted and expected conduct in society.[18] Sociologists often refer to norms as the "rules of behavior," and advocate that norms have great power to motivate human behavior.

Norms may be proscriptive, prescriptive, formal, or informal. *Proscriptive* norms are ones that forbid certain behaviors. A penal statute or code, for example, is a formal proscriptive norm. *Prescriptive* norms are norms that tell us what we can or should do. *Formal* norms are norms that are officially imposed on us by a higher authority, such as the state. Formal norms are generally written and often codified as in a penal code. *Informal* norms are generally created out of face-to-face interaction with others. Informal norms are generally not written down and are generally considered as the appropriate conduct that a person should follow in society. Not cutting in a line ahead of others is an example of an informal norm.

A classic example of an informal norm is the Hawthorne or Western Electric studies that occurred during the time period of the 1920s through 1932 at the Western Electric Company. In the studies, the researchers studied a group of fourteen employees whose duties were involved in the assembly of switches for use in telephone switchboards. The company established a normal day's output of 6,600 wiring connections per day (formal norm). The employees felt that a normal day's output should be only 6,000 connections per day. If an employee became a rate buster, other employees would become hostile, criticize, ostracize, and even use violence to keep the rate buster in line. Management's answer to the situation was to fire the rate buster because the company felt that if the employees were unhappy and had low morale, then production would suffer.[19]

Overview of Delinquency Theories

Multiple theories have been developed to explain the causes of juvenile delinquency. Some of the theories are sophisticated and others are quite basic. The theories may generally be divided into two general themes. The general theme of *free choice* assumes that human behavior is the product of free choice, and the individual chooses to commit crime. The *positivist* theme holds that human behavior is not the result of free choice, and that juvenile crime is determined by internal and external influences. The juvenile does not choose between right and wrong but his or her conduct is determined by biological, psychological, or sociological influences.[20]

The classical school is based on the proposition that individuals have "free will," and any criminal behavior they commit is because they choose to commit the crime. The founders of the classical school are Cesare Beccaria and Jeremy Bentham. The positivist theorists take the opposite approach. They take the position that individuals do not have free will. According to them, human behavior is determined by internal or external differences, or by both. Accordingly, a criminal act is not the result of a freewill discussion, but rather is a symptom of some underlying problem. Both concepts are discussed in more depth in later chapters.

Theories may also be divided into three categories: psychological, sociological, and biological.

The two major *psychological* theories are psychoanalytic theory, which is based on Sigmund Freud's concepts, and social learning theories. The psychoanalytic theory is based on Freud's concepts of id, ego, and superego. According to Freud, these three components combine to create the complex behavior of human beings. Freud contended that the id is the set of uncoordinated instinctual trends; the superego plays the critical and moralizing role; and the ego is the organized, realistic part that mediates between the desires of the id and the superego. Since the id is considered as the drive for immediate gratification, it is frequently used to explain the crimes of shoplifting, burglary, and stealing a car for joyriding. The ego acts according to the reality principle. Accordingly, it seeks to please the id's drive in realistic ways that will benefit in the long term rather than bring grief. The superego is considered as observable by examining how one views themselves as guilty, bad, shameful, and weak, and therefore, feels compelled to do certain things.

The *sociological* theories of juvenile delinquency include the strain, labeling, and social control theories. The sociological theories are the most popular criminological theories in the United States.[21] The theories are based on the belief that society influences a person to become a criminal. The theories explain crime in terms of the social environment, including the family, school, peer group, workplace, community, and society. They differ in that they focus on somewhat different features of the social environment and offer different accounts of why the social environment causes crime.[22]

The *biological* theories are based on the concept that certain individuals are predisposed to commit crime because the juvenile has inherited biochemical and/or genetic factors. Biological theorists contend that the delinquent is biologically different, and this difference results in the higher probability that the juvenile will commit criminal misconduct. Accordingly, the theorists contend that physiological and environmental factors interact in a manner that can render crime more or less likely. This perspective most often supports an indirect relationship between biology and crime: Genes, hormones, diet, and environmental factors such as stress can alter biochemistry, which in turn can shape perception, mood, disposition, and behavior. This relationship is complex, with physiology and the environment both affecting each other.

Biological and psychological approaches to criminal behavior are frequently grouped under trait theories. They attempt to answer the question: Why do people respond differently to identical influences? For example, why do some people give in to peer pressure while others don't, or why some people, when faced with "strain," will commit crime, whereas others continue to practice conformity?[23]

Crime and Age

According to Australian researcher Kelly Richards, responding to juvenile offending is a unique policy and practice challenge. While a substantial proportion of crime is perpetrated by juveniles, Richards points out that most juveniles will "grow out" of offending and adopt law-abiding lifestyles as they mature. It is argued that a range of factors, including juveniles' lack of maturity, propensity to take risks, and susceptibility to peer influence, as well as intellectual disability, mental illness, and victimization, increase juveniles' risks of contact with the criminal justice system. These factors, combined with juveniles' unique capacity to be rehabilitated, can require intensive and often expensive interventions by the juvenile justice system.

According to Richards, it is widely accepted that crime is committed disproportionately by young people, and persons aged fifteen to nineteen are more likely to be processed by police for the commission of a crime than are members of any other population group.[24]

Richards notes that research on adolescent brain development demonstrates that the second decade of life is a period of rapid change, particularly in the areas of the brain associated with response inhibition, the calibration of risks and rewards, and the regulation of emotions. Two key findings have emerged from this body of research that highlight differences between juvenile and adult offenders:

- First, these changes often occur before juveniles develop competence in decision-making. This disjuncture, it has been argued, is akin to "starting an engine without yet having a skilled driver behind the wheel."
- Second, in contrast with the widely held belief that adolescents feel invincible, recent research indicates that young people do understand, and indeed sometimes overestimate, risks to themselves.

Richards noted that adolescents engage in riskier behavior than adults—such as drug and alcohol use, unsafe sexual activity, dangerous driving, and/or delinquent behavior—*despite* understanding the risks involved.

Age–Crime Curve

The age–crime curve discussed in this chapter is related to the pathways to desistance discussed in chapter 2. The prevalence of delinquency tends to increase from late childhood, peak in the teenage years (from fifteen to nineteen), and then decline in the early twenties.[25] This bell-shaped age trend, called the age–crime curve, is universal in studies involving Western countries' populations.[26] Specific versions of the curve vary in significant ways. The curve for violence tends to peak later than that for property crimes. Girls peak earlier than boys. The curve is higher and wider for young males (especially minorities) growing up in the most disadvantaged neighborhoods.

Continuity of offending from the juvenile into the adult years is higher for people who start offending at an early age, chronic delinquents, and violent offenders. A Pittsburgh youth study found that 52 to 57 percent of juvenile delinquents continue to offend up to age twenty-five. This number dropped by two-thirds—to 16 to 19 percent—in the next five years. However, there are large individual differences at play. Juveniles who start offending before the age of twelve are more likely to continue offending into early adulthood.

Not all offense types have the same persistence. One study showed that drug dealing and possession of weapons had the highest likelihood of duration and persistence into early adulthood, while gang membership had a shorter duration. Marijuana use had the longest duration, two to four times longer than theft and violence.

The median age of termination of offending was highest for drug trafficking (age 21.6). Minor offenses, such as shoplifting and vandalism, usually stop before age eighteen. The annual frequency of offending is higher for nonviolent crimes than for violence. The frequency involving violent crimes usually peaks between the ages of seventeen to nineteen, and remains stable over time only for a small number of offenders.

Studies agree that 40 to 60 percent of juvenile delinquents stop offending by early adulthood. For those who do persist, the transition from adolescence to adulthood is a period of increasing severity of offenses and an increase in lethal violence. Most of the violence is directed at victims of the same age, and the age period of sixteen to twenty-four is a high-risk time for violent victimization. Many young people who offend at ages eighteen to twenty, which brings them into the adult justice system, would have been likely to desist naturally in the next few years. Justice system processing may make them worse, rather than better. Developmental studies of late adolescence and early adulthood do not support the notion that there is any naturally occurring break in the prevalence of offending at age eighteen.

Special Categories of Offenders

The average age of onset is earliest for gang membership (average age: 15.9), followed by marijuana use (16.5), drug dealing (17.0), gun carrying (17.3), and hard drug use (17.5). Although drug dealing is rare, drug use is widespread among offenders. Criminals report higher rates of substance use, and substance users report higher rates of offending compared with nonusers. Of all offenses, dealing drugs and illegally carrying guns have the highest persistence from adolescence into adulthood.

Joining a gang increases the rate of offending, but gang involvement is often transient. One study found that most youths who join gangs do so at very early ages, typically between eleven and fifteen; ages fourteen to sixteen are the peak for gang involvement. In contrast, most homicides are single events committed in the nineteen- to twenty-four-year-old age range. However, gang killings take place mostly during adolescence.

The studies looked at risk and protective factors. There is strong evidence that, for males, getting married and holding a stable job foster desistance from offending, and that unstructured activities with peers are associated with persistence.

The sparse research on adult-onset offending provides little information about why some people who were not delinquent during adolescence become adult offenders. However, there is evidence that some factors inhibit offending during adolescence but not during adulthood. One study found that characteristics such as nervousness, anxiousness, social isolation, and social inhibition were associated with adult-onset offending.

Female Delinquency

In one assault report, two sisters, ages thirteen and fourteen, followed another girl home from a charter school in the city of New York, punched her in the face, clawed at her hair, smashed her head into a deli window, and kicked her again and again as she lay on the sidewalk. The allegation was that someone had called someone else a lesbian. The juveniles involved were all honor roll students. In the past several decades, there has been a profound change in the involvement of female delinquents within the juvenile justice system. As noted in figure 1.1, young females account for a growing proportion of the juvenile population involved in the juvenile justice system.

Some criminologists suggest that more-aggressive law enforcement efforts are the cause for the increasing number of females involved in the juvenile justice system. If this were a valid reason, wouldn't there also be an increase in male juveniles arrested? Some professionals suggest that the role of females in society is changing, and that more girls are committing crimes that juvenile males were previously known for, such as assaults. In 2003, according to federal statistics, about one-fourth of juveniles arrested for aggravated assaults were girls. In 1993, only about 10 percent of juveniles arrested for aggravated assaults were females.

Even the findings of a 1993 study by Eileen Poe-Yamagata and Jeffrey A. Butts noted support for the popular contention that female delinquency has increased relatively more than male delinquency in recent years. The authors noted that as far

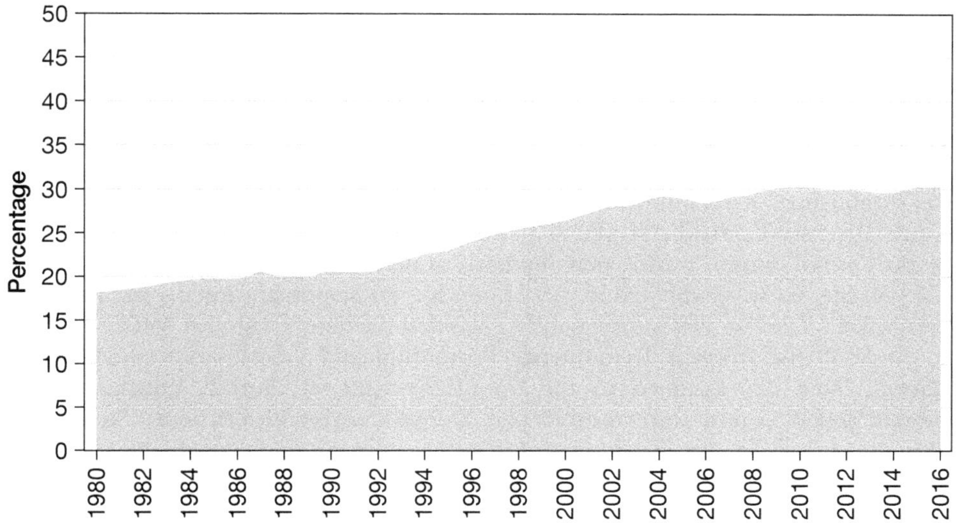

FIG. 1.1 Percentage of Girls among Juveniles in the Justice System. (*Source*: M. Sickmund, M. Sladky, T. J. Kang, and C. Puzzanchera, "Easy Access to the Census of Juveniles in Residential Placement," Washington, DC: Office of Juvenile Justice and Delinquency Prevention, 2015.)

back as 1993, juvenile crime was still predominantly a male problem. In the 1990s, more than three-quarters of juvenile arrests and juvenile court delinquency cases involved males.[27]

Francine Sherman and Annie Balck attribute the gender gap to the juvenile justice system's long-standing "protective and paternalistic" approach to dealing with delinquent girls. According to them, the system tends to detain girls because they're seen as needing protection. It's a strategy that is ill-suited to the personal histories of trauma, physical violence, and poverty that lead many girls into bad behavior. The researchers note that even when the system acknowledges these factors, there are limited options available beyond traditional arrests and detention.[28]

Overview of Federal Action on Juvenile Justice

Juvenile justice, like adult criminal justice, is primarily a state function except in jurisdictions like the District of Columbia, where there is no state jurisdiction. The federal government does provide limited oversight and control of juvenile justice using federal grants and other federal funding. In this section, we will examine federal intervention in the states' juvenile justice systems. (Note: In some cases, the federal action is limited to only those juvenile courts under federal jurisdiction, e.g., the District of Columbia.)[29]

Foundation of Federal Involvement

The Children's Bureau was created by a 1912 Act of Congress. The Act directed the Bureau "to investigate and report . . . on all matters pertaining to the welfare of children and child life among all classes of our people and shall especially investigate the questions of infant mortality, the birth rate, orphanages, juvenile courts, desertion, dangerous occupations, accidents, and diseases of children, employment, [and] legislation affecting children in the several States and Territories."

In 1948, the Interdepartmental Committee on Children and Youth was established. Its purpose was to develop closer relationships among federal agencies concerned with children and youth.

The Midcentury White House Conference on Children and Youth met in Washington, DC, in 1950. The conference considered methods to strengthen juvenile courts and the development of juvenile police services, and studied prevention and treatment services of social agencies, police, courts, institutions, and aftercare agencies.

In 1961 the President's Committee on Juvenile Delinquency and Youth Crime was established. It recommended the enactment of the Juvenile Delinquency and Youth Offenses Control Act of 1961. This Act had a three-year authorization for the purpose of demonstrating new methods of delinquency prevention and control. In 1964, the Act was extended to carry out a special demonstration project in Washington, DC. The Act was subsequently extended through fiscal year 1967.

In 1968 the Juvenile Delinquency Prevention and Control Act of 1968 was enacted. This Act assigned to the US Department of Health, Education, and Welfare (HEW)—now known as the US Department of Health and Human Services—responsibility for developing a national approach to the problem of juvenile delinquency. States were to prepare and implement comprehensive juvenile delinquency plans and, upon approval, receive federal funds to carry out prevention, rehabilitation, training, and research programs.

The Omnibus Crime Control and Safe Streets Act was enacted in 1968. This Act provided block grants to states in order to improve and strengthen law enforcement. While not specifically mentioning juvenile delinquency, this Act's broad crime control and prevention mandate authorized funding of delinquency control and prevention programs.

In 1971 the Juvenile Delinquency Prevention and Control Act was extended for one year. The Interdepartmental Council to Coordinate All Federal Juvenile Delinquency Programs was established by this Act. In 1971 the Omnibus Crime Control and Safe Streets Act was amended, and the definition of law enforcement was changed to specifically include programs related to prevention, control, and reduction of juvenile delinquency. Grants were authorized for community-based juvenile delinquency prevention programming and correctional programs.

The Juvenile Delinquency Prevention Act was enacted in 1972. This Act was an extension of the Juvenile Delinquency Prevention and Control Act of 1971. Under the Act, HEW was to fund preventive programs outside the juvenile justice system. Efforts to combat delinquency within the juvenile justice system were to be assisted through the Omnibus Crime Control and Safe Streets Act by the Law Enforcement Assistance Administration.

In 1973 the Omnibus Crime Control and Safe Streets Act was amended. The Act now specifically required that there be a juvenile delinquency component to any comprehensive state plan for the improvement of law enforcement and criminal justice.

Juvenile Justice and Delinquency Prevention Act of 1974

The US Congress in 1974 enacted the Juvenile Justice and Delinquency Prevention Act. This Act provided, for the first time, a unified national program to deal with juvenile delinquency prevention and control within the context of the total law enforcement and criminal justice effort. The Act has four significant themes:

1. The deinstitutionalization of status offenders and non-offenders. The Act requires that youth who are runaways, truants, or curfew violators cannot be detained in juvenile detention facilities or adult jails.
2. The "Sight and Sound" separation protection disallows contact between juvenile and adult offenders. If juveniles are put in an adult jail or lockup under

the limited circumstances the law allows for, they must be separated from adult inmates.

3. "Jail Removal" disallows the placement of youth in adult jails and lockups except under very limited circumstances.
4. The Disproportionate Minority Confinement (DMC) provision requires states to address the issue of overrepresentation of youths of color and minorities in the justice system.

Key provisions of the Juvenile Justice and Delinquency Prevention Act of 1974:

- Replaced Juvenile Delinquency Prevention and Control Act of 1968.
- Authorized for three years with budget authority of $350 million.
- Provided for discretionary and block grants.
- Created an Office of Juvenile Justice and Delinquency Prevention (OJJDP), with the Runaway Youth Program (Title III) to be administered by HEW.
- Created a National Advisory Committee, a Federal Coordinating Council, a National Institute for Juvenile Justice and Delinquency Prevention; provided formula grants to States based on population under eighteen; and provided discretionary funds to support youth programs developed by public and private youth-serving agencies.
- Mandated that States participating in Act:
  - Remove status offenders within two years of enactment from secure detention and correctional facilities;
  - Not place juveniles in any institutions where they would have regular contact with adults convicted of criminal charges.

In 1977, the Act was reauthorized for three years with the inclusion of programs for learning-disabled children who become involved in the justice system. In 1980, the Act was reauthorized for four years and was amended to include the following:

- Provided for removal of juveniles from adult jails and lockups after five years from date of enactment of amendments.
- Included a new focus on juveniles who have committed serious crimes and on chronic offenders.
- Established the OJJDP as a separate administrative entity within the new Office of Justice Assistance, Research, and Statistics (OJARS) structure.

In 1984 Congress reauthorized the Act for four years, and amended it to:

- Provide for new program for Missing and Exploited Children (Title IV).
- Emphasize programs which strengthen families.
- Extend deadline for full compliance with the jail removal requirement (to after December 8, 1988).
- Abolish the National Advisory Committee.
- Place constraints on the use of Special Emphasis funds, and make changes in application process for Special Emphasis and Institute funds (competition and peer review).
- Prohibit use of funds for biomedical or behavior-control experimentation or research.

In 1988, the Act was reauthorized and an Indian Tribe set-aside was established. In 1990 the Victims of Child Abuse Act was enacted, which provided for:

- Court Appointed Special Advocate Program.
- Child abuse training programs for judicial personnel and prosecutors.
- Treatment for juvenile offenders who are victims of child abuse or neglect.

In 1992, the Act was reauthorized for four years, and amended to include:

- Coordinating council restructured to include nine federal agency members and nine citizen practitioner members.
- Formula grants minimum allocation increased to a maximum base allocation of $600,000 per state and $100,000 per territory.
- State planning and administration allocation increased to 10 percent with requirement for at least one full-time Juvenile Justice Specialist.
- State plan to include focus on educational needs, gender-specific services, rural prevention and treatment, mental health services, and establishment of a comprehensive and coordinated system of services.
- Disproportionate minority confinement made a core protection with 25 percent fund loss for noncompliance with each of four core protections.
- Gang program restructured to focus on gang-free schools and communities and community-based gang intervention programs.
- State Challenge Activities program established to authorize funding for ten challenge activities.
- Treatment program for juvenile sex offenders who are victims of child abuse and neglect.
- Establishment of a Boot Camp program.
- Authorization of a White House Conference on Juvenile Justice.
- Title V Community Prevention Grants program authorized to provide prevention funds to implement local plans.

While federal concern about juvenile delinquency has dated as far back as 1912, the Juvenile Justice and Delinquency Prevention Act of 1974 is landmark legislation in that it represents the first federally supported comprehensive approach to the problem of juvenile justice and delinquency prevention. Its support through the reauthorizations was consistently bipartisan and broadly based, with over one hundred special interest groups advocating for its enactment.

Practicum

Three months before Jimmy's eighteenth birthday, he robs a convenience store. He is not arrested until three days after he has reached the age of eighteen.

Should Jimmy be treated as a juvenile delinquent or as an adult criminal? Justify your answer.

Summary

- The US Constitution does not guarantee a separate court system for juveniles. While a separate system is not protected by the Constitution, all fifty US states and the US federal jurisdictions, including the District of Columbia, have created separate systems for juveniles.
- Prior to the twentieth century, juveniles involved in the justice systems were treated as miniature and immature adults.
- Before the late 1800s, young people who were believed to have committed criminal misconduct were handled in the same criminal courts as adults.
- The term *juvenile delinquent* refers to a person who has committed a criminal act and who is defined by the jurisdiction as a juvenile.
- Juvenile delinquency as an educational discipline developed mainly with the beginning of the twentieth century.

- The age at which children become criminally responsible for their conduct varies by jurisdiction. Each jurisdiction has statutes that establish when a minor may be held criminally liable for his or her criminal misconduct.
- The general rule, which was developed under English common law, is that children under the age of seven years are not held criminally responsible for their conduct.
- As a rule, children fourteen years and older are presumed to have the mental capacity to commit criminal offenses. In most jurisdictions, they are under the jurisdiction of juvenile or family court rather than adult criminal court.
- The two basic types of juvenile misconduct incidents are status offenses and acts that would be considered as a crime regardless of the age of the offender.
- Status offenses involve misconduct that would generally not be considered as an offense if the offender was an adult.
- A 2018 *National Report Series Bulletin* notes that arrests of juveniles in the United States peaked in 1996 at almost 2.7 million juveniles.
- By 2016, the number of juveniles arrested was 68 percent less than the 1996 peak. The arrests of adults also declined during the same period, but only by 20 percent.
- The science of measuring delinquency is not a precise science. It is at best a guess of the extent of delinquent misconduct that has been, or is, occurring. For the most part, the only delinquent acts that are measured are those that are either reported to law enforcement or reported by victims in surveys.
- What causes juvenile delinquency? This is a question frequently asked of researchers who study delinquency. The problem with this question is that there is no single answer.
- Multiple theories have been developed to explain the causes of juvenile delinquency. Some of the theories are sophisticated and others are quite basic. The theories may generally be divided into two general themes. The general theme of *free choice* assumes that human behavior is the product of free choice and the individual chooses to commit crime. The *positivist* theme holds that human behavior is not the result of free choice, and that juvenile crime is determined by internal and external influences.
- While a substantial proportion of crime is perpetrated by juveniles, it is noted that most juveniles will "grow out" of offending and adopt law-abiding lifestyles as they mature.
- The prevalence of delinquency tends to increase from late childhood, peak in the teenage years (from fifteen to nineteen), and then decline in the early twenties.
- In the past several decades, there has been a profound change in the involvement of female delinquents within the juvenile justice system. Young females account for a growing proportion of the juvenile population involved in the juvenile justice system.
- Juvenile justice, like adult criminal justice, is primarily a state function except in jurisdictions like the District of Columbia, where there is no state jurisdiction. The federal government does provide limited oversight and control of juvenile justice using federal grants and other federal funding.

Discussion and Review Questions

1. Define the term *juvenile*.
2. What constitutes a status offender in the juvenile justice system?
3. What is the purpose of a separate system of justice for juveniles?

4. Explain the history of juvenile justice systems.
5. Explain your thoughts as to what age juveniles are capable of understanding the nature of their criminal behavior.
6. What reforms are needed in the juvenile justice system?
7. Why has there been an increase in the percentage of involvement of female delinquents?
8. How are delinquency data collected?
9. What are the goals of the juvenile justice system?
10. How do social norms influence the behavior of juveniles?

Notes

1. D.C. Code §16-2301 (5) (2001).
2. D.C. Superior Court Family Court, Family Guide to the District of Columbia Juvenile Justice System (Washington, DC: GPO, 2011).
3. New York Consolidated Laws, Family Court Act—FCT § 301.2. Definitions (amended October 2018).
4. Application of *Gault*, 387 U.S. 1 (1967).
5. Cliff Roberson and Harvey Wallace, *Principles of Criminal Law*, 6th ed. (Columbus, OH: Pearson, 2016).
6. *State v. Dillon*, 93 Idaho 698, 471 P. 2d 553 (1970).
7. President's Commission on Law Enforcement and Administration of Justice, Washington, DC, 1967, 3–5.
8. Cliff Roberson, *Juvenile Justice: Theory and Practice*, 2nd ed. (Boca Raton, FL: CRC Press, 2010).
9. *United States v. Welch*, 15 F. 3d 1202, 1207 (1st Cir.).
10. Sarah Hockenberry, "Delinquency Cases in Juvenile Court, 2016," *National Report Series Bulletin* (Washington, DC: March 2019). Available at OJJDP website https://www.ojjdp.gov/pubs/251861.pdf (accessed April 8, 2019).
11. The information on measuring the nation's crimes was adapted from the US Department of Justice website at http://bjs.ojp.usdoj.gov/content/pub/html/ntcm.cfm (accessed February 9, 2013).
12. Juvenile Law Center, "Youth in the Justice System: An Overview," posted on the Juvenile Justice Law Center website at https://jlc.org/youth-justice-system-overview (accessed February 18, 2019).
13. Shaunacy Ferro, "Teenagers Can't Help Their Stupid Decision-Making," posted on *Popular Science* website at https://www.salon.com/2013/11/14/teenagers_cant_help_but_make_stupid_decisions_newscred (accessed February 9, 2019).
14. James Ogloff, Margaret Cutajar, Emily Mann, and Paul Mullen, "Child Sexual Abuse and Subsequent Offending and Victimization: A 45-Year Follow-Up Study," *Trends and Issues in Crime and Criminal Justice*, no. 440 (June 2012), 1–6.
15. Janet Currie and Erdal Tekin, "Does Child Abuse Cause Crime," Working Paper 12171, Cambridge, MA: National Bureau of Economic Research, April 2006, available at www.nber.org/papers/w12171.
16. Michelle Alexander, *The New Jim Crow: Mass Incarceration in the Age of Colorblindness* (New York: The New Press, 2012).
17. Tamar R Birckhead, "Delinquent by Reason of Poverty," *Washington University Journal of Law and Policy*, vol. 38 (2012). Available at http://works.bepress.com/tamar_birckhead/17/.
18. Ruth Masters and Cliff Roberson, *Inside Criminology* (Englewood Cliffs, NJ: Prentice Hall, 1990).
19. Masters and Roberson, *Inside Criminology*.
20. Cliff Roberson, *Juvenile Justice: Theory and Practice*, 2nd ed. (Boca Raton, FL: CRC Press, 2010).

21. Neil R. Carlson, Harold L. Miller Jr., Donald S. Heth, John W. Donahoe, G. Neil Martin, *Psychology: The Science of Behavior*, 7th ed. (New York: Pearson, 2010).
22. Robert Winters, Julie Globokar, and Cliff Roberson, *Introduction to Crime and Crime Causation* (Boca Raton, FL: CRC Press, 2014).
23. Winters et al., *Introduction to Crime and Crime Causation*, p. 59.
24. Kelly Richards, "What Makes Juvenile Offenders Different from Adult Offenders," *Trends & Issues in Crime and Criminal Justice*, no. 409 (2011), Canberra: Australian Institute of Criminology, posted on https://aic.gov.au/publications/tandi/tandi409 (accessed March 19, 2019).
25. The information and statistics on age and crime were taken from Rolf Loeber, David P. Farrington, and David Petechuk, "From Juvenile Delinquency to Young Adult Offending," *National Institute of Justice Bulletin* (Washington, DC: US Department of Justice), posted on https://www.nij.gov/topics/crime/Pages/delinquency-to-adult-offending.aspx#reports (accessed March 19, 2019).
26. David P. Farrington, "Age and Crime," in *Crime and Justice: An Annual Review of Research*, vol. 7, eds. Michael Tonry and Norval Morris (Chicago, IL: University of Chicago Press, 1986), 189–250.
27. Eileen Poe-Yamagata and Jeffrey A. Butts, "Female Offenders in the Juvenile Justice System Statistics Summary" (Washington, DC: US Department of Justice, 1993).
28. As reported by Hannah Levintova, "Girls Are the Fastest-Growing Group in the Juvenile Justice System," posted October 1, 2015, on Mother Jones website at https://www.motherjones.com/politics/2015/10/girls-make-ever-growing-proportion-kids-juvenile-justice-system/ (accessed March 20, 2019).
29. Information for this section was taken from the OJJDP website at https://www.ojjdp.gov/compliance/jjdpchronology.pdf (accessed March 25, 2019).

CHAPTER 2

Issues Involving Juvenile Delinquency

CHAPTER OBJECTIVES

After studying this chapter, the reader should be able to:

- Explain why some individuals believe that the juvenile justice system should be abolished and that juveniles accused of criminal misconduct should be processed in the regular criminal court system.
- Discuss the issue of charging juveniles with prostitution.
- Discuss the issues involved in the school-to-prison pipeline concept.
- Analyze the conclusions of the Mexican study involving incarcerated youths.
- Discuss the issues involved in preventing or reducing the bullying of youths.
- Discuss why juveniles are attracted to cyberdelinquency.
- Discuss the findings of the studies on pathways to desistance.

The theoretical theories on delinquency causation are discussed in chapters 3–5. Prior to examining the theoretical causation theories in detail, in this chapter we will look at some of the practical issues and research that are considered as factors in the causation process. These subjects should help the reader to better understand the issues involved in trying to determine delinquency causation.

The first issue discussed is the question of whether we need a separate justice system for juveniles. Next is the "school-to-prison pipeline." Also included in this chapter is a research study by co-author Elena Azaola in which 730 juveniles confined in Mexico juvenile institutions were interviewed. This study is included not only because it is an in-depth study of juvenile delinquency, but also because it indicates that delinquency in other countries follows the patterns of delinquency noted in the United States and the rest of the Western countries.

Do We Need a Separate Court System for Juveniles?

Starting in the late 1970s and until the 2010s, there were many individuals who sought to abolish the juvenile justice system. The movements to abolish the system were based on public opinion that juvenile courts were very lenient and coddled juvenile criminals. With the drop in violent crimes by youths since the 1990s, as discussed in chapter 1, the movements to abolish the system have diminished. However, should there be an increase in crime by youths, this call for abolishment may reemerge. One of the reasons that the authors continually compare the juvenile justice system to the adult system is to help establish the concept that juvenile delinquents should be treated differently from adult criminals.

As noted by one researcher, juvenile courts today bear only a passing similarity to the original concept of juvenile justice formulated over a century ago. Lawmakers built the first juvenile courts around an informal, quasi-civil process. Juvenile court judges had broad discretion with which they could intervene quickly and decisively, even in cases involving hard-to-prove charges. Juvenile offenders received minimal procedural protections in juvenile court, but in return, they were promised a court that would focus on their best interests. The mission of the juvenile court is to help young law violators get back on the right track, not simply to punish them for their illegal behavior.[1] Photo 2.1 depicts an early juvenile court in Denver.

Is the juvenile justice system soft on youths? The critics of the juvenile system contend that it is failing in its rehabilitation efforts and is not punishing serious criminal behavior by young people. One of their strongest arguments is that the system is too lenient on young criminals, and that this leniency compounds the system's failure to rehabilitate by communicating to young people that they can avoid serious consequences for their criminal actions. According to the critics, the current juvenile system promotes a revolving-door process that sends the message to young offenders that they are not accountable for their behavior, and that it would be better to punish a juvenile in the first instance, in order to deter future criminal activity.

PHOTO 2.1 Judge Ben Lindsey of Juvenile Court, Denver, Colorado, circa 1915, taking a weekly report of delinquent children. The children were required to report to the judge every Saturday morning. (Photo courtesy of US Library of Congress Prints and Photographs Division, Washington, DC, LC-USZ62-137720)

Critics also claim it is wrong for juvenile offenders who have committed violent crimes to be released in many juvenile justice systems from the jurisdiction of the juvenile court at age eighteen or twenty-one. Serving a few years in a juvenile correction facility for a crime that if committed by an adult would result in a long prison sentence is unjust. The punishment for a crime, critics argue, should be the same, regardless of the age of the perpetrator. Because of these deficiencies, many critics contend that the juvenile system should be dismantled.

Those critics and others also contend that juveniles should be given full due process rights, including the right to trial by jury, just like adults, and that the juvenile justice system's rehabilitative ideology and restrictions on criminal due process rights prevent the juveniles from standing accountable for their criminal actions. The critics argue that once a juvenile is convicted, a trial court could determine the appropriate sentence.

Jeffrey Butts opines that perhaps the public's frustration with the juvenile justice system is perpetuated by the fact that juvenile courts are a distinct and highly visible component of the criminal justice system. Butts notes that individual, criminal acts by twenty-five-year-olds, or divorced people, or computer programmers, do not often provoke calls for sweeping reforms of the criminal law. There is no separate system set aside for these groups. Every shocking crime by a young person, on the other hand, calls attention to possible problems in the court system especially designed to deal with juveniles. The juvenile justice system acts like a magnet, attracting the public's frustrations about the crime problem, even if juveniles are only a small part of the problem.[2]

Supporters of the system counter with the contention that most of the alleged defects of the juvenile courts could be traced to inadequate funding and to an environment in which many juveniles are forced to live. The supporters contend that violent subcultures and early childhood traumas caused by abuse, neglect, and exposure to violence make it difficult to address individual problems of juveniles. If the systems were adequately funded, they argue, officers and court support personnel could more closely supervise children and monitor rehabilitation efforts. If more energy were put into changing the socioeconomic situation of communities, rehabilitation efforts would improve, and crime would decrease.[3]

Nathan Nelson, in an article on the issue, notes that juveniles are different from adults and therefore should not be required to stand trial in an adult criminal court.[4] Nelson contends that children are not well enough developed mentally, as compared to an adult, to be tried in the adult correctional system. And for these reasons, he states that the juvenile should not be tried in an adult criminal court.

Nelson argues that we should establish a hybrid system for juveniles, one that would be more beneficial for the juvenile and would meet constitutional standards. In order to accomplish all of this, the jurisdictions should be looking at concepts, resources, and management. Applying all three of these criteria will result in the best outcome. The results would end the juvenile system as it currently exists, but instead of getting rid of it altogether, making some changes to the "adult system" to help incorporate these new guidelines.

Nelson points out that the accepted mission of the juvenile justice system is to rehabilitate the juvenile offender and give them the necessary skills to be brought back into society. Nelson opines that society should accept this concept because the juvenile is still young, and therefore, society should be willing to give that individual another chance. He contends that society believes the juvenile is under an obligation to grow himself/herself to be fitted to the perceived values of the society. If this is done effectively, the concept of rehabilitation will work successfully.

Juveniles Involved in Sex Trafficking

In 2019, the Texas governor vetoed a bill that would prevent law enforcement personnel and prosecutors from charging youths under the age of seventeen with prostitution (a safe harbor law). For the most part, juveniles under the age of eighteen may not consent to have sex. Advocates for the bill stated that children forced into prostitution should be treated as victims and not as criminals. The governor justified his veto by stating that while the legislation was well-intentioned, it removed an option that law enforcement and prosecutors could use to separate victims from sex traffickers.

As noted by Sonia Lunn, although no state allows for a child to consent to sex under the age of sixteen, many states still criminalize child prostitution. Statutory rape laws criminalize adults for having sex with underage minors. According to her, safe harbor laws are meant to ensure that 1) minors are not criminalized for prostitution; and that 2) victim services are provided to all sexually exploited youth. However, the definition of sexually exploited youth changes from state to state, making this issue particularly complicated. She notes that few states involved in youth sex trafficking have fully implemented safe harbor laws.[5]

Primary Purpose of Juvenile Justice Courts

As you study this text, an overriding issue is what should be the primary purpose of juvenile courts. Most professionals examining the question have one of three positions:

- To protect juveniles and attempt to correct those who commit criminal misconduct.
- To protect the public first and correct the juvenile delinquents second.
- To protect both the juveniles and the public.

A valid argument could be made that the above principles should also apply to adult criminal courts. In many jurisdictions, the juvenile court is a part of the family court system, and the juvenile court judge lacks any special training regarding the needs and care of juveniles.

The Circuit Court of Cook County, Illinois, justifies the need for juvenile justice courts on its website by examining the purpose of the juvenile courts:[6]

- To protect citizens and the community from crimes committed by young people.
- To hold youth who commit crimes accountable for their actions.
- To provide individualized assessments to rehabilitate and prevent further delinquent behavior through the development of educational, vocational, social, emotional, and basic life skills, which enable youth to grow and mature.
- To provide youth and all other interested parties fair hearings at which legal rights are recognized and enforced.

Privately Operated Juvenile Institutions

According to Michele Deitch, one of the great myths out there is that private prison companies can provide services better and cheaper.[7] According to Deitch, privatization could mean anything from privatizing a particular aspect of operations (e.g., medical, transportation, or food services), to private vendors operating a state-owned facility, to private vendor construction, ownership, and operation of a facility under a contract with the state. Deitch states that she is mostly concerned about situations where the private vendor is running all aspects of correctional operations, and the state's role is limited to contracting, oversight, and funding, and sometimes ownership of the physical building.

Deitch notes that in some jurisdictions in the United States, there is a financial incentive for juvenile court judges to incarcerate the juvenile instead of placing the youth in community corrections. This is because state governments generally fund residential placement for youths that are adjudicated as delinquent, whereas the counties must pay for alternatives to incarceration. She sees this happening as opportunities for expanding privatization abound, in ways that are apparently consistent with the goals of most advocates. She points out that policy-makers may find it difficult to reconcile their desire for small, community-based group homes with opposition to privatization, since they appear to be complementary.

Deitch also notes that these small private facilities can exist under the radar for long periods of time, with little oversight or regulation from government officials, and little scrutiny from concerned citizens, advocates, or the media. Abuses or lack of services can go undetected for years. Deitch states that privatizing large facilities may be more troubling at many levels, but it is far from a safe alternative to simply spread out privatization into smaller, essentially invisible facilities, even if they are well-intended in purpose.

Deitch lists some of the common faults with privately operated institutions as follows:

- Private vendors tend to compromise safety and security to keep down costs. They save money by hiring inexperienced staff at the low end of the wage scale—comparable to local fast-food restaurants. This leads to very high turnover rates. One study found a turnover rate in private prisons of 52 percent, versus 16 percent in government-operated prisons.
- Private vendors skimp on training programs; they've got a very limited budget for this.
- When you've got inexperienced, poorly trained staff, with limited training, you've got a recipe for security and safety problems.
- Combine that with a problem of understaffing. Private vendors often keep staff positions unfilled, so while the position is on the books, there are no costs associated with it.
- Many private facilities are built on the cheap, with design and lack of maintenance contributing to escapes and other security problems.

School-to-Prison Pipeline

The school-to-prison pipeline concept does not fit into any of the recognized theory groups. It is discussed in this initial chapter on delinquency causation. The evidence is clear that students who are disciplined in their schools are also more likely to end up in the juvenile justice system. A Texas study found that, of the students disciplined in middle or high school, 23 percent of them ended up in contact with a juvenile probation officer. That figure stands at 2 percent among those not disciplined in school. And students who have been suspended or expelled are three times more likely to meet the juvenile probation system the following year than the ones who weren't suspended or expelled.[8]

According to the school-to-prison concept, minority groups become delinquents based on discriminatory treatment they have received in schools, especially in the public education system.[9] Many researchers consider that a racial/ethnic disproportionality clearly exists in both the educational and justice systems. While it has been noted that a direct empirical linkage between the experiences of youth in these separate sectors is far from established, researchers Miner P. Marchbanks III and Jamilia J. Blake report that the literature has generated parallel but largely disconnected bodies of scholarship.

The term *school-to-prison pipeline* is used to describe a path through the education system for mostly racial minority and at-risk students. The researchers contend that repeated school disciplinary encounters stigmatize students and interrupt social ties with positive peers. As youth fall out of contact with mainstream friends, they develop new associations with individuals who are genuinely deviant. In this manner, even students who may not have been initially inclined toward serious misbehavior may become delinquent. To the extent that minority youth are more likely to have early school discipline contact, they have a higher chance of entering this school-to-prison pipeline on an accelerated path toward academic failure, delinquency, juvenile justice contact, and, ultimately, adult criminal involvement.[10]

The two key forces that produced and maintain the school-to-prison pipeline are the use of "zero-tolerance" policies that mandate exclusionary punishments, and the presence of police on school campuses, as school resource officers (SROs). These policies and practices became common following a spate of deadly school shootings across the United States in the 1990s. Lawmakers and educators believed they would help to ensure safety on school campuses.[11]

Having a zero-tolerance policy means that a school has zero tolerance for any kind of misbehavior or violation of school rules, no matter how minor, unintentional, or subjectively defined they may be. In a school with a zero-tolerance policy, suspensions and expulsions are normal and common ways of dealing with student misbehavior.

Research shows that the implementation of zero-tolerance policies has led to significant increases in suspensions and expulsions. Scholar Henry Giroux observed that over a four-year period in Chicago public schools, suspensions increased by 51 percent and expulsions by nearly thirty-two times after zero-tolerance policies were implemented.

The labeling theory, discussed in chapter 4, contends that people come to identify and behave in ways that reflect how others label them. Applying this theory to the school-to-prison pipeline suggests that being labeled as a "bad" kid by school authorities and/or SROs, and being treated in a way that reflects that label (punitively), ultimately leads kids to internalize the label and behave in ways that make it real through action. This labeling is a self-fulfilling prophecy.[12]

According to researcher Victor Rios, attempting to control "at-risk" or deviant youth with these methods ultimately fosters the very criminal behavior they are intended to prevent. When social institutions label deviant youths as bad or criminal—stripping them of dignity, failing to acknowledge their struggles, and not treating them with respect—it can lead to rebellion. Thus, criminal misconduct is an act of resistance.

Once suspended or expelled, data show that students are less likely to complete high school, more than twice as likely to be arrested while on forced leave from school, and more likely to be in contact with the juvenile justice system during the year that follows the forced leave. In fact, sociologist David Ramey found, in a nationally representative study, that experiencing school punishment before the age of fifteen is highly associated with contact with the criminal justice system for boys.

A 2014 study of out-of-school suspensions conducted by US Department of Education Office for Civil Rights Data Collection (CRDC) reveals that when categorized by race/ethnicity and gender, non-white students are suspended and expelled at a rate three times greater than that of white students. On average, 4.6 percent of white students are suspended, compared to 16.4 percent of black students. Black boys and girls have higher suspension rates than any of their peers, and 20 percent of black boys and more than 12 percent of black girls received out-of-school suspensions.[13]

The data also noted that students with disabilities are more than twice as likely to receive one or more out-of-school suspensions as students without disabilities. Black students represent 16 percent of student enrollment, but constitute 27 percent of students referred to law enforcement, and 31 percent of students subjected to a school-related arrest. In comparison, white students represent 52 percent of students enrolled, 41 percent of referrals to law enforcement, and 39 percent of those subjected to school-related arrests. In addition, students with disabilities represent one-quarter of the students who are referred to law enforcement or subjected to school-related arrests, while representing just 12 percent of the student population.

Some of the highlights of the CRDC study include:

Out-of-school suspensions: Black and Latino students:

- Three states reported male suspension rates less than the nation for every racial/ethnic group and a smaller gap between black students and their white peers: New Jersey, New York, and North Dakota.
- Five states reported male suspension rates higher than the nation for every racial/ethnic group: Florida, Indiana, North Carolina, Rhode Island, and South Carolina.
- Twelve states or jurisdictions reported higher gaps between the suspension rates of black students and white students for both boys and girls: Alabama, Arkansas, District of Columbia, Indiana, Michigan, Missouri, Nebraska, Ohio, Oklahoma, Pennsylvania, Tennessee, and Wisconsin.

Students with disabilities:

- Six states reported a ten-percentage point or smaller gap in out-of-school suspension rates between students with disabilities and students without disabilities: North Dakota (2%), Utah (3%), Idaho (4%), Mississippi (4%), Wisconsin (4%), and Wyoming (4%).
- Four states reported a ten-percentage point or higher gap in out-of-school suspension rates between students with disabilities and students without disabilities: Florida (18%), Nevada (14%), Louisiana (11%), and Wisconsin (11%).

While the previously stated research study included only the City of Chicago Public Schools, similar studies of other school districts produced similar findings. Is it time for educators to rethink the two main issues in the school-to-prison pipeline concept? First, does the presence of law enforcement officers on school campuses increase the number of incidents where the school administrators refer the students to the justice system? And second, is the zero-tolerance policy worth the costs in young lives?

Juveniles Who Commit Violent Crimes: Mexican Research Study

In 2016, the National Commission for Human Rights requested that co-author Elena Azaola and her associates study a possible correlation between the vulnerability that Mexican juveniles face and their criminal behavior, specifically, the violent crimes that they commit. In this section, we will summarize the findings of the study as it pertains to juvenile delinquency.[14]

Azaola noted that Mexico has about eleven million juveniles ages fourteen to seventeen years of age, which constitutes about 9 percent of the country's total population, and the age range generally under the juvenile justice system's responsibility. While Mexico has the second-largest economy in Latin America, 54 percent of its population lives in poverty, and 39 percent of Mexico's wealth is concentrated in just 1 percent of the population. Mexico is listed among the twenty-five most unequal countries in the world involving economic distribution of income.[15]

In early 2016, there were 3,761 juveniles being held in Mexico's detention centers for the commission of serious crimes. Males accounted for 96 percent of the juveniles in detention. The detention centers are referred to as "internment centers," where juveniles are generally deprived of their freedom for periods ranging from three to ten years.

The research group selected a subgroup of these juveniles. The group developed a survey and conducted personal interviews of 730 juveniles who are deprived of their liberty in detention centers for seventeen institutions representing all regions of the country. The selected juveniles were from the marginalized segment of the population. Juveniles from this segment were selected because the research group believed that these are the juveniles that are most stigmatized and ousted to an almost invisible margin of the population.

An important objective of the study was to listen to the voices and testimonies of the juveniles being held and to provide them with the opportunity to be heard. The researchers' conclusions and findings were based upon the interviews of the juveniles.

The group of interviewees was selected based on recent scientific findings about the development process that takes place during adolescence. Other research studies indicate that during adolescence, the brain is not only going through a process of maturation but is also extraordinarily malleable and vulnerable.[16]

The Mexican researchers noted a report by the US Attorney General, who had ordered the integration of a special working group to study the effects of violence on children and juveniles. This report included a chapter addressing the need to rethink the US juvenile justice system. It was noted in the report that a clear majority of children within the justice system has been exposed to violence throughout their lives and live with the trauma caused by this experience. It stated also that most of these children have been exposed to different kinds of violence throughout their lives and posits that there is a correlation between having been exposed to violence and being subject to punitive measures from the juvenile justice system. Exposure to violence often leads to mistrust, hypervigilance, impulsive behavior, isolation, substance abuse, addictions, lack of empathy, and aggression as means of self-preservation. When children and juveniles are exposed to violence repeatedly or over prolonged periods of time, their bodies and brains adapt to focus on self-preservation. This reduces dramatically their ability to control their impulses and delay gratification. Juveniles that are trying to protect themselves from violence, or do not know how to deal with their violent experiences, are vulnerable to engaging in criminal behavior to obtain a sense of control over their chaotic lives, or as a mechanism for coping with emotional confusion and the barriers to realizing success and safety which are generated by exposure to violence.[17]

The research group concluded that many juveniles confined in juvenile justice institutions seem angry, defiant, or indifferent, but in truth they are scared, depressed, and lonely. They are emotionally damaged, and they feel powerless, abandoned, and subject to double standards both from the adults in their lives and from the institutions. Often, the system views these youngsters as facing a hopeless future, as uncontrollable, and therefore often labels them as "defiant," "willfully irresponsible," and, eventually, "incorrigible." What comes across as intentional defiance and aggressive attitudes are often their defenses against desperation, as the youths face a future which the violence in their lives has deprived of any hope.

Finally, the researchers warn that when the juvenile justice system responds exclusively with punishment, these juveniles may be pushed to become part of the penal justice system for adults, and therefore, a permanent loss to their families and society. By failing to identify and adequately treat children and juveniles that have been exposed to violence, the system misses the opportunity to modify their delinquent behavior.

Methodology

To collect the information, the researchers used a group of research methods and techniques, both quantitative and qualitative. Among them, they surveyed and collected direct testimony from 730 juveniles confined in internment centers in seventeen states throughout the country, which as a group are representative of all the different Mexican regions. This population represented 19 percent of the total population of interned juveniles in Mexico. The result was a thorough and detailed view of the circumstances that this subgroup of vulnerable juveniles faced.

Each juvenile involved in the study completed a survey and was then interviewed by a member of the research group. The survey allowed the research group to develop a clear notion of the characteristics of the total population that is interned in the internment centers in the seventeen states they studied. The interviews provided stories that yielded a deeper perspective about the specific features and individual trajectories of each juvenile.

Crimes Committed

Table 2.1 shows the percentage of the interned juvenile population, disaggregated by type of crime, according to the statistics that were provided by the authorities at the internment centers visited. It is important to point out that these percentages account only for juveniles that have committed serious crimes in Mexico, given that those that commit minor crimes are not confined but subjected to educational and therapeutic measures and remain free, living with their families.

As can be observed, the first four crimes—homicide, violent robbery, kidnap, and rape—represent 83 percent of the total number of serious crimes committed by the juveniles confined in the Mexican states studied. This is consistent with the Mexican guidelines regarding the internment exclusively of those juveniles that commit serious crimes.[18]

Selected Findings of the Study

Family Factors

- 62% have divorced parents.
- 60% have at least one relative who has been in prison.
- 43% ran away from their homes, some of them temporarily, some definitively.
- 31% ran away because of "family problems."
- 27% ran away because they wanted to have "their own lives." Some of them joined criminal groups.
- 22% never met their father.
- 5% never had the chance to meet their mother.
- 30% suffered some type of neglect from their family.

TABLE 2.1 Percentage of Juveniles Confined by Crime, 2016

Crime	%
Homicide	34
Aggravated robbery	24
Kidnap or abduction	13
Rape	12
Vehicle theft	4
Drug related	3
Nonviolent robbery	3
Carrying illegal firearms	2
Pederasty	1
Injuries	1
Others	3
TOTAL	100

Source: Statistics provided by the authorities at the internment centers for adolescents.

- 40% were physically abused.
- 34% were psychologically abused.
- 12% were sexually abused.
- 39% said that while they were being abused, they couldn't find anyone to protect them.
- 24% claimed that it was the father who caused them more damage.
- 12% said they trusted no one.
- 57% lived with adults with alcohol problems.
- 30% lived with adults who consumed drugs.
- 68% of the juveniles have alcohol and drug problems.

Education Factors

- 4% never went to school.
- 15% never completed elementary school.
- 17% only finished elementary school.
- 28% never completed half of high school.
- 20% completed half of high school.
- 53% said they never liked school.

Family Economic Factors

- 51% said they were "poor."
- 31% said they didn't have enough food (extreme poverty).
- 89% of the juveniles had worked before the age of sixteen, receiving very poor salaries.
- 37% started working before reaching the age of twelve.

Characteristics of Their Crimes

- 83% committed violent crimes.
- 34% were accused of homicide.

- 24% committed robbery (with violence).
- 13% committed kidnapping.
- 35% said they had been previously arrested.
- 16% claimed that they were innocent.

Organized Crime Groups

Thirty-five percent of the juveniles reported that they joined an organized crime group. Some of their motivations are listed below:

- The wish to imitate a lifestyle they saw around them, in which having fancy cars, drugs, alcohol, weapons, girlfriends, etc., gave them the impression of having power and a life of luxury.
- The desire to be a member of a group, of belonging, of feeling protected.
- For some, being part of those groups was "natural" because they grew up in families involved in organized crime.
- The cartel chiefs made them believe that the people they were ordered to kill deserved it.
- The cartel chiefs also made them believe they must obey all orders.
- They felt attracted to adrenaline, to "living in danger."
- They also felt attracted to the idea of disputing the power of the State.
- They lived in environments where being a member of an organized crime group gives them a positive image, a higher status.
- The cartel chiefs take advantage of juveniles' immaturity. Even when the juveniles knew they were committing crimes, they didn't have the capacity to measure the impact these acts would have on their future. They frequently said phrases like: "I thought it would be easy"; "I didn't think of the consequences"; "I wanted to know what it felt like"; "I wanted to have the same things the others have"; "I felt attracted to weapons, big vans, etc."

Reasons for Gathering in Gangs

Twenty-seven percent of the juveniles committed a crime as a member of a gang.

- One of the main reasons to be a member of a gang is the need to belong, to have an identity, to be a member of a group, especially when they have dropped out of school and have no job.
- The gangs take the streets, creating their own codes, rituals, rules, and symbols to differentiate themselves from other groups.
- The gangs give their members the opportunity to belong; to be part of an "emotive community"; to have a substitute family that satisfies the emotional needs of juveniles. The gang provides them dignity and gives meaning to their lives.

Interaction with Police

- 57% of the juveniles said they were severely tortured either by police or military members when they were arrested.
- Juveniles considered torture the "normal" behavior they expected from police.

Conditions at Juvenile Institutions

- 31% considered the conditions at the institution in which they were serving time as "bad" or "poor."
- 75% would like to have more courses, workshops, or activities.

- 74% miss their family very much.
- 42% feel "sad" at the institution.
- 39% feel "bored."
- 88% would like to be free to be able to study, work, and be with their families.

Their Hopes for the Future

- 27% hope to become a professional and have a good job.
- 24% hope to build a good family and live in their own home.
- 21% had no dreams regarding their future.
- 8% hope to join the military or the police.
- 8% hope to finish school and get a job.
- 5% hope to become a sports hero.
- 4% want the opportunity to visit many countries.
- 3% hope to be a famous singer or actor.
- 1% hope to be a rich person.

Conclusions of the Research Group

- Generally, teenagers' behavior is a reaction to the circumstances they face.
- Their delinquency was the result of the interactions between the influences from their environment and their own emotional, psychological, cognitive, and brain development.
- Adolescence is a volatile and transitory period of life. Adolescents tend to act impulsively, taking risks without thinking, and they are not capable of considering the long-term consequences of their acts. The great majority abandon participating in criminal acts as a natural part of growing up and gaining maturity.
- In Mexico, most juvenile institutions face all kinds of limitations that do not allow them to provide juveniles with the knowledge, abilities, and capacities they will need to become better and law-abiding citizens.
- In many cases, being at a juvenile institution does not help them to overcome the difficult situations they faced in their childhoods; rather, it could produce more damage to their personalities and compromise their healthy development, creating new vulnerabilities which will reinforce the ones they faced in their childhood.
- The juvenile institutions in Mexico lack the specialized professionals, programs, and resources to provide the attention the juveniles need to mature, to heal, and to understand their responsibilities. They also lack the necessary support and understanding from politicians, who tend to misunderstand the importance of the role these institutions must play, especially in the context of growing violence and criminality.
- The researchers noted that the correctional personnel expressed how little they care about the marginalized juveniles who could be incorporated into society as responsible and law-abiding citizens.

Pathways to Desistance Study

Pathways to Desistance: A Longitudinal Study of Serious Adolescent Offenders was a large, collaborative, multidisciplinary project that followed 1,354 serious juvenile offenders ages fourteen to eighteen and included 184 females and 1,170 males for seven years after their adjudication. The study looked at the factors that lead youth to commit serious criminal misconduct, and their lives in early childhood and late adolescence.[19] (Note: This study supports the age–crime curve discussed in chapter 1.)

Key points of the Pathways to Desistance study include:

- Most youths who commit felonies greatly reduce their offending over time.
- Longer stays in juvenile institutions do not reduce recidivism.
- In the period after incarceration, community-based supervision is more effective for those who have committed serious offenses.
- Substance abuse treatment reduces both substance use and criminal offending for a limited time.

Reduced Reoffending Over Time

Youths who committed felonies greatly reduced their offending over time, regardless of the intervention. Approximately 91.5 percent of youth in the study reported decreased or limited illegal activity during the first three years following their court involvement. Two groups of male offenders—those with high, stable offending rates, and those with high, but declining offending rates—had very different outcomes despite similar treatment by the juvenile justice system. For both groups, approximately 40 percent of offenders were in jail or prison across the three-year follow-up period; each group also had similar percentages under detention or in a contracted residential placement (about 20 percent of each group was in each of these forms of supervision). Overall, approximately 50 percent of the youth in each group were under some form of supervision during the follow-up period, and about 20 percent were receiving community-based services.

The study concluded that institutional placement and the type of setting appeared to have little effect on which high-end offenders persisted in offending and which reduced their offending. Researchers also found that longer stays in juvenile institutions did not reduce recidivism, and some youths who had the lowest offending levels reported committing more crimes after being incarcerated.

Offenders who receive community-based services following incarceration were more likely to attend school, go to work, and reduce offending. Because the project collected monthly data about institutional placement, probation, and involvement in community-based services, investigators were able to examine the effects of aftercare services for six months after a court-ordered placement. Increasing the duration of community supervision reduced reported reoffending. In addition, although returning offenders generally received supervision only, rather than treatment, the research showed that in the six months after release, youth who were involved in community-based services were more likely to avoid further involvement with the juvenile justice system.

The study concluded that substance use among juveniles is linked to serious juvenile offending. The adolescent offenders profiled in the Pathways to Desistance study reported very high levels of substance abuse problems. Substance use was linked to other illegal activities engaged in by the study participants. It is a strong, prevalent predictor of offending. The presence of a drug or alcohol disorder and the level of substance use were both shown to be strongly and independently related to the level of self-reported offending and the number of arrests. This relationship held even when drug-related offenses and behaviors were removed from the offending measures, and characteristics including socioeconomic status, gender, and ethnicity were controlled statistically. Treatment appears to reduce both substance use and offending, at least in the short term. Youth whose treatment lasted for at least ninety days and included significant family involvement showed substantial reductions in alcohol use, marijuana use, and offending over the following six months.

An important conclusion of the study was that even juveniles who have committed serious offenses are not necessarily on track for adult criminal careers. Only a small proportion of the offenders studied continued to offend at a high level throughout the follow-up period. The great majority reported low levels of offending after court involvement, and a significant portion of those with the highest levels of offending reduced their reoffending dramatically. Two factors that appear to distinguish high-end desisters from persisters were lower levels of substance use and greater stability in their daily routines, as measured by stability in living arrangements and work and school attendance.

Another conclusion was that incarceration may not be the most appropriate or effective option, even for many of the most serious adolescent offenders. Longer stays in juvenile facilities did not reduce reoffending; institutional placement even raised offending levels in those with the lowest level of offending. Youth who received community-based supervision and aftercare services were more likely to attend school, go to work, and avoid further offending during the six months after release. It was concluded that longer periods of supervision increased the benefits of supervision.

Deterrence among High-Risk Youth

The Pathways to Desistance study also examined the link between perceptions of the threat of sanctions and deterrence. The study concluded that:[20]

- There was no meaningful reduction in offending or arrests in response to more severe punishment (e.g., correctional placement, longer stays).
- Policies targeting specific types of offending may be more effective at deterring youth from engaging in these specific offenses as opposed to general policies aimed at overall crime reduction.
- In response to an arrest, youth slightly increased their risk perceptions, which is a necessary condition for deterrence.
- Creating ambiguity about detection probabilities in certain areas or for certain types of crime may have a deterrent effect by enhancing the perceived risk of getting caught.

Results from the Pathways to Desistance study addressed two of the three prongs of the deterrence equation—the certainty and severity hypotheses. The idea behind the *certainty hypothesis* is that more-certain punishment should reduce crime because the greater a person's perceived likelihood that he or she will be caught for committing a crime, the less willingness he or she should have to engage in that crime. The *severity hypothesis* assumes that the stronger the penalty associated with a crime, the greater the potential cost of committing the crime, which should also dissuade offenders.

Although the idea that increasing the severity of punishment should serve as a strongly motivating deterrent from crime is intuitive and popular, most of the deterrence research indicates that the certainty of the punishment, rather than its severity, is the primary mechanism through which deterrence works. In other words, all things being equal, offenders typically respond to a threatened punishment that is more likely to occur than to one that is more severe. However, it should be noted that the majority—though certainly not all—of deterrence research has been conducted on adults; that is, much of what researchers know about deterrence and risk has not necessarily been studied in juvenile populations.

Bullying

According to the federal government website, Stopbulling.gov, when adults respond quickly and consistently to bullying behavior, they send the message that it is not acceptable.[21] Research shows this can stop or reduce bullying behavior over time. Parents, school staff, and other adults in the community can help kids prevent bullying by talking about it, building a safe school environment, and creating a community-wide bullying prevention strategy. Bullying is unwanted, aggressive behavior among school-aged children that involves a real or perceived power imbalance. The behavior is repeated, or has the potential to be repeated, over time. Both kids who are bullied and those who bully others may have serious, lasting problems.

In order to be considered bullying, the behavior must be aggressive and include:

- **An imbalance of power:** Kids who bully use their power—such as physical strength, access to embarrassing information, or popularity—to control or harm others. Power imbalances can change over time and in different situations, even if they involve the same people.
- **Repetition:** Bullying behaviors happen more than once or have the potential to happen more than once.

Bullying includes actions such as making threats, spreading rumors, attacking someone physically or verbally, and excluding someone from a group on purpose (see photo 2.2).

Cyberdelinquency

Cybercrime is a broad category of offenses that involve the use of computers and computer networks. Juveniles generally take to computers more quickly and easily than their elders. Today's youths are raised with access to computers, and not just

PHOTO 2.2 Sad-looking youth being bullied. (Photo courtesy of iStock)

PHOTO 2.3 A graphic display of cyberdelinquency. (Photo courtesy of iStock)

standalone computers, but those that are networked to the rest of the world through the Internet. Most have cell phones which are miniature computers. It is not surprising that juveniles love to explore and experiment, as juveniles have always done. However, exploration and experimentation may lead them to sites that are legally off limits, and turn them into delinquents, sometimes without their awareness that they're doing anything criminal.

One popular delinquent act committed online by juveniles is cyberbullying (see photo 2.3). In some cases, computers are the means of committing an offense. It appears that juveniles commit online offenses for the same reasons they commit offenses in the "real world": rebellion, boredom, ignorance of the law, and because everyone else is doing it. In fact, according to a study by researchers at three universities, having friends who engage in cybercrime is one of the biggest determinants in whether juveniles commit such crimes.[22]

Females are more likely than males to be the victims of cyberstalking. This crime characteristic mirrors the demographic qualities of victims of traditional stalking. Unlike physical stalking, however, cyberstalking is perpetrated less by ex-intimate partners and more by acquaintances or strangers.[23] Technological factors allow for easier deceptive practices online. Other factors include easy access to technology, including the Internet. Social factors, such as the anonymity available online and the perpetrator's perception of possessing power and control over the victim, can increase the likelihood of this form of delinquency.

According to researchers Catherine Marcum, George Higgins, and Melissa Ricketts, as the association with deviant peers increases, the likelihood of cyberstalking increases. Marcum and colleagues state that a possible policy implication of their findings is the need for the development of programs for high school students to address the legal implications and punishments of cyberstalking, as juveniles may perceive it to be a crime without punishment. They contend that juveniles involved in cyberstalking lack self-control and need cognitive skill training to better maintain self-control. Furthermore, the researchers feel that juveniles of higher intelligence are more likely to participate in this behavior, and that juvenile groups who have a strong interest in technology and innovation may be the minors to target for this type of intervention.

Practicum

Assume that you are appointed as the administrator of your juvenile justice system. You are asked by the mayor to lead a discussion on issues involving juvenile justice.

Prepare a list of topics you want to cover in the discussion.

Summary

- Starting in the late 1970s and until the 2010s there were many individuals who sought to abolish the juvenile justice system. The movements to abolish the system were based on public opinion that juvenile courts were very lenient and coddled juvenile criminals.
- Juvenile courts today bear only a passing similarity to the original concept of juvenile justice formulated over a century ago. Lawmakers built the first juvenile courts around an informal, quasi-civil process.
- The critics of the juvenile system contend that it is failing in its rehabilitation efforts and is not punishing serious criminal behavior by young people.
- Supporters of a separate juvenile system countered with the contention that most of the alleged defects of the juvenile courts could be traced to inadequate funding and to an environment in which many juveniles are forced to live.
- Researchers contend that children are not developed enough mentally, as compared to adults, to be tried in the adult correctional system.
- In some jurisdictions in the United States, there is a financial incentive for the juvenile court judge to incarcerate the juvenile instead of placing the youth in community corrections; this is because state governments generally fund residential placements for youths that are adjudicated delinquent, whereas the counties must pay for alternatives to incarceration.
- There appears to be a trend toward the privatization of juvenile institutions.
- The small private facilities can ride under the radar for long periods of time, with little oversight or regulation from government officials, and little scrutiny from concerned citizens, advocates, or the media. Abuses or lack of services can go undetected for years.
- The term *school-to-prison pipeline* is used to describe a path through the education system for mostly racial minority and at-risk students.
- The evidence is clear that students who are disciplined by schools are also more likely to end up in the juvenile justice system.
- According to the school-to-prison pipeline concept, minority groups become delinquents based on discriminatory treatment they have received in schools, especially in the public education system.
- The two key forces that produce and maintain the school-to-prison pipeline are the use of "zero-tolerance" policies that mandate exclusionary punishments and the presence of police on school campus as school resource officers (SROs).
- The Mexico study determined that adolescence is a volatile and transitory period of life. Adolescents tend to act impulsively, taking risks without thinking, and they are not capable of considering the long-term consequences of their actions. The great majority naturally abandon participation in criminal acts as they mature.

- In Mexico, most juvenile institutions face all kinds of limitations that do not allow them to provide juveniles with the knowledge, abilities, and capacities they will need to become better and law-abiding citizens.
- Most youths who commit felonies greatly reduce their offending over time.
- Longer stays in juvenile institutions do not reduce recidivism.
- In the period after incarceration, community-based supervision is effective for those who have committed serious offenses.
- *Cybercrime* is a broad category of offenses that involve the use of computers and computer networks. Juveniles generally take to computers more quickly and easily than their elders. Today's youths are raised with access to computers, and not just standalone computers, but those that are networked to the rest of the world through the Internet.

Discussion and Review Questions

1. In your opinion, should there be a separate juvenile justice system? Justify your answer.
2. What are the criticisms pointed out in the school-to-prison pipeline?
3. Explain the issues involved in using privately operated juvenile institutions.
4. What are the most alarming facts noted when reviewing the study of 730 Mexican juveniles who were confined in juvenile institutions?
5. Explain the dynamics of bullying.
6. Why are juveniles involved in cybercrime?

Notes

1. Jeffrey A. Butts, "Can We Do Without Juvenile Justice?" In *You Decide! Current Debates in Criminal Justice*, edited by Bruce N. Waller (Upper Saddle River, NJ: Prentice-Hall, 2009), 321–31.
2. Butts, "Can We Do Without Juvenile Justice?"
3. Robert Dawson, "The Future of Juvenile Justice: Is It Time to Abolish the System," *Journal of Criminal Law and Criminology*, vol. 81, no. 1 (1991), 136–56.
4. Nathan Nelson, "Abolish the Juvenile Justice System" (October 2012), an unpublished paper posted at https://abolishjjs.blogspot.com/2012/11/should-juvenile-justice-system-be.html (accessed April 7, 2019).
5. Sonia Lunn, "Safe Harbor: Does Your State Arrest Minors for Prostitution?" (2018), posted at Human Trafficking Search website, https://humantraffickingsearch.org/safe-harbor-does-your-state-arrest-minors-for-prostitution/ (accessed June 21, 2019).
6. Circuit Court of Cook County, Illinois, website at www.cookcountycourt.org/ABOUTTHECOURT/JuvenileJusticeChildProtection/JuvenileJustice/PurposeofJuvenileJusticeCourts.aspx (accessed April 7, 2019).
7. Michele Deitch, "Oversight of Private Juvenile Facilities," Presentation to the National Juvenile Justice Network Forum, July 28, 2011, posted at www.njjn.org/uploads/digital-library/Oversight of Private Juvenile (accessed April 9, 2019).
8. Donna St. George, "Study Shows Wide Varieties in Discipline Methods among Very Similar Schools," *Washington Post*, July 19, 2011, B-3.
9. Nicki Lisa Cole, "Understanding the School-to-Prison Pipeline," posted on Thought Co. website at https://www.thoughtco.com/school-to-prison-pipeline-4136170 (accessed March 25, 2019).
10. Miner P. Marchbanks III and Jamilia J. Blake, "Assessing the Role of School Discipline in Disproportionate Minority Contact with the Juvenile Justice System: Final Technical Report" (Washington, DC: Office of Justice Programs' National Criminal Justice

Reference Service, August 2018), available on NCJRS website at https://www.ncjrs.gov/pdffiles1/ojjdp/grants/252059.pdf (accessed March 25, 2019).

11. Henry A. Giroux, "Mis/Education and Zero Tolerance: Disposable Youth and the Politics of Domestic Militarization," *Boundary 2: An International Journal of Literature and Culture*, vol. 28, no. 3 (September 1, 2001), 61–92. Article also published at https://docs.google.com/viewer?a=v&pid=sites&srcid=dWljY29sbGVnZXByZXAub3JnfGNvbW11bml0eS1oZWFsdGgtd2ViLXBhZ2V8Z3g6NDA2NThjMmRhZTQyZWM0NQ (accessed March 25, 2019).
12. Victor M. Rios, *Punished: Policing the Lives of Black and Latino Boys (New Perspectives in Crime, Deviance, and Law)* (New York: NYU Press, 2011).
13. US Department of Education, Office for Civil Rights, Issue Brief No. 1, Data Snapshot: School Discipline (2014), posted at https://www.thenation.com/wp-content/uploads/2015/04/CRDC-School-Discipline-Snapshot.pdf (accessed April 8, 2019).
14. The material for this section was taken from the personal notes of co-author Elena Azaola.
15. "Poverty in Mexico," available at http://www.telesurtv.net/telesuragenda/Pobreza-en-Mexico-20160801-0040.html (accessed March 23, 2019).
16. K. C. Monahan, "Trajectories of Antisocial Behavior and Psychosocial Maturity from Adolescence to Young Adulthood," *Developmental Psychology* vol. 45, no. 6 (2009), 1654–68; Richard J. Bonnie, Robert L. Johnson, Betty M. Chemers, and Julie A. Schuck, *Reforming Juvenile Justice: A Developmental Approach* (Washington, DC: National Academies Press, 2013). Available at http://nap.edu/catalog/14685/reforming-juvenile-justice-a-develpmental-approach (accessed April 2, 2019).
17. Department of Justice, *Report of the Attorney General's National Task Force on Children Exposed to Violence* (Washington, DC: Department of Justice, 2012), 171–72.
18. Ley Nacional del Sistema Integral de Justicia Penal para Adolescentes, *Publicada en la Gaceta Parlamentaria de la Cámara de Diputados*, No. 4519-XX (April 29, 2016).
19. Office of Juvenile Justice and Delinquency Prevention, Pathways to Desistance, OJJDP Bulletin Series (Washington, DC: US Department of Justice, 2011). Available on OJJDP website at https://www.ojjdp.gov/pubs/epub/Pathways.epub (accessed March 16, 2019).
20. Thomas A. Loughran, Robert Brame, Jeffrey Fagan, Alex R. Piquero, Edward P. Mulvey, and Carol A. Schubert, "Studying Deterrence Among High-Risk Juveniles," OJJDP Bulletin Series, (Washington, DC: US Department of Justice, August 2015). Available at https://www.ojjdp.gov/pubs/248617.pdf (accessed March 16, 2019).
21. Stopbullying website at https://www.stopbullying.gov/ (accessed May 20, 2019).
22. Andrew Atwal, "Youth Cybercrime Influenced by Peers," *Youth Today*, June 24, 2011, https://youthtoday.org/2011/06/youth-cybercrime-influenced-by-peers/ (accessed April 9, 2019).
23. Catherine Marcum, George E. Higgins, and Melissa L. Ricketts, "Juveniles and Cyber Stalking in the United States: An Analysis of Theoretical Predictors of Patterns of Online Perpetration," *International Journal of Cyber Criminology*, vol. 8, no. 1 (June 2014), 47–56.

PART II

Delinquency Causation Theories

CHAPTER 3

Classical and Positivist Concepts

CHAPTER OBJECTIVES

After studying this chapter, the reader should be able to:

- Discuss the various theoretical explanations of delinquency behavior.
- Describe the nature of the relationship between biology and crime.
- Describe the relationship between drugs and alcohol and criminality.
- Discuss the biological explanations of violence.
- Discuss the importance of the Age of Realism.

Delinquent Behaviors

This chapter contains a discussion of the classical and positivist explanations of delinquency behavior. The discussion is limited only to those acts that are considered as criminal misconduct and therefore excludes status offenses. The classical and positivist theories are the two basic explanations of criminal behavior. Most present-day theories are based on one of these two concepts. Also included in this chapter is a discussion of the rational choice theory, which is an outgrowth of the classical school. The classical school theorists see the juvenile as an individual freely making a choice to commit criminal behavior. The positivist school sees the delinquent as different from the noncriminal because of psychological or biological differences. The psychological differences are generally divided into four different categories:

- Emotional problem theories
- Mental disorder theories
- Sociopathic personality theories
- Thinking pattern theories

Many citizens consider crime as a narrow range of behavior. It is not. As noted earlier, the classic report, "The Challenge of Crime in a Free Society,"[1] states that crime is not just a tough teenager snatching a lady's purse; it is also a professional

TABLE 3.1 How Many of These Transgressions Did You Commit as a Juvenile?

Drinking alcohol as a minor
Shoplifting candy from a local store
Possession of small amounts of controlled substances
Defacing a neighbor's property
Scratching an automobile
Skipping school to have fun
Hiding the textbook of an unfriendly classmate
Cheating on a quiz

thief stealing cars or a well-heeled loan shark. Those of us (like the authors) who reached the age of majority many years ago probably committed serious criminal behavior a couple of times during our juvenile years, but were lucky enough not to have been arrested and adjudged a delinquent. As noted by Roberson, the question of why people commit criminal acts has long been faced by civilization.[2] We tend to forget our own misconduct when judging others. How many of the acts listed in table 3.1 did you commit as a juvenile?

Criminal misconduct refers to those situations where the act committed constitutes a violation of a penal law. Frequently we mix the phrases "criminal misconduct" and "deviance." While many consider them synonymous, they are not. *Deviance* is used to describe conduct that most individuals in a society view as eccentric, dangerous, bizarre, abhorrent, or otherwise outside the bounds of normal behavior. An act may be both criminal misconduct and deviant, but many acts frowned upon by society are not considered as criminal misconduct. Photo 3.1 displays some aspects of juvenile misconduct.

Early Theories of Delinquency

When reviewing early theories of delinquency, it should be remembered that during this time period, juveniles were treated as miniature adults. Early researchers were more interested in why the misconduct was committed, and not whether it was committed by an adult or a juvenile.

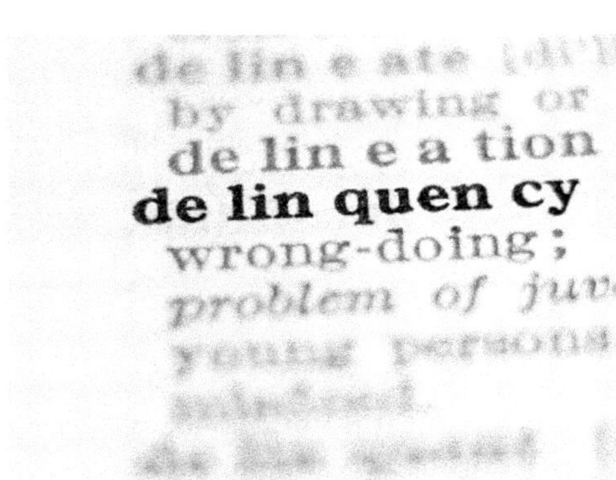

PHOTO 3.1 Graphic display of some aspects of juvenile criminal misconduct. (Photo courtesy of iStock)

The ancient Hebrews considered laws as expressions of God's commands. Accordingly, a violation of the law was a transgression against God—a sin. Deviant behavior, at that time, was believed to destroy the bonds of society. To the ancient Hebrews, any criminal behavior by a member of God's chosen people could incur God's wrath on everyone.

Centuries later, Greek philosophers considered criminal misconduct as an offense against the society or the state. The philosophers considered that individuals who committed crimes were infected with corruption and evil. Later, Greek philosopher Plato (428–348 BC) developed a naturalistic explanation of criminal behavior. Plato theorized that humans have a dual character. While the individual is rational and seeks perfection, he or she is limited by weaknesses and imperfections. Plato concluded that crime would always be present because of our greedy nature. To Plato, punishment was a method to cleanse one's self of evil.

Aristotle (384–322 BC), depicted in this statue (see photo 3.2), concluded that the "ability to reason" was what separated human beings from animals, and that crime was caused by irrational acts. Aristotle, however, failed to explain what caused the irrational acts (crimes).

PHOTO 3.2 Statue of Aristotle located in library lobby, Federal Building and US Courthouse, Erie, Pennsylvania. (Photo courtesy of US Library of Congress Prints and Photographs Division, Washington, DC, LC-DIG-highsm-02522)

Early European churches equated crime with sin, and individuals who committed criminal misconduct were possessed by the devil. St. Augustine (AD 354–430) theorized that crime was caused by the devil's influences. According to him, if the devil was driven out, the criminals would no longer be bad. St. Thomas Aquinas (1225–1274) opined that the "soul," implanted by God, was the source of our reasoning power. Aquinas contended that the "conscience part of the soul" is what drives humans toward rational and just behavior, but that human appetites are often influenced by the devil. According to Aquinas, criminal acts occur when a human's appetite overrules his or her conscience.

During the fifteenth and sixteenth centuries, many individuals thought that astral influences (moon and stars) caused criminal behavior. Hohenheim (1490–1541), a Swiss physician, was a proponent of the concept that criminal behavior was caused by influences of the stars and moon. According to him, people acted strangely and irrationally because of astral influences. The word *lunatic* comes from the Latin word *luna*, meaning "moon." Even today, we comment that it must be a "full moon" when a lot of crazy things happen. For many years in the eighteenth, nineteenth, and early twentieth centuries, farmers even planted their crops based on lunar cycles.

By the late sixteenth century, the European churches' authority had declined. Governments took greater control of the criminal justice system. At that time, the legal codes of many jurisdictions were either confusing, inconsistent, or did not exist. Court procedures were incomplete and left primarily to the whims of judges. It was under these conditions that the classical theory of criminology developed.

Although the classical school marked the beginning of the study of crime causation as a separate field of study, the quest to explain the causes of crime started long before its development. French anthropologist Paul Topinard coined the term *criminology*, and J. Baptiste della Porta (1535–1615) attempted to develop a relationship between physical characteristics and the type of crime the criminal committed.[3]

Classical Concepts

The Age of Enlightenment dominated Europe for most of the eighteenth century. The Enlightenment movement promoted optimism, certainty, reason, tolerance, humanitarianism, the belief that all problems could be solved, and a belief in human progress. The leaders of the movement were philosophers, who with logic and rationality were going to rid the Earth of its problems.

The classical school of crime causation was originally based on Cesare Beccaria's essay, "On Crimes and Punishments." Beccaria (1738–1794) wrote the essay as an attack on the harsh and uneven punishments that were being imposed by Italian criminal courts. There is no evidence to suggest he considered this document as a way to establish a theory of crime causation.

While the background of the classical school involves the entire scope of preceding intellectual history,[4] Beccaria's essay was based on the theories of social contract writers, including Hobbes, Locke, Voltaire, and Rousseau. During the period when Beccaria was writing, the theology of the Church and the doctrine of the divine right of kings were challenged by the intellectualism and rationalism of the social contract thinkers.

Social Contract Theory of Governmental Power

The social contract theorists contended that the state or royalty received their authority to govern based on an implied contract by which the people of a given area agree to live. In this implied contract, citizens agree to live by certain rules or laws in return for their protection. These theorists opined that a social contract was an implicit agreement among the members of an organized society, or between the governed and the government, defining and limiting the rights and duties of each. It was via this social contract that the king or rulers obtained the right to rule over the people. The theorists rejected the concept that the royalty's authority to rule was given to them by God, or a higher being.

The basic assumption of the social contract approach is that law and political order are not natural, but human creations. The social contract and the political order it creates are simply the means toward an end—the benefit of the individuals involved—and legitimate only to the extent that each group fulfills their part of the agreement. Thomas Hobbes argued that government is not a party to the original contract, and citizens are not obligated to submit to the government when it is too weak to act effectively to suppress civil unrest.[5]

Cesare Beccaria and the Development of the Classical School

That Cesare Beccaria had the ability to write his renowned essay on penal reform was not demonstrated in his early life. Scholars quickly note that this was his only publication of any significance. Beccaria was born in Milan in 1738 and died in 1794. His father and mother were members of the aristocracy, and his ancestors achieved distinction in many areas of endeavor. Beccaria attended the Jesuit College in Parma and then studied law at the University of Pavia. During his early years at Jesuit College, he rebelled against the authoritarian methods of instruction and the inflexible and dogmatic demeanor of his teachers.

Beccaria was considered by many as lazy, and that he preferred to explore the world's problems over a beer at a local pub than by working. His mother was reportedly concerned about her son's ability to function in the business world. Accordingly, she sought a safe, prestigious, but not too demanding position for her son, using her influence to get him appointed as a professor at the university.[6]

Beccaria's interest in philosophical works caused him to develop a close association with two brothers, Pietro and Alessandro Verri. During a discussion with the brothers on the social problems of the day, the brothers challenged Beccaria to lead a discussion on the Italian penal system. It was reported that at the time, Beccaria knew little about the penal system, so he set about researching the system, eventually writing his famous essay. Beccaria concluded that human beings were governed by the doctrine of "free will" and rational behavior. The 1764 essay by Beccaria, "On Crimes and Punishments," is considered to be the basic doctrine of the classical school, so named because it was the first formalized school of criminology.

Free Will

Criminal misconduct has long been considered a violation of social imperatives. While most early societies did not treat juveniles differently from adults, they did recognize the need to use social norms as a means of social control.

The classical school's concept of human nature is that human beings are rational, their behavior governed by the doctrine of "free will." In other words, humans, including juveniles, can make a rational choice to commit or refrain from committing criminal misconduct. Crime is the result of a rational decision by an individual to commit the behavior.

Classical school theorists contend that punishment for criminal misconduct should be prompt, certain, useful, and fit the crime. In order for punishment to serve its purpose, it should be proportional to the misconduct committed. In other words, the state should put a price tag on acts of criminal misconduct so that the individual will understand the costs involved in his or her committing the wrongful act. There should be set punishments for the commission of criminal acts without regard to the person who committed the act. For example, if a juvenile commits a certain act of criminal misconduct, the juvenile should be aware before committing the act what the punishment will be if he or she is convicted.

The classical school was developed during the Age of Enlightenment, an intellectual and philosophical movement that dominated the world of ideas during the eighteenth century. The Age of Enlightenment was followed by the Age of Reason, which represented the genesis of the way humans viewed themselves, and was based on the need for the pursuit of knowledge. As discussed later in this chapter, the positivist school of crime causation developed during the Age of Reason.

Principle of Utilitarianism

One of the early supporters of the classical school was Jeremy Bentham (1748–1832). Bentham was considered an "armchair philosopher" because he was a prolific writer and frequently discussed his classical philosophy. Bentham developed the "principle of utilitarianism," based on the concept that an act is not to be judged by an irrational system of absolutes but by a supposedly verifiable principle of the greatest happiness for the greatest number of people.

According to Bentham, the act possesses "utility" if it tends to produce benefit, advantage, pleasure, or happiness, or prevents pain, evil, or unhappiness. An act should be judged by its utility. Bentham contended that all human behavior is reducible to one simple formula of motivation—the pursuit of pleasure and the avoidance of pain.[7]

Crime Causation and Purpose of Punishment

According to the classical school concepts, crime is related to the inequities in the criminal justice system. The criminal, who is a logical and rational person, is aware of the inconsistencies in the administration of justice. The public is aware that punishments are not administered rationally or fairly. Criminals are aware that judges have different biases and that these biases are reflected in sentencing practices.

The general belief is that a "good" attorney makes the difference as to whether punishments will be harsh or lenient.

In the eighteenth century, when the classical school developed, judges had great autonomy and there were many inequities in the justice system. There was no consistency or uniformity in sentencing. It was as if each jurisdiction was an island unto itself. The classical theorists opined that the lack of logic and rationality in the justice system was related to the cause of crime.

In the early classical thinking, there was no room for an individual's reformation or cure. The idea of individualized treatment did not emerge until the second half of the nineteenth century. The only purpose of punishment was to prevent others from committing crime and thus protecting society. The concept of crime prevention, as known today, did not exist.

Neoclassical School

The neoclassical school like the classical school is based on the concept of free will and that people are guided by reason. The neoclassical school differs from the classical school in that it recognizes differences in criminal circumstances and that some people, like juveniles and persons with unstable mental conditions, may not be able to act "reasonably," or may have limited ability to reason.

The neoclassical school advocates providing limited discretion to the trial judges in the sentencing process. According to James Q. Wilson and Richard Herrnstein, the notion of choice is important. No one is inevitably going to commit a crime. According to them, even when a person sneezes on a subway, he or she would probably not sneeze if the person knew that the penalty for sneezing on a subway was automatically ten years in prison.[8]

Overview of the Classical Theory

The key concepts of the classical theory include:

- Human behavior may be explained by the doctrine of free will.
- Delinquents are responsible for their criminal misconduct.
- The reduction in delinquent behavior could be accomplished by inflicting enough pain upon those misbehaving, i.e., place a "price tag" on their criminal misconduct.
- The purpose of punishment should be to deter others from committing criminal acts.
- The degree and amount of punishment should be based only on the crime itself and not on the background of the actor.
- For punishment to be effective it should be prompt, certain, and serve a useful function.

Rational Choice Theory

According to these theorists, juvenile delinquents are rational decision-makers who freely choose to commit criminal misconduct. Rational choice theory (RCT) has been described as a theory based on the principle of self-interest. RCT was first introduced by economists and later adopted by criminology studies in the late 1970s. In some instances, the rational choice theory has been linked with the learning or differential association theories which are discussed later in chapters 5 and 6.

The basic position of RCT is that criminal behavior is no different from noncriminal behavior in that it is conduct that persons intentionally choose to undertake (i.e., they are not compelled or forced to commit a crime). The reason that delinquents choose to commit crime is that they think it will be more rewarding and less costly for them than noncriminal behavior. Under the rational choice concept, criminal misconduct occurs when a rational delinquent decides that the rewards for committing criminal misconduct are greater than the chance of detection and/or punishment. For example, the juvenile who wants a certain item from the local store decides that his or her chance of being detected is small and therefore steals the item by placing it in his or her pocket.

A somewhat similar example may apply to the adult income taxpayer who cheats on his or her income taxes because the chances are less than 1 percent that he or she will get audited by the Internal Revenue Service. Even if the individual does get audited, the penalty will not be very severe; in most cases, he or she will only be required to pay back taxes plus interest.

The reasons that a juvenile may make a rational choice to commit criminal misconduct are frequently based on financial needs, or personal problems that the juvenile is experiencing. A juvenile may be forced to choose to commit the criminal act to help him or her solve those problems. Frequently, the juvenile commits the misconduct to avoid situations that he or she finds uncomfortable. The juvenile misconduct may also be based on economic needs. For example, the juvenile commits a crime to support his or her drug habit.

Overview of the Rational Choice Theory

The concept of human nature as viewed by the rational choice theorists can be summarized as follows:

- All humans, including juveniles, freely choose either paths in conformity with the laws of the society or criminal paths.
- Juveniles will avoid behaviors that will bring pain or discomfort and will engage in behaviors that they perceive will be favorable to them. Prior to deciding which actions to take, the juveniles weigh the expected benefits against the expected pains.
- Juveniles are totally responsible for their behaviors.
- Juveniles are not helpless, passive, or propelled by forces beyond their control.

Donald Shoemaker notes that the degree to which juveniles rationally consider the consequences of their delinquent acts remains a matter of investigation and discussion.[9] He notes that scholars are divided regarding the importance of "free will" versus the concept of determinism when studying human behavior. Shoemaker notes that a reasonable compromise position on this issue is to view human behavior, whether deviant or conformist, as the result of the exercise of choice within given situations.

If juvenile delinquency is the result of rational choice, then what steps should be taken to eliminate or reduce it? If the juvenile believes that he or she can get away with the delinquent act, then he or she is more likely to commit the act. Using the general deterrence concept of punishment, if the juvenile perceives that he or she will be punished, then he or she is less likely to commit the delinquent behavior.

The general *deterrence theory of punishment* is based on the concept that punishment should be certain and prompt. If punishment is certain and prompt, other juveniles will be deterred from committing criminal acts. Thus, even a small sanction may be enough to deter delinquency if juveniles believe punishment will be certain. If, however, a juvenile believes that it is unlikely that he or she will be punished, the juvenile will not be deterred from the misconduct.

BOX 3.1 **A Native American Precept**

If a child is naughty, do not hit it. Make the child fast. When a child is hungry, it will remember his or her past misconduct. Beating a child makes it naughtier.

Chinese Proverb

Based on the classical concept "It is better to hang the wrong fellow than no fellow," this proverb emphasizes that the certainty of punishment is an important factor in reducing criminal misconduct.

Source: Both the precept and proverb were reported in Ruth Masters and Cliff Roberson, *Inside Criminology* (Englewood Cliffs, NJ: Prentice-Hall, 1990), 90–91.

Under the deterrence concept, it is the perception of punishment that is important. Juveniles who wrongly believe that sanctions are unlikely for the criminal conduct generally will not be deterred by the threat of punishment, even if it is in fact certain and prompt. In order to be effective, punishment must be perceived to be fast and certain, and to fit the crime. The basic purpose of punishment or sanctions in the juvenile justice system should be to protect society. Proponents of the rational choice theory and classical theory believe that it is more important to prevent crimes than to sanction delinquents.

How do the two proverbs contained in box 3.1 reflect classical or rational choice concepts?

Mental Capacity Defenses

Insanity Defense

The insanity defense is based on the classical belief that humans have "free will" to choose between good and bad behavior. Sometimes, however, a person, because of mental issues, lacks the ability to make a rational choice. In this situation, the theorists who advocate the concept of free will contend that the person should not be sanctioned for the choice to commit a delinquent act. The question as to whether the insanity defense should be available to delinquent juveniles is not an easy question to answer for classical or rational choice theorists.

Researchers Jamison Rogers and Wade Myers contend that juveniles, like adults, should be afforded the right to raise an insanity defense.[10] They note that few juveniles across the United States are granted access to the insanity defense and the reasons they should have that option. The researchers note that currently, each year, hundreds of thousands of youths who appear in juvenile court do not have access to the insanity defense. They also note that forty-six states and the federal government jurisdictions allow the insanity defense to be used in adult criminal courts, but only ten states allow juveniles to use the defense.

Individuals who oppose allowing juveniles the defense of insanity rely on the following argument: The purpose of the juvenile system is rehabilitative and treatment-oriented, as opposed to punitive and adversarial. Accordingly, there is no need for mentally ill children to have the ability to raise an insanity defense.

Age Rules on Culpability

Rogers and Myers note that the premise that children have diminished culpability when compared with adults is not new idea. They state that Plato noted in the fourth century BCE that children should not be held criminally responsible for many of their acts. Prior to the establishment of juvenile courts, an 1883 Kentucky case recognized the right of juveniles to raise the insanity defense.[11]

Rogers and Myers note that as a rule, children aged six years and younger are viewed as incapable of forming the intent to commit a crime (infancy defense). From ages seven to thirteen, they are presumed not criminally responsible, but the presumption is rebuttable if a child's immaturity does not cause him to be incapable of understanding the wrongfulness of the act. Children aged fourteen and older are typically considered criminally responsible. Juveniles waived to adult court are held to the same standard, or lack of one, for pleading not guilty by reason of insanity (NGRI) as adult defendants.

Early Positivist Concepts

The positivist approach to criminal misconduct developed during the Age of Reason, or the "realism" movement. This movement encouraged an attitude of "matter-of-fact detachment," and supported a close, precise description of various phenomena, including the use of scientific methods. Hugh Barlow, in describing the mood of that time, stated: "The armchair philosophy that for centuries had dominated learned discourse on the nature of man and society was replaced by the logic and methodology of objective empirical science."[12]

One of the leaders of the positivist school was Cesare Lombroso, who advocated the concept that human beings do not have free will. With the rejection of the concept of free will, the positivist theorists adopted the concept of *determinism*, which holds that individuals have no choice in their behavior. The positivists believed that the individual who commits criminal misconduct is propelled by social, biological, emotional, and/or spiritual forces beyond his or her control.

Positivist Concepts

To understand the different viewpoints between the positivist school and the classical school, we need to examine the marked shift in the thinking of intellectual leaders that took place with the end of the Age of Enlightenment and the beginning of the Age of Realism.[13] It was of such magnitude that it can be considered an intellectual revolution.

Realism was the prevailing intellectual temper during the third quarter of the nineteenth century, discounting sentiment, idealism, mysticism, and the belief in the supernatural. During the century between Cesare Beccaria and Cesare Lombroso (1835–1909), the logic and basic methodology of objective science became entrenched. These interpretations of scientific investigations provide a new intellectual approach that looked for the answers of all phenomena in terms of objective science rather than religion or philosophy.[14]

As noted earlier in the chapter, the positivist theorists did not accept that humans have free will. Instead, they accepted the concept of social determinism and that a delinquent was propelled by social or biological forces beyond the individual's control. The positivists believed that the delinquent was ill, sick, and/or deprived, and the delinquent should be treated rather than sanctioned.

An important contribution of the positivists to the juvenile justice system is the concept that treatment and sanctions should be directed toward what's best for the delinquent rather than simply determining what punishment the delinquent should receive for his or her misconduct.[15] The theorists also accept the concept that the treatment should be individually tailored to meet the needs of the delinquent.

Specific assumptions of positivist criminologists include the following:

- Human behavior is shaped in predictable ways by factors that can be observed and identified.
- Human behavior is thus best understood through an application of the scientific method (observation and hypothesis testing).
- Once the factors that shape human behavior are identified, steps can be taken to alter those factors in order to modify human behavior.

This is a more deterministic approach to delinquency than is true of the rational choice theory or the classical school; rather than stressing free will, positivists believe that human behavior is largely determined by a wide range of factors that may be outside of a person's control.

Cesare Lombroso was the first clinical criminologist who "got his hands dirty" by spending numerous hours measuring the skulls of criminally insane persons and epileptics, earning him the nickname "scientific Columbus." Lombroso categorized and classified types of offenders, developing the first criminal topology. Although his system of classification is considered crude by today's standards, Lombroso concluded that criminals are different from noncriminals because of the manifestation of multiple physical anomalies which are of atavistic or degenerative origin. He classified criminals as follows:

- epileptic;
- insane;
- born; or
- occasional.

Lombroso considered the epileptic criminal, the insane criminal, and the born criminal as separate types, but all stemming from an epileptoid base. Lombroso believed that the moral imbecile and the criminal were fundamentally alike in physical constitution and mental characteristics. Lombroso noted that the born criminal had sensory and functional peculiarities, including a greater insensitivity to pain and touch, more-acute sight, and less-than-average acuteness of hearing, smell, and taste. The born criminal had a lack of moral sense, including an absence of repentance and remorse. The occasional criminal refers to individuals who do not necessarily seek out the occasion for the crime, but are drawn or fall into criminal conduct for very insignificant reasons.[16]

Biological Explanations of Delinquency

The biological approach to delinquency cases assumes that the misconduct is caused or triggered by an internal mechanism. The earliest biological explanations failed to distinguish between biological and psychological characteristics. Most of the early biological theorists were educated as medical doctors, and thus tended to focus on the physical properties of the body in their research.

Charles Darwin's book *On the Origin of Species* (1859) is considered by most researchers as the final break with the Age of Enlightenment and the start of the Age of Realism.[17] Darwin presented evidence to prove that humans were the same general kind of creatures as other animals, but were more highly evolved or developed—that humans were merely one type of creature with no divinity links. According to Darwin (pictured in photo 3.3), our ancestors were less highly evolved and were part of a continuous chain linking humans to the earliest and simplest forms of animal life.

In the late 1700s, Franz Joseph Gall (1758–1828) investigated the bumps and other irregularities of the skulls of deceased criminals. As a result of Gall's work, phrenology emerged as a discipline. Phrenology is based on the theory that the exterior of the skull corresponds to the interior and the brain's conformation. According to this discipline, the brain can be divided into functions, and those functions are related to the shape of the skull. By examining the shape of a person's skull, one can measure their behavior.

PHOTO 3.3 Sir Charles Carlyle Darwin. (Photo courtesy of US Library of Congress Prints and Photographs Division, Washington, DC, LC-DIG-ggbain-03485)

The works upon which the positivist school is based were developed about seventy years before the contributions of Cesare Lombroso. Along with Gall, the works of Auguste Comte (1798–1857) also contributed to the development of the school. Comte originally called his research methods and conclusions "social physics," but dropped this term when Belgian social statistician Adolphe Quetelet also referred to his work the same way.[18] Comte envisioned a society in which all social problems would be solved by scientific methods and research. He contended that by studying large groups of people, we could learn the specific laws that govern human behavior.

Comte theorized that there are three stages in the evolution of human thinking:

- Theological stage, characterized by mythological thinking.
- Metaphysical or abstract stage, characterized by classical thinking.
- Scientific or positivist stage, which Comte considered the highest stage in human thinking.

As noted earlier, Cesare Lombroso is credited with the development of the positivist school of criminology, and the one who truly made it popular. More has been written by and about Cesare Lombroso (1835–1909) than any other criminologist. Lombroso is generally referred to as "the father of modern criminology." His influence is still alive in European contemporary research. In America, he is often used as a straw man for an attack on biological analyses of crime causation.

While a professor of legal medicine at the University of Turin, Lombroso's name became prominent with the publication of his book, *L'uomo delinquente* (The Criminal Man), in 1876. In the book, Lombroso proposed that criminals were biological throwbacks to an earlier evolutionary stage when people were more primitive and less highly evolved than their noncriminal counterparts. He described those people as "atavistic." The word is apparently taken from the Latin word *atavus*, which means "ancestor." Darwin had previously written: "With mankind some of the worst dispositions which occasionally without any assignable cause make their appearance in families, may perhaps be reversions to a savage state, from which we are not removed by many generations."[19]

Lombroso's personal life was apparently normal. At the age of thirty-four, he married a young Jewish girl. They had two daughters, both of whom married professional men who were involved in Lombroso's work. With his daughter

Gina's husband, G. Ferrero, Lombroso spent many hours examining human skulls. Together, Ferrero and Lombroso published *The Female Offender*.

According to George Vold, some researchers contend that it is something of an anomaly that Lombroso's fate was to be known principally for the earliest formulation of his theory of criminality of the atavistic criminal. Vold points out that the real basis for the positivist school is the search for the causes of criminal behavior, based on the multiple factor causation approach, and that while some of the factors may be biological, others may be psychological, and still others, social.[20] Lombroso's thinking changed over the years; later on, he looked more and more to environmental factors rather than biological factors.[21]

Cesare Lombroso advocated that the first objective of punishment should be the protection of society. The second objective was the improvement of the criminal. He objected to the classical approach, where delinquents are treated based on the crime committed and not the differences in the individuals who commit the crime. Lombroso contended that we should make the punishment fit the offender. Like a physician applying remedies according to the illnesses, we should adapt the punishments to fit individuals. There should be different treatments based on whether we have been considering a born criminal, an occasional criminal, or a criminal who committed an act due to passion. Lombroso recommended the concept of indeterminate sentencing, thus restraining the criminal until he or she has been treated and/or corrected.

Most scholars believe that positivism was a reaction to the inflexible harshness of the classical school. The positivist researchers emphasized that what should be considered is not the crime, but the actor as an individual, and the concept that the punishment should be tailored to fit the actor, who had no rational choice in the crime because of determinism. According to positivism, crime can only be eliminated by treating the criminal, not merely punishing him or her. The positivists advocated scientific methodologies for studying the causes of crime. By careful studies and scientific observations, the causes of crime can be determined and eliminated. An important contribution by the school is evidenced by the juvenile justice system, where treatment and punishment is directed toward what's best for the juvenile.

The positivists rejected the freewill concept and substituted the doctrine of determinism and the position that punishment should be tailored to fit the needs of the criminal. Determinism is based on the belief that the delinquent has no choice in his or her behavior because of biological or other factors. The individual is propelled by social, biological, emotional, and/or spiritual forces beyond his or her control. Using this logic, the delinquent did not voluntarily commit the crime.

The positivists recognize two types of determinism: hard and soft determinism. *Hard determinism* is based on the concept that the individual has no freedom of choice. *Soft determinism* is based on the concept that the individual has limited choice in the matter.

Modern biological theorists assume that in addition to delinquency being caused by internal or physical properties, the delinquent is also predisposed to criminality. This predisposition toward criminal behavior often interacts with environmental factors, which may affect biological factors, pushing the juvenile toward delinquency. David Rowe and Wayne Osgood note that the predisposition connection between biology and delinquency is a reciprocal one, and that environmental factors may be both shaped by and influence biological factors. This results in the reciprocal influence that contributes to delinquency.[22]

The modern view on biological causes is that biological factors are seen as predisposing juveniles toward criminality rather than determining delinquency. Most of the biological theorists do not see biological factors as the sole explanation for delinquent behavior, but they are still a significant factor.

Heredity as a Factor

Do criminals inherit bad genes, and are they the cause of their antisocial behavior? Two studies in the early part of the twentieth century examined heredity as a factor. One was about the famous Juke family and the other involved the Kallikak family. Henry Goddard, an advocate of heredity and crime, conducted the research on the Kallikak family. Researchers in both studies concluded there was evidence of hereditary transmission of criminality. The modern view is that there is little evidence to support the findings of hereditary transmission of criminality in the studies of the Jukes and Kallikaks.

A 1992 publication by the National Research Council discussed the findings of a team of Dutch and American scientists who had discovered a Dutch family in which for the past five generations the men had been unusually prone to aggressive outbursts, rape, and arson. The report determined that the men in that family had a genetic defect that made them deficient in an enzyme that regulates levels of the neurotransmitter serotonin. The report, however, cautioned that the results concerned only one family and should not be generalized to the population at large. Researchers Bettyann Kevles and Daniel Kevles concluded that the findings of this team of Dutch and American scientists were recently exaggerated not only by the lay media but by the technical press as well.[23]

Biological explanations of crime causation assume that structure determines behavior. People behave differently because their body structures are different. The structural differences may be the result of chromosomes, genes, chemistry, hormones, or even body type. The biological theories assume that the cause of criminal misconduct is because the person is different, which is often beyond his or her control.

According to many researchers, brain scans seem to give a dramatic view into the biological dynamics of violence. In the 1980s, brain scan studies indicated that the brains of many convicted criminals had areas of inactivity relative to the brain scans of control subjects. In 1997, one psychologist at the University of Texas, Medical Branch, conjured up red-and-blue reconstructions of the brains of violent offenders and used them to support his thesis that hair-trigger tempers are the result of an impairment of the frontal and parietal lobes of their brains. Neuroscientists are attempting to isolate and study the roles of several neurotransmitters in suicidal patients, depressives, and people prone to impulsive violence.[24]

Body Type as a Factor

Ernst Kretschmer (1888–1964) studied the relationship between physique and mental illness. Kretschmer concluded that bodies could be divided into three distinct types:

- *Asthenic*: The asthenic type has a thin and narrow build, with long arms, and is delicate in bone structure and appearance. This type of person tends to be idealistic, introverted, and withdrawn; often associated with schizophrenia. He concluded that this type of person is generally associated with violent crimes.
- *Pyknic*: The pyknic type has a round body and is fat and fleshy. This body type is associated with manic-depressiveness, and tends to exhibit moodiness, extroversion, joviality, and realism. He concluded that this type of person is generally associated with larceny and fraud crimes.

- *Dysplastic*: The dysplastic type has a body type that is part pyknic and part asthenic. He did not indicate an identifiable mental illness for this type of person.[25]

Earnest A. Hooton, a Harvard physical anthropologist, attempted to establish that Lombroso was correct in his biological theories. Hooton concluded that there were key differences between criminals and noncriminals:

- Criminals were more likely to have long, thin necks, thinner beards and body hair, more red-brown hair, and thinner lips than noncriminals.
- Criminals also had low foreheads, compressed faces, and narrow jaws.
- Criminals were physically inferior to noncriminals, and differences were due to hereditary factors.[26]

William Sheldon studied delinquent male youths between the ages of fifteen and twenty-one. He concluded that delinquents had greater mesomorphy (tendency to be big-boned and muscular) than did nondelinquents. He developed his own method of body typing, attempting to isolate three poles of physique which he called somatypes:

- *Endomorph*: A person who is fat, round, and fleshy with short tapering limbs and small bones;
- *Ectomorph*: A person who is thin, small, and bony with a small face, sharp nose, fine hair, relatively little body mass and relatively great surface area; and
- *Mesomorph*: A person who is big-boned and muscular and tends to have a large trunk, heavy chest, and large wrists and hands.[27]

Sheldon Glueck and Eleanor Glueck studied physical types and delinquency. They concluded that strength, physical ability, and activity level of mesomorphy can, under certain circumstances, become antisocial and criminal.[28]

These body-type theories have been criticized for a variety of reasons, some of which are listed below:

- Most body-type theories have not actually demonstrated the relationship between physique and behavior.
- In most studies on body types, cultural factors were not considered.
- Most body-type tests were conducted only on males.
- Most body-type theories were conducted on confined individuals and probably do not represent a normal sample.

Difference and Defectiveness Theories

The difference and defectiveness theories are based on the concept that criminals are biochemically different from noncriminals. Linus Pauling (pictured in photo 3.4) suggested that behavior disorders are mostly caused by "abnormal reaction rates" in the body, which result from constitutional defects, faulty diets, and abnormal concentrations of essential body elements.[29]

Crime and Diet

While links have been established between diet and hyperactivity, the main culprits being cited as sugar, processed, and refined foods, there is controversy as to whether diet can be correlated with criminal behavior. Several studies have indicated that biochemical imbalances in the body may be the result of an inadequate or improper diet.[30] Additional studies have indicated that delinquents generally suffer from vitamin deficiencies, allergies, and low blood sugar. It appears that more research is

PHOTO 3.4 Linus Pauling. (Photo courtesy of US Library of Congress Prints and Photographs Division, Washington, DC, LC-USZ62-76925)

PHOTO 3.5 Sigmund Freud. (Photo courtesy of US Library of Congress Prints and Photographs Division, Washington, DC, LC-USZ62-139124)

needed in this area before positive conclusions can be reached regarding the effect of diet on delinquency.

Psychological Concepts

Generally, psychological approaches to delinquency causation contend that criminal misconduct originates primarily in the personalities of the delinquent. Some of the psychological causation theorists focus on learning patterns to explain the delinquency. Early theorists used demonology to explain criminal behavior, declaring that the delinquent was possessed by evil spirits, and to change their behavior, the evil spirits would need to be driven out. *The Exorcist* horror films are based on this concept, with the series grossing over $660 million at the box office.

Psychological/psychiatric approaches to delinquency causation include psychoanalytic theories, emotional problem theories, mental disorder theories, sociopathic personality theories, and thinking pattern theories.

Psychoanalytic Theories

Sigmund Freud, pictured here in 1909 (see photo 3.5), is considered the chief developer of psychoanalytic theories of delinquency causation, even though he did not discuss criminal behavior to any great extent. According to him, criminals were their own worst punishers. Freud focused on the pathological part of human beings and not on the healthy part. He believed that aggression and violence had their roots in instinct. He developed the concept of a "death wish," a constant source of aggressive impulses that tries to reduce the organism to an inanimate state. He contended that the death wish may be expressed directly, manifested indirectly, as in hunting, or sublimated into sadomasochism.

According to Freud's well-known concepts, the id, ego, and superego form the basis of personality. The id is the primary, rash, impulsive part of the personality, governed by the pleasure principle. The id has no regard for responsibility and sensible things. The ego is considered the sensible and responsible part of the personality, governed by the reality principle. It appraises the external situation and then enables a person to make rational decisions. The ego should repress unacceptable social impulses. The superego is the conscience, the unconscious part of the personality that allows a person to feel pride, shame, or guilt. It is the individual's moral faculty and sets a person's moral and ethical standards.

According to Freud, there are certain psychosexual development stages that humans go through: oral, anal, phallic, latency, and genital. The first is the oral stage, and occurs during the first year of life. During this stage, the infant is totally antisocial and laden with primitive urges, including oral. The second is the anal stage, which lasts until the child is about three years old. During this stage, the child is stubborn, spiteful, and cruel. The next stage is the phallic stage, which lasts until the child is approximately six years old. During the phallic stage the child's genitals are a major focus. During the latency stage, which lasts until about the age of twelve, there are no urges present. The last is the genital stage, where the preteen is once again obsessed with his or her genitals, as well as sex, oral urges, and anal urges.

The psychoanalytic theories were summarized by Louis Yablonski and Martin Haskell as:[31]

- An inability to control criminal drives (id) because of a deficiency in ego or superego development.
- Antisocial character formation resulting from a disturbed ego development, which occurred during the first three years of life.
- An overdeveloped superego, which makes no provision for the satisfaction of the demands of the id.

Emotional Problem Theories

The emotional problem theories assume that delinquency is caused by the inability to cope with everyday problems. The delinquent is responding to very subtle psychological factors that prevent him or her from functioning normally. For the most part, these theories assume that the delinquent is normal in psychological makeup and is not psychotic, neurotic, or sociopathic. The theorists assume that the individual's coping skills have deteriorated. The deterioration could be caused by problems such as those caused by relationships, crises, financial difficulty, employment, sickness, or lack of an adequate self-concept. If the delinquent's coping ability is restored, it is unlikely that the individual will commit additional crimes. Both the emotional problem theories and the mental disorder theories (discussed next) consider that there is something wrong with the delinquent, and that he or she is not a normal person.

Mental Disorder Theories

There is a lot of disagreement among mental disorder theorists as to the actual cause of the delinquency. They all agree that the delinquent is not a normal person. The mental disorder theories attempt to classify the delinquent behavior using certain mental disorders, such as psychosis, neurosis, and/or impulse disorders. The most commonly mentioned disorder is psychosis. According to these theorists, the psychoses can be functional and/or organic. Psychotic individuals lose contact with reality and have difficulty distinguishing between reality and fantasy.

Neurosis is a type of disorder that was first used to cover a group of diseases that affected the nervous system. It appears that neurosis has no demonstrable organic cause, and that neurotic behaviors are those that do not grossly violate social norms or represent severely disordered personalities.

Impulse disorders are frequently sudden and explosive, driving the person to action. An individual with impulse disorder may not necessarily lose touch with reality or lose the ability to communicate. Impulse disorders include compulsive thievery, an irresistible impulse to set fires, or other destructive behaviors that occur in persons with otherwise good self-control.

There is a common tendency to view deviant behavior or irrational behavior as psychologically abnormal behavior. Frequently, unacceptable behavior is associated with mental illness; the individual is guilty by association. Research has indicated that psychotic or disturbed individuals are no more likely to commit serious crimes than others in the general population.

Sociopathic Personality Theories

The term *psychopath* is used by psychiatrists to describe individuals who exhibit a certain group of behaviors and attitudes. It is often used in conjunction with the current terms *sociopath* and *antisocial personality*. The terms are used interchangeably, and are reserved for those individuals who are basically unsocialized, and whose behavior patterns bring them repeatedly into conflicts with society. These individuals are considered incapable of significant loyalty to individuals or groups and social values. They are also considered selfish, callous, irresponsible, impulsive, and unable to feel guilt or to learn from experience and punishment. Their frustration tolerance is low, and they tend to blame others for their behavior.[32]

Many theorists believe that delinquent behaviors originate in the personality of the individual. Others contend that it is possible the behaviors can be explained by factors other than personality, and that sociopathy, alcoholism, and drug addiction are only psychiatric conditions consistently associated with delinquent behavior.

Starting with the *Diagnostic and Statistical Manual of Mental Disorders (DSM-III)* and continued in *DSM-5*, the American Psychiatric Association has replaced the terms *psychopath* and *sociopath* with the term *antisocial personality disorder*. As many researchers have pointed out, the term is so broad that it might be applied to almost any criminal. Hervey Cleckley notes that the term may be found in any profession, and that most are not criminal.[33]

Thinking Pattern Theories

The thinking pattern theories are psychological theories that focus on the delinquent's cognitive processes. Assuming that there is a link between crime and intelligence, the theorists see low intelligence as the cause of crime. Yet, they fail to explain why many intelligent youths are also involved in delinquent behaviors. The two most popular thinking pattern theories are cognitive development theories and the criminal personality.

Cognitive development theories are based on the works of Jean Piaget. Piaget's theory of cognitive development is a comprehensive theory about the nature and development of human intelligence. Piaget believed that one's childhood plays a vital and active role in a person's development. Piaget's idea is primarily known as a developmental stage theory, which deals with the nature of knowledge itself, and how humans gradually come to acquire, construct, and use it. These theorists contend that the ways in which people organize their thoughts about rules and laws result in either criminal or noncriminal behavior. The organization of thoughts is referred to as moral reasoning.

The later cognitive development theorists developed the thesis that both criminal and noncriminal behaviors are related to cognitive development, and that people choose the behaviors in which they wish to engage. The theorists argue that criminal behavior exists because of the way people think.

Samuel Yochelson and Stanton Samenow conducted the most detailed study on the criminal mind and the way that offenders think.[34] Based on their experience working with criminal offenders in a psychiatric hospital, the authors concluded that criminal behavior resulted primarily from the thinking patterns of offenders. They identified fifty-two "thinking errors" that characterized criminal thought processes. For example, they found that offenders were often closed to criticism, refused to accept responsibility for their own behaviors, and were present- rather than future-oriented. Yochelson and Samenow held that these thinking errors are deeply ingrained within the offender. They argued that for them to change, offenders must undergo rehabilitation and learn new ways of thinking that will enable them to pursue a responsible path in life.

Practicum

Assume that you are a juvenile court judge and are deciding the disposition of a case involving a juvenile who, without authorization of the owner, took a motor vehicle for a "joyride." If you accept the concept of free will, then you would believe the juvenile made a rational decision to commit the act. If, however, you accept the concept of determinism, you would believe that the juvenile did not make a rational decision to take the vehicle.

How would your choice of concept affect your disposition of the juvenile's case?

Summary

- Classical and positivist theories are the two basic explanations of criminal behavior. Most present-day theories are based on one of these two schools of thought.
- The positivist school sees the delinquent as different from the noncriminal because of psychological or biological differences.
- The ancient Hebrews considered laws as expressions of God's commands. Accordingly, a violation of the law was a transgression against God—a sin. Deviant behavior, at that time, was believed to destroy the bonds of society.
- Greek philosophers considered criminal misconduct as an offense against society or the state. The philosophers considered that individuals who committed crimes were infected with corruption and evil.
- Early European churches equated crime with sin. Individuals who committed criminal misconduct were possessed by the devil.
- The classical school was originally based on Cesare Beccaria's essay, "On Crimes and Punishments."
- Social contract theorists contended that the state or royalty received their authority to govern based on an implied contract by which the people of a given area agree to live.
- The classical school's concept of human nature was that human beings were rational, and their behavior was governed by the doctrine of "free will."
- The classical school theorists contended that punishment for criminal misconduct should be prompt, certain, useful, and fit the crime. To serve its purpose, punishment should be proportional to the misconduct.

- The neoclassical school differs from the classical school in that it recognizes differences in criminal circumstances, and that some people, like juveniles and persons with unstable mental conditions, may not be able to act "reasonably," or have limited ability to reason.
- The rational choice theory is a modified and updated version of the classical school. The basic concepts of the classical school are retained by the rational choice theorists.
- Rational choice theorists advocate that criminal behavior is based on the use of calculations, reasoning, and "rational considerations."
- Specific assumptions of positivist criminologists include the following: Human behavior is shaped in predictable ways by factors that can be observed and identified; human behavior is thus best understood through an application of the scientific method (observation and hypothesis testing); and once the factors that shape human behavior are identified, steps can be taken to alter those factors in order to modify human behavior.
- The biological approach to delinquency cases assumes that the misconduct is caused or triggered by an internal mechanism.
- The psychological approaches to delinquency causation contend that criminal misconduct originates primarily in the personalities of the delinquent.

Discussion and Review Questions

1. Explain the concept of free will.
2. How do the classical and positivist schools differ in their approach to juvenile delinquency?
3. Explain why Lombroso is considered the father of modern criminology.
4. Discuss the conclusions of Auguste Comte.
5. How does Freud explain criminal behavior?
6. What are the basic concepts of the psychological theories of crime causation?

Notes

1. President's Commission on Law Enforcement and Administration of Justice, "The Challenge of Crime in a Free Society" (Washington, DC: GPO, 1967), 3–5.
2. Cliff Roberson and Harvey Wallace, *Introduction to Criminology* (Incline Village, NV: Copperhouse Publishing, 1998).
3. Jodie Jenkinson, "Face Facts: A History of Physiognomy from Ancient Mesopotamia to the End of the 19th Century," *Journal of Biocommunication*, vol. 24, no. 3 (1997), 2–7.
4. George B. Vold and Thomas J. Bernard, *Theoretical Criminology*, 3rd ed. (New York: Oxford University Press, 1986).
5. Patrick Riley, "The Social Contract and Its Critics," chapter 12 in *The Cambridge History of Eighteenth-Century Political Thought*, edited by Mark Goldie and Robert Wokler, vol. 4 of *The Cambridge History of Political Thought* (London: Cambridge University Press, 2006), 347–75.
6. John Hostettler, *Cesare Beccaria: The Genius of "On Crimes and Punishments"* (Hampshire, UK: Waterside Press, 2011).
7. Roberson and Wallace, *Introduction to Criminology*, 1998.
8. James Q. Wilson and Richard J. Herrnstein, *Crime and Human Nature* (New York: Simon & Schuster, 1986).
9. Donald J. Shoemaker, *Theories of Delinquency: An Examination of Explanations of Delinquent Behavior*, 7th ed. (New York: Oxford University Press, 2018), 18.
10. Jamison Rogers and Wade Myers, "Commentary: The Insanity Defense and Youths in Juvenile Court," *Journal of the American Academy of Psychiatry and the Law*, vol. 41, no. 4 (December 2013), 496–500.

11. *McClure v. Commonwealth*, 81 Ky. L. Rptr. 448, 451 (1883).
12. Hugh D. Barlow, *Introduction to Criminology* (Boston: Little, Brown, 1984), 132.
13. Roberson and Wallace, *Introduction to Criminology*, 1998.
14. Roberson and Wallace, *Introduction to Criminology*, 1998.
15. Ruth E. Masters and Cliff Roberson, *Inside Criminology* (Upper Saddle River, NJ: Prentice-Hall, 1990).
16. Roberson and Wallace, *Introduction to Criminology*, 1998.
17. George B. Vold and Thomas J. Bernard, *Theoretical Criminology*, 3rd ed. (New York: Oxford University, 1986).
18. Lewis Coser, "The Sociology of Poverty," *Social Problems*, vol. 13 (Fall 1971).
19. Charles Darwin, *The Descent of Man* (London: John Murray, 1871), 137.
20. Vold and Bernard, *Theoretical Criminology*, 37.
21. Vold and Bernard, *Theoretical Criminology*.
22. David Rowe and Wayne Osgood, "Heredity and Sociological Theories of Delinquency," *American Sociological Review*, vol. 49 (1984), 526–40.
23. Frank H. Marsh and Janet Katz, eds. *Biology, Crime and Ethics* (Cincinnati, OH: Anderson, 1985).
24. Bettyann H. Kevles and Daniel J. Kevles, "Scapegoat Biology," *Discovery* (October 1997), 58–64.
25. Ernst Kretschmer, *Physique and Character* (translated by W. J. H. Sprott) (London: Trubner, 1925).
26. Earnest A. Hooton, *The American Criminal: An Anthropological Study* (Cambridge: Harvard University Press, 1939).
27. W. H. Sheldon, *Varieties of Delinquent Youths* (New York: Harper, 1949).
28. Sheldon Glueck and Eleanor Glueck, *Unraveling Juvenile Delinquency* (New York: Commonwealth Fund, 1950).
29. A. Hoffer, "Some Theoretical Principles Basic to Orthomolecular Psychiatric Treatment," in L. J. Hippen, ed. *Ecologic-Biochemical Approaches to Treatment of Delinquents and Criminals* (New York: Van Nostrand Reinhold, 1978).
30. Vold and Bernard, *Theoretical Criminology*.
31. Louis Yablonsky and Martin R. Haskell, *Juvenile Delinquency* (New York: Harper & Row, 1988).
32. *Diagnostic and Statistical Manual of Mental Disorders*, 5th ed. (Washington, DC: American Psychiatric Association, 2013).
33. Hervey Cleckley, *The Mask of Insanity*, 5th ed. (St. Louis: Mosby, 1981).
34. Samuel Yochelson and Stanton Samenow, *The Criminal Personality, Volume I: A Profile for Change* (Northvale, NJ: Jason Aronson, 1976).

CHAPTER 4

Social Structure Concepts

CHAPTER OBJECTIVES

After studying this chapter, the reader should be able to:

- Explain the social structural approach to crime causation.
- Discuss the concept of social disorganization.
- Explain the broken windows theory.
- Discuss the symbolic interactionist theories.
- Explain the concept of "anomie."
- Compare the social structure theories with the classical theories.

Causation Theories

Grouping delinquency causation theories into certain categories is based largely on the opinions of the authors. It is difficult and subject to interpretation as to which theory belongs in which general category. In addition, many of the theories can logically be placed in different groups. In chapter 3, for example, we explored the rational choice theory. It was placed in chapter 3 because it was a continuation of the classical theory of crime causation. Rational choice theory, however, could justifiably be included in this chapter on social theories. The approach that the authors recommend is to consider each individual theory and determine if the logic and assumptions of that theory are rational, and not be too concerned with which general group it is placed in by the authors.

In this chapter, the social structural explanations of delinquency are discussed, including the concept of *structural disadvantage*. According to this concept, crime is more likely to occur in neighborhoods with deteriorated housing, low rates of home ownership, high rates of residential mobility, and low collective efficacy. Structural disadvantage can lead to crime in three ways:

- It creates social disorganization, causes strain, and encourages the development of subcultural values that clash with the dominant culture.
- Race- and class-based social exclusion perpetuate disadvantage and, by extension, encourage crime.

- Crime can be reduced through neighborhood-level interventions and changes in the overall social structure.

Central to the social structural perspective is the idea that human behavior is more than a matter of choice or personal characteristics. Two people with similar dispositions can have different propensities toward crime depending upon their position in the social structure.

Social Norms

A norm is a basic sociological concept that is used to explain human behavior. Norms have also been referred to as "rules of conduct." They are also seen as blueprints for behavior. As discussed in chapter 1, norms can be proscriptive, prescriptive, formal, or informal.[1] *Proscriptive* norms are norms that forbid certain actions. For example, you should not commit murder. *Prescriptive* norms are norms that tell us what we should do or what we may do, i.e., we should give up our seat on the bus to a disabled person. *Formal* norms are those that are formally imposed upon a society or group. For example, the penal code of your home state contains formal proscriptive norms. *Informal* norms are those social actions that are not formally written down. An example of a proscriptive informal norm would be that in a line of people waiting to enter an airplane, you should not cut in line.

Socialization

Socialization refers to the learning process by which a person becomes part of a social group and learns the group's norms. When a person joins the US Marines, for example, he or she is required to attend boot camp, during which the individual is socialized as a marine. The same concepts apply when individuals attend police academies. The persons are being socialized as police officers. Similar processes take place when a person becomes a teacher or an attorney.

When a person is socialized as a member of his or her family, the socialization starts at birth and continues during the period that the person is a member of the family. During this socialization process, the individual learns the skills, knowledge, attitudes, values, and behaviors that are acceptable to the family. Socialization may also result in the learning of negative behavior, such as that depicted in photo 4.1.

The concept of *resocialization* refers to an extreme change or shift in values, attitudes, and behaviors that were once an integral part of the person's life. For example, when a military person is released from active military duty and returns to civilian life, he or she goes through the process of resocialization from military life to civilian life.

Anomie

In his text, *The Division of Labor in Society*, Emile Durkheim introduced the term *anomie*.[2] At the time (1893), Durkheim was focused on the transformation of societies from folk to modern societies. Durkheim used the Greek term *anomie* to refer to a state or condition that exists when a society evolves from a primitive society to a modern one. While the term is officially defined as "a state of lawlessness," Durkheim used it to describe a condition of normlessness. According to his definition, norms have lost their meaning and have become inoperative for a large portion of society.

For a modern concept of anomie, consider the fact that if you lived in a small town you would hesitate to violate community norms because it would cause

PHOTO 4.1 Female student being bullied by her classmates. Frequently such behavior can be learned by socialization. (Photo courtesy of iStock)

embarrassment to your family. When you move to a major city where you do not know your next-door neighbor and you are isolated, then norms would not be as strong in controlling your behavior. In the latter example, community members would not even be aware of your violation of society norms unless the violation was particularly grievous.

Durkheim believed that anomie was caused by the division of labor as society changed from a primitive one to a modern one. In a primitive society, the family was almost self-sufficient. You raised your own food and built your own shelters. In a modern society, under a division of labor, you buy your groceries, rent or buy a prebuilt home, and are dependent on numerous other individuals in the society.

Durkheim noted that when society is in transition and anomie is high, institutions and laws become meaningless to people, and criminal behavior results. He opined that even crime in a society serves a purpose. A person who is convicted of a crime is marked as not a good member of the community, whereas those who have not been convicted of a crime can consider themselves good members of the community. Box 4.1 looks at the situation described by Durkheim: a society where the most serious crimes have been eliminated, and therefore the most severe punishments are used for minor offenses.

Social Structure Processes

The social structural theorists believe that we need to look at the dynamics of social status, relationships, and institutions such as the "economy, polity, family, and education" to understand the concentration of crime in disadvantaged urban communities.[3] Robert Merton authored an article entitled "Social Structure and Anomie" in which he applied Durkheim's theory of anomie to deviant behavior. Merton opined that deviant behavior was caused by conditions in the social structure. He believed that society created a strain between culturally prescribed goals and the socially structured means to achieve them. Merton described *culturally*

BOX 4.1 **Should a Person Guilty of a Minor Offense Receive the Maximum Allowable Punishment?**

Roberson and Wallace discuss punishments in a society without serious crime. Consider the consequences of such a society. As noted by Emil Durkheim, this would be a pathological state. Using the concept that the most serious crimes should receive the maximum punishments permitted in a society, if aggravated murder is the most serious crime, then a person who commits this crime should receive the maximum punishment. But if the society has no serious crime, then would the maximum punishment be reserved for those individuals who commit minor transgressions, such as jaywalking?

Source: Cliff Roberson and Harvey Wallace, *Introduction to Criminology* (Incline Village, NV: Copperhouse, 1998).

prescribed goals as the values in a society and the *socially structured means* as the norms in a society.[4] Merton developed five different modes of adaptations to an anomic society:

- **Conformity** occurs when a person accepts both the goals and means of a society.
- **Innovation** exists when a person accepts the goals but rejects the accepted means for achieving the goals.
- **Ritualism** describes the situation when a person rejects the goals but accepts the means.
- **Retreatism** is when a person rejects both the goals and the means.
- **Rebellion** is when a person does not accept the goals and the means of society, and wishes to change the social structure.

The assumptions of social structural theorists include:

- Crime is a normal response under certain social conditions.
- Social problems tend to cluster among structurally disadvantaged populations, and among the geographic spaces in which disadvantage is concentrated.
- Crime is more likely to occur in neighborhoods with structural disadvantage, including deteriorated housing, low rates of home ownership, high rates of residential mobility, and low collective efficacy. This can lead to crime in three ways:
  - It creates social disorganization;
  - causes strain; and
  - encourages the development of subcultural values that clash with the dominant culture.
- Race- and class-based social exclusion perpetuate disadvantage and, by extension, encourage crime.
- Crime can be reduced through neighborhood-level interventions and changes in the overall social structure.
- Rehabilitative programs targeted at individual offenders are unlikely to be successful at reducing crime unless they also address criminogenic social conditions. *Criminogenic* refers to the factors or conditions that produce or tend to cause crime or criminals.

Strain Theories

The general assumptions of the strain theories are based on the following principles:

- When an individual does not conform to society's norms and laws, it is because there are excessive pressures or strains placed on the individual, which cause the misconduct.
- It is not normal for individuals to engage in lawbreaking or criminal deviance.
- Most criminal misconduct is caused by pressures placed on the individual by society's expectations.
- People are basically moral and desire to conform to society's laws and norms.
- The principal question for strain theorists is: What is the nature of the strains or pressures that cause an individual to commit criminal misconduct?[5]

Robert Merton and the Strain Theory

Robert Merton is credited with the development of the strain theory in the 1940s to explain the rising crime rates experienced at that time. The theory quickly became popular with contemporary sociologists. Using Durkheim's conception of anomie and applying it to the United States, Merton discussed the question of how malintegration in society was a cause of criminal deviance. Merton concluded that anomie was the greatest in societies like that found in the United States, where certain ends or goals were elevated but many individuals lacked the means of attaining those goals.

Merton opined that our cultural system in the United States developed based on the "American Dream," which he defined as a set of meritocratic principles in which people assumed that the equality of opportunity was available to all, regardless of class, gender, or ethnicity. This dream encouraged individuals to pursue a goal of success, largely measured in terms of the acquisition of wealth and material possessions. People were expected to pursue this goal through legitimate means, such as education and work. Excerpts of Merton's comments are contained in box 4.2. Merton noted that the culture of a society defines certain goals that the society deems worth striving for, and that there are certain approved methods to use in obtaining those goals. For example, in the United States, the society in general desires to acquire wealth, which is generally equated with a high degree of prestige and social status. The accepted and approved mode of attaining wealth is to get a good education, a good job, and then to work hard.

BOX 4.2 **Robert Merton's Comments**

Certain aspects of the social structure may generate counter mores and antisocial behavior precisely because of differential emphases on goals and regulations. In the extreme case, the latter may be so vitiated by the goal-emphasis that the range of behavior is limited only by considerations of technical expediency. [. . .] As this process continues, the integration of the society becomes tenuous and anomie ensues.

Source: Robert K. Merton, "Social Structure and Anomie," *American Sociological Review*, vol. 3, no. 5 (1938), 673.

But since not all individuals have an equal opportunity to get a good education and a good job, some use methods that are not approved by society's norms in order to obtain the goals. The pressure to attain wealth causes many individuals to take shortcuts and commit criminal misconduct to acquire it. For example, a person may deal in drugs, which, in addition to being criminal, is not a socially approved method of attaining wealth. It sends a powerful message when youths living in an impoverished area see that the fancy cars are all driven by drug dealers.

Merton observed that while success in the United States is almost universally measured by individual economic achievement, conventional pathways for economic success are not universally accessible. Merton used the phrase "goals–means dysfunction" to describe the situation where a person accepts society's goals but is blocked from attaining these goals by society's accepted means. According to Merton, when the dysfunction exists, the individual makes specific adaptations to obtain the goals.

Merton contended that there are five modes of adaptation a person can make to deal with anomie. He noted that they are designed to account for some but not all forms of criminal misconduct. Table 4.1 is a comparison of the modes and goals of society.

The five modes of adaptation are:

- **Conformity:** The person accepts both society's goals and the means for attaining those goals. For example, the individual accepts the goal of acquiring wealth and gets a good education to qualify for a high-paying job in order to acquire the wealth.
- **Innovation:** The individual accepts the goals, but rejects the approved means for acquiring the goal. For example, an individual accepts the goal of acquiring wealth but looks for different ways to obtain that goal, like theft.
- **Ritualism:** The person rejects society's goals yet accepts the approved means to achieve the goals. For example, even though the person believes that the goal of acquiring wealth is not important, he or she still qualifies for a profession, but then expends minimum effort (i.e., he or she plays the game). Merton indicated that this was a common lower-middle-class socioeconomic status response.
- **Retreatism:** Individuals using this adaptation reject both the goals and the approved means for obtaining those goals. For example, the individual is a dropout from society.
- **Rebellion:** The person rejects both the goals and the approved means of obtaining those goals, and replaces them with his or her own goals. An illegal drug

TABLE 4.1 Merton's Modes of Adaptation

Modes	Approved Goals	Approved Means
Conformity	+	+
Innovation	+	-
Ritualism	-	+
Retreatism	-	-
Rebellion	+/-	+/-

\+ signifies acceptance.
\- signifies rejection.
+/- signifies rejection of prevailing values and substitution of new values.

user would fit in this group if the individual did not care about wealth and stole to feed his or her drug habit.

Differential Opportunity Theory

Richard Cloward in his differential opportunity theory concludes that just as access to conventional means is differentially distributed, so are the opportunities to engage in criminal misconduct.[6] According to Cloward and L. E. Ohlin, even the juveniles who are motivated to engage in delinquent misconduct may not have enough knowledge regarding how to engage in the conduct and where to start.[7] The limitations they may face include:

- Few opportunities to learn illegitimate skills, such as theft or burglary;
- Lack of access to criminal networks, as with accessing a distributor for drug dealing; and
- Greater disapproval and intolerance from the surrounding community.

Differential opportunity theory integrated the ideas from two distinctly different theories. The motivation for deviance from the strain theory was combined with the theories about means to learn criminal behavior. Differential opportunity theory attempts to explain the emergence of three different delinquent subcultures: the criminal, the conflict, and the retreatist subcultures. Over the years since its inception, differential opportunity theory has received mixed empirical support.

General Strain Theory

Robert Agnew formulated the general strain theory based on Merton's initial focus on goal attainment as a cause of strain. Agnew concluded that in addition to the pursuit of desired states, people are also motivated to avoid undesirable states. The concept of the general strain theory is that crime may result from either an inability to obtain a desired state or the inability to escape a negative circumstance. Agnew contended that both pathways result in strain. Individuals who found themselves powerless to leave stressful situations, such as a negative home environment or harassment from peers, may be compelled to commit crimes.[8] Agnew's contributions expanded the strain theory. Those contributions include:

- Not all crime is related to blocked goal attainment.
- Youths typically have less power than adults to choose their circumstances, which is one explanation for why crime peaks during adolescence and young adulthood and then declines with age.
- Crime may be committed to escape the undesired situation, or out of anger and frustration for being unable to do so.

Agnew later added to his theory the different types of strain that may lead to crime:

- **Failure to achieve positively valued goals.** This is the type of strain most consistent with Merton's conceptualization of strain.[9]
- **The removal of positively valued stimuli.** Divorce, family breakups, the death of loved ones, and other forms of loss can result in an immense amount of stress. These activities may lead to crime through drug use, attempts at revenge, or efforts to "retrieve the lost stimuli or obtain substitute stimuli."
- **The presentation of negative stimuli.** Victimization, poor-quality relationships, and physically uncomfortable environments can stimulate crime among those trying to escape or cope with those circumstances.

Agnew in his fully developed general strain theory concluded that strains are most likely to result in crime when they:[10]

- are seen as unjust;
- are seen as high in magnitude;
- are associated with low social control;
- create pressure or incentive to engage in criminal coping; and
- can be addressed through the reduction of strain or an increase in the accessibility of noncriminal coping mechanisms.

Subcultural Theories

Subcultural theories developed from symbolic interaction theories and the Chicago School. The latter started in 1920 when members of the Department of Sociology at the University of Chicago conducted the first large-scale study of crime in the United States. Subcultural theorists contend that certain groups or subcultures in society have values and attitudes that are conducive to crime and violence. These theorists believe that if this pattern of offending can be understood and controlled, it would stop the transition from teenage offender into habitual criminal. Some of the theories are functionalist and assume that criminal activity is motivated by economic needs; other subcultural theories are based on societal rationale to explain delinquency. Generally, the subcultural theories identify alternative value systems that arise from disadvantaged economic or social circumstances.

Albert Cohen

Albert Cohen developed the concept of "the middle-class measuring rod." Cohen saw our society as primarily consisting of middle and working classes. According to him, society places a high premium on ambition, getting ahead, and achievement. Both the middle and lower classes teach these values to their children, but the children from the lower classes, while their success is measured by the middle-class measuring rod, are not properly trained or lack the resources to fulfill the expectations. In addition, the lower-class children have different values from the middle-class children. Table 4.2 contains a comparison of the values of the two classes.

Albert Cohen's delinquent subculture theory,[11] like strain theories, places an emphasis on low-income youths' difficulty in obtaining conventional markers of

TABLE 4.2 Values Comparison

Middle-class values	Lower-class values
Self-control	Nonchalance
Postponement of immediate gratification in favor of long-term goals	Easygoing
Planning for future	Lack of order
Being orderly	Lack of punctuality
Individual responsibility	Lack of responsibility
Ambition	Lack of ambition
Development and growth of skills	Taking care of today
Respect for property	Little respect for property
Control of aggression and anger	Toughness

success. Cohen, however, focused attention on understanding the resultant formation of delinquent subcultures. Cohen contended that efforts to obtain upward mobility were subject to the decision-making of gatekeepers such as teachers and businesspeople who have the power to grant or deny access to others.

The gatekeepers value traditional "middle-class" values, such as ambition, personal responsibility, and the acceptance of delayed gratification, while lower-class youth have limited access to the tools needed to meet these middle-class goals. Cohen argued that the pursuit of social mobility in the face of repeated rejection results in psychological stress. In order to relieve this uncomfortable state, low-income individuals create an oppositional value system that conveys status based on the rejection of the mainstream values of the system that has rejected them. Unlike Merton's utilitarian argument—that crime is often committed as a means to an end—Cohen instead contends that crime is "non-utilitarian, malicious, and negativistic," reactions adopted in overt rejection of middle-class values.[12]

Institutional Anomie Theory

The institutional anomie theory (IAT) was developed in the 1990s by Stephen Messner and Richard Rosenfeld. The theory is based on Merton's strain theory and Durkheim's conceptualization of anomie. The aim of the researchers was to explain crime rates at the aggregate level.[13]

Messner and Rosenfeld opine that an institutional arrangement where the economy can dominate without enough restraints from other institutional components, such as the family and the polity, will foster criminal behavior. The researchers propose that US society is an example of such a social system. Their conclusions are partially based on the concept that capitalism developed in the United States, a territory without preexisting institutional structures. According to the researchers, crime resulted from a lack of the restraining potential of families and other conventional institutions.

In 2004, using the IAT, Sang-Weon Kim and William Pridemore examined socioeconomic change, social institutions, and serious property crime in transitional Russia.[14] Using crime data from the Russian Ministry of the Interior and an index of socioeconomic change, the researchers concluded that socioeconomic changes had no effect on two different measures of robbery; only very limited support for the hypothesis of direct effects of social institutions on crime; and no support for the hypothesis that institutions moderate the effect of these changes on crime. The researchers interpreted these findings in the context of transitional Russia and concluded that rigorous research in other nations was important in determining the generalizability of criminological theories developed to explain crime in Western nations.

Symbolic Interaction Theories

The leading symbolic interaction (SI) theories of delinquent causation are labeling and differential association (DA). Both examine the influence of an individual's associations with peers, family, and other social units on the individual. The general assumptions of SI theories are:

- Symbols that we learn and use become our social reality.
- We are socialized by the people with whom we associate.
- The causes of our behavior are based on our interpretations of reality.

The term *symbolic interaction* was coined by George Herbert Bloomer in 1937. Bloomer focused on situations and interactions with society that lead up to delinquent behavior rather than the differences or defectiveness of the delinquent. The basic positions of SI theories include the fact that people act toward things based on the meanings that these things have for them; and that the meanings these things have are derived from social interactions with others.

Differential Association

Edwin Sutherland, considered by most criminologists as the father of American criminology, developed his differential association (DA) theory to explain career criminal behavior. It is a very popular theory in the United States. Differential association has been the most influential sociopsychological theory since the 1930s. After Sutherland's death in 1950, his student, Donald Cressey, continued Sutherland's work and advocated the theory's basic principles.[15]

There is a general agreement among criminologists that differential association is not a good descriptive title for Sutherland's theory. While *differential association* sounds like it refers to people in association, it does not. What is differentially associated are definitions of situations. Sutherland contended that the individual has a limited choice regarding his or her conduct, but he has a conflict orientation to society. Sutherland concluded that we learn to accept antisocial values and thus commit antisocial acts because of the people with whom we associate. Accordingly, we learn to commit delinquent acts the same way we learn to play basketball or baseball. Sutherland did not see social factors as being innately good or bad, but simply present, to be acted upon by others.

Sutherland developed the following set of propositions to explain differential association theory:

1. Criminal behavior is learned and not a necessary outcome of a socially disorganized society or because the offender is different from the noncriminal.
2. Criminal behavior is learned with other persons in the process of communication. Simply being in a criminogenic environment does not cause criminal behavior.
3. The primary part of learning criminal behavior occurs within intimate personal groups. We identify with our reference groups and they, in turn, guide our values. The reference group includes the groups with which we really identify. The contacts that have the greatest influence on our behavior are those that have the greatest significance and meaning to us.
4. When criminal behavior is learned, the delinquent also learns the techniques of committing the misbehavior and the specific direction of motives, drives, rationalizations, and attitudes.
5. The specific direction of motives and drives are learned from definitions of the legal codes as favorable or unfavorable to violation of the law. A person's attitude about what is right or wrong is influenced by the attitude of those the person considers to be important and have meaning to him or her.
6. A person becomes delinquent because of an excess of definitions favorable to violation of the law over definitions unfavorable to violation of the law.
7. Differential associations vary in frequency, duration, priority, and intensity.
8. The process of learning criminal behavior by association with criminal and noncriminal patterns involves all the mechanisms that are involved in any other learning.
9. Although criminal behavior is an expression of general needs and values, it is not explained by those general needs and values, since noncriminal behavior is also an expression of the same needs and values.

Sutherland's proposition 6, listed above, is considered as the key to DA. While William J. Chambliss states that differential association theory explains a wide range of behavior, this is a single straightforward generalization, and he notes that the theory has never been adequately tested. Chambliss sees that the theory and Sutherland's propositions are difficult to conceptualize in a manner that leads to empirical measurement.[16]

Differential Association Reinforcement

Researchers Robert Burgess and Ronald Akers are credited with developing the differential association reinforcement theory. Using Sutherland's differential association, the researchers broaden the theory to include a more-general concept of behaviorism, incorporating the works of B. F. Skinner. Their theory may be summarized as follows:[17]

- The primary learning of social behavior occurs with operant conditions in which behavior is shaped by the stimuli that follows or are the consequences of the behavior.
- Direct conditioning and imitations of others are important in determining behavior.
- Rewards or positive reinforcement as well as the desire to avoid pain and punishment strengthen behavior.
- Differential reinforcement determines whether the behavior is considered as deviant or conforming.
- People learn the norms of behavior from those who are important to them.

An example of this theory may be observed in the following scenario:

> While standing in a checkout line at grocery store you observe that a father and his child are waiting in the line ahead of you. The child sees a display of candy bars and demands one. The father refuses the request. The child throws a temper tantrum. After several minutes of screaming and foot stomping the child stops. The child then apologizes for his behavior and asks for a candy bar in a very polite voice. The father thanks the child for his or her polite manners and buys the child a candy bar.

This sequence of interactions between the father and his child is an example of differential association reinforcement. (Note: This is very similar to the rational choice theory, which suggests that people weigh the rewards and risks involved in certain types of behavior and then decide which course of action to follow.)[18]

Labeling

Researcher Frank Tannenbaum wrote the following in his book *Crime and the Community*, in 1938:

> The first dramatization of the "evil" which separates a child out of his group for specialized treatment plays a greater role in making the criminal than perhaps any other experience. It cannot be emphasized enough that for the child, the whole situation has become different. He now lives in a different world. He has been tagged.[19]

The labeling theory, originally referred to as the societal reaction school, became popular in the early 1960s. It was developed by noted researchers, including Frank Tannenbaum (pictured in photo 4.2), David Matza, Edward Matza, Edwin Lemert, Howard Becker, Austin Turk, and Edwin Shur. The labeling theorists contended

PHOTO 4.2 A 1940 picture of Frank Tannenbaum (1893–1969). (Photo courtesy of US Library of Congress Prints and Photographs Division, Washington, DC, LC-DIG-ggbain-19596)

that the popular theories of crime causation placed too much emphasis on individual deviance and neglected the reactions of people to the deviance. For example, Tannenbaum believed that we tend to overemphasize the original deviant act as well as the character of the deviant. He challenged the concept that because crime is bad, those who commit crime are also bad.

The original development of the labeling perspective can be traced to Frank Tannenbaum and his book, *Crime and the Community*.[20] He developed the concept of "dramatization of evil," which holds that deviant behavior is not so much a product of the deviant's lack of adjustment to society as it is to the fact that the delinquent has adjusted to a special group, and his or her criminal behavior is the product of a conflict between that group and the community.

After an act of misconduct, the community places a "label" on the child, identifying him or her as a delinquent. This labeling causes the child to change his or her self-image. It also causes others to react to the label and not the child. Based on this concept, the process of labeling a person as a delinquent causes crime.

Tannenbaum noted that once a youth is arrested and labeled as a criminal, the youth is forced into companionship with other similarly defined youths, resulting in the youth being exposed to criminal mores and new sets of experiences that lead directly to a criminal career. Recall the discussion in chapter 2 regarding the school-to-prison pipeline, where many youths are sanctioned under a zero-tolerance policy, effectively labeling them as delinquents.

A concept used by the labeling theorists is the "looking-glass self." This concept defines the social self as made up of what a person sees others seeing in him or her. To the child, others are a mirror (looking-glass) to one's self. Accordingly, the looking-glass is a predictor of future behavior, because if a person thinks that others see him or her as criminal, the person will tend to commit delinquent acts. If, however, the person thinks others tend to see him or her as good, then he or she will assume the part of a good child. This concept is based on a "self-fulfilling prophecy" concept. Many individuals would counter-argue that by ignoring the primary act, we are encouraging the juvenile to commit additional deviant acts.

The basic principles of the labeling theory are:[21]

- Society tends to have multiple values with differing degrees of overlap.
- The quality of behavior is determined by the application of societal values to an individual's behavior.
- The identification of the behavior as deviant occurs because of the reaction to that behavior.
- Deviance exists only because there is a reaction to the behavior.
- Once behavior is perceived and labeled deviant by the social audience, the individual who is responsible for the behavior is labeled as deviant.
- The adverse reaction to behavior and the invocation of the labeling process is more likely to occur when the actor is a member of a less socially powerful class.
- Society tends to observe more closely those whom have been identified as deviant and therefore will find even more deviance in those persons. Subsequent

deviant acts are reacted to more quickly and the deviant label becomes more firmly affixed.

- Depending on the strength of an individual's original self-concept, once a person is labeled as deviant, the individual will accept the label as his or her self-identity.
- A person who is labeled as criminal is also perceived to be first and foremost a criminal; the individual's other attributes are generally ignored.
- Further deviant behavior (secondary deviance) is a product of living and acting within the deviant label.

The labeling theory has had significant influence on the study of crime causation. It has also had its critics. One serious criticism is that it is not a theory, but a perspective, and that it has no systemic theoretical basis. In addition, like differential association theory, empirical testing of the labeling theory is impossible.

Ecological Theories

The ecological theories used to explain delinquency developed from the work of the Chicago School on gangs. The study produced a large mass of data and many observations about crime.[22]

The term *ecology* is currently linked to the idea of protecting the environment. In its original meaning, ecology was considered as a branch of biology in which plants and animals are studied in their relationship to each other and to their habitat. Robert Park considered that there was a parallel between the distribution of plant life in nature and the organization of human life in society. He viewed the city of Chicago not as a geographic phenomenon, but as a social organism. He viewed the city as a functional unit in which the relations among the individuals are determined and that the city was not merely a physical structure.[23]

Chicago School

The Chicago School viewed the urban environment as the appropriate landscape for studying human nature. These theorists contended that urban life magnified natural tendencies because it:

- encourages people to seek out individuals with shared interests;
- reduces informal social controls because of its anonymity; and
- introduces delinquents to greater temptations.

Robert Park, one of the developers of the school, stated:

> A small community often tolerates eccentricity. The city, on the contrary, rewards it. Neither the criminal, the defective, nor the genius has the same opportunity to develop his innate disposition in a small town than he invariably finds in a great city.[24]

According to Park, by simultaneously presenting new temptations and the weakening of inhibiting social forces, the city becomes a perfect laboratory for the examination of a range of human behaviors, including vice.[25]

Ernest Watson Burgess, who developed the concentric zone(s) model (also known as the Burgess model) in 1925, used his theory to explain urban social structures. Burgess opined that urban areas tended to develop in certain patterned ways just as ants structure colonies or beavers construct dams.[26] According to his model, the natural pattern of urban development starts with the formation of central business districts and develops outward in a process of succession. As the area immediately surrounding the city center becomes more heavily populated and is encroached upon by industry, it results in urban decay. Those with adequate financial resources move to newer developments farther from the city center to escape the deteriorating conditions. Burgess explained the resulting urban pattern as follows:[27]

Zone 1: Central Business District. The downtown area that serves as the center of "economic, cultural, and political life," typified by the presence of government offices, a substantial retail presence, office buildings, transportation hubs, museums, and other businesses.[28]
Zone 2: Area of Transition. The least desirable space in the city. As the housing stock deteriorates, it becomes inhabited by those who can't afford to live elsewhere, including recently settled immigrant populations. The proximity to factories further decreases its desirability as a residential area.
Zone 3: Workingmen's Homes. Occupied by those who want to reside close to their employment, but have attained enough economic success to move from Zone 2.
Zone 4: Residential Zone. Dominated by expensive apartments or gated communities.
Zone 5: Commuters' Zone. Composed of suburban areas that allow an escape from urban life while remaining within commutable distance to the city center.

According to Burgess, recent immigrants and other city newcomers tend to live in the affordable zone of transition. As they adjust to city life, they undergo a reorganization of attitudes and conduct as they stop their old habits and beliefs and adopt new goals and ways of life.[29] At the individual level, anomie is a transitory experience during adjustment to urban life, and the constant influx of new residents through the zone of transition results in the presence of anomie within the zone. It was determined that the neighborhoods with the highest delinquency rates were located within or adjacent to the zone where heavy industry or commerce were located. Also, the highest rates of delinquency occurred in the neighborhoods with the lowest economic status.

Social Disorganization Theory

The social disorganization theory was developed by Clifford Shaw and Henry McKay of the Chicago School. Shaw concluded that delinquency was closely related to the process of invasion, dominance, and succession. According to him, when the location of a city is invaded by new residents, the established relationships that have bound the neighborhood together are destroyed and the natural organization of the neighborhood is severely impaired. This condition creates a state of social disorganization. Because the neighborhood is in transition, the residents no longer identify with it and thus do not care as much about its appearance or reputation.

Shaw and McKay contended that there are four specific assumptions that explain delinquency:

- With the collapse of community-based controls, people living in these disadvantaged urban neighborhoods are responding naturally to environmental conditions.
- The rapid growth of immigration in disadvantaged urban neighborhoods.
- Businesses located closely to the disadvantaged neighborhoods are influenced by the "ecological approach" of competition and dominance.
- The disadvantaged urban neighborhoods lead to the development of criminal values that replace normal societal values.

Social disorganization theory suggests that a person's residential location is more significant than the person's characteristics when predicting criminal activity, and that juveniles living in those areas acquire criminality by the culture's approval within the disadvantaged urban neighborhoods. According to this theory, location matters when it comes to criminality.

Broken Windows Theory

The broken windows theory of delinquency causation was highlighted in a March 1982 article in *Atlantic Monthly* magazine, co-authored by George L. Kelling and James Q. Wilson.[30] The authors used broken windows as a metaphor for disorder in the community. Broken windows in a community indicates that the community is in disorder and unsafe. There are two types of disorder: physical disorder, which is typified by vacant buildings, broken windows, abandoned vehicles, and vacant lots filled with trash. The second type of disorder is of a social nature. This type is typified by aggressive panhandlers, noisy neighbors, and groups of youths standing on street corners. While disorder is not directly linked to serious crime, Kelling and Wilson opined that it leads to increased fear and withdrawal from residents, which then allows more serious crime to move in because of decreased levels of informal social control.

The authors reported that a mid-1970s "Safe and Clean Neighborhoods Program" was started by the State of New Jersey. The program was designed to improve the quality of community life in twenty-eight cities, and included money to take police officers out of their patrol cars and assist them in walking local beats as a way of reducing crime.

Five years after the program was started, an evaluation of the foot patrol was published by the Police Foundation in Washington, DC. The foundation opined that while the foot-patrol program had not reduced delinquency, the citizens in those neighborhoods did feel safer and had a more positive view of the police.

The authors noted that the study may be taken as evidence that foot patrols have no effect on crime; however, they concluded that officers walking the beats did in fact make the neighborhoods safer. The authors contended that we need to understand what most frightens people in public places, and in this study, they found it was the fear of being bothered by disorderly people. The authors opined that unintended behavior leads to a breakdown of community controls, and the neighborhood declines and becomes vulnerable to criminal invasion.

According to the authors, the essence of the police role in maintaining order is to reinforce the informal control mechanisms of the community itself. The police cannot provide a substitute for that informal control without committing extraordinary resources. On the other hand, to strengthen those natural informal controls, the police must accommodate them. As a result, police activity must shift from maintaining order to law enforcement. Police work is seen as involving the application of universal rules, and behavior that does not hurt another person is ignored.

The authors contend that we must return to the long-abandoned view that the police ought to protect communities as well as individuals. To reduce crime, they advocate the importance of maintaining intact communities, without broken windows. The broken windows theory holds that urban disorder is a direct cue that residents are reluctant to intervene in the community; consequently, their neighborhoods become vulnerable to perceptive criminals.

Collective Efficacy

The concept of collective efficacy developed following the broken windows theory. According to Brian Higgins and Joel Hunt, collective efficacy is the glue that binds neighborhoods together. The researchers contend that it helps explain why some communities fight crime and disorder and others do not. According to them, it can be small actions, such as asking questions of strangers, calling the police when a neighbor needs help, shoveling snow off an elderly neighbor's driveway, and attending city council meetings. Local governments and police departments can work with community members and organizations to take larger actions to eliminate nuisances and help improve collective efficacy: cleaning up litter and graffiti, repairing and restoring dilapidated houses, and bringing in new businesses.[31]

The researchers found that residents with high perceptions of collective efficacy and social cohesion saw themselves and their neighbors as protectors of their community; they perceived their communities as having fewer incivilities (e.g., litter, disorder, graffiti); and they were more satisfied with the work of the police. In addition, the perception of social cohesion had a statistically significant effect on residents' fear of crime: Those who had higher perceptions of social cohesion had less fear of crime.

Practicum

Assume you accept the labelist concepts on the causes of delinquent misconduct and you are invited to lead a discussion by the local school board on whether the school district should adopt a zero-tolerance policy.

What points would you want to bring up in the discussion?

Summary

- Social structural theorists conclude that crime is a normal response to certain social conditions. Social problems tend to cluster among structurally disadvantaged populations, and among the geographic spaces in which disadvantage is concentrated.
- Central to the social structural perspective is the idea that human behavior is more than a matter of choice or personal characteristics. Two people with similar dispositions can have different propensities toward crime depending upon their position in the social structure.
- A social norm is a basic sociological concept that is used to explain human behavior. Norms have also been referred to as "rules of conduct," and are seen as blueprints for behavior. Norms can be prescriptive, proscriptive, formal, or informal.
- Socialization refers to the learning process by which a person becomes part of a social group and learns the group's norms.
- Durkheim used the Greek term *anomie* to mean a state or condition that exists when a society evolves from a primitive society to a modern one. *Anomie* is defined as "a state of lawlessness." Durkheim used the term to describe a condition of normlessness.
- Durkheim believed that anomie was caused by the division of labor as the society changed from a primitive one to a modern one. In the primitive society, the family was almost self-sufficient.
- Merton opined that deviant behavior was caused by conditions in the social structure. He believed that society created a strain between culturally prescribed goals and the socially structured means to achieve them.
- Merton described "culturally prescribed goals" as the values in a society and the socially structured means as the norms in a society.
- It is not normal for individuals to engage in lawbreaking or criminal deviance.

- Most criminal misconduct is caused by pressures placed on the individual by societal expectations.
- The concept of the general strain theory is that crime may result from either an inability to obtain a desired state or the inability to escape a negative circumstance.
- Subcultural theorists contend that certain groups or subcultures in society have values and attitudes that are conducive to crime and violence.
- The leading symbolic interaction (SI) theories of delinquent causation are labeling and differential association (DA). Both examine the influence of an individual's associations with peers, family, and other social units on the individual.
- Edwin Sutherland contended that the individual has a limited choice regarding his or her conduct, but he has a conflict orientation to society. Sutherland concluded that we learn to accept antisocial values and thus commit antisocial acts because of the people with whom we associate.
- Frank Tannenbaum noted that once a youth is arrested and labeled as a criminal, the youth is forced into companionship with other similarly defined youths, the result of which is that the youth is exposed to criminal mores and a new set of experiences that lead directly to a criminal career.
- The ecological theories used to explain delinquency developed from the work of the Chicago School on gangs.
- The social disorganization theory was developed by Clifford Shaw and Henry McKay of the Chicago School. Shaw concluded that delinquency was closely related to the process of invasion, dominance, and succession.
- Broken windows in a community indicate that the community is in disorder and unsafe. There are two types of disorder: physical disorder, which is typified by vacant buildings, broken windows, abandoned vehicles, and vacant lots filled with trash; and disorder of a social nature, typified by aggressive panhandlers, noisy neighbors, and groups of youths standing on street corners.

Discussion and Review Questions

1. Explain the concepts involved in the broken windows theory.
2. How does the strain theory differ from the general strain theory?
3. Explain the differential association theory.
4. How does the labeling theory explain secondary deviation?
5. Explain the importance of the anomie concept.
6. What were the significant achievements discussed in the chapter regarding Robert Merton?
7. Discuss how the Chicago School explains the existence of crime.

Notes

1. Ruth Masters and Cliff Roberson, *Inside Criminology* (Englewood Cliffs, NJ: Prentice-Hall, 1990).
2. Emile Durkheim, *The Division of Labor in Society*, transl. John A. Spaulding and George Simpson (New York: Free Press, 1965).
3. W. J. Wilson, *When Work Disappears: The World of the New Urban Poor* (New York: Vintage Books, 1996).
4. Robert K. Merton, "Anomie, Anomia, and Social Interaction: Contexts of Deviant Behavior." In *Anomie and Deviant Behavior: A Discussion and Critique*, edited by Marshall B. Clinard (New York: Free Press, 1964), 213–42.
5. Cliff Roberson and Harvey Wallace, *Introduction to Criminology* (Incline Village, NV: Copperhouse Publishing, 1998).

6. Richard Cloward, "Illegitimate Means, Anomie, and Deviant Behavior," *American Sociological Review*, vol. 24, no. 2 (1959), 164–76.
7. Richard A. Cloward and L. E. Ohlin, *Delinquency and Opportunity: A Theory of Delinquent Gangs* (Glencoe, IL: Free Press, 1960).
8. R. Agnew, "A Revised Strain Theory of Delinquency," *Social Forces*, vol. 64, no. 1 (1985), 151–67.
9. R. Agnew, "Foundations for a General Strain Theory of Crime and Delinquency," *Criminology*, vol. 30, no. 1 (1992), 47–87.
10. R. Agnew, "Building on the Foundation of General Strain Theory: Specifying the Types of Strain Most Likely to Lead to Crime and Delinquency," *Journal of Research in Crime and Delinquency*, vol. 38, no. 4 (2001), 319–61, 326.
11. Albert K. Cohen, *Delinquent Boys: The Culture of the Gang* (Glencoe, IL: Free Press, 1955).
12. Cohen, *Delinquent Boys*, 25.
13. Steven Messner and Richard Rosenfeld, "Institutions, Anomie, and Violent Crime: Clarifying and Elaborating Institutional-Anomie Theory," *International Journal of Conflict and Violence*, vol. 2, no. 2 (2008), 163–82.
14. Sang-Weon Kim and William Alex Pridemore, "Social Change, Institutional Anomie, and Serious Property Crime in Transitional Russia," *British Journal of Criminology*, vol. 45, no. 1 (January 1, 2005), 81–97.
15. Masters and Roberson, *Inside Criminology*.
16. Sue Titus Reid, *Crime and Criminology*, 4th ed. (New York: Holt, Rinehart, and Winston, 1982), 180.
17. Reid, *Crime and Criminology*.
18. Heart Funding Foundation website at https://healthresearchfunding.org/akers-differential-association-reinforcement-theory-explained (accessed March 7, 2019).
19. Frank Tannenbaum, *Crime and the Community* (Boston: Ginn, 1938), 19–20.
20. Tannenbaum, *Crime and the Community*.
21. Masters and Roberson, *Inside Criminology*.
22. George B. Vold and Thomas J. Bernard, *Theoretical Criminology*, 3rd ed. (New York: Oxford University Press, 1986).
23. Vold and Bernard, *Theoretical Criminology*.
24. R. E. Park, "The City: Suggestions for the Investigation of Human Behavior in the Urban Environment." In R. E. Park, E. W. Burgess, and R. D. McKenzie, eds., *The City* (Chicago: University of Chicago Press, 1925), 1–46, 41.
25. Park, "The City: Suggestions," 1–46.
26. E. W. Burgess, "The Growth of the City: An Introduction to a Research Project." In R. E. Park, E. W. Burgess, and R. D. McKenzie, eds., *The City* (Chicago: University of Chicago Press, 1925), 47–62.
27. Burgess, "The Growth of the City," 47–62.
28. Burgess, "The Growth of the City," 52.
29. Burgess, "The Growth of the City," 54.
30. George L. Kelling and James Q. Wilson, "Broken Windows: The Police and Neighborhood Safety," *Atlantic Monthly* (March 1982), 38–52.
31. Brian Higgins and Joel Hunt, "Collective Efficacy: Taking Action to Improve Neighborhoods," *National Institute of Justice Journal*, NCJ 249823, May 2016.

CHAPTER 5

Social Process and Integrated Theories

CHAPTER OBJECTIVES

After studying this chapter, the reader should be able to:

- Explain why the social control theories are also considered as socialization theories.
- Discuss the importance of the socialization process.
- Discuss Durkheim's contributions to the development of causation theories.
- Explain the social bond theory.
- Describe the key tenets of the social learning theory.
- Differentiate between the social process theories and the integrated theories.

Social Control Theories

The social control theories are also described as socialization theories. According to the social control theorists, the process of socialization is the dominant method by which groups control individuals. We are taught the "right way" to act and to perform. The basic theme of the social control theories is that the social bond of an individual to society determines whether the individual commits criminal behavior. The socialization process was discussed in chapter 4.

The earliest form of social control theory can be traced to Emile Durkheim.[1] Durkheim contended that a society without deviance would be an abnormal society, and even deviance has social utility. According to Durkheim, deviance helps societies to maintain social order. Durkheim stated that even punishment plays a role in the maintenance of social solidarity. According to him, when the rules of the collective conscience are violated, society responds with repressive sanctions—not for retribution or deterrence, but because those of us who conform will not be demoralized. Durkheim noted that when an offender is punished, those of us who are not punished receive the reward of "not being punished" because of our "good" behavior.

Durkheim theorized that it would be a pathological state of society if there was no criminal misconduct. A society that had no crime would be one in which the constraints of the collective conscience were so rigid that no one could oppose them. Crime would be eliminated, but so would the possibility of any progressive social change, because no one would dare to deviate from the norm. Individual growth could not occur in a child if it was impossible for the child to misbehave. A child who never did anything wrong would be pathologically over-controlled. Elimination of criminal misbehavior would also eliminate the possibility of independent growth. In a perfect society, one without crime or deviance, what would be the subject matter of our novels, television programs, and movies? Durkheim would probably hold that it would be quite boring. In addition, many jobs would be lost if there was no need for police officers, courts, judges, correctional officers, or school crossing guards.

Social control theorists hold that people's relationships, commitments, values, norms, and beliefs encourage them not to break the law. Accordingly, if a person's moral codes are internalized and the individual has accepted them, and they have a stake in their wider community, he or she will voluntarily limit the propensity to commit deviant acts.

The social control theorist is looking to understand the ways in which it is possible to reduce the likelihood of criminality developing in individuals. The theorists do not consider motivational issues. They simply state that human beings may choose to engage in a wide range of activities, unless the range is limited by the processes of socialization and social learning.[2]

Social Bond Theories

Travis Hirschi is given credit for developing the social bond theory of delinquency. He concluded that delinquent behavior was caused by a lack of social attachments. He modified his ideas later and renamed his theory as the self-control theory of crime. The latter theory holds that misconduct is committed because of the available opportunity and lack of self-control on the part of the delinquent. He also contended that the degree of parenting a child receives is a determining factor in whether the child will commit criminal misconduct.[3]

In 1969, Travis Hirschi put forth his social bond theory in his book *Causes of Delinquency*. He claimed that the absence of social bonds and lack of social interaction with parents, teachers, friends, and others caused a decrease in acceptance of social norms and recognition of morals, exacerbating tendencies toward juvenile delinquency.

The social bond theory developed as Hirschi continued to redefine his concepts of delinquent behavior causation. In 1990 Hirschi collaborated with Michael R. Gottfredson on the book *A General Theory of Crime*, in which they proposed that a person's level of self-control stabilizes by the age of eight, depending on how he or she is reared as a child.[4] The theory places a lot of responsibility on the parents regarding whether or not a child would eventually become deviant and commit criminal misbehavior. According to Hirschi and Gottfredson, a child reared in a stable environment is far less likely to commit crimes than a child that was neglected or abused.

Hirschi contended that humans are born to violate social norms and commit criminal misbehavior. According to Hirschi, individuals refrain from doing so only if special circumstances exist. Special circumstances exist only when an individual's bond to society is strong. The bond to society is based on the following four elements:

- **Attachment.** Attachment refers to the person's ability to be sensitive to the thoughts, feelings, and desires of other humans.
- **Commitment.** By commitment, Hirschi is referring to the rational component in conformity. Commitment assumes that the organization of society is such that the interests of most of the society would be endangered if they were to engage in criminal misbehavior.
- **Involvement.** According to Hirschi, the more a person is involved in conventional things, the less the opportunity the person must commit criminal behavior.
- **Belief.** Hirschi believed that when the individual's personal belief in the values of his or her society or community are weakened, the individual is more likely to commit criminal conduct.

The social control theorists take the position that the desire to commit criminal behavior is a part of human nature; humans are basically bad; and with ineffective social controls, humans will commit crime. When social controls break down, the result is that crime and other uncontrolled behavior occurs.[5]

The term *control* in the social control theories label refers to one's perspective on what tends to control people. There are differences between the various control theories, but they all share one basic principle: People without social restraints will commit deviant behavior. Whereas most theories ask "Why do people commit crime?" the control theorist asks "Why do people obey laws?"

The social control theorist is looking to understand the ways in which it is possible to reduce the likelihood of criminality developing in individuals. The theorists do not consider motivational issues; they simply state that human beings may choose to engage in a wide range of activities, unless the range is limited by the processes of socialization and social learning.[6]

Albert J. Reiss

In 1951, Albert J. Reiss published the results of his study of 1,110 white male working-class juvenile probationers between the ages of eleven and seventeen. He classified the juveniles according to psychological types. The study also examined several factors that are related to the control perspective.[7] Reiss concluded that revocation of probation was more likely when boys had weak ego and superego controls which prevented them from internalizing society's norms. He contended that his study affirmed that control was related to the attachment people had for others, and that people were controlled by the norms of those to whom they were attached. Reiss concluded that juvenile delinquency emerges from the failure of personal and social controls to produce behavior in conformity with the norms of the social system.[8]

Delinquency and Drift

Two of the leading control theorists are David Matza and Gresham Sykes. Matza in his text, *Delinquency and Drift*, indicates that a delinquent youth has no commitment to either societal or criminal norms.[9] Matza states that delinquents drift in and out of crime. He points out that even delinquents spend most of their time involved in law-abiding activities. Matza contends that delinquents are not immune from the demands made by society, and that they have values that support the dominant society.

An interview with Charles Manson supports the contention that most individuals spend most of their time involved in law-abiding activities. During the interview, Manson—who gained national notoriety after the murder of actress Sharon Tate and four others in her home on August 8 and 9, 1969—remarked that he did not like to drive in Los Angeles because nobody obeyed the traffic laws.

Matza opined that most delinquents are not wholly committed to criminal behavior; rather, they are only dabbling in it. He believed that delinquents act out society's "subterranean values"—what he described as those values that exist in society but are not generally approved by the society.

Both Matza and Sykes contended that people do not commit crimes when they are controlled by morals. But, when the morals are neutralized, the controls are lessened and the individuals are more prone to commit criminal behavior. According to the researchers, we need to neutralize our morals before violating laws we believe in; in other words, we need to make acceptable the behavior we know is wrong before we commit the misconduct. Sykes and Matza developed five "techniques of neutralization" used to enable delinquents to break laws they believe in:[10]

- **Denial of responsibility.** The delinquent defines him- or herself as lacking responsibility for the behavior. The delinquents' acts are the result of outside forces, such as unloving parents.
- **Denial of injury.** No one will really be injured or harmed by the act. For example, stealing an automobile will not hurt the owner because the automobile is insured.
- **Denial of the victim.** The injury that results from the criminal act is not wrong considering the circumstances. The victim deserves to have something happen to him or her. For example, rape is justified because the victim really wanted sex.
- **Condemnation of the condemners.** This technique involves a change of focus. It is a rejection of those who would condemn the act. For example, the victim is a corrupt businessperson.
- **Appeal to higher loyalties.** The delinquent sacrifices the demands of society for the good of the gang or peer group.

A review of the five techniques of neutralization indicates that they are used to lessen the effectiveness of social controls placed on the delinquent. Critics of the theory ask: If humans are bad and will commit crime without societal controls, why does the delinquent need to neutralize his or her conduct? In addition, the theory fails to indicate why some kids deviate and others do not.

Containment Theory

Walter Reckless's containment theory holds that people have several social controls, containments, or protective barriers which help them to resist pressures to commit criminal misbehavior.[11] Reckless stated that we all have pushes and pulls toward crime, but not all people have the same ones. He attempted to explain why some people submit to certain pushes and pulls while others do not.

Reckless identified two types of containments: internal and external. *Internal containments* are those social bonds and ties that we perceive of ourselves (e.g., good self-image, goal-directedness, inner strength, and self-control). *External containments* are strong social bonds and ties that are placed on us by others, such as family, peers, schools, and churches. Reckless saw internal containments as the most effective controls on a person, but taken together, internal and external containments prevent us from becoming a criminal.

Reckless also contended that people have many social pressures that pull and push them and interact with their containments. The pulls are environmental factors, such as poverty, poor family life, and lack of a solid education. The pushes are individual factors, such as hostility, personality, and aggressiveness. In the best situations, the internal and external containments interact with the pushes and pulls on the individual and prevent the person from committing delinquent behavior.

Conflict Theories

> Criminal law . . . is a direct expression of the ruling class; it is concerned with the protection of their property and the consolidation of their political power. The "real" function of policing is political rather than the control of crime per se. (Excerpt of statement by Jock Young, "The Failure of Criminology")[12]

The two major views of sociologically based causation theories are the consensus approach and the conflict approach. The *consensus approach* sees society as based on a consensus of social values, with the state organized to protect those closely held values. The *conflict approach* sees a society composed of groups of people with conflicting values and interests, and the state does not represent the values and interests of society as a whole.

The conflict view holds that society supports and upholds the values and interests of those groups who have enough power to control the state. Accordingly, the state represents only the rich and powerful members of society.

While the consensus approach holds that societal norms and laws represent the general and common view of what is right and wrong, the conflict approach views society's values and laws as the values and laws of the rich and powerful.

Scholars have divided the conflict orientation into two general groups: the conservative conflict approach and the critical radical approach. While the less-radical critical theorists contend that reforms of our capitalist economic system will result in a true consensus-based state, the more-radical critical theorists contend that a revolution is necessary to cure the ills of society.

Charles McCaghy reported that conflict criminology has two important advantages over the traditional causation theories. First, conflict criminology acknowledges that there is a relationship between deviant behavior and the process of making and enforcing laws. Second, unlike traditional causation theories, conflict theorists recognize that many acts of rule-breaking are committed in the name of a group or cause.[13] The rioting committed during the Black Lives Matter (BLM) demonstrations in 2020 may be considered as an example of rule-breaking in the name of a cause. While the overwhelming number of law enforcement and protestors during the BLM demonstrations were peaceful, a few individuals from both sides committed criminal violations, such as looting and excessive use of force.

Critical Theories

While the two sub-areas of critical thought are clearly distinct from one another, they share key underlying assumptions:

- Society is composed of groups with differing priorities, cultures, and interests.
- These groups vary in their access to political power, which in turn shapes their relative ability to influence the law.
- The law tends to protect the interests and values of those in power and works to the relative detriment of others.

While most theorists assume that the law reflects broad moral consensus, critical theorists subscribe to the conflict model of law: They believe that those in power write laws to maintain their position of advantage while systematically subjugating the norms, values, and/or best interests of others. To them the acts are seen as "criminal" in the context of a broader sociopolitical struggle.

Critical criminologists claim that mainstream theorists are misguided in their efforts to explain and prevent violations of criminal law, and that the violations of criminal law are not an accurate representation of social harm to all society members. Critical theorists note that criminal law has a tendency to overlook the harmful actions of the powerful, and that laws tend to "over-criminalize" behaviors of disadvantaged populations. In addition, the focus on law-violators overlooks the macro-social conditions that underlie much lower-class criminality.

Critical theorists argue that mainstream criminologists' uncritical acceptance of the legal definition of "crime" serves to perpetuate stereotypes about who criminals are, which distracts from the more-substantial injustices perpetrated every day by those in power. According to this perspective, it is absurd to focus solely on those who break the law without also trying to understand other forms of exploitative, uncompassionate, or otherwise harmful behavior. From the critical perspective, all forms of social harm are fair game in the study of crime.

Austin Turk

In his book *Criminality and Legal Order*, Austin Turk describes his theory of criminalization and normative-legal conflict. According to Turk, there are conditions under which differences between authorities and subjects will result in overt conflict. By authorities, he is referring to the decision-makers (e.g., police, judges, lawyers, prosecutors), and by subjects, he is referring to individuals affected by those decisions. Turk notes that subjects are distinguished from authorities by their inability to manipulate the legal processes.[14]

According to Turk, the potential for authority–subject conflict is always present. But not all authorities have equal opportunity to influence the law. Turk sees the police as the "first-line enforcers" with the greatest impact on the criminalization of an individual, and that the police may rely upon coercion to gain compliance. Turk refers to situations where the police use force to gain compliance as "nightstick law."

Turk states that criminality is the result of cultural conflicts. Subjects may be unaware of or may not accept specific legal rules. According to Turk, the greater the cultural differences between the evaluator and violator, the less likely are the psychological sanctions, which assume a capacity and readiness to subtle cues to get through to the violator. Therefore, sanctioning will need to be more physically coercive in order to enforce the norm. In this situation, nonviolent forms of persuasion by authorities, such as verbal announcements or body language, may be insufficient to achieve the compliance of people who have different or conflicting views or values.

Turk notes four situations that are subject to authority–subject conflict:

- The congruence of norms for both authorities and subjects is high.
- The congruence of norms for subjects, but not authorities, is high.
- The congruence of norms for authorities is high, but not for subjects.
- The congruence of norms for both authorities and subjects is not high.

Conflict is more likely to occur when the norms for both authorities and subjects are high. Turk also notes that the odds are higher for conflict when authorities and subjects are unsophisticated, because unsophisticated persons are less skilled in assessing the strengths and weaknesses of their position relative to the other party. Turk contends that when cultural norms clash, authorities and subjects will appeal to their own distinct values. Accordingly, authorities are inclined to appeal to legal rules or written policies, whereas subjects tend to appeal to extralegal norms, such as their right to privacy or natural law.

Turk's theory has been criticized by both conflict and consensus criminologists. According to his critics, his attempt to generate a non-ideological conflict theory is submissive, abstract, and tautological. His critics suggest that criminologists should focus instead on the origin of conflict, which they view as social and economic inequality. In addition, Turk is less troubled with the sources of conflict than with the conditions in which it is manifested. Consensus theorists have criticized Turk for dismissing a significant body of knowledge which has shown that consensus rather than conflict characterizes American society. Turk maintains, however, that the idea a consensus actually exists is just an illusion. He claims that whether they realize it or not, people are inevitably involved in intergroup struggles over who will have what resources in a finite world.

Richard Quinney

The leading modern spokesperson for conflict criminology is Richard Quinney. Quinney used the conflict theory in an attempt to explain why some acts are defined and prosecuted as criminal whereas others are not.[15] In his book, *The Social Reality of Crime*, he concludes that public conceptions of crime are constructed in the political arena to serve political purposes. In a later article, he introduced a theory of legal order intended to demystify the false consciousness that he maintained was created by official reality. He argued that crime is a function of society's structure, that the law is created by those in power to protect and serve their interests (as opposed to the interests of the broader public), and that the criminal justice system is an agent of oppression designed to perpetuate the status quo.

Key Concepts in Critical Criminology

1. Traditional theorists, in accepting the state and legal definition of crime, have excluded behavior which is not legally defined as "crime" (e.g., imperialism, exploitation, racism, and sexism), as well as behavior which is not typically prosecuted (e.g., tax evasion, price-fixing, consumer fraud, government corruption, police homicides, etc.).
2. Critical criminologists note that the focus on legally defined crimes—behaviors that violate criminal laws—overlooks a broad array of truly criminal behaviors, the wide range of socially harmful behaviors that may or may not be legally defined as "criminal," and which are more equitably distributed throughout society.
3. Critical theorists note that since the ruling class holds the power to shape criminal law, the law will tend to overlook their harmful behaviors and leave the disadvantaged to bear the brunt of the stigma and punishment of the criminal justice system. Specifically, critical criminologists note the tendency for the criminal justice system to systematically:
   - Assign low penalties to white-collar crimes, including those that are more harmful to society than many street offenses;
   - Punish corporate crimes through corporate fines rather than criminal penalties for the individuals responsible; and
   - Enforce laws most stringently against disadvantaged populations.

   These inequalities pathologize "street offenders" while often turning a blind eye to the harmful acts of the powerful, as when businesses release potentially fatal toxins into the air and water supply, fail to take precautions for their workers' safety, or cut corners in ways that may put consumers at risk.[16]

Radical Criminology

Radical criminology is based on the economic determinism theses of Karl Marx.[17] Both Marx and Friedrich Engels contended that delinquency and economic conditions were linked. Marx based his delinquent causation theory on the conflict between the material forces of production and the social relations to production. He stated that the material forces of production referred to society's ability to produce material goods. The social relations of production referred to the relationship between people involved in producing and consuming the material goods, and included property relationships. Marx predicted that as the material forces of production continued to develop under capitalism, the social relations would restrict them, until eventually there would be a violent restructuring of society. When this happened, capitalism would be replaced by socialism.

A disciple of Marx and Engels, William Bonger concluded that primitive societies were characterized by altruism—that people in primitive societies produced goods for personal consumption. It is only when people start producing goods for exchange that society loses its altruistic nature and replaces it with selfishness. When this change occurs, the change provides a climate of motivation for delinquency. Bonger saw the definition of crime as social in nature, and believed that for certain conduct to be considered criminal, the behavior must be harmful to society.

Social Learning Theory

Social learning theory can be traced back to the teachings of behaviorist B. F. Skinner. In the 1940s Skinner delivered a series of lectures on verbal behavior, stressing a more-empirical approach to the subject of social learning than was generally used in psychology at the time. Skinner proposed the use of stimulus-response theories to describe language use and development, and contended that all verbal behavior was underpinned by operant conditioning.

Skinner was famous for his thesis that humans were born neither good nor bad. He once stated that he could take a child and develop the child into either a surgeon or a plumber according to the training of the child.

Skinner did state that some forms of speech derived from words and sounds that had previously been heard (echoic response), and that reinforcement from parents allowed these echoic responses to be pared down to understandable speech. Skinner denied that there was any instinct or faculty of imitation. Skinner's behaviorist theories formed a basis for redevelopment into social learning theory.

Social learning theory is based on the concept that new behaviors can be acquired by observing and imitating others. According to the theory, learning is a cognitive process that takes place in a social context and can occur purely through observation or direct instruction, even in the absence of motor reproduction or direct reinforcement. Learning also occurs through the observation of rewards and punishments, a process known as *vicarious reinforcement*. According to the theory, when certain behavior is rewarded on a regular basis, it will most likely persist. If certain behavior is constantly punished, it will most likely not be repeated. The theory is an expansion of traditional behavioral theories, which contend that behavior is governed solely by reinforcements, and by placing emphasis on the important roles of various internal processes in the learning individual.

Social learning theory is used to explain the emergence and maintenance of delinquent misconduct, including misconduct involving aggression. As noted in chapter 4, Akers and Burgess integrated the principles of social learning and operant conditioning with the differential association theory to create their theory of delinquent misconduct. Burgess and Akers emphasized that criminal behavior is learned in both social and nonsocial situations through combinations of direct reinforcement, vicarious reinforcement, explicit instruction, and observation. According to them, both the probability of being exposed to certain behaviors and the nature of the reinforcement are dependent on group norms.

Social learning theory uses integrated behavioral and cognitive theories of learning in order to provide a comprehensive model that could account for the wide range of learning experiences that occur in society. Some key concepts of the theory include:

- Learning is not entirely behavioral; rather, it is a cognitive process that takes place in a social context.
- Learning mostly occurs by observing a behavior and by observing the consequences of the behavior. This process is known as *vicarious reinforcement.*
- Learning involves observation, extraction of information from those observations, and making decisions about the performance of the behavior, also known as *observational learning* or *modeling.*
- Learning can occur without an observable change in behavior.
- Reinforcement plays a role in learning, but is not entirely responsible for learning.
- The learner is not a passive recipient of information. Cognition, environment, and behavior all mutually influence each other. This process is known as *reciprocal determinism.*

Multiple-Factor Theories of Crime

A common criticism of the crime causation theories is that they emphasize a single factor as the cause of crime. Factors like inherited physical traits, biological inferiority, feeblemindedness, emotional disturbances, or poverty have been described as the single cause of crime. We don't accept the concept that a single factor causes all types of medical illness, so why should we accept the concept that different types of crime are caused by just one factor? For example, the crime of a stockbroker who embezzles from his or her clients is most likely caused by different factors than the crimes committed by a sexual predator.

The multiple-factor approach in criminology grew out of discrepancies in single-factor approaches. The multiple-factor theorists argue that crime should be understood in terms of varied contributions made by a variety of factors. Their basic assumption is that criminal behavior is the product of many factors—biological, psychological, economic, and social—and that different crimes will be the result of different combinations of factors. The correct approach in criminology is an eclectic one, emphasizing identification and analysis of multiple factors. Scholars who advocate this approach include William Healy, Cyril Burt, and Sheldon and Eleanor Glueck.

Integrated Theories

The integrated theories are those that expand upon the arguments of other theories to provide more-complete explanations of delinquent misconduct. These theories involve the linking and synthesizing of different theories of delinquent causation to explain why individuals commit criminal misconduct. These theories vary in scope. Researchers generally divide the integrated theories into two broad groups: *developmental theories*, which prioritize explanations of change over time within individual offenders; and multi-factor theories, which focus on building an explanation of crime that crosscuts through different layers of analysis.

Developmental Theories of Delinquency

Developmental theories of delinquency were popular during the 1980s and 1990s. Their success during this period is credited to the enormous amount of significant longitudinal research on delinquent misconduct published during that period. Development theories of delinquency tend to be concerned with:

- Development of antisocial behavior from birth to death;
- Influence of risk and protective factors at different ages; and
- Effects of life events on an individual's development.

Unlike traditional theories of delinquency causation, developmental theories are focused on explaining the differences in offending rates of delinquents over a certain period.[18]

Integrated Cognitive Antisocial Potential Theory

The integrated cognitive antisocial potential (ICAP) theory was developed by David Farrington, and is based on the concept that an individual's antisocial propensity (AP) determines whether or not the juvenile will commit criminal misconduct. A person's AP refers to their risk or propensity to engage in crime, and the decision-making process that turns this potential process into an actual process. The key construct is antisocial propensity, which tends to persist over time, and has a wide variety of behavioral manifestations.[19]

Social Development Model

The social development model developed by Richard Catalano and J. David Hawkins is a general theory of antisocial behavior. By using this model, researchers were attempting to explain the key elements of a career in criminal misconduct, researching the onset and persistence of this behavior. This model compares general overarching principles and anchors individuals to a progression through elementary school, high school, and across multiple development stages. The key tenets of the model take on a holistic, multi-domain approach to explain delinquent misconduct.

According to the model, a social bond consisting of attachment to conventional others, commitment to conventional lines of action, and a belief in the conventional moral order inhibits delinquency. The social bond results from a social process involving the following constructs:[20]

- Opportunities for involvement in conventional activities and interactions with conventional others;
- Degree of involvement and interaction;
- Possessing the skills to participate in conventional involvements and interactions; and
- The rewards that an individual perceives as forthcoming from performance in conventional involvement and interactions.

Control Balance Theory

The control balance theory developed by Charles R. Tittle states that a person lives his or her life in one of three states: control surplus, control equilibrium, or control deficit.[21] Tittle predicted deviance by positing that the amount of control to which an individual is subject, relative to the amount of control he or she can exercise, determines the probability of deviance occurring, as well as the type of deviance that is likely to occur. This is referred to as the *control ratio*.

Tittle contended that an individual commits criminal misconduct or deviance when there is an imbalance in the control ratio. The imbalance results when three situations exist simultaneously: predisposition, motivation, and opportunity. Accordingly, an individual is predisposed toward deviance when the balance of control is not equal.

The inequality may favor the individual (a control surplus) or may not favor the individual (a control deficit). In the control surplus situation, the individual is predisposed toward delinquent behavior that expresses exploitation, plunder, and defiance. In the control deficit situation, the person acts in a manner that expresses defiance, submissiveness, or predation.

According to the control balance theory, the second element required for delinquent behavior is motivation. The motivation for delinquency could come from the imbalance that exists in control. The result of the motivation would be deviance, in order to overcome the deficit or enlarge the surplus. Other possible sources for motivation could be a situation or issue that causes the need to act in a delinquent manner in order to remedy the situation.

The existence of motivation or predisposition alone is not, according to Tittle, enough to cause delinquent behavior. A third element is necessary. For delinquency to take place, the opportunity to commit an offense must also be present.

When all three prongs of the theory are satisfied, one may engage in delinquency that is said to be a result of an issue of control imbalance. If there is no imbalance in control, deviant behavior is less likely to occur.

Differential Coercion Theory

The differential coercion theory outlines the relationship between coercion and crime. According to the theory, coercion is identified as a force that compels or intimidates an individual to act because of the fear and anxiety it creates. The theory emphasizes the link between coercion and the development of a range of social-psychological deficits. These deficits include anger, low self-control, coercive behavior modeling, control balance deficits, low social bonds, low self-efficacy, and an external locus of control.

Stephen W. Baron studied three hundred homeless street youths in his attempt to test differential coercion theory, and the role that coercion and the social-psychological deficits of anger, low self-control, coercive modeling, coercive ideation, and control imbalances play in the generation of violent crime. Individual mediators revealed that coercion has a direct relationship with violent offending, as well as a relationship mediated by low self-control, anger, coercive modeling, and coercive ideation.[22]

Baron based his study on the differential coercion theory as explained in Mark Colvin's monograph, published in 2000.[23] Colvin discussed an integrated theory that outlined how coercive forces can lead to the development of serious chronic offending. Colvin contended that coercion takes place when individuals are forced by others to behave in a particular manner by using threats, intimidation, or direct force, or when behavior is constrained by way of impersonal social or economic pressures.

The sources of direct or interpersonal coercion come from family, school, peer groups, the workplace, welfare agencies, and the criminal justice system. Coercion takes place in these environments when "compliance" is achieved through the generation of fear, which stems from the threatened or actual removal of emotional and material supports and through threats of, or actual use of, physical force.

Colvin states that the impersonal coercion stems from larger structural conditions that force an individual in a direction that generates desperation and certain lines of action. These impersonal forces—such as violent competition among groups, poverty, and structural unemployment—can create social and economic stresses that force individuals to react in certain ways. Both direct and indirect coercion are viewed as punitive, generating emotional and physical pain that induce individuals to act in response to force. Colvin states that although it is often overlooked in research on crime and delinquency, studying the effects of coercion offers great potential for understanding the link between various social settings and criminal behavior.

Practicum

Thomas, the son of a wealthy local businessman, is stopped for shoplifting. The police officer, rather than taking Thomas to the police station and booking him, calls Thomas's father and requests that the father come down to the store and pick Thomas up to take him home. The same week, Joseph, a member of a homeless family, is arrested for shoplifting and taken to the local police department and booked.

As a critical criminologist, compare and discuss the differences in these two cases.

Summary

- The social control theories are also described as socialization theories. According to the social control theorists, the process of socialization is the dominant method by which groups control individuals. We are taught the "right way" to act and to perform.
- Travis Hirschi concluded that delinquent behavior was caused by a lack of social attachments. He modified his ideas later and renamed his theory the "self-control theory" of crime. The latter theory holds that misconduct is committed because of an available opportunity and a lack of self-control on the part of the delinquent.
- The social control theorists take the position that the desire to commit criminal behavior is a part of human nature; humans are basically bad; and with ineffective social controls, humans will commit crime.
- According to the concept of delinquency and drift, a delinquent youth has no commitment to either societal or criminal norms. Matza states that delinquents drift in and out of crime. He points out that even delinquents spend most of their time involved in law-abiding activities. Matza contends that delinquents are not immune from the demands made by society, and that delinquents have values that support the dominant society.
- Reckless's containment theory holds that people have several social controls, containments, or protective barriers which help them to resist pressures to commit criminal misbehavior. Reckless stated that we all have pushes and pulls toward crime, but not all people have the same ones.

- The two major views of sociologically based causation theories are the consensus approach and the conflict approach.
- The consensus approach sees society as based on a consensus of social values, with the state organized to protect those closely held values.
- The conflict approach sees a society composed of groups of people with conflicting values and interests, and the state does not represent the values and interests of society as a whole.
- Radical criminology is based on the economic determinism theses of Karl Marx. Marx based his delinquent causation theory on the conflict between the material forces of production and the social relations to production.
- The social learning theories can be traced back to the teaching of behaviorist B. F. Skinner.
- Skinner was famous for his thesis that humans were born neither good nor bad. He once stated that he could take a child and develop the child into either a surgeon or a plumber according to the training of the child.
- Skinner's behaviorist theories formed a basis for redevelopment into social learning theory.
- A common criticism of the crime causation theories is that they emphasize a single factor as the cause of crime. Factors like inherited physical traits, biological inferiority, feeblemindedness, emotional disturbances, or poverty have been described as the single cause of crime.
- The control balance theory states that a person lives his or her life in one of three states: control surplus, control equilibrium, or control deficit.
- Tittle predicted deviance by positing that the amount of control to which an individual is subject, relative to the amount of control he or she can exercise, determines the probability of deviance occurring, as well as the type of deviance likely to occur.
- The differential coercion theory outlines the relationship between coercion and crime. According to the theory, coercion is identified as a force that compels or intimidates an individual to act because of the fear and anxiety it creates.
- The differential coercion theory emphasizes the link between coercion and the development of a range of social-psychological deficits. These deficits include anger, low self-control, coercive behavior modeling, control balance deficits, low social bonds, low self-efficacy, and an external locus of control.

Discussion and Review Questions

1. Why are social control theories also described as socialization theories?
2. What were Durkheim's contributions to the development of social control theory?
3. How would society be affected if we developed a society that was void of deviance?
4. Explain Travis Hirschi's social bond theory.
5. Explain the general thesis of the concept of delinquency and drift.
6. What does Reckless mean when he states that we all have pushes and pulls toward crime?
7. Explain the differences between the conflict and radical theories.
8. How does Skinner view the nature of human beings?
9. Explain the multiple-factor approach to crime causation.
10. What are the three states involved in Tittle's control balance theory?

Notes

1. Emile Durkheim, *The Rules of the Sociological Method*, translated by Sarah A. Solovay and John Mueller (New York: Free Press, 1895).
2. Albert J. Reiss, "Delinquency and the Failure of Personal and Social Controls," *American Sociological Review*, vol. 16 (1951), 196–207.
3. Donald J. Shoemaker, *Theories of Delinquency: An Examination of Explanations of Delinquent Behavior*, 7th ed. (New York: Oxford University Press, 2018).
4. Michael Gottfredson and Travis Hirschi, *A General Theory of Crime* (Redwood City, CA: Stanford University Press, 1990).
5. Ruth Masters and Cliff Roberson, *Inside Criminology* (Englewood Cliffs, NJ: Prentice-Hall, 1990).
6. Reiss, "Delinquency and the Failure of Personal and Social Controls," 196–207.
7. George B. Vold and Thomas J. Bernard, *Theoretical Criminology* (New York: Oxford University Press, 1986).
8. Reiss, "Delinquency and the Failure of Personal and Social Controls," 196–207.
9. David Matza, *Delinquency and Drift* (New York: Wiley, 1964).
10. Gresham Sykes and David Matza, "Techniques of Neutralization: A Theory of Delinquency," *American Sociological Review*, vol. 22 (December 1957), 667–70.
11. Walter Reckless, *The Crime Problem*, 5th ed. (Englewood Cliffs, NJ: Prentice-Hall, 1973).
12. Jock Young, *The Failure of Criminology: The Need for a Radical Realism*. Abridged from *Confronting Crime*, eds. R. Matthews and J. Young (London: Sage, 1986), 9–30. Republished chapter 40 (pp. 442–52) in J. Muncie, E. McLaughlin, and M. Langan, eds., *Criminological Perspectives: A Reader* (Thousand Oaks, CA: Sage Publications, 1996), 445.
13. Charles McCaghy, *Deviant Behavior: Crime, Conflict, and Interest Groups* (New York: Macmillan, 1976).
14. Austin Turk, "The Criminalization Process," in Francis Cullen and Pamela Wilcox, eds., *Encyclopedia of Criminological Theory* (Thousand Oaks, CA: Sage, 2010), 969–72.
15. Richard Quinney, *The Social Reality of Crime* (Boston: Little, Brown, 1970).
16. Robert Winters, Julie Globokar, and Cliff Roberson, *An Introduction to Crime and Crime Causation* (Boca Raton, FL: CRC Press, 2014).
17. Masters and Roberson, *Inside Criminology*.
18. Winters et al., *An Introduction to Crime*.
19. Winters et al., *An Introduction to Crime*.
20. Winters et al., *An Introduction to Crime*.
21. Charles R. Tittle, *Control Balance: Toward a General Theory of Deviance* (Boulder, CO: Westview Press, 1995).
22. Stephen W. Baron, "Differential Coercion, Street Youth, and Violent Crime," *Criminology*, vol. 47, no. 1 (2009), 239–301.
23. Mark Colvin, *Crime and Coercion: An Integrated Theory of Chronic Criminality* (New York: St. Martin's Press, 2000).

PART III

Delinquency Influences

CHAPTER 6

Families and Peers Delinquency Influences

CHAPTER OBJECTIVES

After studying this chapter, the reader should be able to:

- Discuss the link between family relationships and juvenile misconduct.
- Explain the importance of birth order in predicting juvenile misconduct.
- Discuss how child abuse and neglect is related to juvenile delinquency.
- Explain the issues involved with early childhood disruptive behavior.
- Discuss the importance of peer influence in delinquency prevention.

Family Influences

This chapter examines families and peer influences on juveniles and how those influences may cause or prevent juvenile misconduct. In chapter 2, the authors reviewed the study of 730 violent juveniles incarcerated in seventeen Mexico institutions. The authors noted that 62 percent of the juveniles had divorced parents, that 43 percent had ran away from home, 30 percent perceived that they suffered neglect from their family, 22 percent had never met their fathers, and 60 percent had at least one relative who was in or had been in prison. Those statistics indicate that having a stable family—or not having one—has a significant impact on whether or not the juvenile will commit criminal misconduct.

As noted in another study, children learn positive and negative behaviors from interactions with others, and parents are particularly important when it comes to influencing children's prosocial and antisocial behavior. Parents who endorse attitudes favoring deviant behavior or who fail to correct children's misbehavior increase the likelihood that children will view delinquent activities as acceptable means to achieve certain outcomes, particularly when the juveniles perceive more benefits than negative consequences from engaging in delinquent misconduct.[1]

Family Structure and Delinquency

In discussing family structure or family type, the authors are referring to whether the family is composed of mother and father living as a unit (intact) or a family composed of a father only, a mother only, or stepparent and other. The families in all types of structures may also include siblings. Table 6.1 indicates the percentage of juveniles involved in misconduct by family structure.

Terence P. Thornberry, Carolyn A. Smith, Craig Rivera, David Huizinga, and Magda Stouthamer-Loeber noted in a study that the composition of families is one aspect of family life that is consistently associated with delinquency. Children who live in homes with only one parent or in which marital relationships have been disrupted by divorce or separation are more likely to display a range of emotional and behavioral problems, including delinquency, than children from two-parent families.[2] Photo 6.1 depicts the range of family support services available.

Thornberry et al. noted that since the 1970s, the proportion of American households that have children who live with both parents has declined substantially. In 1970, 64 percent of African-American children lived with two parents, compared with 35 percent in 1997; comparable figures for white children are 90 percent and 74 percent, respectively. According to some estimates, as many as 40 percent of white children and 75 percent of African-American children will experience parental separation or divorce before they reach the age of sixteen, and many of these children will experience multiple family disruptions over time.

The Thornberry study notes that most research on the issue does not address the impact of family transitions on individual children. These transitions can set into motion changes in residence, financial conditions, family roles, and relationships along with increased stress and conflict in the home. All these factors have major implications for children's adjustment. The study notes that while some research finds that the number of family transitions is linked to delinquency, there is little information on the impact of multiple family transitions on serious adolescent problem behavior, such as delinquency and drug use.

Even in two-parent families, the family may still be dysfunctional, and the youth may not receive the supervision, training, and advocacy needed to ensure a positive developmental course. Many studies have concluded that poor parental

TABLE 6.1 Family Structure and Misconduct: A Self-Reported Study

Experiences in percentages	Females Both biological parents	Females All other families	Males Both biological parents	Males All other families
Suspended from school	9%	29%	23%	45%
Runaway ever	7%	17%	22%	40%
Petty theft ever	25%	34%	33%	43%
Major theft in last year	2%	4%	4%	8%
Arrested in past year	2%	5%	4%	10%

Note: For example, only 9 percent of the female delinquent juveniles in the study who lived in a family with both biological parents reported that they had been suspended from school compared to 29 percent who lived in another type of family. Percentages were rounded off to the nearest whole number.
Source: Adapted from Howard N. Snyder and Melissa Sickmund, "Juvenile Offenders and Victims: 2006 National Report," Office of Juvenile Justice and Delinquency Prevention (Washington, DC: US Department of Justice, March 2006). Available at www.ojp.usdoj.gov/ojjdp (accessed April 24, 2019).

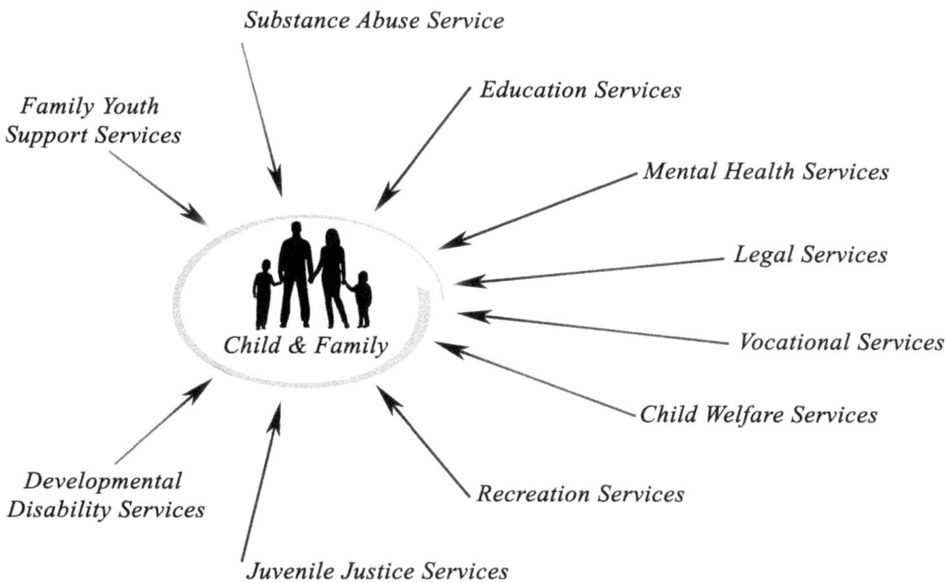

PHOTO 6.1 Graphic depiction of family support services. (Photo courtesy of iStock)

management and disciplinary practices are associated with the development of delinquent behavior. Several of the studies blame the high misconduct rate in two-parent families on the failure of the parents to set clear expectations for children's behavior, inconsistent discipline, and excessively severe or aggressive discipline.[3]

Juveniles who grow up in foster care are destined to grow up in uncertainty. The lack of a permanent home and "foster care drift" are obviously frustrating to a developing child who must find his or her elemental identity without roots and stability. A child requires a stable base to understand who he or she is and to have the courage to venture out on one's own.

Birth Order

One research study found that birth order apparently has an effect on the decision to be involved in criminal behavior. The researchers concluded that second-born boys are substantially more likely to exhibit delinquency problems compared to their older sibling in both Denmark and Florida. Incarceration by age twenty-one was also found to be 40 percent higher in both Florida and Denmark for the second-born child. The researchers noted that this trend was particularly strong for more-severe violent crimes. In Florida, similar birth-order effects were found for school suspensions, but the effects on truancy were much more moderate and heterogeneous.[4]

The researchers ruled out many explanations for the differences in delinquency based on birth order. The differences include: worse health at birth (second-born children appeared healthier) or in childhood disabilities (second-born children have fewer disabilities); schooling decisions, including the age of entry and the quality of schools chosen (second-born children attend similar schools and are more likely to attend prekindergarten and daycare); as well as maternal employment (measured by maternity leave) in the first year of life. The researchers did find that maternal employment and the use of daycare was higher for second-born two- to four-year-olds compared to firstborn siblings.

The researchers opined that it was well known that firstborns have undivided attention until the arrival of the second-born, but these results show that the arrival of the second-born child has the potential to extend the early-childhood parental investment in the firstborn child and a concomitant bifurcation of parental attention between first- and second-born children.

Child Abuse and Neglect

If a child is abused in early childhood, does this create a greater chance that the child will later become involved in delinquent misconduct? This is a question that has been researched by several studies, and the studies have concluded that the answer is yes. According to the studies, early child abuse or child neglect increases the chances that the child will later become involved in delinquency.

Janet Currie and Erdal Tekin conducted a study to determine if child abuse causes crime.[5] They concluded that when a child is maltreated, it approximately doubles the probability of the child later engaging in many types of crime. According to the study, children in families that are considered as low socioeconomic status are both more likely to be mistreated and suffer more damaging effects. Boys are at greater risk than girls, at least in terms of increased propensity to commit crime. Sexual abuse appears to have the largest negative effects. The researchers concluded that the probability of engaging in crime increases with the experience of multiple forms of maltreatment, as well as the experience of a Child Protective Services investigation.

Currie and Tekin concluded that a potential explanation for the increased likelihood that abused and neglected children will be involved in criminal activities is that the abused children start engaging in crime earlier. The researchers concluded that abused or neglected children are more likely to be arrested as both juveniles and adults. Starting to engage in criminal behavior early may increase illegal human capital by raising experience in criminal activities, and decrease human capital in legitimate activities, such as schooling or being in the labor market. This would further increase their criminal propensities. The researchers opined that the apparent negative effects of maltreatment on children's propensity to engage in crime are real and not simply artifacts of other features of dysfunctional families.

Currie and Tekin also concluded that having access to a gun at home increases the propensity to commit a variety of crimes by about 30 percent among adolescents. They noted that decreases in gun ownership can explain up to a third of the decline in youth crimes. According to them, exposure to firearm violence approximately doubles the probability that an adolescent will engage in serious violence over the subsequent two years, and that effects of maltreatment are like those of exposure to gun violence.

The family environment plays a major role in the development of noncognitive skills and subsequent delinquency. Cathy Widom noted in her study that there exists a "cycle of violence" where delinquency among parents is passed on to children. She noted that the sheer amount of time children spend with their family and the influences each member has on one another imply that the family influence must have large effects.[6] "Cycle of violence" or "intergenerational transmission of violence" are terms used to describe the relationship between maltreatment in childhood and violence by the youth in adolescence and adulthood. According to Widom, research has indicated higher rates of violent offending among survivors of childhood maltreatment than among individuals not abused in childhood.[7]

Widom later conducted research that is considered one of the best-known studies of the long-term effects of maltreatment. In this study, she matched a sample of 908 children with substantiated cases of maltreatment to controls (non-abused children) who were selected to be similar in terms of age, sex, race, and socioeconomic status. Her study is unusual in that it distinguished between physical abuse, neglect, and sexual abuse. It also involved long-term follow-up of the subjects. She found substantial effects of both abuse and neglect on arrest both as a juvenile and as an adult. She found that being abused or neglected as a child increases an individual's risk for an arrest as a juvenile by 53 percent; increases the probability of arrest as an adult by 38 percent; and increases the probability of an arrest for a violent crime by 38 percent.

Numerous research studies have indicated that families are one of the strongest socializing forces in life. Children learn to control unacceptable behavior, to delay gratification, and to respect the rights of others from their families. Families can also teach children aggressive, antisocial, and violent behavior.[8] Juveniles are more likely to become juvenile delinquents if there is little structure provided for them in their families. Families are one of the strongest socializing forces in life. But when a child is abused, the socializing force will probably be negative in nature.

Beverly Rivera and Cathy Widom examined the link between childhood abuse and neglect and later violent criminality.[9] The researchers found that maltreated males were at greater risk of committing a violent offense than a matched control group, while this was not true among females. However, in a different study conducted six years later by Michael Maxfield and Cathy Widom, the researchers found that abused and neglected females were at a greater risk of arrest for violence than females who were in the control group.[10]

Biological Factors

Are juvenile delinquents genetically different from nondelinquent juveniles? It appears that all behavior, including delinquency, is influenced by biological factors. These factors include not only physical strength but also brain functioning, such as neurotransmitters that pass signals to the brain. Serotonin receptors, for instance, are neurotransmitters that have been associated with impulsive behavior. Other biological factors have also been associated with delinquency. Compared to nondelinquents, delinquents tend to have a lower heart rate and a lower skin response, which are measures of autonomic nervous activity. One line of research has concentrated on hormones, including testosterone. While a high level of testosterone during the elementary school years is not known to predict later delinquency, it is far from clear to what extent biological processes determine delinquency at a young age.[11]

Children Exposed to Violence

According to the *Report of the Attorney General's National Task Force on Children Exposed to Violence*, most youths involved in the criminal justice system have survived exposure to violence and are living with the trauma of those experiences.[12] The report notes that by the time children come into contact with the juvenile justice system, the juveniles have been exposed to several types of traumatic violence over the course of many years. The report notes that in one study conducted in a juvenile detention center in Cook County, Illinois, 90 percent of the youths reported past exposure to traumatic violence, which included being threatened with weapons and/or physically abused. A study that used a national sample determined that youths in juvenile detention centers were three times as likely as those in a national sample of juveniles not involved in the justice system to have been exposed to multiple types of violence and traumatic events.

The task force concluded that the relationship between exposure to violence and involvement in the juvenile justice system was not a coincidence. That exposure to violence frequently leads to distrust, hypervigilance, impulsive behavior, isolation, addiction, lack of empathy or concern for others, and self-protective aggression. According to the report, when young people experience prolonged or repeated violence, their bodies and brains adapt by becoming focused on survival. This reduces their ability to delay impulses and gratification to a degree beyond that of normal children. The report also concludes that youths who are trying to protect themselves from more violence, or who do not know how to deal with violence they have already experienced, may engage in delinquent or criminal behavior as a way to gain a sense of control in their chaotic lives and to cope with the emotional turmoil and barriers to security and success that violence creates.

The task force concluded that while many youths in the juvenile justice system appear to be angry, defiant, or indifferent, they are actually fearful, depressed, and lonely. (Note: This conclusion coincides with the Azaola et al. study of Mexican juveniles discussed in chapter 2.) According to the task force, the youths are hurting emotionally and feel powerless, abandoned, and subject to a double standard by the adults in their lives and in the system.

Hyperactivity

Children who are restless, squirmy, and fidgety are more likely to be involved in later delinquent behavior. Clinical studies of hyperactive children have shown that they are at high risk of delinquency. For example, motor restlessness (hyperactive or hyperkinetic behavior), as rated by kindergarten teachers, was a better predictor of delinquency between the ages of ten and thirteen than a lack of prosocial behavior and low anxiety. Another study concluded that hyperactivity leads to delinquency only when it occurs in tandem with physical aggression or oppositional behavior.[13]

Antisocial Behavior

Early antisocial behavior is a strong predictor of later delinquency.[14] Antisocial behaviors generally include various forms of oppositional rule violation and aggression, such as theft, physical fighting, and vandalism. In fact, early aggression appears to be the most significant social behavior characteristic to predict delinquent behavior before the age of thirteen. In one study, physical aggression in kindergarten was the best and only predictor of later involvement in property crimes. In contrast, prosocial behavior (such as helping, sharing, and cooperation), as rated by teachers, appeared to be a protective factor, specifically for those who have risk factors for committing violent and property crimes before age thirteen.

Studies conducted in Canada, England, New Zealand, Sweden, and the United States have confirmed that early antisocial behavior tends to be a strong predictor of early-onset delinquency for boys. For example, in one study, antisocial behavior was the best predictor of age at first arrest when compared with family social disadvantage, parental monitoring, and parental discipline. Long-term results also indicated that those with an early arrest (before age thirteen) were most likely to be chronic offenders by age eighteen. A Cambridge study in delinquent development in London, England, showed that one of the strongest predictors of a conviction between ages ten and thirteen was troublesome behavior between the ages of eight and ten, as rated by teachers and peers.

The Terrible Twos

Mothers will tell you that two-year-old children are very unruly. This is probably correct, but most children outgrow early problem behaviors. The ones who do not outgrow such behaviors are of concern because of the increased risk that they may become child delinquents.

Family Structure and Juvenile Court

Does family stability influence the juvenile judge in making the decision to incarcerate a juvenile delinquent? Researchers Nancy Rodriguez, Hilary Smith, and Marjorie S. Zatz concluded that juvenile court decisions are influenced by perceptions of juveniles' family backgrounds, which include family structure, quality of care, and economic resources. They noted that central to the family and home life of the juvenile was the social class of the family, and opined that court officials tend to perceive lower-class families as unstable and inadequate in providing appropriate supervision for juveniles. Conversely, researchers noted that judges perceive middle-class families as offering the ideal home environment. The researchers asked whether court officials' perceptions of ideal homes translate into less-severe treatment for youths from ideal homes.

Rodriguez et al. also noted that family dysfunction has been identified as a risk factor in juvenile court processes and outcomes, which in some cases leads to court intervention and removal of juveniles from the home. An immediate indicator of family dysfunction for the court is likely to be the criminal involvement and imprisonment of a parent.[15]

Most studies on the effects of the family on a juvenile's decision to commit criminal misconduct are based on research involving juveniles who are incarcerated in institutions. If the juvenile court judges are influenced by the family status when they make the decision on whether to incarcerate the juvenile, the statistics on family influences and juveniles, as noted in co-author Azaola's study of interned Mexican juveniles, may need to be revisited.

The task force noted that when children are exposed to violence, the convergence between real-life events and their worst fears—about physical injury and loss of life, risk to their loved ones, and control of their actions—is an experience of overwhelming and often unanticipated danger. This danger may trigger a traumatic disruption of biological, cognitive, social, and emotional regulation that has different behavioral manifestations depending on the developmental stage of the youth. According to the report, early exposure to violence deprives a child of as much as 10 percent of his or her potential intelligence. This leaves the child vulnerable to serious emotional, learning, and behavioral problems when they reach school age. Studies emphasize that a delinquent sibling can greatly encourage a child to become delinquent, as well, especially when the siblings are close in age and have a close relationship.

Early Childhood Disruptive Behavior

According to researchers Rolf Loeber, David P. Farrington, and David Petechuk, generations of studies indicate that one of the best predictors of future behavior is past behavior.[16] Children showing persistent disruptive behavior are likely to become child delinquents and, in turn, child delinquents are likely to become serious, violent, or chronic juvenile offenders.

In more than twenty studies reviewed by Loeber et al., the researchers concluded that there is a significant relationship between early onset of delinquency and later crime and delinquency. Child delinquents, compared with juveniles who have a later onset of delinquency, are at greater risk of becoming serious, violent, and chronic offenders, and have longer delinquency careers.

While the researchers noted that not all disruptive children become child delinquents, and not all child delinquents will become serious, violent, or chronic juvenile offenders, they concluded that many of the eventual serious, violent, and chronic juvenile offenders had a history of problem behaviors that went back to their childhood years. They noted that the antisocial careers of male juvenile offenders start, on average, at age seven, much earlier than the average age of first court contact for Crime Index offenses, which is fourteen and a half. They recommended that since it is not possible to accurately predict which children will progress from serious problem behaviors to delinquency, it is better to tackle these problem behaviors before the youths become serious, violent, or chronic juvenile offenders.

The researchers noted that the preschool period is critical in setting a foundation for preventing the development of disruptive behavior and, eventually, child delinquency. They pointed out four primary reasons why the preschool period may have important implications for understanding and preventing very young offending:

- Disruptive problem behavior, including serious aggression and chronic violation of the rights and property of others, is the most common source of referral to mental health services for preschool children.
- Studies have documented a predictive relationship between problem behaviors in preschool and later conduct disorder and child delinquency.
- Many important developmental skills (such as language development) begin during this period, and difficulties in developing these skills may weaken the foundation of learning and contribute to later disruptive behavior and child delinquency.
- Understanding the early emergence of problem behaviors may help in the creation of earlier, effective interventions for the prevention of child delinquency.

Behaviors that place a child at risk for an early career of disruptive behavior and child delinquency may be present as early as two years of age. Although many child delinquents have a history of disruptive behavior—such as aggressive, inattentive, or sensation-seeking behavior in the preschool period—most preschoolers with such behavior problems do not go on to become young offenders.

The researchers stated that the following factors may affect the development of pro- and antisocial behavior during preschool and beyond:

- Language is the primary means by which parents and others affect children's behavior. Delayed language development may increase a child's stress level, impede normal socialization, and be associated with later criminality up to the age of thirty.
- Temperamental characteristics are individual predispositions for certain behavior characteristics that can be modified by environmental influences.
- Difficult temperament (predominance of negative moods, such as anger and difficulty in controlling behaviors and emotions) early in life may be a marker for the early antecedents of antisocial behavior and behavior problems.
- Low attachment to caregivers, as in the early mother–infant bond, plays an important role in later behavior and delinquency problems.
- The closer the relationship that a child has to the mother, the less likely a child is to be at risk for delinquency.

The researchers noted that one of the difficulties in dealing with preschool children is the use of inappropriate labels, such as "disruptive," for behaviors that may be developmentally normal. For example, aggression, noncompliance, and lying are common behaviors in the second year of life, and are part of the development of self-identity, self-control, and understanding the nature of social relations.

Another issue is whether young children can commit willful acts of aggression. Several developmental researchers have demonstrated that preschool children do have a basic understanding of the impact of their behavior on others and can control their behavior based on internalized social norms. The researchers found enough evidence to conclude that some preschool children can engage in very serious antisocial behavior and that, in some but not all cases, preschool behavior problems foreshadow early delinquency.

The researchers pointed out that in addition to early antisocial behavior, family characteristics are important predictors of early-onset offending. It is also important to consider the number of family risk factors to which a child is exposed and how long the child is exposed to them.

Some family characteristics that may contribute to early-onset child delinquency include the following:

- Antisocial parents;
- Substance-abusing parents;
- Parental psychopathology;
- Poor parenting practices, such as lack of monitoring and/or a lack of positive reinforcement;
- The prevalence of physical abuse;
- A history of family violence; and
- Large family size.

The researchers noted that many of the family risk factors interact with other social systems, such as peers and the community environment. One study found that the strongest predictors of early-onset violence included large family size, poor parenting skills, and antisocial parents. They concluded that an accelerated path toward child delinquency and subsequent more-serious offending may be the result of a combination of the following factors:

- Antisocial tendencies of children with persistent early disruptive behaviors;
- Associations with peers who already show deviant behavior; and
- Negative consequences of peer rejection.

According to the researchers' conclusions, as children get older, attend school, and become integrated into their community, the array of risk factors for child delinquency expands. Many studies show a relation between deviant peer associations and juvenile offending. A major issue is whether "birds of a feather flock together" or "bad company corrupts." Most hypotheses suggest that deviant peers can lead some youth with no previous history of delinquent behavior to initiate delinquent acts, and may influence already-delinquent youth to increase their delinquency. Youth who associate with deviant peers are likely to be arrested earlier than youth who do not associate with such peers.

Functional Family Theory

An interesting approach to delinquency prevention is functional family theory (FFT). As noted by Thomas Sexton and James Alexander, FFT is a family-based prevention and intervention program that has been applied successfully in a variety of contexts to treat a range of these high-risk youth and their families.[17] As such, FFT is a good example of the current generation of family-based treatments for adolescent behavior problems. FFT integrates the following elements into a clear and comprehensive clinical model: established clinical theory, empirically supported principles, and extensive clinical experience. The FFT model allows for successful intervention in complex and multidimensional problems through clinical practice that is flexibly structured and culturally sensitive—and is accountable to youth, their families, and the community.

Although commonly used as an intervention program, FFT is also an effective prevention program for at-risk adolescents and their families. Whether implemented as an intervention or a prevention program, FFT may include diversion, probation, alternatives to incarceration, and/or reentry programs for youth returning to the community following release from a high-security, severely restrictive institutional setting.

According to the researchers, based on the results of extensive independent reviews, FFT has been designated variously as a "blueprint program," an "exemplary model" program, and "family-based empirically supported treatment." These designations reflect FFT's thirty years of clinical and research experience and its use at a wide range of intervention sites in the United States and other countries.

FFT targets youth between the ages of eleven and eighteen from a variety of ethnic and cultural groups. It also provides treatment to the younger siblings of referred adolescents. FFT is a short-term intervention including, on average, eight to twelve sessions for mild cases and up to thirty hours of direct service (e.g., clinical sessions, telephone calls, and meetings involving community resources) for more-difficult cases. In most cases, sessions are spread over a three-month period. Regardless of the target population, FFT emphasizes the importance of respecting all family members on their own terms (i.e., as they experience the intervention process).

Goals

Functional family therapy is so named to identify the primary focus of intervention (the family) and reflect an understanding that positive and negative behaviors both influence and are influenced by multiple relational systems (i.e., are functional). FFT is a multisystemic prevention program, meaning that it focuses on the multiple domains and systems within which adolescents and their families live. FFT is also multisystemic and multilevel as an intervention in that it focuses on the treatment system, family and individual functioning, and the therapist as major components. Within this context, FFT works first to develop family members' inner strengths and sense of being able to improve their situations—even if modestly at first. These characteristics provide the family with a platform for change and future functioning that extends beyond the direct support of the therapist and other social systems. In the long run, the FFT philosophy leads to greater self-sufficiency, fewer total treatment needs, and considerably lower costs.

At the level of clinical practice, FFT includes a systematic and multiphase intervention map—phase task analysis—that forms the basis for responsive clinical decisions. This map gives FFT a flexible structure by identifying treatment strategies with a high probability of success and facilitating therapists' clinical options. FFT's flexibility extends to all family members and thereby results in effective moment-by-moment decisions in the intervention setting. Thus, FFT practice is both systematic and individualized.

Intervention Phases

FFT's three specific intervention phases—engagement and motivation, behavior change, and generalization—are interdependent and sequentially linked. Each has distinct goals and assessment objectives, each addresses different risk and protective factors, and each calls for particular skills from the interventionist or therapist providing treatment. The interventions in each phase are organized coherently, which allows clinicians to maintain focus in contexts that often involve considerable family and individual disruption. The three intervention phases are described in the sections that follow.

Phase 1: Engagement and Motivation. This phase places primary emphasis on maximizing factors that enhance intervention credibility (i.e., the perception that positive change might occur) and minimizing factors likely to decrease that perception (e.g., poor program image, difficult location, insensitive referrals, personal and/or cultural insensitivity, and inadequate resources). Therapists apply reattribution (e.g., reframing, developing positive themes) and related techniques to address maladaptive perceptions, beliefs, and emotions. Use of such techniques establishes a family-focused perception of the presenting problem that serves to increase families' hope and expectation of change, decrease resistance, improve alliance and trust between family and therapist, reduce oppressive negativity within families and between families and the community, and help build respect for individual differences and values.

Phase 2: Behavior Change. During this phase, FFT clinicians develop and implement intermediate and, ultimately, long-term behavior change plans that are culturally appropriate, context-sensitive, and tailored to the unique characteristics of each family member. The assessment focus in this phase includes cognitive (e.g., attributional processes and coping strategies), interactive (e.g., reciprocity of positive rather than negative behaviors, competent parenting, and understanding of behavior sequences involved in delinquency), and emotional components (e.g., blaming and negativity). Clinicians provide concrete behavioral intervention to guide and model specific behavior changes (e.g., parenting, communication, and conflict management). Emphasis is placed on using individualized and developmentally appropriate techniques that fit the family relational system.

Phase 3: Generalization. This FFT phase is guided by the need to apply (i.e., generalize) positive family change to other problem areas and/or situations. FFT clinicians help families maintain change and prevent relapses. To ensure long-term support of changes, FFT links families with available community resources. The primary goal of the generalization phase is to improve a family's ability to affect the multiple systems in which it is embedded (e.g., school, juvenile justice system, community), thereby allowing the family to mobilize community support systems and modify deteriorated family-system relationships. If necessary, FFT clinicians intervene directly with the systems in which a family is embedded until the family develops the ability to do so itself.

Assessment

Assessment is an ongoing, multifaceted process that is part of each phase of the FFT clinical model. In FFT, assessment focuses on understanding the ways in which behavioral problems function within family relationship systems. The focus of assessment depends on the phase of treatment. In general, assessment in FFT is based on the following principles:

- FFT assessment should focus on the ways that family relational systems are related to the presenting behavior problems—in both adaptive and maladaptive ways.
- FFT should identify risk and protective factors through clinical and formal assessment. In doing so, FFT helps identify family, individual, and contextual issues that might become the targets of treatment.

- Assessment should be multilevel, multidimensional, and multimethod. Individual factors include the adolescent's cognitive and developmental level and any psychological conditions that he or she may have (e.g., depression/anxiety, thought disorders).
- Assessment should also consider the adolescent's family, because the family is the psychosocial context in which the adolescent lives. Family factors considered in an FFT assessment include what goes on during daily family life (e.g., parenting, teaching, supporting, providing, and relating).
- Behavioral and contextual factors include external and social factors that influence the adolescent (e.g., the presence or absence of risk and protective factors and the availability of community resources).
- Assessment of family functioning—rather than completion of a diagnostic assessment—is the most helpful way to identify appropriate treatment options and approaches. The goal of assessment is to plan the most appropriate treatment.
- Clinical, outcome, and adherence assessment are critical to successful implementation of the FFT model.

FFT has identified formal and clinical tools for model, adherence, and outcome assessment. These tools are incorporated into the Functional Family Assessment Protocol—a systematic approach to understanding families—and the Clinical Services System (CSS)—an implementation tool that allows therapists to track the activities (i.e., session process goals, comprehensive client assessments, and clinical outcomes) essential to successful implementation.

CSS seeks to improve therapists' competence and skill by keeping them focused on the goals, skills, and interventions needed for each phase of FFT. CSS's computer-based format gives therapists easy access to a variety of process and assessment information which, in turn, allows them to make good clinical decisions and provides them with the complete outcome information needed to evaluate case success.

Shifting of Parenting Styles and Delinquency

Parenting style can affect everything from how much a child weighs to how she feels about herself. Sociologists contend that it is important to ensure that the parenting style is supporting healthy growth and development, because the way the parent interacts with a child and how the parent disciplines the child will influence him or her for the rest of the child's life.

Researchers have identified four types of parenting style:

- *Authoritarian* parents believe that children are, by nature, strong-willed and self-indulgent and need strict discipline. Authoritarian parents see their primary job to be bending the will of the child to that of authority.
- *Authoritative* parents are also strict, consistent, and loving, but their values and beliefs about parenting and children are markedly different. Authoritative parents are issue-oriented and pragmatic, rather than motivated by an external, absolute standard. They tend to adjust their expectations to the needs of the child.
- *Permissive* parents have a style characterized by low demands with high responsiveness. Permissive parents tend to be very loving, yet provide few guidelines and rules for their children.
- *Uninvolved* parents, sometimes referred to as neglectful, have a style characterized by a lack of responsiveness to a child's needs. Uninvolved parents make few to no demands of their children.

Each style takes a different approach to raising children, and can be identified by several different characteristics. Most sociologists will agree that parenting styles are changing. How do these changes affect juvenile delinquency?

Diana Baumrind in the 1960s concluded that parenting styles have been influential in not only explaining delinquency but other outcomes as well, such as self-esteem, academic performance, and sexual risk-taking.[18] Baumrind concluded that juveniles with neglectful or authoritarian parents were more likely to be delinquent. The researcher found some differences by race but not by gender. Her findings were based on studies that are currently over fifty years old.

Baumrind stated that parenting can be grouped under two dimensions: responsiveness and demandingness (control). Responsiveness involves the parent being attuned, supportive, and acquiescent to children's needs and demands. Demandingness, on the other hand, refers to the nature of direct confrontations, parental monitoring, and discipline.

Nancy Darling and Laurence Steinberg indicated that demandingness refers to the parent's willingness to act as a socializing agent, whereas responsiveness refers to the parent's recognition of the child's individuality. The two dimensions reflect two types of demands: those made by society on the child as conveyed through the parent, and those made by the child on society.[19]

In a 2009 study, a group of researchers tested the connection between parenting and delinquency.[20] They focused on parenting from different perspectives, analyzing parenting dimensions, styles, and behaviors in relation to delinquency. The researchers concluded that their meta-analysis demonstrated the following:

- A significant relationship exists between parenting styles and delinquency, confirming previous research that behavioral control, such as parental monitoring, is negatively linked to delinquency;
- Negative aspects of support, including rejection, hostility and neglect, and psychological control, had the strongest links to delinquency; and
- Several indicators of parental monitoring, including parental knowledge, child disclosure, and active monitoring by parents, had similar links to delinquency.

They noted that a lack of support by the parent had a relatively strong link to delinquency if that parent and child were of the same gender. In addition, the parenting–delinquency link was stronger in school-age children and early adolescents than in older adolescents. In addition, they found that parental monitoring was more strongly linked to overt delinquency than covert delinquency, stressing the importance of distinguishing between different types of delinquency.

There are several other studies on the effects of parenting styles and delinquency, but they are not as thorough or as current as this 2009 study (which was completed more than a decade ago). This is an issue that needs to be revisited, since parenting styles are continuingly changing.

These findings have important implications for intervention and prevention policies related to delinquency. Interventions should focus not only on aspects of behavioral control, such as restrictiveness, consistency in discipline, and monitoring, but should also target parenting dimensions, such as psychological control and negative aspects of support. Furthermore, the findings suggest that fathers should be involved in intervention programs for violent youth, particularly those aimed at delinquent boys, if the fathers themselves are not offenders. Finally, the finding that parenting is more strongly linked to delinquency in school-age children and early adolescents underscores the importance of prevention strategies early in life.

Peers and Delinquency

Impact of Peer Relationships

Studies seem to prove that the effects of deviant peers on criminal misconduct are heightened if the juveniles believe that their peers approve of their behavior, especially if they are closely attached to those peers. By "closely attached," we mean that they spend considerable time with them, and that they perceive pressure from those peers to engage in delinquent acts.

A teen tends to make riskier decisions when a peer is watching their decision-making process. The presence of a peer can activate reward circuitry in the brain, which makes teens act in a riskier fashion. These peers do not necessarily have to convince a teen to act in a riskier fashion, as their mere presence can change the mind-set of a teen. These patterns do not exist in adults, meaning that the adult brain can filter out this reward circuitry from the decision-making process.[21]

According to Jeremi Davidson, many teens go through a stage of moral reasoning, where their opinions of themselves come from what others think. This outer-directed behavior can change the way a teen acts, since he or she gets his or her image of him- or herself from his or her friends. At this stage of life, a teen might start experimenting with drinking, drugs, and sex because of this pressure to conform to what others do. The teen may start acting like everyone else, even if everyone else's behavior goes against the morals that a parent has instilled in a teen.[22]

According to one study, there is a dramatic increase during childhood in the amount of importance peer relationships assume during late adolescence, with their importance peaking at about age seventeen and declining thereafter.[23] The decline in delinquency after about age eighteen parallels the decline in the importance of peers, including those with deviant influences. Peer influences appear to have a particularly strong relationship to delinquency in the context of family conflict. For example, this study found that adolescents' lack of respect for their parents influenced their antisocial behavior only because it led to increases in antisocial peer affiliations. Other research suggests that adolescents usually become involved with delinquent peers before they become delinquent themselves. In those cases in which an adolescent was delinquent prior to having delinquent friends, the delinquency was exacerbated by association with deviant peers.[24]

Peer groups can play an important role as the child develops into adulthood. But one thing we should keep in mind is that peer groups may have a positive effect on youth. Peers may have a positive influence on a teen's life, especially if that friend has a commitment to succeeding. Two friends who spend frequent time together can push each other toward academic and sports-related goals, making both more successful. Having positive friends in a teen's life can also provide feedback when an individual makes a bad decision. The encouragement and social skills acquired through a solid network of friends teaches young people how to act in social situations, which sets them up well for adulthood.[25]

Studies have indicated that grouping younger children with prosocial juveniles can reduce antisocial behaviors and increase prosocial behaviors. A problem in this regard is that grouping at-risk juveniles together may provide additional opportunities to reinforce deviant behavior. In addition, at-risk juveniles may adjust their values in a negative manner after associating with peers who approve of misbehavior.

Peer Rejection

Researchers refer to an Oregon youth study where investigators found, after controlling for earlier antisocial behavior, that peer rejection in the fourth grade predicted antisocial behavior two years later.[26] Another study that followed children from first through fourth grade found that aggressive behavior and rejection by peers in the first grade predicted later self-reported delinquency. This indicates that first-grade rejection may be a useful marker for the early-starter pathway to antisocial behavior.[27]

Peer rejection can influence child and adolescent delinquency by inducing the rejected child to associate with deviant peer groups and gangs. Gang membership provides a ready source of co-offenders for juvenile delinquency and reflects the greatest degree of deviant peer influence on offending. Youths tend to join gangs at younger ages than in the past, which leads to an increased number of youthful offenders. The impact of accomplices is very important. One recent study found that less than 5 percent of offenders who committed their first offense at age twelve or younger acted alone.

Practicum

Diane's father has alcohol problems and frequently comes home from work and abuses her. Diane's mother is afraid to say anything to protect Diane and allows the father to mistreat Diane. To avoid an unhappy situation at home, Diane tends to hang out at the local mall.

In the above scenario, what factors would tend to push Diane toward delinquent misconduct?

Summary

- Children learn positive and negative behaviors from interactions with others, and parents are particularly important when it comes to influencing children's prosocial and antisocial behavior.
- Parents who endorse attitudes favoring deviant behavior or who fail to correct children's misbehavior increase the likelihood that children will view delinquent activities as acceptable means to achieve certain outcomes, particularly when the juveniles perceive more benefits than negative consequences from engaging in delinquent misconduct.
- Children who live in homes with only one parent or in which marital relationships have been disrupted by divorce or separation are more likely to display a range of emotional and behavioral problems, including delinquency, than children from two-parent families.
- Even in two-parent families, the family may still be dysfunctional, and the youth may not receive the supervision, training, and advocacy needed to ensure a positive developmental course.
- Many studies have concluded that poor parental management and disciplinary practices are associated with the development of delinquent behavior.
- Birth order apparently has an effect on the decision to be involved in criminal behavior. Second-born boys are substantially more likely to exhibit delinquency problems compared to their older sibling.
- Early child abuse or child neglect increases the chances that the child will later become involved in delinquency.
- The family environment plays a major role in the development of non-cognitive skills and subsequent delinquency.
- Most youths involved in the criminal justice system have survived exposure to violence and are living with the trauma of those experiences.
- Clinical studies of hyperactive children have shown that they are at high risk of delinquency.

- Early antisocial behavior is a strong predictor of later delinquency.
- Juvenile court decisions are influenced by perceptions of juveniles' family backgrounds, which include family structure, quality of care, and economic resources.
- Children showing persistent disruptive behavior are likely to become child delinquents and, in turn, child delinquents are likely to become serious, violent, or chronic juvenile offenders.
- Functional family therapy (FFT) is a family-based prevention and intervention program that has been applied successfully in a variety of contexts to treat a range of these high-risk youth and their families.
- The effects of deviant peers on criminal misconduct are heightened if the juveniles believe that their peers approve of their behavior, especially if they are closely attached to those peers.

Discussion and Review Questions

1. Explain the influences that the family has on the propensity to commit delinquency.
2. Why is early childhood disruptive behavior a concern?
3. What are the important concepts in functional family therapy?
4. How significant is the concept of peer rejection in determining whether a child will commit delinquent misconduct?
5. What are the early indicators that a child may have a propensity to commit delinquency?
6. How does the presence of a peer influence a child's behavior?
7. Discuss the relationship between child neglect and delinquent behavior.
8. Explain the issues involved in birth order and delinquent behavior.

Notes

1. Abigail A. Fagan, "Family-Focused Interventions to Prevent Juvenile Delinquency: A Case Where Science and Policy Can Find Common Ground," *Criminology & Public Policy*, vol. 12 (2013), 617–50.
2. Terence P. Thornberry, Carolyn A. Smith, Craig Rivera, David Huizinga, and Magda Stouthamer-Loeber, "Family Disruption and Delinquency," *Juvenile Justice Bulletin* (Washington, DC: US Department of Justice, September 1999).
3. Joan McCord, Cathy S. Widom, and Nancy A. Crowell, *Juvenile Crime, Juvenile Justice*, National Research Council and Institute of Medicine (Washington, DC: National Academies Press, 2001). Available at https://doi.org/10.17226/9747.
4. Sanni N. Breining, Joseph J. Doyle Jr., David N. Figlio, Krzysztof Karbownik, and Jeffrey Roth, "Birth Order and Delinquency: Evidence from Denmark and Florida," Working Paper No. 23038 (Cambridge, MA: National Bureau of Economic Research, 2017). Available at http://www.nber.org/papers/w23038 (accessed April 25, 2019).
5. Janet Currie and Erdal Tekin, "Does Child Abuse Cause Crime?" National Bureau of Economic Research Working Paper, No. 12171 (April 2006), posted online at https://www.nber.org/papers/w12171 (accessed April 25, 2019).
6. Cathy S. Widom, "The Cycle of Violence," *Science*, vol. 244 (1989), 160–66.
7. Breining et al., "Birth Order and Delinquency."
8. Nisar Muhammad, Ullah Shakir, Ali Madad, and Alam Sadiq, "Juvenile Delinquency: The Influence of Family, Peer and Economic Factors on Juvenile Delinquents," *Scientia Agriculturae*, vol. 9, no. 1 (2015), 37–48. Retrieved from www.pscipub.com (DOI: 10.15192/PSCP.SA.2015.9.1.3748) (accessed April 23, 2019).

9. Beverly Rivera and Cathy S. Widom, "Childhood Victimization and Violent Offending," *Violence and Victims*, vol. 5 (1990), 19–35.
10. Michael G. Maxfield and Cathy S. Widom, "The Cycle of Violence: Revised 6 Years Later," *Archives of Pediatrics and Adolescent Medicine*, vol. 150 (1996), 390–95.
11. Gail A. Wasserman, Kate Keenan, Richard E. Tremblay, John D. Coie, Todd I. Herrenkohl, Rolf Loeber, and David Petechuk, "Risk and Protective Factors of Child Delinquency," *Child Delinquency Bulletin Series* (Washington, DC: Office of Juvenile Justice and Delinquency Prevention, April 2003).
12. Office of Juvenile Justice and Delinquency Prevention, "Report of the Attorney General's National Task Force on Children Exposed to Violence" (Washington, DC: US Department of Justice, December 2012).
13. Wasserman et al., "Risk and Protective Factors of Child Delinquency."
14. Wasserman et al., "Risk and Protective Factors of Child Delinquency."
15. Nancy Rodriguez, Hilary Smith, and Marjorie S. Zatz, "Youth Is Enmeshed in a Highly Dysfunctional Family System: Exploring the Relationship among Dysfunctional Families, Parental Incarceration, and Juvenile Court Decision Making," *Criminology*, vol. 47 (2009), 177–208.
16. The information for this section was adapted from: Rolf Loeber, David P. Farrington, and David Petechuk, "Child Delinquency: Early Intervention and Prevention," *Child Delinquency Bulletin Series* (Washington, DC: Office of Juvenile Justice and Delinquency Prevention, May 2003).
17. The information for this section was taken from: Thomas L. Sexton and James Alexander, "Functional Family Therapy," *OJJDP Bulletin* (Washington, DC: US Department of Justice, December 2000).
18. Diana Baumrind, "Effects of Authoritative Parental Control on Child Behavior," *Child Development*, vol. 37, no. 4 (1966), 887–907.
19. Nancy Darling and Laurence Steinberg, "Parenting Style as Context: An Integrative Model," *Psychological Bulletin*, vol. 113, no. 3 (1993), 487–96.
20. Machteld Hoeve, Judith Semon Dubas, Veroini L. Eichelsheim, Peter H. van der Laan, Wilma Smeenk, and Jan R. M. Gerris, "The Relationship Between Parenting and Delinquency: A Meta-Analysis," *Journal of Abnormal Child Psychology*, vol. 37, no. 6 (August 2009), 749–75.
21. Jeremi Davidson, "How Much Do Friends Affect Teen Behavior?" (June 2017), posted on Healthfully website at https://healthfully.com/488271-how-much-do-friends-affect-teen-behavior.html (accessed April 25, 2019).
22. Davidson, "How Much Do Friends Affect Teen Behavior?"
23. Howard N. Snyder and Melissa Sickmund, "Juvenile Offenders and Victims: 2006 National Report," Office of Juvenile Justice and Delinquency Prevention (Washington, DC: US Department of Justice, May 2006), www.ojp.usdoj.gov/ojjdp (accessed April 24, 2019).
24. McCord et al., *Juvenile Crime, Juvenile Justice.*
25. Davidson, "How Much Do Friends Affect Teen Behavior?"
26. G. R. Patterson and L. Bank, "Some Amplifying Mechanisms for Pathologic Processes in Families," in *Systems and Development: The Minnesota Symposia on Child Psychology*, edited by M. R. Gunnar and E. Thelen (Hillsdale, NJ: Erlbaum, 1989), 167–209.
27. S. Miller-Johnson, J. D. Coie, A. Maumary Gremand, and K. Bierman, "Peer Rejection and Aggression and Early Starter Models of Conduct Disorder," Conduct Problems Prevention Research Group Paper presented at the meeting of the Society for Research in Child Development, April 1997, Indianapolis, Indiana.

CHAPTER 7

Youth Gangs

CHAPTER OBJECTIVES

After studying this chapter, the reader should be able to:

- Understand why youths join gangs.
- Be able to recommend steps for preventing gang membership.
- Explain what constitutes a youth gang.
- Discuss how to determine if there are youth gangs in your area.
- List the indicators that a youth is involved in a gang.
- Discuss the purpose of the National Youth Gang Center.

Youth Gang Issues

The Network of Care website states that although once thought to be an inner-city problem, gang violence has spread to communities throughout the United States. At last count in 2019, there were more than 24,500 different youth gangs around the country, and more than 772,500 teens and young adults were members of gangs.[1]

According to the Philadelphia-based website, teens join gangs for a variety of reasons. Some are seeking excitement; others are looking for prestige, protection, a chance to make money, or a sense of belonging. Few teens are forced to join gangs; in most cases, teens can refuse to join without fear of retaliation. The website concludes that for most teens, gang membership is a brief phase. Three studies that tracked teens over time found that one-half to two-thirds of youth gang members leave the gang by the one-year mark.

The website notes that male youths are much more likely to join gangs than female youths. But it is difficult to get a good estimate of the number of female gangs and gang members, because many police jurisdictions fail to count girls as gang members. While the national estimates are based on police reports, which indicate that only about 8 percent of gang members are female, one eleven-city survey of eighth graders concluded that 38 percent of gang members are female. Female gangs are somewhat more likely to be found in small cities and rural areas than in large cities, and female gang members tend to be younger, on average, than male gang members.

Female gang members are involved in less delinquent or criminal activity than male gang members, and they commit fewer violent crimes. However, female gang members are still an important concern. In one survey, 78 percent of female gang members reported being involved in gang fights, 65 percent reported carrying a weapon for protection, and 39 percent reported attacking someone with a weapon.

The website article points out that although many people think of gangs as a problem confined to inner-city neighborhoods, this is clearly no longer the case. In the past few decades there has been a dramatic increase in the growth of gang problems in smaller cities, towns, and villages. Gangs in suburban, small-town, and rural areas are different from the gangs in large cities. The gangs in suburban areas include more females, white, and younger youth, and are more likely to have ethnically and racially mixed memberships.

Youth gangs are linked with serious crime problems in elementary and secondary schools in the United States. Students report much higher drug availability when gangs are active at their school. Schools with gangs have nearly double the likelihood of violent victimization at school than those without a gang presence. Teens that are gang members are much more likely than other teens to commit serious and violent crimes. Photo 7.1 is a graphic display of gang issues.

Defining Youth Gangs

What is a youth gang? There is no single, accepted definition. The term *youth gang* is ambiguous and without a clear-cut distinction, and is widely used alongside *gangs* and *street gangs*. A reference to a "gang" often implies a youth gang. In some cases, youth gangs are distinguished from other types of gangs; how a gang member is defined as a youth varies as well.[2]

Federal Definition

The federal definition of a gang as used by the Department of Justice and the Department of Homeland Security's Immigration and Customs Enforcement (ICE)[3] is:

A. An association of three or more individuals.
B. Whose members collectively identify themselves by adopting a group identity, which they use to create an atmosphere of fear or intimidation, frequently by employing one or more of the following: a common name, slogan, identifying

PHOTO 7.1 A graphic display of gang issues. (Photo courtesy of iStock)

sign, symbol, tattoo, or other physical marking, style, or color of clothing, hairstyle, hand sign, or graffiti.

C. Whose purpose in part is to engage in criminal activity and which uses violence or intimidation to further its criminal objectives.
D. Whose members engage in criminal misconduct with the intent to enhance or preserve the association's power, reputation, or economic resources.
E. The association may also possess some of the following characteristics:
    1. The members may employ rules for joining and operating within the association.
    2. The members may meet on a recurring basis.
    3. The association may provide physical protection of its members from others.
    4. The association may seek to exercise control over a geographic location or region, or it may simply defend its perceived interests against rivals.
    5. The association may have an identifiable structure.

The federal definition of gangs excludes drug trafficking organizations, terrorist organizations, traditional organized crime groups, such as La Cosa Nostra, and groups that fall within the Department of Justice's definition of transnational organized crime.

Defining "Youth Gangs"

The typical age range for a youth gang member is from twelve to twenty-four, with the average age around seventeen to eighteen years old. The average age tends to be older in cities like Los Angeles and Chicago, where gangs are well established and have been in existence for longer periods of time. The generally accepted definition that researchers use for classifying groups as youth gangs includes the following:[4]

- The group has three or more members, generally ranging in age from twelve to twenty-four years old.
- Members share an identity, typically linked to a name, and often other symbols.
- Members view themselves as a gang, and they are recognized by others as a gang.
- The group has some permanence and a degree of organization.
- The group is involved in an elevated level of criminal activity.

State and Local Definitions

State and local jurisdictions tend to develop their own definitions of what constitutes a youth gang. Nevertheless, a youth gang is commonly thought of as a self-formed association of peers having the following characteristics: a gang name and recognizable symbols, identifiable leadership, a geographic territory, a regular meeting pattern, and collective actions to carry out illegal activities.[5]

History of Youth Gangs

According to the Office of Juvenile Justice and Delinquency Prevention (OJJDP), youth gangs probably first appeared in Europe and Mexico.[6] No one is sure when or why they emerged in the United States. The earliest record of their appearance in the United States is 1783, as the American Revolution ended. They may have emerged spontaneously from adolescent play groups or as a collective response to urban conditions in this country.

Some researchers suggest they first emerged in the United States following the Mexican migration to the Southwest after the Mexican Revolution in 1813. They may have grown out of difficulties Mexican youth encountered with social and cultural adjustment to the US way of life under extremely poor conditions in the Southwest. Gangs appear to have spread in New England in the early 1800s as the Industrial Revolution gained momentum in the first large cities in the United States: New York, Boston, and Philadelphia.

Youth gangs began to flourish in Chicago and other large cities during the industrial era, when immigration and population shifts reached peak levels. Early in American history, gangs seem to have been most visible and most violent during periods of rapid population shifts. The United States has seen four distinct periods of gang growth and peak activity: the late 1800s, the 1920s, the 1960s, and the 1990s. Gang proliferation, in other words, has not been constant.[7]

Youth gangs have been influenced by several trends. In the 1970s and 1980s, because of increased mobility and access to more-lethal weapons, many gangs became more dangerous. Gangs of the 1980s and 1990s appear to consist of both younger and more older members than before. An increased number of members have prison records or ties to prison inmates.

According to researchers, current gang members are less concerned with territorial affiliations, use alcohol and drugs more extensively, and are more involved in drug trafficking. Many youth gangs have been transformed into entrepreneurial organizations by the crack cocaine epidemic that began in the mid-1980s. The extent to which they have become drug-trafficking organizations is unclear.

Not all youth groups are considered as gangs. Many of the youth groups are not seriously involved in illegal activities, and provide mainly social opportunities for their membership. Some groups seldom use drugs and alcohol or commit criminal misconduct. Some have close community ties.

Gang Indicators

We often don't want to admit there is youth gang activity in our hometowns. The OJJDP in their series on youth gangs and other noted research into gang activities suggest that youth-serving organizations should be alert to signs that indicate possible gang involvement of youths. According to Ronald D. Stephens, executive director of the National School Safety Center at Pepperdine University, the signs of gang activity in your area include:[8]

- **Presence of graffiti:** Gangs use graffiti to mark their territory. When another gang disputes territory, they often replace the rival gang's graffiti with their own.
- **Youths wearing colors, jewelry, or distinctive clothing:** Gangs generally establish distinctive clothing to signify affiliation with a gang. Unwary youths wearing similar clothing may become victims of gang rivalries.
- **Increased violent confrontations:** An increase in violence may signal the presence of gangs.
- **The excessive use of electronic communications:** Youths who carry electronic communications tools may be involved with gang drug activity.
- **An increase in the number of drive-by shootings:** Drive-by shootings are most often the result of competition between gangs for territory.
- **Open display of firearms:** Usually a precursor to drive-by shootings; gang members will drive by brandishing weapons to demonstrate their capacity for deadly violence.

- **Increased racial conflict:** There is a high correlation between racial conflict and gang membership. Many gangs are formed along racial and ethnic lines for protection and affiliation.
- **Tattoos:** Gang members often have tattoos that symbolize their gang affiliation.

Indicators of Youth Gang Involvement

The county government of Fairfax County, Virginia, has published a handout of the common signs that indicate possible involvement by a youth in a gang. According to the Fairfax County website, the signs that a youth has become involved with a gang include:[9]

- Withdrawing from family activities.
- Suddenly changing friends and spending time with undesirable people.
- Social media posts with signs of teens falling prey to gang recruitment.
- Developing a bad attitude toward family, school, and authorities.
- Sudden drop in school grades.
- Staying out later than usual.
- Wanting excessive privacy.
- Using a new nickname.
- Using hand signs.
- Using unfamiliar slang words.
- Purchasing or wanting to buy or wear clothing of all one color or style.
- Modifying clothing to indicate membership in a special group.
- Changing appearance with special haircuts, eyebrow markings, or tattoos.
- Suddenly having more money or possessions.
- Using gang graffiti on folders, desks, walls, and buildings.
- Evidence of drug or alcohol use.
- Carrying objects that can be used as weapons.

Dynamics of Youth Gangs

According to professors David C. Pyrooz and Gary Sweeten, gang members are disproportionately male, black or Hispanic, from single-parent households, and from families living below the poverty level.[10] The professors estimated that there are more than one million youth gang members in the United States. (Note: The earlier study mentioned at the start of this chapter had a lower estimate of the number of gang members in the United States.) Pyrooz and Sweeten also concluded that significantly more youths are involved with gangs than previous estimates would suggest, and that clinicians and policy-makers must recognize that youth gang members may not conform to popular perceptions of gang demographics. This strengthens the statement that it is very difficult to know how many youths are involved in gangs.

Pyrooz and Sweeten also estimated that youth gang membership peaks at the age of fourteen, and has a turnover or exit rate of about 36 percent per year.[11] They concluded that once youth get involved, they soon realize that being a gang member is not all it's cracked up to be, and that the money, cars, girls, and protection is more myth than reality. They recommend that prevention programs aimed at children before they enter their teen years would be more successful.

Gang Specialization

According to the OJJDP, certain offenses are related to different racial/ethnic youth gangs. African-American gangs are relatively more involved in drug offenses;

Hispanic gangs, in "turf-related" violence; Asian and white gangs, in property crimes.[12]

The Hispanic gangs in Los Angeles tend to be structured around age-based cohorts, based in a specific territory (barrio), and characterized by fighting. The gang provides family-like relationships for adolescents who feel isolated, drifting between their native and adopted cultures and feeling alienated from both. Hispanic gangs have strong links to the neighborhood, or barrio, which tie them to the larger culture. Much of their violence is related to the defense of neighborhood turf. African-American gangs in large cities tend to replace traditional social networks that link youth with legitimate work opportunities. These gangs tend to be involved in entrepreneurial activities more than other ethnic/racial gangs, and may evolve from "scavenger" groups to turf gangs and drug-trafficking gangs.

The use of violence to protect the neighborhood, or gang turf, from rival gangs is also a predominant goal in Chicago, San Diego, and St. Louis. Violence is rarely planned and generally occurs spontaneously among gangs in response to a wide variety of situations.

One way of viewing gangs is along a continuum of degree of organization, from youth groups who hang out together in shopping malls and other places; to criminal groups—small clusters of friends who band together to commit crimes, such as fencing operations; to street gangs composed of groups of adolescents and young adults who form a semi-structured operation and engage in delinquent and criminal behavior. In some areas, gangs may evolve from less-formal to more-formal organizations along this continuum. Photo 7.2 depicts the arrest of a youth gang.

Female Gang Delinquency

The OJJDP estimates that approximately 10 percent of gang members are female. The OJJDP's Program of Research on the Causes and Correlates of Delinquency

PHOTO 7.2 Youth gang arrested in New York City in 1959. (Photo courtesy of US Library of Congress Prints and Photographs Division, Washington, DC, LC-USZ62-136366)

reports that female membership is higher in early adolescence. Among all adolescents, female involvement may be increasing proportionally with male gang involvement.

Are female gang members becoming involved in more serious and violent offending? The researchers working with OJJDP state that this question cannot be answered definitively because national trend data are not available. According to one study, female gang violence was more likely to involve simple battery or assault than homicide, and female nonviolent crimes consisted mainly of liquor law violations.[13]

Why Youths Join Gangs

According to James C. Howell, senior research associate with the National Gang Center, studies have shown that the gang-joining process is similar to the way most of us would go about joining an organization—that is, gradually, as familiarity and acceptance grow. A youth typically begins hanging out with gang members at age eleven or twelve, and joins the gang between the ages of twelve and fifteen. In other words, the process typically takes from six months to one to two years from the initial association with a gang to gang membership.[14]

Howell notes that some widely held beliefs on why youth join gangs are misleading. For example, there is a common misperception that many youths are coerced into joining a gang. Quite to the contrary, most youth who join a gang very much want to belong to a gang, but their reasons for joining may vary. The major reason youth give for joining a gang is the need for protection, followed by fun, respect, money, and because a friend was in the gang.

Gang-joining typically has several steps, particularly in communities where gangs are well-established. In elementary school, children may hear about gangs, and some may be in awe when they see gang members in middle school. Seeing gang members for the first time can validate their importance in a young adolescent's mind. Also, the schoolyard may have separate gang hangouts toward which youngsters gravitate. In addition, the most vulnerable children enter middle school with poor academic achievement, and their street exposure renders them prime candidates for gang membership.

Consequences of Gang Membership

At the individual level, youths who join a gang develop an increased propensity for violence and, in turn, are more likely to be victims of violence. In addition, the likelihood of favorable life-course outcomes is significantly reduced. Communities are negatively affected by gangs, particularly in terms of quality of life, crime, victimization, and economic costs.[15]

Studies of increased involvement in violence of large representative samples in several large US cities indicate that many gang members are actively involved in violent crimes. Youths commit many more serious and violent acts while they are gang members than before they joined and after they leave the gang. During the time they are actively involved in a gang, youth commit serious and violent offenses at a rate several times higher than youth who are not in a gang. In late adolescence, gang involvement leads to drug trafficking and persistent gun carrying. Gang members account for a disproportionate amount of crime in communities where gangs are particularly active. In several cities, gang members accounted for more than seven in ten self-reported violent offenses in the study sample.

Preventing Gang Membership

According to James Howell, it is important to prevent gang membership if possible. He justifies this rationale based on the following factors:[16]

- Gangs are a serious, persistent problem in the United States; according to the National Youth Gang Survey, from 2002 to 2010 the estimated number of youth gangs increased by nearly 35 percent—from 21,800 to 29,400 nationwide.
- Because high-rate gang offenders impose enormous costs on society, successful prevention and early intervention programs potentially can produce large monetary cost savings to communities.
- Programs and strategies are most urgently needed with high-risk youth, families, schools, and communities.
- The most successful comprehensive gang initiatives are communitywide in scope; have broad community involvement in planning and delivery; and employ integrated prevention, outreach, support, and services.

Howell concludes that youth gangs are not a new social problem in the United States; this has been a serious issue since the early nineteenth century, and remains a persistent problem today. Overall, one-third of cities, towns, and rural counties reported gang problems in 2010, and this number is estimated to be significantly higher in the following years. Recent data indicate that nearly half of high school students report that there are students at their school who consider themselves to be part of a gang, and one in five students in grades six through twelve report that gangs are present in their school.

Howell notes that the consequences of joining a gang are potentially very serious, both for youth and for their communities. The frequency with which someone commits serious and violent acts typically increases while they are gang members, compared with periods before and after gang involvement. Adolescents who are in a gang commit many more serious and violent offenses than non-gang adolescents. In samples from several US cities, gang members account for approximately three-fourths of the violent offenses committed by delinquents in those samples. Gang involvement also elevates drug use and gun carrying, leading to arrest, conviction, incarceration, and a greater likelihood of violent victimization. These experiences bring disorder to the life course through a cascading series of difficulties, including school dropout, teen parenthood, and unstable employment.

Prevention Options

Howell notes that because gang membership typically occurs along a pathway toward serious and violent delinquency, delinquency prevention programs can help to prevent gang involvement. Involvement in juvenile delinquency, almost without exception, precedes gang-joining, and very early involvement in delinquency has been shown to be a precursor behavior for gang-joining in several independent studies. One study suggests that fighting and other delinquent acts by age ten, and perhaps even younger, may be a key factor leading to gang involvement. Another study found that academic failure as early as the elementary-school level is a main risk factor for later gang involvement.

Children who are on a trajectory of increasing antisocial behavior are more likely to join gangs during their late childhood or early adolescence. The early onset of behavioral problems can escalate to gang involvement and, in turn, to serious and violent offending. Howell contends that there are multiple strategies for working with pre-delinquent and delinquent youth in early prevention of gang-joining. For example, it is possible to focus at the individual level on at-risk children, particularly disruptive children. Other strategies work at family, school, or community levels to reduce risk and to enhance protective influences for those youth who are exposed to violence and are victims themselves.

In addition, more attention needs to be given to within-gang victimization and victimization of non-gang youth by gang members in individual, family, school, and community contexts. In this regard, here are some priorities recommended by Howell:

- Mental health professionals should be placed in schools to immediately identify children needing services and deliver or coordinate those services.
- Interventions must focus on families and peer group affiliations.
- Prevention services at multiple levels and across multiple systems must address youths at risk and in need of protection.
- Prevention services must also give priority to the development of positive coping skills, competencies, and problem-solving skills in children and adolescents so they can deal effectively with high levels of exposure to violence and victimization.
- The most successful comprehensive gang initiatives are communitywide in scope, with broad community involvement in the planning and delivery of interventions, and offer a wide variety of integrated programs and services from multiple agencies that are coordinated by an intervention team.
- Statewide implementation of prevention programming also appears feasible.

Promising Programs for Dealing with Youth Gangs

Gang Resistance Education and Training

The Gang Resistance Education and Training (G.R.E.A.T.) Program is an evidence-based, national, and international gang and violence prevention program that has been building trust between law enforcement and communities for decades.[17] G.R.E.A.T. is intended to act as an immunization against delinquency, youth violence, and gang membership. It is designed to help children in the years immediately before the prime age for introduction into gangs and delinquent behavior.

The program started in Phoenix, Arizona, in 1992, and expanded into a nationally based program in 1993 because of its perceived success. The program's goal is to prevent youth crime, violence, and gang involvement by developing a positive relationship among law enforcement, families, and young people to create a much safer community.[18]

G.R.E.A.T. is a school-based program that uses law enforcement officer–instructed classroom curricula, providing a continuum of components for children and their families. The program has a thirteen-lesson middle school curriculum, a six-lesson elementary school curriculum, a summer component, and a family's component. More than 13,000 sworn officers from around the United States and various Central American countries have been trained and certified to teach the G.R.E.A.T. curricula. The G.R.E.A.T. curricula have been delivered to more than six million children, allowing law enforcement to foster strong relationships with these students, as well as their schools and communities.

Since its inception, G.R.E.A.T. has developed partnerships with nationally recognized organizations, such as Boys & Girls Clubs of America, Inc.; Families and Schools Together; and the National Association of Police Athletic/Activities Leagues, Inc. These partnerships encourage positive collaboration among the community, parents, schools, and law enforcement.

The OJJDP Comprehensive Gang Model

The OJJDP Comprehensive Gang Model is an evidence-based framework for the coordination of multiple data-driven anti-gang and violence-reduction strategies to address serious, violent, and entrenched youth street gang problems. The Model combines prevention, intervention, and suppression tactics that reach beyond enforcement to address the root causes of criminal gang activity within a community. This framework provides a mechanism to pull together disjointed, fragmented approaches into an organized plan of action.[19]

Implementation is guided by a steering committee made up of decision-makers from local agencies and organizations that hold responsibility for addressing a community's gang problem. The Model facilitates community involvement and uses a multidisciplinary team, along with street outreach, to directly intervene with those gang-involved youths and young adults most likely to be involved in violent gang-related behaviors. Suppression strategies are focused on addressing the most serious crime problems, including violence.

The Model provides a response to gangs on multiple levels that works by coordinating strategies among sectors, including law enforcement, education, criminal justice, social services, community-based agencies, outreach programs, and grassroots community groups. The Model has been tested with more than twenty years of implementation experience in communities large and small, and has shown positive results in reducing serious gang-related crimes in affected communities.

The Five Core Strategies of the Model are:

1. Community Mobilization—community engagement and collaboration
2. Social Intervention—outreach and access to provision of services for gang-involved youth and their families
3. Organizational Change and Development—development of policy for effective use of resources
4. Opportunities Provision—education, training, and employment programs
5. Suppression—community policing with formal and informal social controls and accountability measures

The advantages of using the Model include:

- Encourages communitywide acknowledgment of the gang problem.
- Spreads responsibility and accountability for the gang problem across the community—it is no longer solely a law enforcement issue.
- Connects a wide array of resources into an organized system of mutually reinforcing strategies.
- Supports community-oriented policing efforts by fostering partnerships, improving community safety, and reducing fear.
- Provides a comprehensive assessment that helps focus limited law enforcement resources based on intelligence analysis.

Homeboy Industries

Homeboy Industries is an organization that offers a variety of services to people who are no longer involved in gangs. The organization was started in 1988 by Father Greg in Los Angeles, California. The organization's goal is to help people get the education and services they need so they can go out into the world and find jobs. According to the program directors, full-time jobs are probably about 80 percent of what these folks need in order to redirect their lives. The other 20 percent is a mixture of therapeutic and support services. The program offers legal, medical, employment, and other services, such as tattoo removal. They also employ some of the individuals in their bakery and café, among other businesses.[20]

Gang Rescue and Support Project

The Gang Rescue and Support (GRASP) Project is a program for youth who are at risk of gang involvement. The program has achieved success and is run by ex-gang members. GRASP has been around for forty-five years and offers a lot of different services, including parent awareness training, tattoo removal, healing circles, and hospital intervention.[21]

Project Safe Neighborhoods

Project Safe Neighborhoods (PSN) is designed to create and foster safer neighborhoods through a sustained reduction in violent crime, including, but not limited to, addressing criminal youth gangs and the felonious possession and use of firearms. The program's effectiveness depends upon the ongoing coordination, cooperation, and partnerships of local, state, tribal, and federal law enforcement agencies—and the communities they serve—engaged in a unified approach led by the US Attorney in all ninety-four federal districts.

Through the PSN task force, each district implements the following PSN design features to address violent crime in their respective districts:

- **Leadership:** US Attorneys (USAs), working with state, local, and tribal law enforcement, are the cornerstone of the law enforcement response to crime in their jurisdictions, and are best positioned to take the leadership role in developing and implementing a crime-reduction program.
- **Partnership:** The USA must work in partnership with federal, state, local, and tribal law enforcement and prosecutors, as well as the community. Under the leadership of the US Attorney's Office (USAO), the PSN task force typically includes federal and local prosecutors; federal, local, and state law enforcement agencies; probation and parole agencies; and the certified fiscal agent. The involvement of local government leaders, social service providers, neighborhood leaders, members of the faith community, and business leaders also enhance a task force's effectiveness. PSN sites also have the option of engaging a research partner.
- **Targeted and prioritized enforcement:** PSN requires each district to develop data-driven strategies to target enforcement efforts in locations with significant violent crime problems and against offenders who are driving the violence. District-based enforcement efforts must accomplish three goals: 1) identify the locations within the district that have the most significant issues with violence; 2) identify the offenders who are driving the violence in those areas; and 3) prosecute those offenders to provide the most certain and appropriate sanctions.
- **Prevention:** The PSN task force must develop effective relationships with community leaders and residents, understand the needs and priorities of the community, and effectively communicate how law enforcement efforts are helping to reduce crime and increase public safety. Additionally, PSN encourages partnerships with local prevention and offender reentry programs that can help prevent violent crime.
- **Accountability:** PSN maintains accountability by measuring outcomes (i.e., reduction of violent crime), as well as number and quality of investigations and prosecutions. PSN task forces must collect and analyze relevant data that focus on these relevant outcomes.

PSN also encourages the development of practitioner-researcher partnerships that use data, evidence, and innovation to create strategies and interventions that are effective and make communities safer. This data-driven approach enables jurisdictions to understand the full nature and extent of the crime challenges they are facing and to direct resources to the highest priorities.

BUILD Program

The BUILD, Inc. program is based in Chicago. Since 1969, they have helped thousands of kids stay out of gangs by creating programs for them to keep them off the streets. The program provides restorative justice programs and helps to build stronger community ties with at-risk youth through connections with former gang members, the police, and neighbors. They also provide education programs to help kids academically and to keep them from failing in school. The program also helps with GED classes for those who have dropped out of high school, encouraging them to pursue further education at trade schools or college. The program provides for kids with troubled pasts so that they may grow into upstanding members of the community. Overall, this program is built on the foundation of helping kids who may be at risk, who are attempting to get out of a gang, or who may be in a gang still and need the tools to be successful.[22]

Seattle Youth Violence Prevention Initiative

The Seattle Youth Violence Prevention Initiative (SYVPI) was launched in 2009 as a partnership between the City of Seattle and several community-based organizations designed to reduce youth violence in Seattle, keep young people out of trouble, and get them back in school. SYVPI focuses on youths ages twelve to seventeen who are at the highest risk of committing or being victimized by violence. These teenagers include repeat offenders; middle school truants or students at risk of suspension; youth arrested for crimes, such as shoplifting, that do not automatically require jail time; and victims of violence, including by their friends and relatives. SYVPI is broken into neighborhood networks where indicators of future violent behaviors, including school discipline rates, absences, or dropout rates, are the highest.

Since 2010, Therapeutic Health Services (THS) has supervised the management of the SYVPI neighborhood networks. They provide intake and referral, intensive case management, outreach, family support, youth employment and pre-apprenticeships, recreation, mentorship, and anger management training. Youth are referred to SYVPI services through juvenile court, police, community outreach workers, schools, Seattle Parks and Recreation Youth Centers, and other neighborhood network agencies. The goals of the initiative are a 50 percent reduction in juvenile violent crime court referrals in the three network neighborhoods and a 50 percent reduction in the number of suspensions/expulsions due to violent incidents in five selected middle schools.

National Youth Gang Center

As part of its comprehensive, coordinated response to America's gang problem, the OJJDP funds the National Youth Gang Center (NYGC). The NYGC assists state and local jurisdictions in the collection, analysis, and exchange of information on gang-related demographics, legislation, literature, research, and promising program strategies. The NYGC coordinates activities of the OJJDP Gang Consortium, a group of federal agencies, gang program representatives, and service providers that works to coordinate gang information and programs. The NYGC also provides training and technical assistance for the OJJDP's Rural Gang, Gang-Free Schools, and Gang-Free Communities Initiatives. The contact information for the center is as follows:

National Youth Gang Center
P. O. Box 12729
Tallahassee, FL 32317
(850) 385-0600
nygc@iir.com www.iir.com/nygc

Practicum

In Baltimore, Rickey Prince, a seventeen-year-old who witnessed a gang murder and agreed to testify against the killer, was shot in the back of the head a few days after a prosecutor read Mr. Prince's name aloud in a packed courtroom. In Boston, a witness to a shooting by a member of a street gang recently found copies of his grand jury testimony taped to all the doors in the housing project where he lives.

The above incidents indicate the problems inherent with finding witnesses to prosecute gang crime. These two examples highlight what police, prosecutors, and judges say is a growing national problem of witness intimidation by youth gangs that in some cities is jeopardizing the legal system, and bears striking similarities to the way organized crime has often silenced witnesses.[23]

What steps should a prosecutor take to encourage those who have witnessed crimes committed by gangs to report and testify against criminals who commit these crimes?

Summary

- At last count in 2019, there were more than 24,500 different youth gangs around the country, with more than 772,500 teen and young adult members.
- Teens join gangs for a variety of reasons. Some are seeking excitement; others are looking for prestige, protection, a chance to make money, or a sense of belonging.
- Few teens are forced to join gangs; in most cases, teens can refuse to join without fear of retaliation.
- Male youths are much more likely to join gangs than female youths.
- Female gang members are involved in less delinquent or criminal activity than male gang members, and they commit fewer violent crimes.
- There has been a dramatic increase in the growth of gang problems in smaller cities, towns, and villages.
- Gangs in suburban, small-town, and rural areas are different from the gangs in large cities.
- The gangs in suburban areas include more females, white, and younger youth, and are more likely to have ethnically and racially mixed memberships.
- There is no single, accepted definition for the term *youth gangs*, which is ambiguous and without a clear-cut distinction.
- The typical age range for a youth gang member is twelve to twenty-four, with the average age seventeen or eighteen years old.
- The average age of a gang member tends to be older in cities like Los Angeles and Chicago, where gangs are well-established and have been in existence for longer periods of time.

- No one is sure when or why youth gangs emerged in the United States. The earliest record of their appearance in the United States may have been as early as 1783, as the American Revolution ended.
- Youth gangs began to flourish in Chicago and other large cities during the industrial era, when immigration and population shifts reached peak levels.
- The United States has seen four distinct periods of gang growth and peak activity: the late 1800s, the 1920s, the 1960s, and the 1990s.
- Gang proliferation has not been constant.
- Gang members are disproportionately male, black, Hispanic, from single-parent households, and families living below the poverty level.
- According to the OJJDP, certain offenses are related to different racial/ethnic youth gangs. African-American gangs are relatively more involved in drug offenses; Hispanic gangs, in "turf-related" violence; Asian and white gangs, in property crimes.
- A youth typically begins hanging out with gang members at age eleven or twelve, and joins the gang between the ages of twelve and fifteen.
- At the individual level, youths who join a gang develop an increased propensity for violence and, in turn, are more likely to be victims of violence.
- As part of its comprehensive, coordinated response to America's gang problem, the Office of Juvenile Justice and Delinquency Prevention (OJJDP) funds the National Youth Gang Center (NYGC).

Discussion and Review Questions

1. What constitutes a youth gang?
2. Why do youths join gangs?
3. Explain the history of gangs in the United States.
4. Explain Project Safe Neighborhoods.
5. Why are there problems in determining the number of gangs in the United States?
6. How are female gangs different from male gangs?
7. What are the signs that indicate a youth is involved in a gang?
8. What are the indicators of gang activity in your home community?

Notes

1. Network of Care website posted at http://philadelphia.pa.networkofcare.org/ps/library/article.aspx?id=2363 (accessed April 28, 2019).
2. National Institute of Justice website, "What is a Gang?" at https://nij.gov/topics/crime/gangs/Pages/definitions.aspx#note1 (accessed April 27, 2019).
3. US Department of Justice website at https://www.justice.gov/criminal-ocgs/about-violent-gangs (accessed April 27, 2019).
4. National Institute of Justice website, "What is a Gang?"
5. James C. Howell, "Gangs" Office of Juvenile Justice and Delinquency Prevention Fact Sheet (Washington, DC: US Department of Justice, December 1997).
6. James C. Howell, "Youth Gangs: An Overview," *Juvenile Justice Bulletin* (Washington, DC: US Department of Justice, August 1998), posted at https://www.ojjdp.gov/jjbulletin/9808/contents.html (accessed April 27, 2019).
7. Howell, "Youth Gangs: An Overview."
8. Nonprofit Risk Management Center website, "Perspectives on Gangs and Gang Violence," posted at https://www.nonprofitrisk.org/resources/articles/perspectives-on-gangs-and-gang-violence/ (accessed April 27, 2019).

9. County of Fairfax website at https://www.fairfaxcounty.gov/news2/gang-activity-on-the-rise-17-signs-to-look-for-in-kids-who-may-join/ (accessed April 27, 2019).
10. David C. Pyrooz and Gary Sweeten, "Gang Membership between Ages 5 and 17 Years in the United States," *Journal of Adolescent Health*, vol. 56, no. 4 (April 2015), 414–19.
11. Pyrooz and Sweeten, "Gang Membership."
12. Research for this section is based on Howell, "Youth Gangs: An Overview."
13. Information for this section was provided from Joan Moore and John Hagedorn, "Female Gangs: Focus on Research," *Juvenile Justice Bulletin* (Washington, DC: US Department of Justice, March 2001), available at https://www.ncjrs.gov/pdffiles1/ojjdp/186159.pdf (accessed July 24, 2020).
14. James C. Howell, "Why Is Gang-Membership Prevention Important?" In Thomas Simon, Nancy Ritter, Reshma Mahendra, eds. *Changing Course: Preventing Gang Membership* (Washington, DC: US Department of Justice, 2012), 7–12.
15. Howell, "Why Is Gang-Membership Prevention Important?"
16. Howell, "Why Is Gang-Membership Prevention Important?"
17. G.R.E.A.T. website at https://www.great-online.org/Home/GREAT (accessed April 27, 2019).
18. Barry S. McCrary, "Identifying Various Gang Prevention and Intervention Programs to Reduce Gang Violence and Understand Why Youth Join Gangs," *Law Enforcement Executive Forum*, vol. 19, no. 1 (March 2019), 30–34.
19. "A Law Enforcement Official's Guide to OJJDP: Comprehensive Gang Model," posted on website at https://www.nationalgangcenter.gov/Content/Documents/LE-Officials-Guide-to-OJJDP-Comprehensive-Gang-Model.pdf (accessed April 27, 2019).
20. McCrary, "Identifying Various Gang Prevention and Intervention Programs."
21. McCrary, "Identifying Various Gang Prevention and Intervention Programs."
22. Barry S. McCrary (March 2019) and Therapeutic Health Services (2018), "Seattle Youth Violence Prevention Initiative," retrieved from http://ths-wa.org/wordpress/programs-and-services/youth-programs-and-services/seattle-youth-violenceprevention-initiative (accessed April 28, 2019).
23. Fox Butterfield, "Guns and Jeers Used by Gangs to Buy Silence," *New York Times*, January 16, 2005, https://www.nytimes.com/2005/01/16/us/guns-and-jeers-used-by-gangs-to-buy-silence.html (accessed April 28, 2019).

CHAPTER 8

Juveniles and Police

CHAPTER OBJECTIVES

After studying this chapter, the reader should be able to:

- Analyze why youth arrest rates have declined in recent years.
- Discuss the importance of the initial on-the-street contact between the police officer and a youth.
- Discuss the issues involved in the use of police discretion.
- Discuss the issues involved with the use of school resource officers.
- Explain the concept of "contempt of cop."
- Explain the special issues involved when police search or interrogate a youth.
- Discuss evidence of bias in police decision-making.

Police and Juvenile Offenders

In 2016, law enforcement agencies in the United States made more than 856,000 arrests of persons younger than the age of eighteen.[1] This was the lowest number of yearly arrests in more than forty years. The number of arrests of juveniles in 2016 was 58 percent fewer than the number of arrests in 2007. Juvenile arrests for violent crimes fell 67 percent from 1994 to 2016. Table 8.1 charts the decline in arrests for both adults and juveniles from 2007 to 2016. While there were declines in all categories listed, the decline for youths under the age of eighteen was much more significant. Note that the crime of rape is omitted in this table. This was based on the change in definition of what constitutes rape. Since 1927, the FBI had defined forcible rape as "the carnal knowledge of a female, forcibly and against her will." Beginning in 2013, the FBI adopted a broader definition of rape: "Penetration, no matter how slight, of the vagina or anus with any body part or object, or oral penetration by a sex organ of another person, without the consent of the victim." Unlike the definition in place for more than eighty years, the new definition does not require force and is gender-neutral. Accordingly, a comparison of the arrest rates for rape would be meaningless.

TABLE 8.1 Percentage of Decline in Arrests for Juveniles and Adults (2007–2016)

Most serious crime	Juveniles	Adults
All violent crimes	-48	-8
Murder	-36	-10
Robbery	-44	-17
Aggravated assault	-51	-6
All property crimes	-56	-2
Burglary	-61	-21
Larceny-theft	-55	-5
Simple assault	-47	-11
Weapons law violations	-55	-5
Drug abuse violations	-50	-10

Violent crimes include murder, robbery, and aggravated assault.
Source: Charles Puzzanchera, "Juvenile Arrests," *Juvenile Justice Statistics National Report Series Bulletin* (Washington, DC: US Department of Justice, December 2018).

In 2016, about one in five juvenile violent crime arrests involved females and more than half involved minority youths. Females accounted for 29 percent of juvenile arrests in 2016. In 2016, law enforcement agencies made 252,520 arrests of females younger than the age of eighteen and 603,610 arrests of males, also younger than age eighteen. Although males accounted for the majority (71%) of juvenile arrests overall in 2016, the female share was relatively high for certain offenses, including larceny-theft (41%), liquor law violations (40%), simple assault (37%), and disorderly conduct (36%). Females accounted for 19 percent of juvenile violent crime arrests and 26 percent of aggravated assault arrests in 2016. From 2007 through 2016, arrests of juvenile females decreased less than male arrests in several offense categories (e.g., aggravated and simple assault, robbery, vandalism, drug abuse violations, and liquor law violations).

For more-detailed information and the latest statistics on juvenile arrests, visit the US Office of Juvenile Justice and Delinquency Prevention's (OJJDP) Statistical Briefing Book. The online Statistical Briefing Book (SBB) offers access to a wealth of information about juvenile crime and victimization and about youth involved in the juvenile justice system. Visit the "Law Enforcement and Juvenile Crime" section of the SBB at ojjdp.gov/ojstatbb/crime/faqs.asp. Photo 8.1 depicts a sixteen-year-old boy arrested for robbery.

Police Discretion

Generally, the first contact between a youth and the juvenile justice system, in a non-school situation, is an initial contact with a police officer. At this point, the officer has wide discretion in deciding whether the youth will be involved in the criminal justice system. The officer may lecture the youth and allow him or her to go on his or her way. Or, the officer may decide that official action needs to be taken, and that the juvenile should be referred to the justice system. At no other point on the juvenile justice continuum does an individual have as much discretion as the police officer making this initial contact. According to Erika Gebo and Carolyn Boyes-Watson,

PHOTO 8.1 Youth arrested for robbery. (Photo courtesy of iStock)

discretionary responses for police–youth encounters range from ignoring the incident completely to issuing a formal arrest and the use of lethal force.[2]

The process is very similar to a traffic officer stopping a driver for a traffic violation. The officer may warn, or ticket, the driver. If the driver only receives a warning, nothing further happens regarding the violation. It is only after the ticket is issued that the driver becomes involved with the traffic court system.

When making decisions regarding the juvenile's disposition, the police officer is faced with multifaceted perspectives. While an officer is expected to enforce the laws, at the same time, he or she is also expected to take into consideration the welfare of the youth; that is, will it be more beneficial to the youth to impose legal sanctions upon him or her, or will it be more beneficial to release him or her with a warning? The officer is faced with interpreting and enforcing laws designed to protect society while at the same time considering what is best for the youth.[3]

To accomplish this assigned dual task, the officer must depend upon the information that is available to the officer at the time of contact with the youthful offender. Often, however, the information is limited and sketchy. In most cases the officer has only "cues," such as attitude, age, sex, and physical or mental appearance of the youth, to assist in arriving at a dispositional decision.

Contempt of Cop

The phrase *contempt of cop* was coined by former Los Angeles police officer and later author Joseph Wambaugh in his novel, *The Blue Knight*, in 1972. According to the novel, when a citizen doesn't give a police officer a "Yes, sir!" and immediately obey his or her requests, the cop gets mad. The officer turns his or her back on what they consider important business, choosing instead to get into the citizen's face, making an arrest they know will not stand up in court. This has become a slang phrase used when an individual does not act with "proper" respect toward an officer when the individual, often a youth, is stopped by the officer. The phrase is an analogy to *contempt of court*, which, unlike contempt of cop, is a criminal offense. The situation has also been referred to as "flunking the attitude test."

Many researchers consider an individual's attitude toward an officer when stopped an important factor in the officer's decision-making process as to whether to formally invoke the justice system. For example, an officer stops a youth on the street at night and asks the youth what he is doing. If the youth makes a smart remark to the officer, researchers contend that the youth is more likely to be arrested than if he or she had politely answered the officer.

Discussions with police officers reveal that many times when an officer stops a youth, the youth is disrespectful and fails to answer the officer's legitimate questions; however, the officers deny that the youth's attitude influences their decision regarding whether or not to arrest the youth.

Racial Bias

According to researchers Carl E. Pope and Howard N. Snyder, few research studies have focused on police encounters with juveniles.[4] Pope and Snyder state that these encounters are rather difficult to measure because they tend to be low-visibility events that take place spontaneously on the streets. However, studies that have examined such encounters have generally found that police decision-making does contribute to minority overrepresentation in the juvenile justice system. The researchers opine that police in their scope of responsibility decide when to arrest and when not to arrest, and to a great extent, this decision-making process results in the arrest of African-American youths at a higher rate than white youths. They conclude that without more information, it is impossible to say whether this overrepresentation is the result of police bias or differential behavior.

Many observers argue that the justice system is biased against minority offenders (the race-related selection bias perspective), pointing to the fact that African-American youths are more likely to be arrested than other youths. Some research has focused on a somewhat neglected area: the role that race plays in police decision-making. The research compared arrest probabilities of white and nonwhite juveniles for violent crimes and found no direct evidence that a youth's race affects police decisions to take him or her into custody.

The MacArthur Foundation in 2018 noted that youths of color constitute approximately one-third of the adolescent population in the United States, but two-thirds of incarcerated youth.[5] The disproportional confinement of minorities has been recognized as a problem by the US government. In 1988, Congress amended the Juvenile Justice and Delinquency Prevention Act of 1974 to require that states participating in the act's formula grants program address the disproportionate confinement of minority juveniles in secure facilities.[6] States were required to assess the level of confinement of minority juveniles and to implement strategies to reduce disproportionate minority representation where it was found to exist.

In 1991, the Office of Juvenile Justice and Delinquency Prevention (OJJDP) created the Disproportionate Minority Confinement Initiative to help states comply with the mandate by testing various approaches for addressing the problem. Since 1988, the OJJDP has been a leader in efforts to reduce the overrepresentation of minority youth in the nation's juvenile justice system. The OJJDP has recognized that disproportionate minority contact (DMC) is a definite issue in the juvenile justice system.[7]

A 2018 report by the Georgia Criminal Justice Coordinating Council concluded that research suggests members of law enforcement treat African-American youths differently than they treat white youths. Studies have found that an

African-American youth who commits the same offense as a white youth is likely to be treated more harshly. Likewise, race has been found to be a key predictor of a youth's outcome in the juvenile justice system after controlling for socioeconomic status, sex, and age. The Council also noted that African Americans account for about one-third of the United States' youth population yet make up about half of the juvenile justice population.[8]

Ethnic Identity and Attitudes toward Police

Joanna M. Lee, Laurence Steinberg, and Alex R. Piquero reported on a study that examined the attitudes toward the police by considering adolescents' ethnic identity and how it related to perceptions of police legitimacy.[9] The researchers identified four key findings of the study. First, a stronger sense of ethnic identity was related to higher perceived discrimination by the police. Second, using two different measures of procedural justice (perceptions of general discrimination and event-specific legal processes) made it clear that the salience of race affected perceptions of global police prejudice toward others rather than specific inequities during legal processing. Both the affective (i.e., feelings of belongingness) and cognitive (i.e., feelings of identity achievement) components of ethnic identity were significant in predicting perceived police biases.

Third, with respect to youths' views of the police as a legitimate authority, as expected, both procedural justice experiences and offending affected perceptions of police legitimacy. The researchers noted that youth who felt the police treated groups of people in a more-equitable manner also rated them more positively on the legitimacy scale, while youth who reported a greater variety of offending gave the police a more-negative legitimacy rating. The effects of ethnic identity on police legitimacy were significant above and beyond the impact of youths' sense of procedural justice and offending involvement. After controlling for these factors, a stronger sense of ethnic identity predicted more-positive ratings of police legitimacy.

Finally, although ethnic identity predicted perceptions of police discrimination, it did not moderate the effects of discrimination on police legitimacy as expected. Not only were the main effects of ethnic identity on legitimacy independent of procedural justice experiences, the direction of the effect was also unexpected: After controlling for perceptions of police discrimination, youth with higher ethnic identity rated police authority as more legitimate.

The Lee et al. study concluded that it was useful to bear in mind that the overrepresentation of African-American youth in the juvenile justice system was the result of a larger number of direct and indirect factors that cannot be explained by differential involvement in crime alone. Increased police presence in low-income, non-white neighborhoods most likely makes black youths feel like targets of unjust policing. A hostile attitude may be a response to real or perceived police prejudice, especially if police concentrate surveillance on underclass areas and differentially stop minority youths.

The study indicated that the salience of ethnic identity can exacerbate this perception of prejudice. The process leading to a more-coherent sense of identity becomes a double-edged sword for many youths of color. Although some may internalize the negative effect of discrimination or employ maladaptive strategies to deal with it, for others, the cognitive maturity necessary for the development of a stronger ethnic identity can provide them with more-positive coping strategies and ultimately serve as a protective factor against the adverse effects of racial discrimination.

School Resource Officers

School resource officers (SROs) are uniformed, armed police officers assigned to work directly in schools. SROs' duties involve a combination of law enforcement, teaching, and mentoring. Their law enforcement duties include investigating criminal complaints and ensuring the safety of the school by patrolling school grounds. Teaching duties generally include providing educational programs such as Drug Abuse Resistance Education (DARE) and the Gang Resistance Education and Training program (G.R.E.A.T.). They also serve as mentors to students and advisors to school administrators and teachers. It is estimated that SROs spend about 50 percent of their time doing law enforcement activities, about 25 percent advising and mentoring, and the remaining time on presenting educational programs and other projects, such as paperwork, community meetings, and other school events.

History of School Resource Officers

SROs were first employed in Flint, Michigan, in the 1950s as a means of community policing to deal with increased levels of gun violence.[10] Currently their prevalence and purpose within schools has increased to include the handling of school discipline problems involving racial tension, drug use, and school violence, including mass shootings. The National Association of School Resource Officers (NASRO) estimates that between 14,000 and 20,000 SROs are assigned to approximately one-third of the public schools in the United States. The largest increase in SROs has occurred in large urban high schools.

The broader use of SROs started in the mid-1990s based on legislative initiatives such as the Safe Schools Act of 1994, and a 1998 amendment to the Omnibus Crime Control and Safe Streets Act of 1968. Legislation during that period encouraged partnerships between schools and law enforcement. Funding for SROs was provided through the US Department of Justice's "COPS in Schools" grant program.

Issues with SROs

Most states do not have any requirements regarding the use of SROs or any specialized training requirements before an officer is assigned as an SRO. In the few states that do have requirements, they vary greatly. In many schools, the SROs are increasingly involved in discipline issues, and they are frequently misused. The results have been greater numbers of school arrests for school behavior.

Using SROs to manage schools' discipline problems increases the likelihood that students will end up involved in the juvenile justice system. As noted in chapter 2, the use of SROs has promoted concerns about the school-to-prison pipeline. Jennifer Counts and her colleagues recommend that states establish policies regarding the use of SROs, and increase training requirements before assignment as an SRO to include behavior management, child development, communication techniques, and disability awareness.[11] According to the researchers, if the SRO programs are going to be effectively used to positively impact school climate, school administrators need to be proactive in working with the SROs. It also appears that the use of SROs to handle school discipline problems should be limited only to incidents involving serious criminal misconduct.

Juvenile Police Officers

Many large police departments have officers assigned as juvenile police officers. These officers differ from SROs in that the juvenile police officer performs his or her duties under the supervision of the law enforcement agency and not school officials.

While their duties vary, generally the juvenile police officers handle cases involving minors who are involved in the juvenile justice system or who are detained by the police. The position of juvenile officer encompasses many different duties and responsibilities, including handling and coordinating the various filings and paperwork that go to juvenile court on each juvenile charged with an offense. Juvenile officers frequently conduct follow-up investigations when the juvenile is involved in serious criminal activity, and they act as liaisons between police departments and the Department of Children and Family Services or Child Protective Services Agency. Another significant duty is the juvenile officer's oversight and coordination of youth community diversion programs sanctioned by the juvenile court.

National Association of School Resource Officers and State Associations

The National Association of School Resource Officers (NASRO) is a not-for-profit organization founded in 1991, with a commitment to school safety. Their mission is to provide the highest-quality training to school-based law enforcement officers to promote safer schools and safer children. NASRO includes school-based law enforcement officers, school administrators, and school security/safety professionals working as partners to protect students, faculty, and staff, and their school community.

Some states have a juvenile police officers' association. The one in Massachusetts has been in existence for over fifty years, and includes a combination of SROs, juvenile officers, DARE officers, detectives, supervisors, probation officers, principals, assistant principals, teachers, counselors, and school safety/security personnel. They provide information and training for law enforcement and school personnel to keep its members up-to-date on juvenile issues, school issues, and recent court decisions. The stated goal of the association is to assist police and school personnel in creating a safe learning environment for all students and staff while stressing the importance of building partnerships between the school and police and fire departments. One of the greatest values of association membership is the constant networking and sharing of information among law enforcement personnel and school personnel.

The State of New York also has a Police Juvenile Officers Association that was established in 1975. Its mission is to provide a training and advocacy organization comprised primarily of police officers and other professionals who specialize in the field of juvenile justice and prevention.

Police and the Rule of Law

Generally, each jurisdiction has statutes or regulations regarding how police should handle youths taken into custody. Box 8.1 contains a summary of the requirements in the State of Texas for law enforcement officers who are taking youths into custody. The requirements in other jurisdictions are similar, with minor differences. Texas, like many other states, has a Juvenile Justice Handbook for citizens that explains the procedures that law enforcement officers must comply with when taking juveniles into custody. The Texas handbook may be downloaded from the following website: https://www.texasattorneygeneral.gov/sites/default/files/files/divisions/juvenile-justice/JuvenileJusticeHandbook.pdf. (The authors suggest that you conduct an online search to find the appropriate handbook or guide for your jurisdiction.)

BOX 8.1 **Texas Family Code, Article 52**

Taking a Child into Custody

If a peace officer decides to take a child into custody, the officer may transport the child to an officially designated juvenile processing office, where the juvenile may be kept for up to six hours (§52.025(d), F.C.). A child may be detained in a juvenile processing office only for:

- return of the child to a parent or other responsible adult;
- completion of essential forms and records;
- photographing and fingerprinting of the child if authorized;
- issuance of warning to the child as required by law; or
- taking a statement from the child (§52.025(d), F.C.).

An exception to this rule is that an officer who has probable cause to believe a child is truant is able to take the child into custody for the purpose of returning the child to the appropriate school campus if the school agrees to assume responsibility.

A juvenile detention facility must keep juveniles separated by sight and sound from adults detained in the same building. Children and adults are separated by sight and sound only if they are unable to see or talk to each other. The separation must extend to all areas of the facility and can be accomplished through architectural design (§51.12(f), F.C.).

A directive to apprehend is a juvenile court order authorizing any law enforcement or probation officer to take a child into custody if the court finds there is probable cause to do so (§52.015, F.C.).

A child may not be left unattended in a juvenile processing office and is entitled to be accompanied by a parent, guardian, or other custodian, or by the child's attorney (§52.025(c), F.C.). A law guarantees the parent of a child taken into custody the right to communicate in person privately with the child for reasonable periods of time while the child is in a juvenile processing office (§61.103(a)(1), F.C.).

If the child is not released to the parent or guardian, it becomes the law enforcement officer's duty to transport the child to the appropriate juvenile detention facility. If the detention facility is located outside the county in which the child is taken into custody, it becomes the responsibility of the law enforcement officer who took the child into custody to transport the child to an out-of-county facility (§52.026(a) and (b), F.C.). A parent also has the right to communicate in person privately with the child for reasonable periods of time while the child is in a secure detention or correctional facility (§61.103(a)(1), F.C.).

Texas law permits a juvenile to be taken into custody under the following circumstances:

- pursuant to an order of the juvenile court;
- pursuant to the laws of arrest;

- by a law enforcement officer if there is probable cause to believe a child has violated a penal law of this state, has committed delinquent conduct or CINS, or conduct that violates a condition of probation imposed by the juvenile court;
- by a probation officer if there is probable cause to believe a child has violated a condition of probation or release imposed by the juvenile court; or
- pursuant to a directive to apprehend (§52.01(a), F.C.).

Taking a child into custody is not considered an arrest (§52.01(b), F.C.). If asked, a child who has been taken into custody may truthfully state that he or she has never been arrested.

Juvenile Curfews and the Police

The use of curfews to control youth movements during peak crime periods is a hotly contested issue in the academic, police, and civil liberty communities.[12] Curfew supporters believe that these measures are effective and appropriate methods for communities to control delinquent behavior. Those who oppose curfews argue that they are mere "Band-Aid" solutions that violate the rights of young people.

Many police officials believe that curfews help "keep kids off the streets," whether by personal decision or parental edict. They believe this will decrease the likelihood of juvenile involvement in disorder and minor criminal offenses, such as destruction of property or thefts, probably reducing victimization by keeping youth "out of harm's way" during nighttime hours. In addition, they believe curfews can be used as a tool to lawfully investigate young people who may be involved in more-serious criminality, such as membership in gangs or crime rings.

The use of curfews as a mechanism of social control is not new. They can be traced back more than 1,100 years to the rule of Alfred the Great (849–899) in England. During that era, an evening bell was rung to signal to residents of Oxford that they should douse their fires and return to their homes for the night. Later, during the reign of William the Conqueror (1066–1087), a ringing bell signaled citizens that it was time to retire from the streets for the evening. Curfews were enforced as a control mechanism to prevent the Saxons from assembling and causing any disorders during the evening hours.

In the United States, areas in the pre–Civil War South used curfews to restrict the activities of both slaves and free blacks. Currently curfews are used by many US communities to control the hours during which youth can be out in public.

There are several unresolved issues relating to juvenile curfews. The most obvious question is whether curfews really work to reduce criminal behavior. Is it appropriate to restrict the freedom and liberties of nondelinquent youth? Is the imposition of a curfew an individual matter between a parent and a child, or is it a legitimate concern of the state? Even if curfews are enacted in part to protect youth from victimization, is this reason compelling enough to justify the loss of liberty? Is it appropriate to punish a large segment of the population because of their status (being under a certain age)? Isn't criminal law intended to punish people because of their behavior? Do curfews prevent crime, or do they simply displace crime to other locations?

Individuals who have opposed curfews have relied on several long-standing principles in arguing that curfew laws directed at youths are unconstitutional.

They claim that the laws infringe on the fundamental rights of youth and parents; they violate the right to travel and the First Amendment right to free speech; and they are overbroad or vague.

The US Supreme Court has never taken up the issue of juvenile curfew laws, leaving the states to sort out the issues for themselves, with mixed results. The federal circuit courts are divided on whether juveniles have a fundamental right to travel, whether curfew laws impact the rights of parents in raising their children, and how and when First Amendment rights are implicated under the ordinances.[13]

Searches

When do police have the right to search a juvenile? Law enforcement officers may conduct a police search of a juvenile and their property. Generally, officers must provide juveniles with the same Fourth Amendment search and seizure protections as adults: Except under certain circumstances, the search must be reasonable and conducted with a search warrant. The exceptions of the warrant requirements include the following:

- When the youth is in a vehicle and the police have probable cause to search the vehicle.
- If the youth is lawfully arrested, then a search may be conducted.
- Under *Terry v. Ohio* (stop-and-frisk rule), where the officer may stop and detain a youth if the officer has a reasonable suspicion that criminal activity is ongoing. The officer may also pat down the youth if the officer has reasonable suspicion that the youth may be armed.[14] Under the stop-and-frisk rule, the officer must have reasonable suspicion that a crime has occurred or is in the process of occurring in order to stop the youth. After the youth has been stopped, the officer must have reasonable suspicion that the youth is armed before the officer may pat down the youth for weapons. If an object is detected that may be a weapon during the pat-down, then the officer probably has reasonable suspicion to conduct a complete search of the youth.
- Under certain recognized exigent circumstances, such as when there is an immediate danger to the safety of others if the youth is not searched.
- Border searches when the youth is entering this country. A nation has the right to protect its borders.
- Good faith exception under the *Massachusetts v. Shepherd* rule;[15] the good faith exception does not apply to police officer mistakes, only mistakes made by other public officials.
- School search rules set forth in the *New Jersey v. T.L.O.* case.[16]
- Consent searches.
- Airport searches prior to entering the boarding area of an airport. The individual may prevent the search by leaving the area and not entering the boarding area.

All of the above searches pertain to both adults and juveniles, except for the school searches, which are discussed in the *New Jersey v. T.L.O.* case below.

New Jersey v. T.L.O.

In *New Jersey v. T.L.O.*, the US Supreme Court held that the assistant vice principal's search of a student's purse in his office did not violate the Fourth Amendment.[17] The Court held that the Amendment's prohibition on unreasonable searches and seizures applies to searches conducted by public school officials, but that school officials need not obtain a warrant before searching a student who is under their authority.

The facts of the case are as follows: In 1980, a teacher at Piscataway High School in Middlesex County, New Jersey, discovered two girls smoking in a lavatory. One of the two girls was the respondent, T.L.O., who at that time was a fourteen-year-old high school freshman. Because smoking in the lavatory was a violation of a school rule, the teacher took the two girls to the principal's office, where they met with an assistant principal. In response to questioning, T.L.O.'s companion admitted that she had violated the rule. T.L.O., however, denied that she had been smoking in the lavatory, and claimed that she did not smoke at all.

The assistant principal asked T.L.O. to come into his private office and demanded to see her purse. Opening the purse, he found a pack of cigarettes, which he removed from the purse and held before T.L.O. as he accused her of having lied to him. As he reached into the purse for the cigarettes, he also noticed a package of cigarette rolling papers. In his experience, possession of rolling papers by high school students was closely associated with the use of marijuana. Suspecting that a closer examination of the purse might yield further evidence of drug use, he proceeded to search the purse thoroughly. The search revealed a small amount of marijuana, a pipe, a number of empty plastic bags, a substantial quantity of money in one-dollar bills, an index card that appeared to be a list of students who owed T.L.O. money, and two letters that implicated T.L.O. in marijuana dealing.

The assistant principal notified T.L.O.'s mother and the police, and turned the evidence of drug dealing over to the police. The State brought delinquency charges against T.L.O. in the Juvenile and Domestic Relations Court of Middlesex County. Contending that the search of her purse violated the Fourth Amendment, T.L.O.'s counsel moved to suppress the evidence found in her purse, as well as her confession, which, counsel argued, was tainted by the allegedly unlawful search.

The case eventually reached the US Supreme Court. Associate Justice White, who authored the Court's opinion, noted that in determining whether the search at issue in this case had violated the Fourth Amendment, said that the Court was faced initially with the question of whether that Amendment's prohibition on unreasonable searches and seizures applied to searches conducted by public school officials. The Supreme Court held that it does.

Justice White noted that it is now beyond dispute that "the Federal Constitution, by virtue of the Fourteenth Amendment, prohibits unreasonable searches and seizures by state officers." Equally indisputable is the proposition that the Fourteenth Amendment protects the rights of students against encroachment by public school officials.

The Court noted that the State of New Jersey had argued that the history of the Fourth Amendment indicates that the Amendment was intended to regulate only searches and seizures carried out by law enforcement officers. Accordingly, the State contended that although public school officials are concededly State agents for purposes of the Fourteenth Amendment, the Fourth Amendment creates no rights enforceable against them.

The Court also noted that it had held school officials were subject to the commands of the First Amendment, and the Due Process Clause of the Fourteenth Amendment purposes of the constitutional guarantees of freedom of expression and due process. Accordingly, it is difficult to understand why they should be deemed to be exercising parental rather than public authority when conducting searches of their students.

The Court stated that to hold that the Fourth Amendment applies to searches conducted by school authorities is only to begin the inquiry into the standards governing such searches. Although the underlying command of the Fourth Amendment is always that searches and seizures be reasonable, what is reasonable depends on the context within which a search takes place. The determination of the standard of reasonableness governing any specific class of searches requires "balancing the need to search against the invasion which the search entails." On one side of the balance are arrayed the individual's legitimate expectations of privacy and personal security; on the other, the government's need for effective methods to deal with breaches of public order.

The Court stated that against the child's interest in privacy must be set the substantial interest of teachers and administrators in maintaining discipline in the classroom and on school grounds. Maintaining order in the classroom has never been easy, but in recent years, school disorder has often taken particularly ugly forms: Drug use and violent crime in schools have become major social problems. Even in schools that have been spared the most severe disciplinary problems, the preservation of order and a proper educational environment requires close supervision of schoolchildren, as well as the enforcement of rules against conduct that would be perfectly permissible if undertaken by an adult.

According to Justice White, it is important to strike the proper balance between the schoolchild's legitimate expectations of privacy and the school's equally legitimate need to maintain an environment in which learning can take place. It is evident that the school setting requires some easing of the restrictions to which searches by public authorities are ordinarily subject. The warrant requirement, in particular, is unsuited to the school environment: Requiring a teacher to obtain a warrant before searching a child suspected of an infraction of school rules (or of the criminal law) would unduly interfere with the maintenance of the swift and informal disciplinary procedures needed in schools. The Court held that school officials need not obtain a warrant before searching a student who is under their authority.

Justice White then concluded that there remains the question of the legality of the search in this case. He stated: "Our review of the facts surrounding the search leads us to conclude that the search was in no sense unreasonable for Fourth Amendment purposes."

SRO Search of Student: *In the Matter of S.W.*

The *T.L.O.* case stated that school officials may conduct a reasonable search of a student's possessions without the requirement of obtaining a search warrant. What about an SRO? When conducting a search, is an SRO a school official or a police officer? While the US Supreme Court has not yet ruled on this issue as of this date, several state courts have, reaching decisions like the case of *In the Matter of S.W.*

Facts of the case: At Riverside High School in Durham, North Carolina, a student walked by an SRO, who was also a deputy in the Durham sheriff's department.[18] The SRO noticed a strong odor of marijuana emanating from the student, and requested that the student accompany him in the hallway. The SRO then located two school administrators. The SRO asked the two administrators and two unidentified students to accompany him and the student into the school's weight room. Once in the room, the SRO asked the student if he "had anything on him." The student responded, "No." Then, the SRO asked the student, "Do you mind if I search you?" The student indicated that he did not want to be searched. The SRO conducted a search. When the SRO requested that the student empty his pockets, the student produced a plastic bag that contained ten small plastic bags of marijuana.

A juvenile petition was filed alleging the juvenile possessed with intent to sell or deliver a schedule VI substance in violation of N.C. Gen. Stat. § 90-95(a)(1). During the hearing, the SRO testified for the State and the juvenile testified on his own behalf. The trial court found the juvenile to be delinquent and placed him on level I supervised probation for six months. The juvenile appealed.

The juvenile's counsel argued that the trial court erred by denying the motion to suppress evidence obtained during an alleged unlawful search. (Other errors alleged by counsel are not discussed in this overview of the case.) The North Carolina court noted that the United States Supreme Court discussed warrantless searches of students at school in *New Jersey v. T.L.O.*, which held that a juvenile's consent is not needed to conduct a search of a student while at school. The court noted that under ordinary circumstances, a search of a student by a teacher or other school official will be justified at its inception when there are reasonable grounds for suspecting that the search will turn up evidence that the student has violated or is violating either the law or the rules of the school. Such a search will be permissible in its scope when the measures adopted are reasonably related to the objectives of the search and not excessively intrusive considering the age and sex of the student and the nature of the infraction.

The state court noted that while the holding in *T.L.O.* was limited to searches by school administrators and officials, the court has since held that the *T.L.O.* standard governs searches conducted by school resource officers working in conjunction with school officials, where these officers are primarily responsible to the school district rather than the local police department.

The state court noted that the courts draw a clear distinction between the categories of cases and those cases in which outside law enforcement officers search students as part of an independent investigation or in which school officials search students at the request or behest of the outside law enforcement officers and law enforcement agencies. The state appellate court noted that courts do not apply the *T.L.O.* rule to these cases, but instead require the traditional probable cause requirement to justify the search.

The state court affirmed that the SRO was assigned to permanent full-time duty as the Riverside High School resource officer, and held that the *T.L.O.* standard applies to law enforcement officers who serve as school resource officers, acting in conjunction with school officials. According to this ruling, the SRO in question assisted school officials with school discipline matters and taught law enforcement–related subjects. The SRO was exclusively a school resource officer, who was present in the school hallways during school hours and was furthering the school's education-related goals when he stopped the juvenile. He was not an outside police officer conducting an investigation. The SRO did not conduct the investigation at the behest of an outside officer who was investigating a non-school-related crime. In maintaining a proper educational environment, the SRO's employment as a resource officer mandates that he help maintain a drug-free environment at the school. The state court upheld the trial court's ruling that the search by the SRO was constitutional.

Interrogation

Any discussion regarding the rights of youths when questioned by law enforcement officers should start with the US Supreme Court case of *J.D.B. v. North Carolina*.[19] In that case, the police stopped and questioned J.D.B., a thirteen-year-old, seventh-grade student, upon seeing him near the site of two home break-ins. Five days later, a digital camera matching one of the stolen items was found at J.D.B.'s school and seen in his possession.

After finding the item, a uniformed police officer on detail to the school took J.D.B. from his classroom to a closed-door conference room, where police and school administrators questioned him for at least thirty minutes. Before beginning the questioning, they did not give him Miranda warnings or the opportunity to call his grandmother, his legal guardian, nor tell him he was free to leave the room. He first denied his involvement, but later confessed after officials urged him to tell the truth and told him about the prospect of juvenile detention. Only then did the officer tell J.D.B. that he could refuse to answer questions and was free to leave. Asked whether he understood, J.D.B. nodded and provided further details, including the location of the stolen items.

Two juvenile petitions were filed against J.D.B., charging him with breaking and entering and with larceny. His public defender moved to suppress his statements and the evidence derived therefrom, arguing that J.D.B. had been interrogated in a custodial setting without being afforded Miranda warnings and that his statements were involuntary. The trial court denied the motion. J.D.B. entered a transcript of admission to the charges, but renewed his objection to the denial of his motion to suppress. The case eventually came before the US Supreme Court.

A summary of the Court's decision follows: The Supreme Court noted that any police interview of an individual suspected of a crime has "coercive aspects to it." Those interrogations that occur while a suspect is in police custody, however, heighten the risk that statements obtained are not the product of the suspect's free choice. The State contended that a child's age has no place in the custody analysis, no matter how young the child subjected to police questioning. The Court did not agree. In some circumstances, a child's age would have affected how a reasonable person in the suspect's position would perceive his or her freedom to leave. That is, a reasonable child subjected to police questioning will sometimes feel pressured to submit when a reasonable adult would feel free to go.

The Court concluded that a child's age is far "more than a chronological fact." It is a fact that generates commonsense conclusions about behavior and perception that apply broadly to children as a class. Children generally are less mature and responsible than adults; they often lack the experience, perspective, and judgment to recognize and avoid choices that could be detrimental to them; and they are more vulnerable or susceptible to outside pressures than adults. In the specific context of police interrogation, events that would leave a man cold and unimpressed can overawe and overwhelm a teen.

The law has historically reflected the same assumption that children characteristically lack the capacity to exercise mature judgment and possess only an incomplete ability to understand the world around them.

The effect of the schoolhouse setting cannot be disentangled from the identity of the person questioned. A student—whose presence at school is compulsory and whose disobedience at school is cause for disciplinary action—is in a far different position than, say, a parent volunteer on school grounds to chaperone an event, or an adult from the community on school grounds to attend a basketball game. Without asking whether the person "questioned in school" is a "minor," the coercive effect of the schoolhouse setting is unknowable.

The Court stated that our history is replete with laws and judicial recognition that children cannot be viewed simply as miniature adults. The Court saw no justification for taking a different course here. Courts should be instructed to take particular care to ensure that young children's incriminating statements are not obtained involuntarily. But Miranda's procedural safeguards exist precisely because the voluntariness test is an inadequate barrier when custodial interrogation is at stake.

Parents' Right to be Present during Interrogation

Do parents have the right to be present when youth are questioned? The right varies from state to state. For example, in the State of Nevada the police can question any child (whether seventeen years old or ten years old) without telling his or her parents first, or even asking the child whether he or she wants a parent present before being questioned.

Most jurisdictions, however, require parents be notified any time police take a child into custody, and many others will ask for parental consent before questioning a minor, even though doing so is not constitutionally required. Frequently the interrogation is an informal one between an officer and a youth on the street. Generally, in these situations, the parents are not notified of the questioning.

If it is a formal interrogation, typically, law enforcement officers will attempt to contact parents for the sake of health and safety, as there may be important information for officers to know about, such as a severe peanut allergy. Often the youth may benefit from the absence of the parents. Frequently parents unwittingly provide helpful information to officers. In addition, more mature children, such as teenagers, might be more willing to talk to officers if parents are not notified.

Practicum

Jerry is a sixteen-year-old student in a public high school. Recently there has been a rash of thefts from school lockers. For some reason, the SRO thinks that Jerry may be involved. The SRO calls Jerry into his office and starts questioning him regarding the thefts.

What actions should the SRO take prior to the questioning of the student, and what warnings should he give the student prior to the questioning?

Summary

- In 2016, law enforcement agencies in the United States made more than 856,000 arrests of persons younger than the age of eighteen. This was their lowest total of yearly arrests in more than forty years.
- In 2016, about one in five juvenile violent crime arrests involved females, and more than half involved minority youths.
- Generally, the first contact between a youth and the juvenile justice system, in a non-school situation, is an initial contact with a police officer. At this point, the officer has wide discretion in deciding whether the youth will be involved in the criminal justice system.
- Many researchers consider that an individual's attitude toward an officer when stopped is an important factor in the officer's decision-making process as to whether to formally invoke the justice system.
- The salience of ethnic identity can exacerbate this perception of prejudice. The process leading to a more-coherent sense of identity becomes a double-edged sword for many youths of color.
- Although some may internalize the negative effect of discrimination or employ maladaptive strategies to deal with it, for others, the cognitive maturity necessary for the development of a stronger ethnic identity can provide them with more-positive coping strategies and ultimately serve as a protective factor against the adverse effects of racial discrimination.
- School resource officers (SROs) are uniformed, armed police officers assigned to work directly in schools. SROs' duties involve a combination of law

enforcement, teaching, and mentoring. Their law enforcement duties include investigating criminal complaints and ensuring the safety of the school by patrolling the school grounds.

- Most states do not have any requirements regarding the use of SROs or any specialized training requirements before an officer is assigned as an SRO. In the few states that do have requirements, they vary greatly.
- Generally, each jurisdiction has statutes or regulations regarding how police should handle youths taken into custody.
- The use of curfews to control youth movement during peak crime periods is a hotly contested issue in the academic, police, and civil liberty communities.
- Generally, officers must provide juveniles with the same Fourth Amendment search and seizure protections as adults, and except under certain circumstances, the search must be reasonable and conducted with a search warrant.
- In *New Jersey v. T.L.O.*, the US Supreme Court held that the Fourth Amendment's prohibition on unreasonable searches and seizures applies to searches conducted by public school officials, but that school officials need not obtain a warrant before searching a student who is under their authority.
- Any discussion regarding the rights of youths when questioned by law enforcement officers should start with the US Supreme Court case of *J.D.B. v. North Carolina*. In that case, the Court stated that because of his or her age, a juvenile needs certain protections during an interrogation.

Discussion and Review Questions

1. Why does a police officer have wide discretion when he or she stops a youth on the street for questioning regarding a crime?
2. Why is the *T.L.O.* case important?
3. Why are minorities overrepresented in the juvenile justice system?
4. What precautions should be taken by the police before questioning a youth?
5. What are the general duties of an SRO?
6. How do SROs differ from juvenile police officers?
7. What specialized training should an SRO have before being assigned to a public school?
8. How has the increased use of SROs increased the school-to-prison pipeline?

Notes

1. Charles Puzzanchera, "Juvenile Arrests," *Juvenile Justice Statistics National Report Series Bulletin* (Washington, DC: US Department of Justice, December 2018), posted at https://www.ojjdp.gov/pubs/251861.pdf (accessed April 29, 2019).
2. Erika Gebo and Carolyn Boyes-Watson, *Youth, Crime, and Justice: Learning Through Cases* (Lanham, MD: Rowman and Littlefield, 2018).
3. Muriel Bridges and Monty Merritt, "Police Discretion with Respect to the Juvenile Offender, Department of Public Safety, Multnomah County, Oregon" (1974), Dissertations and Theses, Paper 1717-39.
4. Carl E. Pope and Howard N. Snyder, "Race as a Factor in Juvenile Arrests," *Juvenile Justice Bulletin* (Washington, DC: US Department of Justice, April 2003).
5. "Racial and Ethnic Disparities in the Juvenile Justice System," National Conference of State Legislatures website, November 11, 2018, posted at http://www.ncsl.org/research/civil-and-criminal-justice/racial-and-ethnic-disparities-in-the-juvenile-justice-system.aspx (accessed May 1, 2019).
6. P.L. 93-415, 42 U.S.C. 5601 et seq.

7. "In Focus: Disproportionate Minority Contact," (2012), posted at the OJJPD website at https://www.ojjdp.gov/pubs/239457.pdf (accessed May 1, 2019).
8. Georgia Criminal Justice Coordinating Council, "Disproportionate Minority Contact in Georgia's Juvenile Justice System: A Three-Prong Approach to Analyzing DMC in Georgia" (March 2018), posted online at https://cjcc.georgia.gov/sites/cjcc.georgia.gov/files/2018%20DMC%20Assessment%20-%206.26.18.pdf (accessed May 1, 2019).
9. Joanna M. Lee, Laurence Steinberg, and Alex R. Piquero, "Ethnic Identity and Attitudes toward the Police among African-American Juvenile Offenders," *Journal of Criminal Justice*, vol. 38 (2010), 781–89.
10. Jennifer Counts, Kristina N. Randall, Joseph B. Ryan, and Antonis Katsiyannis, "School Resource Officers in Public Schools: A National Review," *Education & Treatment of Children*, vol. 41, no. 4 (November 2018), 405–30.
11. Counts et al., "School Resource Officers in Public Schools."
12. Andra J. Bannister, David L Carter, and Joseph Schafe, "A National Police Survey on the Use of Juvenile Curfews," *Journal of Criminal Justice*, vol. 29, no. 3 (May 2001), 233–40.
13. Angie Schwartz and Lucy Wang, "Proliferating Curfew Laws Keep Kids at Home, But Fail to Curb Juvenile Crime," June 2018, National Center for Youth Law website at https://youthlaw.org/publication/proliferating-curfew-laws-keep-kids-at-home-but-fail-to-curb-juvenile-crime/ (accessed April 30, 2019).
14. *Terry v. Ohio*, 392 U.S. 1 (1968).
15. *Massachusetts v. Shepherd*, 468 U.S. 897 (1984).
16. *New Jersey v. T.L.O.*, 469 U.S. 325 (1985).
17. *New Jersey v. T.L.O.*
18. *In the Matter of S.W.*, 614 S.E.2d 424 (2005, Court of Appeals of North Carolina).
19. *J.D.B. v. North Carolina*, 564 U.S. 261 (2011).

PART IV

Juvenile Justice System

CHAPTER 9

Juvenile Justice

CHAPTER OBJECTIVES

After studying this chapter, the reader should be able to:

- Explain the development of the juvenile justice system.
- Discuss the US Supreme Court decisions on the rights of juveniles.
- Understand the differences in court procedures in juvenile cases when compared to adult criminal cases.
- Explain the juvenile court procedures and the disposition and aftercare programs available to the juvenile court.

Development of Juvenile Justice

In the study of juvenile delinquency and the juvenile justice system, it is essential for the reader to understand that in the United States and its jurisdictions, juvenile justice, like adult criminal justice, is mainly a function of the state or the federal jurisdictions that are not in a state, like the District of Columbia or Puerto Rico. Each of the fifty states and the federal jurisdictions differ to some degree in responding to juvenile crime.

In addition, the US Supreme Court has imposed guidelines on how the states should handle juveniles. For example, in the case of *Kent v. United States*, the Supreme Court in 1966 set forth the procedural guidelines that states should use in transferring a juvenile delinquent from juvenile court to adult criminal court.[1] The Court has based their guidelines on the due process clause contained in the Fourteenth Amendment to the US Constitution. Table 9.1 provides a comparison between the terms used in the juvenile justice system and those used in the adult criminal justice system.

Early Justice

As primitive tribes began to exercise social control over the behavior of their members, generally children were subject to the same control and held to the same

TABLE 9.1 Terms Used in Juvenile Justice

Adult Terms	Juvenile Justice Terms
Criminal	Delinquent
Crime	Delinquent act
Incarceration	Commitment
Defendant	Defendant
Indictment	Petition
Not guilty plea	Deny petition
Guilty plea	Agree to a finding
Sentence	Disposition
Parole	Aftercare

standards as the adults. At that time, incarceration or imprisonment was not used as a form of punishment. The most severe punishment was banishment. When a person was banished from the tribe, that person was considered outside of the law—thus, an outlaw. A banished person received no protection or help from the tribe, and was vulnerable to wild animals and other outlaws.[2]

In the eighteenth and early nineteenth centuries, delinquent juveniles were tried in adult criminal courts. Those found guilty were punished and confined in jails and penitentiaries. There were few other options available, so youths of all ages and genders were indiscriminately confined with adult criminals in penal institutions. Many juveniles were confined for noncriminal behavior because there were no other options. During this time period, many cities were confronting high rates of child poverty and neglect.[3]

The juvenile justice system functioned for many years with only occasional appellate court interventions. Remember that the original juvenile courts were very informal; many concluded that the US Constitution did not apply to them as it did to adult criminal courts. This all changed in the 1960s and 1970s, when the US Supreme Court altered the juvenile court system by issuing a series of key decisions that established certain constitutional rights for juveniles (discussed later in this chapter). Box 9.1 contains the comments of noted English jurist William Blackstone.

Houses of Refuge

Thomas Eddy and John Griscom were two penal reformers who organized the Society for the Prevention of Pauperism to oppose the practice of housing youth in adult jails and prisons. They urged the creation of new types of juvenile institutions, and their work led to the establishment of the New York House of Refuge in 1825. This was the first US institution designed to house poor, destitute, and vagrant youth who were deemed by authorities to be on the path toward delinquency. The New York House of Refuge is considered the first step toward the development of a juvenile justice system. Similar institutions were opened in Boston and Philadelphia. By the 1840s, approximately twenty-five comparable facilities were opened throughout the United States.[4]

Houses of Refuge were very similar to adult penitentiaries. They were large fortress-like congregate-style institutions located in urban areas for youth who had been designated as abandoned, delinquent, or incorrigible. The average number of

BOX 9.1 **William Blackstone on Persons Capable of Committing Crimes**

William Blackstone was an eighteenth-century British lawyer noted for writing "Commentaries on the Laws of England." Here are some excerpts:

> But by the law, as it now stands, . . . the capacity of doing ill, or contracting guilt, is not so much measured by years and days, as by the strength of the delinquent's understanding and judgment. For one lad of eleven years old may have as much cunning as another of fourteen; and in these cases, our maxim is, that *malitia supplet aetatem* ["malice supplies the age"]. Under seven years of age indeed an infant cannot be guilty of felony; for then a felonious discretion is almost an impossibility in nature: but at eight years old he may be guilty of felony. Also, under fourteen . . . if it appears to the court and jury, that he . . . could discern between good and evil, he may be convicted and suffer death. Thus, a girl of thirteen has been burnt for killing her mistress: and one boy of ten, and another of nine years old, who had killed their companions, have been sentenced to death, and he of ten years actually hanged; because it appeared upon their trials, that the one hid himself, and the other hid the body he had killed; which hiding manifested a consciousness of guilt, and a discretion to discern between good and evil. . . . Thus also, in very modern times, a boy of ten years old was convicted on [his] own confession of murdering his bedfellow; there appearing in his whole behaviour plain tokens of a mischievous discretion: and, as the sparing this boy merely on account of his tender years might be of dangerous consequence to the public, by propagating a notion that children might commit such atrocious crimes with impunity, it was unanimously agreed by all the judges that he was a proper subject of capital punishment.

Source: William Blackstone, "Of the Persons Capable of Committing Crimes," Book IV, Chapter 2, in *Commentaries on the Laws of England* (Oxford, England: Clarendon Press, 1765).

youths housed in these institutions was two hundred, but some, like the New York House of Refuge, housed more than one thousand youths.

Juvenile Courts

As noted by Melanie King, the State of Illinois (Cook County) established the first juvenile court in the United States in July 1899. The act that established the juvenile court was one of the first pieces of legislation that made a distinction between juveniles who were neglected and those who were delinquent.[5] The Act established a special court and probation program for children under the age of sixteen, and was based on the following principles:

- Juveniles, because of their immaturity, should not be held accountable as adult criminals.
- The objective of juvenile court was not to punish juveniles, but to treat and rehabilitate them.

BOX 9.2 Excerpts of Juvenile Court Judge Julian Mack's Comments

Judge Julian Mack was one of the first judges to preside over the nation's first juvenile court in Cook County, Illinois. Here he describes the goals of the juvenile court in 1909:

> The child who must be brought into court should, of course, be made to know that he is face to face with the power of the state, but he should at the same time, and more emphatically, be made to feel that he is the object of its care and solicitude. The ordinary trappings of the courtroom are out of place in such hearings. The judge on a bench, looking down upon the boy standing at the bar, can never evoke a proper sympathetic spirit. Seated at a desk, with the child at his side, where he can on occasion put his arm around his shoulder and draw the lad to him, the judge, while losing none of his judicial dignity, will gain immensely in the effectiveness of his work.

Source: Julian Mack, "The Juvenile Court," *Harvard Law Review*, vol. 23 (1909), 120.

- Disposition of the juvenile cases should be based on the individual juvenile's circumstances and needs.
- Juvenile court, following informal procedures, should avoid adult criminal procedures because of the complexity and confusing rules and procedures of adult criminal court.
- The role of the juvenile court judges and juvenile probation was to diagnose the child's condition and wrongful conduct and prescribe corrective programs to alleviate them.

By 1925, juvenile courts existed in every state. While some states established elaborate juvenile court systems, others passed juvenile court legislation, albeit, with limited or no implementation. Similar situations existed in many juvenile probation systems. In 1926, Sanford Fox noted that five out of every six juvenile courts failed to meet the minimum standards set forth by the US Children Bureau.[6] Box 9.2 contains the comments of an early juvenile court judge.

Juvenile courts today exercise jurisdiction over two types of offenders: status offenders and criminal delinquents. A *status offender* is a juvenile who has committed at least one activity that is deemed offensive when committed by juveniles, because of their age at the time of the activity. Common status offenses include truancy, possession and consumption of alcohol, curfew violations, failure to attend school, and purchase of cigarettes. The basis for status offenses stems from the legal theory of *parens patriae*, in that status offenses are harmful to minors, and the courts need to protect minors from such activities. Status offenses are discussed in chapter 14.

Juvenile courts with delinquency jurisdiction handle cases involving *criminal delinquents*, in which juveniles are accused of criminal acts that would be crimes if committed by an adult. In forty-five states, the maximum age of juvenile court jurisdiction is age seventeen. Five states—Georgia, Michigan, Missouri, Texas, and Wisconsin—now draw the juvenile/adult line at age sixteen. Missouri raised the age of juvenile court jurisdiction to age seventeen in 2018, and the law will go into effect

BOX 9.3 **California Welfare and Institutions Code, Section 602 and Subsection 707(a)(1) (2017)**

(Typical state statute establishing juvenile court jurisdiction)

Section 602

Except as provided in Section 707, any person who is under eighteen years of age when he or she violates any law of this state or of the United States, or any ordinance of any city or county of this state, defining crime other than an ordinance establishing a curfew based solely on age, is within the jurisdiction of the juvenile court, which may adjudge such person to be a ward of the court.

Subsection 707(a)(1)

In any case in which a minor is alleged to be a person described in Section 602 by reason of the violation, when he or she was sixteen years of age or older, of any felony criminal statute, or of an offense listed in subdivision (b) when he or she was fourteen or fifteen years of age, the district attorney or other appropriate prosecuting officer may make a motion to transfer the minor from juvenile court to a court of criminal jurisdiction. The motion must be made prior to the attachment of jeopardy. Upon such motion, the juvenile court shall order the probation officer to submit a report on the behavioral patterns and social history of the minor. The report shall include any written or oral statement offered by the victim pursuant to Section 656.2.

January 1, 2021. However, all states have transfer laws that allow or require young offenders to be prosecuted as adults for more-serious offenses. Box 9.3 contains excerpts from the State of California's Welfare and Institutions Code, which establishes their juvenile court jurisdiction. The transfer of a juvenile to adult criminal court is discussed in chapter 13.

According to a booklet published by the National Conference of State Legislatures, public sentiment shifted drastically beginning in the 1980s as juvenile crime rates rose, especially for homicides. The increase in juvenile crime, accompanied by heightened media attention, prompted a shift from a sympathetic view of juveniles to one of fear. Juvenile offenders were viewed as savvy criminals who had access to guns and could commit serious, violent crimes. Rehabilitative policies were considered inadequate due to high recidivism rates, and some serious offenders were termed *super-predators*, unreceptive to treatment-oriented sentences. Consequently, more-punitive policies began to replace rehabilitative ones, and the transfer of juveniles to criminal courts became more common. Several states lowered the age at which juveniles could be within criminal court jurisdiction; many states eased the methods for transferring juveniles; and some states expanded the list of offenses for which transfer is possible. Policies increasingly reflected the popular mantra: "Adult time for adult crime."[7] There presently appears to be a tendency to increase the number of individuals subject to juvenile court jurisdiction as noted in recent changes made by the State of New York. Photo 9.1 depicts a youth who has been arrested and is now in the juvenile justice system.

PHOTO 9.1 Once a youth has been arrested, he or she is now involved in the juvenile justice system. (Photo courtesy of iStock)

Juvenile Justice Reform

Louisiana Case Study

In 2016, the State of Louisiana modified the Raise the Age Act to include seventeen-year-olds in the juvenile justice system. This Act took effect in two parts:[8]

- As of March 1, 2019, seventeen-year-olds charged with nonviolent offenses—the vast majority of those arrested—were included in the juvenile justice system.
- As of July 1, 2020, seventeen-year-olds charged with any offense were included in the juvenile justice system.

The increase in jurisdiction of the Louisiana juvenile justice system began in 2003, initiated because the state juvenile justice system was notorious for its brutal treatment of youths. In addition, Louisiana is attempting to adopt the "Missouri Model of Care" for juveniles, discussed below.

In 2017, the state legislature commissioned a task force to determine if there was an issue with the state's secure juvenile care facilities. The task force recommended that the state appoint an independent contractor to monitor the facilities that the state entrusts to house and rehabilitate some of the most vulnerable youth. The task force noted that the legislature approved in 2003 a commission to see the continued reform of the state's juvenile justice system, and that the commission had not met since 2016. The task force noted that the Louisiana Office of Juvenile Justice (OJJ) did not conduct quality assurance audits on secure care facilities from calendar years 2010 through 2015, and between fiscal years 2013 and 2017, OJJ did not address 19 percent of youth grievances within the time frames set in OJJ policy.

The task force noted that in 2017, the OJJ began participating in Performance-based Standards (PbS), a data-driven improvement model that sets national standards and compares juvenile justice agency performance to that of national averages. The goal of PbS is to assist the OJJ in monitoring safety through the development of improvement plans for measures that are below the national average. Currently, thirty-six states participate in PbS. In addition to participating in PbS, the OJJ has adopted the following policies and practices nationwide to help ensure safety at secure juvenile facilities:

- Required staffing ratios to ensure that enough employees properly oversee youth
- Continuous quality improvement system (CQIS) audits of secure care facilities

- Collecting information on fights, use of restraints, drug testing, and contraband
- Guidelines for the use and monitoring of room confinement
- Processes for youth to file grievances

Missouri Model of Care in Juvenile Lockups

In 2001, the State of Missouri juvenile justice system was recognized by the American Youth Policy Center as the "guiding light" for reform of its juvenile justice system. Since that time, officials representing thirty states have visited Missouri to tour its youth corrections facilities and learn about its juvenile treatment model. Highlights of the Missouri Model include:

- Placing youths who require confinement into smaller facilities located near the youths' homes and families, rather than incarcerating delinquent youth in large, faraway, prisonlike training schools.
- Placing those youths into closely supervised small groups and applying a rigorous group treatment process that offers extensive and ongoing individual attention, rather than isolating confined youth in individual cells or leaving them to fend for themselves among a crowd of delinquent peers.
- Placing emphasis on (and achieving admirable success in) keeping youths safe not only from physical aggression but also from ridicule and emotional abuse; and it does so through constant staff supervision and using supportive peer relationships rather than through coercive techniques that are commonplace in most youth corrections systems.
- Helping confined youths develop academic, pre-vocational, and communications skills that improve their ability to succeed following release—along with crucial insights into the roots of their delinquent behavior and new social competence to acknowledge and solve personal problems.
- The state reaches out to family members and involves them both as partners in the treatment process and as allies in planning for success in the aftercare transition, rather than keeping families at a distance and treating them as the source of delinquent youths' problems.
- The state provides considerable support and supervision for youth transitioning home from a residential facility—conducting intensive aftercare planning prior to release, monitoring and mentoring youth closely in the first crucial weeks following release, and working hard to enroll them in school, place them in jobs, and/or sign them up for extracurricular activities in their home communities.[9]

Development of Dependency Jurisdiction

The Illinois Juvenile Court Act of 1899 included delinquent children in its jurisdictional mandate. The Act did not include abused and dependent children. The focus of the early juvenile court was "saving" potentially criminal children from becoming criminal, irrespective of whether the condition which brought them to the court was delinquent conduct or dependent status. According to Marvin Ventrell, it would be unfair to say that the focus of the juvenile court founders was in no way altruistic. He states that it is a misunderstanding of history to believe that the dependency component of the court was a movement to protect abused and neglected children.[10] The dependency court is that part of the juvenile court which handles child maltreatment cases. A child who has been adjudicated as maltreated or is under state custody is referred to as a "dependent child."

Dependency proceedings are based on the doctrine of *parens patriae*. Accordingly, the right of a state or federal government to take actions to protect children

BOX 9.4 ***Ex parte Crouse***

SUPREME COURT OF PENNSYLVANIA
EASTERN DISTRICT, PHILADELPHIA
4 Whart. 9; 1839 Pa. LEXIS 171 January 5, 1839

The 1839 Pennsylvania Supreme Court decision of *Ex parte Crouse* in 1839 was the first case upholding the Refuge System. The child (Mary Ann Crouse) was committed to the Philadelphia House of Refuge by a justice of the peace. The justice's warrant, executed by the child's mother, contended that it would be in the child's interests to be incarcerated in the House because she was "beyond her parents' control." The father filed a habeas corpus petition for his daughter's return. The father contended that allowing the child's commitment without a trial was unconstitutional. The court denied the father's appeal on the basis that the House was not a prison. The court concluded that the child was there for her own reformation, not punishment. The decision of the court acknowledged and sanctioned the state's authority to intervene into the family as ultimate parent via the doctrine of *parens patriae*. The holding of the case was relied on as the authority for the right of the state to make coercive predictions about deviant children. The Court's decision set the precedent that the state has the right to intervene into the parent–child relationship for the good of the child.

Source: *Ex parte Crouse* case and Marvin Ventrell, "Evolution of the Dependency Component of the Juvenile Court, in A Centennial Celebration of the Juvenile Court 1899–1999," *Juvenile and Family Court Journal*, vol. 49, no. 4 (Fall 1998).

is based on this doctrine. The doctrine developed in early English common law and refers to the right of the ruler to protect the people. In the United States, the doctrine refers to the government's responsibility as the supreme guardian of children, mentally ill adults, and people who are incompetent to protect themselves. Under this doctrine, both federal and state governments have held that they have the obligation to intervene on behalf of the best interests of the child or incompetent person when his or her welfare is in jeopardy. Box 9.4 discusses the 1839 case of *Ex parte Crouse*, which was one of the earliest cases that approved the doctrine of *parens patriae*.

US Supreme Court and the Rights of Juveniles

Cases Involving Juvenile Justice Proceedings

The *Kent* and *In re Gault* cases provided notice to all that the US Supreme Court would require the juvenile justice system and its courts to follow the constitutional requirements of due process. Many justice professionals consider these cases as signaling an end to the informal processes that were being used in the juvenile justice system, and making the juvenile justice system a mirror of the adult criminal justice system. However, as discussed in chapter 2, the requirement of "due process" in juvenile proceedings did not end the juvenile justice system.

Kent v. United States

The US Supreme Court in 1966 issued its opinion in the case of *Kent v. United States*. The *Kent* case established the procedural guidelines to be used in the waiver of a juvenile delinquent from juvenile to adult court jurisdiction.[11]

Facts of the case: Morris Kent, a sixteen-year-old with a police record, was arrested and charged with housebreaking, robbery, and rape. He admitted to committing the crimes. After being held in a juvenile detention center for six days, the juvenile judge, without holding a hearing, waived jurisdiction and transferred the case to an adult criminal court.

The case was appealed to the Supreme Court on the single issue of whether juveniles have a right to a hearing before their cases are transferred to adult criminal court. However, the Supreme Court's decision went far beyond the single issue of the need for a juvenile hearing before waiving jurisdiction. It was a warning to juvenile courts that the traditional laxity toward procedural and evidentiary standards would be subject to scrutiny by the Supreme Court. The Court had previously indicated its concern regarding juveniles as early as 1948, in *Haley v. Ohio*.[12] The *Haley* case involved a juvenile tried in adult criminal court for first-degree murder. The Court held that the due process clause barred the use of a confession obtained by force by juvenile authorities.

The Supreme Court noted that the authority of a juvenile court judge to waive or transfer jurisdiction to the US District Court for the District of Columbia was contained in the Juvenile Court Act (§ 11-914 D.C. Code, 1951 Ed.). The section permitted the judge to waive jurisdiction after a full investigation of any child sixteen years of age or older who is charged with an offense which is a felony in the case of an adult, or any child charged with an offense which if committed by an adult was punishable by death or life imprisonment.

The Court pointed out that the statute contains no specific standards for the exercise of this important discretionary act, but leaves the formulation to the juvenile court judge. The Court noted that knowledge of the criteria used by the judge is important to the child, his or her parents, his or her attorney, the judges of the US District Court for the District of Columbia, the US Attorney and his assistants, and to the Metropolitan Police Department, as well as to the staff of the juvenile court.

The Court held that an offense falling within the statutory limitations may be waived if it has prosecutive merit and if it is heinous or of an aggravated character, or—even though less serious—if it represents a pattern of repeated offenses which indicate that the juvenile may be beyond rehabilitation under juvenile court procedures, or if the public needs the protection afforded by such action.

Under D.C. statute, the juvenile court is vested with "original and exclusive jurisdiction" of the child. This jurisdiction confers special rights and immunities. The juvenile is shielded from publicity. He or she may be confined, but with rare exceptions he or she may not be jailed along with adults. The juvenile may be detained, but only until he or she is twenty-one years of age. The Court pointed out that the statute gave preference to retaining the child in the custody of his parents unless his or her welfare and the safety and protection of the public couldn't be adequately safeguarded without removal. In addition, the child is protected against consequences of adult conviction, such as the loss of civil rights, the use of adjudication against him or her in subsequent proceedings, and disqualification for public employment.

The Court noted that a determination of whether to transfer a child from juvenile court jurisdiction to the adult criminal processes of the district court is "critically important." The Juvenile Court Act confers upon the child a right to avail him- or herself of that court's "exclusive" jurisdiction. The Court held that it is implicit in the juvenile court scheme that noncriminal treatment is to be the rule—and adult criminal treatment, the exception—and that the latter must be governed by the factors of each individual case.

The Court concluded that, as a condition to a valid waiver order, a juvenile is entitled to a hearing, including access by his counsel to the social records and probation or similar reports which were considered by the juvenile court judge, and to a statement of reasons for the juvenile judge's decision.

The Court held that it is incumbent upon the juvenile court to accompany its waiver order with a statement of the reasons or considerations. While the statement does not need to be formal or include conventional findings of fact, it must be sufficient to demonstrate that the statutory requirement of a "full investigation" has been met, and that the question has received careful consideration by the juvenile court. It must also set forth the basis for the order with sufficient specificity to permit meaningful review.

The Court concluded that an opportunity for a hearing, which may be informal, must be given the child prior to entry of a waiver order. The child is entitled to counsel in connection with a waiver proceeding, and counsel is entitled to see the child's social records. These rights are meaningless—an illusion, a mockery—unless counsel is given an opportunity to function.

The Court held that the right to representation by counsel is not a formality. It is not a grudging gesture to a ritualistic requirement. It is the very essence of justice. Appointment of counsel without affording an opportunity for a hearing on a "critically important" decision is tantamount to denial of counsel. A waiver hearing to be held under D.C. Code Ann. § 11-1553 (1965) need not conform with all requirements of a criminal trial, or even of the usual administrative hearing, but the hearing must measure up to the essentials of due process and fair treatment.

The waiver question is primarily and initially one for the juvenile court to decide, and its failure to do so in a valid manner cannot be said to be a harmless error. It is the juvenile court, not the district or adult criminal court, which has the facilities, personnel, and expertise for a proper determination of the waiver issue.

In an appendix to the Court's decision, the Court set forth the criteria to be used by juvenile courts in determining whether to waive jurisdiction of juveniles. The determinative factors which should be considered by the judge in deciding whether the juvenile court's jurisdiction over such offenses will be waived are:

- The seriousness of the alleged offense to the community and whether the protection of the community requires a waiver.
- Whether the alleged offense was committed in an aggressive, violent, premeditated, or willful manner.
- Whether the alleged offense was against persons or against property, with greater weight being given to offenses against persons, especially if personal injury resulted.
- The prosecutive merit of the complaint, i.e., whether there is evidence upon which a grand jury may be expected to return an indictment (to be determined by consultation with the prosecutor).
- The desirability of trial and disposition of the entire offense in one court when the juvenile's associates in the alleged offense are adults who will be charged with a crime in the US District Court for the District of Columbia.

- The sophistication and maturity of the juvenile as determined by consideration of his home, environmental situation, emotional attitude, and pattern of living.
- The record and previous history of the juvenile, including previous contacts with the Youth Aid Division, other law enforcement agencies, juvenile courts and other jurisdictions, prior periods of probation to this Court, or prior commitments to juvenile institutions.
- The prospects for adequate protection of the public and the likelihood of reasonable rehabilitation of the juvenile (if he or she is found to have committed the alleged offense) using procedures, services, and facilities currently available to the juvenile court.

In re Gault

The US Supreme Court decision in the 1967 case of *In re Gault* provides guidelines for juvenile court procedures.[13]

Facts of the case: Gerald Francis Gault was fifteen years old at the time he was committed to the State Industrial School by the Juvenile Court of Gila County, Arizona. On June 8, 1964, Gault and a friend were taken into custody by the Gila County sheriff based on a verbal complaint of a neighbor. The neighbor claimed that Gault had made a telephone call to her that contained lewd and indecent remarks. At the time of the alleged call, Gerald was on six months' probation from a court order issued because he was in the company of another boy who had stolen a wallet from a lady's purse.

When Gault was taken into custody his parents were at work. No notice was provided to the parents that he was in custody, nor was it posted at their residence. No steps were taken to advise the parents of the location of their son. When Gault's mother arrived home and found Gault was not present, she sent his oldest brother to look for him. Later that evening, they learned that Gault was in custody at the Children's Detention Home. When his mother contacted the home, she was informed by a deputy probation officer that Gerald was in custody and that a hearing in his case would be held in juvenile court at 3:00 p.m. the following day.

The Court noted that the arresting officer, Flagg, filed a petition with the court on the day of the hearing, but no copy was served on the parents or on Gault. They did not see the petition until August 17, 1964, at a habeas corpus hearing filed by the parents to set aside the commitment. The petition for delinquency adjuration was stated in formal language but contained no supporting factual statements regarding the basis for the action. The petition alleged only that "said minor is under the age of eighteen years, and is in need of the protection of this Honorable Court." The petition requested that "a hearing be held and that an order be issued regarding the care and custody of the said minor."

Gault, his mother, his older brother, the probation officer, and Officer Flagg appeared before the juvenile court judge on June 9, 1964. Mrs. Cook, the complainant, was not present. No one was sworn. No witnesses were called. No transcript of the proceeding or memorandum of the substance of the hearing was made.

There was a conflict over what occurred at the hearing. According to Gault's mother, Gault admitted dialing the telephone, but claimed that he gave the telephone to his friend who made the remarks. Officer Flagg stated that Gault admitted making the lewd remarks. After the hearing, Gault was taken back to the detention home. He was released from custody on either June 11 or 12. There was no explanation as to why he was released.

When he was released, the mother received a letter signed by Officer Flagg. The entire text of the letter is as follows:

Mrs. Gault:
Judge McGhee has set Monday, June 15, 1964, at 11:00 a.m. as the date and time for further hearing on Gerald's delinquency.
Signed,
Flagg

At the June 15 hearing, a probation report was filed with the juvenile court. The contents of the report were not disclosed to Gault or his parents. The report listed the charge against Gault as "lewd phone calls." Gault's mother requested that Mrs. Cook be called so that she could identify which youth made the remarks. The judge denied her request.

After the hearing, the judge committed Gault as a delinquent to the State Industrial School until he was twenty-one unless sooner discharged by due process of law. The Court noted that had Gault been tried in adult criminal court, the maximum jail term would have been six months. At that time, Arizona law did not provide for an appeal from a juvenile court holding. The parents filed a writ of habeas corpus to get Gault released from the institution. After a court denied the appeal, the denial was appealed to the US Supreme Court.

The Court noted that the state was proceeding as *parens patriae* of Gault. The doctrine of *parens patriae* was currently being used by juvenile courts to rationalize the exclusion of juveniles from the due process clause of the US Constitution. The Court held that the *parens patriae* doctrine's meaning was murky and its historic credentials were of dubious relevance. The Court also noted that there was no history of the doctrine of *parens patriae* being used in criminal procedures.

The Supreme Court noted that from the inception of the juvenile court system, wide differences had been tolerated between the procedural rights accorded to adults and those accorded to juveniles. From the start, the idea of crime and punishment was to be abandoned. The child was to be treated and rehabilitated. The right of the state, as *parens patriae*, to deny to the child the procedural rights available to his or her elders was elaborated by the assertion that a child, unlike an adult, has a right not to liberty but to custody. He or she can be made to heed parents, go to school, etc. If his or her parents default in effectively performing their custodial functions—that is, if the child is delinquent—the state may intervene. In doing so, it does not deprive the child of any rights because he or she has none. It merely provides the custody to which the child is entitled. On this basis, proceedings involving juveniles were described as civil, not criminal, and therefore not subject to the requirements which restrict a state when it seeks to deprive a person of liberty.

The Supreme Court determined that the initial hearing in the case was not a hearing on the merits, notice was not timely, and there was no conceivable purpose served by the deferral proposed by the juvenile justice court. The Court held that it requires that the child and his parents or guardian be notified, in writing, of the specific charge of factual allegations to be considered at the hearing, and that such written notice be given at the earliest practicable time.

The Court also decided that the concept of fundamental fairness must be made applicable to juvenile delinquency proceedings, and that the due process clause of the Fourteenth Amendment required that certain procedural guarantees were essential to the adjudication of delinquency.

Gault stands for the proposition that juveniles who have violated a criminal statute and who may be committed to an institution in which their freedom may be curtailed are entitled to:

- Fair notice of the charges against them.
- The right to be represented by counsel.
- The right to confrontation and cross-examination of witnesses against them.
- The right to the privilege against self-incrimination.

The Court, however, did not hold that juvenile offenders were entitled to all the procedural guarantees applicable to adults charged in criminal cases. The Court's decision was not clear as to what rights should apply to nondelinquent children before the juvenile court. The practical effects of the *Gault* decision were that juvenile courts could no longer deal with children in a benign and paternalistic fashion (that the courts must process juvenile offenders within the framework of appropriate constitutional procedures). *Gault* stands for the proposition that the right to counsel, the privilege against self-incrimination, and the right to fair notice are applied at all stages of the juvenile justice process.

Breed v. Jones

In *Breed v. Jones* the US Supreme Court provided additional answers to questions involving transfer proceedings.[14] The case is discussed in more detail in chapter 13. The Breed case held:

- Due process prohibits trying a juvenile in adult court after there has been a prior adjudicatory juvenile hearing involving the same misconduct.
- A finding of probable cause to hold the youth may be established at the transfer hearing without violating the double jeopardy protection if the child is transferred to adult criminal court.
- Since the same evidence is often used in both the transfer hearing and the subsequent trial in either adult or juvenile court, a different judge is required at trial from the judge that was involved in the transfer hearing.

In re Winship

In the case of *In re Winship*, the Supreme Court held that due process requires the standard of proof beyond a reasonable doubt for juvenile adjudication proceedings.[15] The New York Family Act (at the time) defined a juvenile delinquent as any person over the age of seven and less than sixteen years of age who does any act which, if done by an adult, would constitute a crime.

Facts of the case: The family court found that the youth had entered a locker and stolen $112 from a woman's pocketbook. The family court judge noted that proof of guilt might not be established beyond a reasonable doubt, but that the New York Family Act required that any determination at the conclusion of an adjudicatory hearing must be based on a preponderance of evidence. The New York Court of Appeals affirmed the decision, and the case was appealed to the US Supreme Court.

The Court traced the history of the requirement that guilt of a criminal charge be established by proof beyond a reasonable doubt, noting that this requirement dates at least from our early years as a nation. The Court determined that "observance of the standard of proof beyond a reasonable doubt will not compel the States to abandon or displace any of the substantive benefits of the juvenile justice process." The Court determined that the constitutional safeguard of proof beyond a reasonable doubt is as much required during the adjudicatory stage of a delinquency proceeding as are those safeguards applied in *Gault*.

McKeiver v. Pennsylvania

In *McKeiver v. Pennsylvania* in 1971, the US Supreme Court not only denied juveniles the constitutional right to a jury trial, but it also retreated from the previously standard practice of judicial equalization of procedure in adult and juvenile courts. In the case, the Court recognized that while recent constitutional cases had focused on the issue of fundamental fairness in fact-finding procedures, juries are not actually an essential part of due process for juvenile justice.[16]

Facts of the case: Joseph McKeiver, a sixteen-year-old juvenile, was charged with the crimes of robbery, larceny, and receiving stolen goods. His counsel requested a jury trial at the adjudication hearing. His request was denied in accordance with Pennsylvania law. On appeal, the case was consolidated with the *Terry v. Pennsylvania* case. Both cases involved the same issue: the right of juveniles to a jury trial. Edward Terry was charged with assault and battery on a police officer and conspiracy. At the time of the acts, Terry was fifteen years old. Like Joseph McKeiver's case, counsel also requested a jury trial and was denied. At the adjudication hearings, both youths were adjudged to be delinquents.

The Supreme Court stated that the right to an impartial jury in all federal criminal prosecutions is guaranteed by the Sixth Amendment. The Court also noted that trial by jury in serious criminal cases is fundamental to the United States' scheme of justice. The Court held that trial by jury in the juvenile court's adjudicative stage is not a constitutional requirement for state juvenile justice systems. The Court opined that if the formalities of the criminal adjudicative process are to be superimposed upon juvenile courts, there is little need for a separate court system.

Sentencing and Commitment Issues

Roper v. Simmons

The *Roper v. Simmons* case, decided by the US Supreme Court in 2005, examined whether the death penalty could be imposed on individuals who were under the age of eighteen when the crime was committed.[17]

Facts of the case: Simmons was accused of committing a capital murder when he was seventeen years old. After he had turned eighteen, he was sentenced to death for the crime. His direct appeal and subsequent petitions for state and federal post-conviction relief were rejected. The Court noted in *Atkins v. Virginia* that the Eighth Amendment, applicable to the States through the Fourteenth Amendment, prohibits the execution of a mentally retarded person.[18] Simmons filed a new petition for state post-conviction relief, arguing that *Atkins*' reasoning established that the Constitution prohibits the execution of a juvenile who was under eighteen—by this reasoning, not fully developed mentally or morally—when he committed his crime. The Missouri Supreme Court agreed and set aside Simmons's death sentence in favor of life imprisonment without eligibility for release. The Court ruled that the Eighth and Fourteenth Amendments forbid the imposition of the death penalty on offenders who were under the age of eighteen when their crimes were committed.

The Court noted that the Eighth Amendment's prohibition against "cruel and unusual punishments" must be interpreted according to its text, by considering history, tradition, and precedent, and with due regard for its purpose and function in the constitutional design. The Court established the propriety and affirmed the necessity of referring to "the evolving standards of decency that mark the progress of a maturing society" to determine which punishments are so disproportionate as to be "cruel and unusual." The Court determined that the death penalty was a disproportionate punishment for juveniles.

The Court noted that capital punishment must be limited to those offenders who commit "a narrow category of the most serious crimes," and whose extreme culpability makes them "the most deserving of execution." The Court pointed out that the general differences between juveniles under eighteen and adults demonstrate that juvenile offenders cannot be classified among the worst offenders. Juveniles' susceptibility to immature and irresponsible behavior means "their irresponsible conduct is not as morally reprehensible as that of an adult." Their vulnerability and comparative lack of control over their immediate surroundings mean juveniles have a greater claim than adults to be forgiven for failing to escape negative influences in their whole environment.

The Court noted that juveniles' struggle to define their identity means it is less supportable to conclude that even a heinous crime committed by a juvenile is evidence of irretrievably depraved character. The Court stated that once juveniles' diminished culpability is recognized, it is evident that neither of the two penological justifications for the death penalty—retribution and deterrence of capital crimes by prospective offenders—provides justification for imposing that penalty on juveniles.

The Court concluded that a juvenile offender's objective immaturity, vulnerability, and lack of true depravity should require a penalty less severe than death. When a juvenile commits a heinous crime, the State can exact forfeiture of some of the most basic liberties, but the State cannot extinguish his life and his potential to attain a mature understanding of his own humanity. While drawing the line at eighteen is subject to the objections always raised against categorical rules, this is the point where society draws the line for many purposes between childhood and adulthood, and the age at which the line for death eligibility ought to rest.

Graham v. Florida

In *Graham v. Florida*, the Supreme Court held that sentencing a juvenile defendant to life imprisonment without the possibility of parole violated the Eighth Amendment.[19]

Facts of the case: Terrance Graham was sixteen when he committed armed burglary and another crime. Under a plea agreement, the Florida trial court sentenced Graham to probation and withheld adjudication of guilt. Subsequently, the trial court found that Graham had violated the terms of his probation by committing additional crimes. The trial court adjudicated Graham guilty of the earlier charges, revoked his probation, and sentenced him to life in prison. Because Florida has abolished its parole system, the life sentence left Graham with no possibility of release except via executive clemency. His counsel challenged the sentence under the Eighth Amendment's Cruel and Unusual Punishments Clause. The case was affirmed by Florida's First District Court of Appeal.

The Court held that the Eighth Amendment's Cruel and Unusual Punishment Clause did not permit a juvenile offender to be sentenced to life in prison without parole for a non-homicide crime. The Court noted that embodied in the cruel and unusual punishments ban is the precept that punishment for a crime should be graduated and proportioned to the offense.

The Court stated that implementing the proportionality standard falls within two general classifications: cruel and unusual. In cases of the first type, the Court considers all of the circumstances to determine whether the length of a term-of-years sentence is unconstitutionally excessive for a defendant's crime.

Schall v. Martin

In the *Schall v. Martin* case, the US Supreme Court discussed pretrial detention of juveniles.[20] Section 320.5(3)(b) of the New York Family Court Act authorized pretrial detention of an accused juvenile delinquent based on a finding that there was a "serious risk" that the juvenile "may before the return date commit an act which if committed by an adult would constitute a crime." Appellees—juveniles who had been detained under the Act—brought a habeas corpus class action in Federal District Court, seeking a declaratory judgment that the section violated the Due Process Clause of the Fourteenth Amendment. The District Court struck down the statute as permitting detention without due process and ordered the release of all class members. The Court of Appeals affirmed the decision, holding that, since most of the juveniles detained under the statute either had their cases dismissed before an adjudication of delinquency or were released after adjudication, the statute as administered—not for preventive purposes, but to impose punishment for unadjudicated criminal acts—was therefore unconstitutional as to all juveniles.

The Supreme Court disagreed and held that preventive detention under the statute serves a legitimate state objective, held in common with every state, of protecting both the juvenile and society from the hazards of pretrial crime. That objective is compatible with the "fundamental fairness" demanded by the Due Process Clause in juvenile proceedings, and is compatible with that objective. The Court noted that pretrial detention need not be considered punishment merely because a juvenile is subsequently discharged subject to conditions or put on probation.

The Court also held that the procedural safeguards afforded by the Family Court Act to juveniles detained prior to fact-finding provide enough protection against erroneous and unnecessary deprivations of liberty. The Court noted that notice, a hearing, and a statement of facts and reasons are given to the juvenile prior to any detention, and a formal probable cause hearing is then held within a short time thereafter, if the fact-finding hearing is not itself scheduled within three days.

Other Issues Involving Juvenile Rights and Protections

Oklahoma Publishing Company v. District Court in and for Oklahoma City

The *Oklahoma Publishing Company* case involved a court order prohibiting the press from publishing the name and photograph of a youth involved in a juvenile court proceeding.[21] The material in question was obtained legally from a source outside the court. The US Supreme Court found the court order to be an unconstitutional infringement on freedom of the press.

Smith v. Daily Mail Publishing Company

The *Daily Mail* case held that state law cannot stop the press from publishing a juvenile's name that it obtained independently of the court.[22] Although the decision did not hold that the press should have access to juvenile court files, it held that if information regarding a juvenile case is lawfully obtained by the media, the First Amendment interest in a free press takes precedence over the interests of preserving the anonymity of juvenile defendants.

Justice Rehnquist stated in his concurring opinion (citations omitted):

> Historically, we have viewed freedom of speech and of the press as indispensable to a free society and its government. But recognition of this proposition has not meant that the public interest in free speech and press always has prevailed over competing interests of the public. Freedom of speech thus does not comprehend the right to speak on any subject at any time, and the press is not free to publish with impunity everything and anything it desires to publish . . . While we have shown a special solicitude for freedom of speech and of the press, we have eschewed absolutes in favor of a more delicate calculus that carefully weighs the conflicting interests to determine which demands the greater protection under the particular circumstances presented.
>
> The Court does not depart from these principles today. Instead, it concludes that the asserted state interest is not enough to justify punishment of publication of truthful, lawfully obtained information about a matter of public significance. So valued is the liberty of speech and of the press that there is a tendency in cases such as this to accept virtually any contention supported by a claim of interference with speech or the press. I would resist that temptation. In my view, a State's interest in preserving the anonymity of its juvenile offenders—an interest that I consider to be, in the words of the Court, of the "highest order"—far outweighs any minimal interference with freedom of the press that a ban on publication of the youth's names entails.

Lassiter v. Department of Social Services

In the *Lassiter* case, the US Supreme Court held that the Constitution does not require the appointment of counsel for indigent parents in every parental status termination proceeding. The Court noted that the decision regarding whether due process calls for the appointment of counsel is to be answered in the first instance by the trial court.[23]

Facts of the case: In 1975, a North Carolina state court adjudicated the petitioner's infant son to be a neglected child and transferred him to the custody of respondent Durham County Department of Social Services. A year later, the mother was convicted of second-degree murder, and she began a sentence of twenty-five to forty years of imprisonment. In 1978, the county petitioned the court to terminate the mother's parental rights.

The petitioner mother was brought from prison to the hearing on the petition, and the court, after determining that she had been given ample opportunity to obtain counsel and that her failure to do so was without just cause, did not postpone the proceedings. The petitioner did not aver that she was indigent, and the court did not appoint counsel for her. At the hearing, the petitioner cross-examined a social worker from the respondent, and both the petitioner and her mother testified under the court's questioning. The court thereafter terminated the petitioner's parental status, finding that she had not contacted the respondent about her child since December 1975, and that she had "willfully failed to maintain concern or responsibility for the welfare of the minor." The North Carolina Court of Appeals rejected the petitioner's sole contention on appeal that, because she was indigent, the Due Process Clause of the Fourteenth Amendment required the State to provide counsel for her. The North Carolina Supreme Court summarily denied discretionary review.

The Court stated that in the circumstances of this case, the trial judge did not deny the petitioner due process of law when he did not appoint counsel for her. The record shows that the petition to terminate the petitioner's parental rights contained no allegations of neglect or abuse upon which criminal charges could be based; no expert witnesses testified; the case presented no especially troublesome points of law; the presence of counsel could not have made a determinative difference for the petitioner; she had expressly declined to appear at the 1975 child custody hearing; and the trial court found that her failure to make an effort to contest the termination proceeding was without cause.

New Jersey v. T.L.O.

In the 1985 case of *New Jersey v. T.L.O.*, the US Supreme Court discusses the issue of what rights a student has under the Fourth Amendment of the US Constitution.[24] The *T.L.O.* case was discussed in chapter 8.

Vernonia School District 47J v. Acton

In *Vernonia School District 47J v. Acton*, the US Supreme Court upheld the constitutionality of a random drug-testing regimen implemented by the local public schools in Vernonia, Oregon.[25] The regimen required student athletes to submit to random drug testing before being permitted to participate in sports. During the season, 10 percent of all athletes were selected at random for testing. The Supreme Court held that although the tests were searches under the Fourth Amendment, they were reasonable, considering the schools' interest in preventing teenage drug use.

United States v. Lopez

The US Supreme Court case of *United States v. Lopez* involved the constitutionality of the Gun-Free School Zones Act of 1990.[26] As a result of the Act, Congress made it a federal offense "for any individual knowingly to possess a firearm at a place that the individual knows, or has reasonable cause to believe, is a school zone."[27]

Facts of the case: On March 10, 1992, the respondent, who was then a twelfth-grade student, arrived at Edison High School in San Antonio, Texas, carrying a concealed .38 caliber handgun and five bullets. Acting upon an anonymous tip, school authorities confronted the respondent, who admitted that he was carrying the weapon. He was arrested and charged under Texas law with firearm possession on school premises. The next day, the state charges were dismissed after federal agents charged the respondent by complaint with violating the Gun-Free School Zones Act of 1990.

The Supreme Court held that the Act neither regulated a commercial activity nor contained a requirement that the possession be connected in any way to interstate commerce. The Court held since the Act exceeds the authority of Congress "[t]o regulate Commerce . . . among the several States . . . ." it was unconstitutional.[28]

Practicum

Dennis is sixteen years old. His parents were divorced, and his mother was awarded custody of Dennis. Dennis does not like living with his mother. He runs away and is taken into custody when he attempts to find his father. He states that if he is returned to his mother, he will again attempt to run away.

What type of juvenile offender is Dennis? If you were the juvenile court judge in this case, how would you dispose of the case?

Summary

- Juvenile justice, like adult criminal justice, is mainly a function of the state or the federal jurisdictions that are not in a state, like the District of Columbia or Puerto Rico.

- Each of the fifty states and the federal jurisdictions differ to some degree in responding to juvenile crime.
- The US Supreme Court has imposed guidelines on how the states should handle juveniles.
- As primitive tribes began to exercise social control over the behavior of their members, generally children were subject to the same control and held to the same standards as the adults.
- In the eighteenth and early nineteenth centuries, delinquent juveniles were tried in adult criminal courts. Those found guilty were punished and confined in jails and penitentiaries.
- The juvenile justice system functioned for many years with only occasional appellate court intervention. That changed in the 1960s and 1970s, when the US Supreme Court altered the juvenile court system by issuing a series of decisions to establish certain constitutional rights for juveniles.
- Houses of refuge were very similar to adult penitentiaries. They were large, fortress-like, congregate-style institutions located in urban areas for youth designated as abandoned, delinquent, or incorrigible.
- The State of Illinois (Cook County) established the first juvenile court in the United States in July 1899. It was one of the first governmental acts that established juvenile delinquency as a legal concept.
- The objective of juvenile court was not to punish juveniles, but to treat and rehabilitate them.
- Juvenile courts today exercise jurisdiction over two categories of offenders: status offenders and criminal delinquents.
- State juvenile courts with delinquency jurisdiction handle cases in which juveniles are accused of acts that would be crimes if adults committed them.
- Dependency proceedings are based on the doctrine of *parens patriae*. Accordingly, the right of a state or federal government to take actions to protect children is based on this doctrine. The doctrine developed in early English common law and refers to the right of the ruler to protect the people.
- In the United States, the *parens patriae* doctrine refers to the government's responsibility as the supreme guardian of children, mentally ill adults, and people who are incompetent to protect themselves.
- The *Kent* and the *In re Gault* cases provided notice that the US Supreme Court would require that the juvenile justice system and its courts follow the constitutional requirements of due process.
- The court that can issue child or juvenile protective orders varies in different states. In most states they are issued by the family or domestic court. For the most part these orders are issued to protect the child or juvenile.

Discussion and Review Questions

1. What is the significance of the *Kent* and *Gault* cases?
2. Explain the differences between status offenses and criminal delinquency offenses.
3. Explain the differences between terminology used in juvenile proceedings and that used in adult criminal courts.
4. Discuss the development of the juvenile justice system.
5. Explain the purpose and goal of the juvenile justice system.
6. Discuss the development of dependency jurisdiction of juvenile courts.

Notes

1. *Kent v. United States*, 383 U.S. 541 (1966).
2. Cliff Roberson, *Juvenile Justice: Theory and Practice* (Boca Raton, FL: CRC Press, 2010).
3. Center on Juvenile and Criminal Justice website posted at www.cjcj.org (accessed February 11, 2019).
4. Center on Juvenile and Criminal Justice website.
5. Marvin Ventrell, "Evolution of the Dependency Component of the Juvenile Court, in A Centennial Celebration of the Juvenile Court 1899–1999," *Juvenile and Family Court Journal*, vol. 49, no. 4 (Fall 1998).
6. Sanford Fox, "The Early History of the Court" in *The Future of Children* (Princeton, NJ: Princeton University), vol. 6, no. 3 (Winter 1996), 29–39.
7. Rich Williams, "Adolescent Development & Competency: Juvenile Justice GuideBook for Legislatures, Briefing Papers on the Important Issues of the Day," vol. 23, no. 39, National Conference of State Legislatures, Denver, Colorado, October 2015.
8. Daryl Purpera, "Evaluation of the Office of Juvenile Justice's Oversight of Safety in Secure Care Facilities," Office of Juvenile Justice, Baton Rouge, State of Louisiana, June 2018.
9. Richard A. Mendel, *The Missouri Model* (Baltimore, MD: Annie C. Casey Foundation, 2010).
10. Ventrell, "Evolution of the Dependency Component of the Juvenile Court."
11. *Kent v. United States*, 383 U.S. 541, 566–67 (U.S. 1966).
12. 322 U.S. 596 1948.
13. *In re Gault* (387 U.S. 1 [1967]).
14. 421 U.S. 519 (1975).
15. 397 U.S. 358 (1970).
16. 403 U.S. 528 (1971).
17. 543 U.S. 551 (2005).
18. 536 U.S. 304 (2005).
19. 560 U.S. 48 (2010).
20. 467 U.S. 253 (1984).
21. 480 U.S. 308, 97 S. Ct. 1045 (1977).
22. 443 U.S. 97, 99 S. Ct. 2667 (1979).
23. 452 U.S. 18 (1981).
24. 469 U.S. 325 (1985).
25. 515 U.S. 646 (1995).
26. 514 U.S. 549 (1995).
27. 18 U.S.C. § 922(q)(1)(A) (1988 ed., Supp. V).
28. U.S. Const., Art. I, §8, cl. 3.

CHAPTER 10

Juvenile Court Hearings

CHAPTER OBJECTIVES

After studying this chapter, the reader should be able to:

- Explain the adjudication process in juvenile court proceedings.
- Understand the requirements before a juvenile may be placed in temporary custody prior to adjudication.
- Explain the importance of the petition in juvenile court.
- Discuss the duties of the juvenile court judge at the detention hearing.
- Understand what rights a juvenile has during the adjudication hearing.

Overview

Juveniles younger than age sixteen at the time of referral to court account for about half of all delinquency cases handled by the juvenile courts. This age group accounts for about 60 percent of person offense cases (assault, battery, rape, homicides, etc.), about 53 percent of property offense cases, and about 49 percent of public order offense cases. Personal offense cases have the largest proportion (about 11%) of very young juveniles (younger than age thirteen at referral), followed by property offense cases (8%) and public order offense cases (7%). There are a smaller proportion of cases involving juveniles younger than age thirteen for drug offense cases (3%).[1]

While a juvenile may be placed in secure detention at various times during case processing, detention is primarily used for temporary holding while youths await adjudication, disposition, or placement elsewhere. Many jurisdictions detain youths if there is reason to believe they are a threat to the community, will be at risk if returned to the community, or may fail to appear at an upcoming hearing. Intake staff may also detain juveniles for diagnostic evaluation purposes. All states require that a detention hearing be held within a few hours or days of placement in detention (usually within twenty-four hours). More than one-quarter of the overall delinquency caseload involves females. In 2016, juvenile courts handled

PHOTO 10.1 Judge Lindsey, a woman, another man, and three boys sitting around a table in the judge's chambers; several other persons sit and stand against the walls of the room in an early informal juvenile court hearing. (Photo courtesy of US Library of Congress Prints and Photographs Division, Washington, DC, LC-USZ62-137719)

235,600 cases involving females, compared with 614,900 cases involving males. Photo 10.1 depicts an early informal juvenile court hearing in 1915.

The racial disproportionality in delinquency cases varies across offense categories. White youth account for a larger proportion of drug offense cases (56%) than any of the other general offense categories. In contrast, black youth are involved in only 18 percent of drug offense cases, accounting for a larger proportion of person offense cases (40%) than any other general offense category. Hispanic youth are involved in 22 percent of drug offense cases, accounting for their largest share across offense categories. Asian and American Indian youth account for a small proportion of cases across all offense categories.

When a juvenile is adjudicated (judged delinquent), it is like a conviction in criminal court. Generally, juveniles are adjudicated in about 58 percent of petitioned cases. After a juvenile has been adjudicated as a delinquent, the court holds disposition hearings to decide what sanctions it should impose on the youth, and whether the court should place him or her under court supervision. Many cases result in multifaceted dispositions, and most involve some type of supervision. A probation order often includes additional requirements, such as drug counseling, restitution to the victim, or community service. In those cases where the court has placed the juvenile under court supervision, formal probation is the most severe disposition ordered in about 50 percent of the cases. About 25 percent of cases are ordered to residential placement as the most severe disposition. A smaller proportion of cases receive some other sanction as their most severe disposition.[2]

According to retired juvenile court judge Leonard Edwards, the decision as to which youth cases should proceed through the court system and which should be resolved less formally is an important, if rarely discussed, issue in our juvenile and family courts. Social workers, probation officers, and prosecutors make the decision on which cases will proceed through the formal court process, resolving most cases that come to their attention in the community with warnings, referrals to services, or agreements for participation in services.[3]

According to Judge Edwards, some juvenile and family court judges worry that many cases are resolved without formal judicial intervention, and that the children in these cases remain at high risk of future harm. He notes that the juvenile court judge decides which cases are permitted through the juvenile courthouse door. These judges act as the gatekeepers and ultimately determine the extent to which the State intervenes in the lives of children and families.

Judge Edwards states that in both delinquency and abuse and neglect matters, the cases that the formal juvenile court system processes set the standard for decisions made throughout the community. Social workers and probation officers know what the judge ultimately decides in their cases, whether the judge dismisses the petition, refers the matter for informal services, or rules that the case will be formally processed through the court system.

Judge Edwards concludes that it is important that the juvenile court judge engage with social work and probation department offices, as well as prosecutors, defense attorneys, and law enforcement representatives, concerning the intake process so that it operates fairly and is consistent with best practices.

The juvenile court intake function is the responsibility of the juvenile probation department or the prosecutor's office. At intake, authorities decide whether to dismiss the case, handle it informally (without filing a petition), or file a petition to formally request an adjudicatory hearing or waiver hearing. About 20 percent of all delinquency cases are dismissed at intake, generally for lack of legal sufficiency. An additional 36 percent are handled informally, with the juvenile agreeing to some sort of voluntary sanction (e.g., restitution). In 50 percent of all delinquency cases, authorities file a petition and handle the case formally.

In all jurisdictions, juvenile court judges may waive juvenile court jurisdiction in certain cases and transfer jurisdiction to criminal court so the juvenile can be tried as an adult. The court decision in these matters follows a review of the case and a determination that probable cause exists to believe the juvenile committed the criminal act. The judge's decision generally centers on the issue of whether the juvenile is amenable to treatment in the juvenile justice system.

The prosecutor may argue that the juvenile has been adjudicated several times previously and that interventions the juvenile court ordered have not prevented the youth from committing subsequent criminal acts. The prosecutor may also argue that the crime is so serious that the juvenile court cannot intervene for the time period necessary to rehabilitate the youth. Waiver and transfer to adult criminal court decisions are discussed in more detail in chapter 13.

The Petition

In adult criminal court, a guilty or not guilty finding is determined at a trial. In juvenile justice, the equivalent process is called the adjudication hearing, and the terms *guilty* or *not guilty* are replaced with terms that are appropriate to the juvenile justice system.

Temporary Custody

In most cases while awaiting disposition of the case, the juvenile will be released to the parents, a guardian, or a responsible relative. Temporary custody while awaiting disposition of the case is generally used only in one of the following situations:

- The juvenile does not have a responsible parent or adult who can and will take care and control of the juvenile.
- The juvenile does not have a suitable place to live.
- The juvenile needs to be in custody for his or her own protection.
- The public or another person needs to be protected from the juvenile.
- The juvenile will probably run away.
- The juvenile has previously disobeyed a court order.
- The juvenile is considered dangerous to the public.

If the juvenile is released rather than placed in temporary custody, certain restrictions may be part of the release, such as the juvenile must submit to searches by law enforcement or may not visit certain areas. A frequent condition of the release is that the juvenile does not commit any criminal behavior while awaiting the disposition of his or her case.

In most states a juvenile can be held in temporary custody for forty-eight hours, not counting weekends or holidays, unless the district attorney files a petition in juvenile court or files charges in adult criminal court.

Case Development

A case in the juvenile system generally starts with the moment a law enforcement officer forms an opinion that a juvenile has committed criminal misconduct. As discussed in chapter 8, as in the adult system, the officer probably has the greatest amount of discretion in the system. The officer may give the juvenile a warning and then release him or her, taking no further action. Another option the officer has is to take the youth to a community program or to a children's shelter for abused or neglected children. The third option the officer has is to write the youth a citation and require the juvenile to appear with his or her parents at a juvenile center.

The fourth and most severe option available to the officer is to detain the juvenile and take him or her to a juvenile intake center. In most states, this option means the juvenile is processed by a probation officer or an investigation officer who investigates the incident. If the misconduct is serious, the officer will usually recommend that charges be filed. If the misconduct is not serious, the officer will most likely recommend informal measures be taken, such as issuing a warning or placing the juvenile on informal probation.

Box 10.1 contains an excerpt from the *State of California's Guide to Juvenile Court*, which explains what is required to file a petition in the state of California. (Other states use similar requirements.)

In general, after the petition is filed in juvenile court, a detention hearing is held to determine if the juvenile should continue in temporary custody, or whether he or she should be detained in custody until the adjudicatory or dispositional hearing is held. The juvenile can contest the reasons that he or she is in custody and has a right to counsel at the detention hearing. The juvenile or his or her counsel may call witnesses to support the youth's position on custody.

A juvenile may be placed in secure detention at various times during treatment in the juvenile justice system. Detention is primarily used for temporary holding while youth await adjudication, disposition, or placement elsewhere. Many states detain youth if there is reason to believe they are a threat to the community, will be

BOX 10.1 Filing of a Petition in Juvenile Court (State of California)

A petition asks the court to get involved. The petition says what the state thinks your child did, and it is the judge's job to decide if the petition is true.

There are two kinds of petitions:

- 601 Petition. The probation department files this petition. It says that a child ran away, skipped school, broke curfew, or disobeyed his or her parents—things that are only against the law because they are done by children. If the judge decides the petition is true, the child can become a "ward" of the court and be called a "status offender."
- 602 Petition. The district attorney's office files this petition. It says that a child did something that would still be a crime if he or she was eighteen or older. This can be a felony, like car theft, drug sales, rape, or murder, or a misdemeanor, like assault or drunk driving. If the judge decides the petition is true, the child becomes a "ward" of the court as a "delinquent." The punishment depends on what the child did.

You have the right to get a copy of the petition. It says what your child is accused of; it does not mean your child is guilty. Make sure you read the petition carefully so you know what your child is being charged with.

Once you receive the petition, you will also receive a notice that tells you about the first hearing, called a "detention hearing."

- If your child is eight years old or older, he or she will also get a notice.
- If your child is locked up, you will get the notice at least five days before the hearing.
- If your child is not locked up, you will get the petition and a notice at least ten days before the hearing.
- If the hearing is less than five days after the petition is filed, you will get the notice at least twenty-four hours before the hearing.

Source: State of California, Judicial Branch, "Guide to Juvenile Court," Sacramento, CA: Judicial Branch, 2019), 1–2. Available at www.courts.ca.gov/1216.htm (accessed March 13, 2019).

at risk if returned to the community, or may fail to appear at an upcoming hearing. Intake staff may also detain a juvenile for diagnostic evaluation purposes. At the detention hearing, the judge reviews the initial detention decision, considers what is in the best interests of the community and/or the youth, and decides whether to continue the youth's detention.

Most states also use detention for sanctioning purposes: Juveniles may be committed to a detention facility as part of a disposition order or as a sanction for a probation violation. Actual detention practices vary substantially across jurisdictions. A youth may be detained and released more than once between referral to court and case disposition. In most delinquency cases, the juvenile is not detained (73% in 2016).

The juvenile court has the duty to make a decision at the detention hearing as to the best place for the juvenile pending the disposition hearing. In most cases, if the court removes the juvenile from the home, the judge must state a reason. The reasons may include:

- The juvenile has failed to obey court orders.
- The juvenile has run away from a detention center.
- There is a high probability that the juvenile would run away if not detained.
- The juvenile needs protection because:
  - The home is not a safe place.
  - The juvenile is addicted to drugs or alcohol.
  - The juvenile has mental issues or physical injuries.
  - The juvenile has committed a serious crime.
  - The court needs to protect other persons from the juvenile.

Waiver of Counsel

An issue in many states is the ability to waive counsel in a juvenile hearing. A related issue is whether the parents or guardian may waive counsel for a juvenile. Various jurisdictions have different rules regarding this developing issue. (For a definitive discussion on the right to waive counsel, please see "Waiver of Counsel in Juvenile Court" by Jennifer Woolard, Document Number 253015 (June 2019), available online at National Institute of Justice website, https://nij.gov.)

Juvenile Justice Hearings

In most jurisdictions, the juvenile justice process includes four hearings: a temporary custody hearing; a jurisdiction or intake hearing; an adjudicatory hearing; and a judicial disposition hearing.

Temporary Custody Hearing

The temporary custody hearing was discussed earlier in this chapter.

Jurisdiction or Intake Hearing

Before a juvenile court may accept a petition, it must have jurisdiction in the case. Jurisdiction equals the power of the court to decide the issues involved. In most jurisdictions the jurisdiction or intake hearing must take place as soon as reasonably possible if the juvenile is in temporary custody. At the jurisdiction or intake hearing, the judge advises the juvenile of the facts and misconduct alleged in the petition, and what can happen at the hearing. The judge should also advise the parents that if a fine or restitution is imposed at the disposition hearing, the family or guardian may be liable to make those payments.

If the juvenile admits to the misconduct in the petition and the judge decides that the juvenile understands the allegations and possible consequences of admitting that they are true, the judge can immediately hold a disposition hearing or schedule a date for it. If the juvenile denies the allegations in the petition or the judge feels it is in the best interests of the juvenile not to accept the juvenile's admission that the allegations are true, the judge can set an adjudicatory hearing to determine if the petition's allegations should be accepted by the court as true.

Waiver of juvenile court jurisdiction and transferring the case to adult criminal court is discussed in chapter 13. The waiver and transfer is not as frequent as most people think. In 2016, juvenile court judges waived jurisdiction in an estimated 3,500 delinquency cases nationwide, sending them to criminal court. This represents only about 1 percent of all formally handled delinquency cases.

Adjudicatory Hearing

The adjudicatory hearing is the fact-finding hearing, and determines if the allegations against the juvenile stated in the petition are true. If they are found to be true, then the trial judge sets a disposition hearing, at which time the judge determines what is best for the juvenile's care, treatment, and/or guidance.

The adjudicatory hearing is used when the case has not been dismissed, referred to other agencies, dropped, or found to be subject to a consent order. It is the trial for the juvenile and determines if the misconduct alleged in the petition is true. At this hearing, the juvenile has certain due process rights, which include right to counsel, and the requirement that the misconduct be established beyond a reasonable doubt. Two rights that an adult criminal defendant has that do not apply to the juvenile adjudicatory hearing are the right to a jury trial and the right to a public trial. There are, however, a minority of jurisdictions in the United States that do provide these two rights to the juvenile. In some of the jurisdictions, the juvenile's right to a jury trial is limited to certain crimes or circumstances. The US Supreme Court has stated that a juvenile does not have these rights under the due process clause of the US Constitution.

As with an adult criminal court, the burden of producing evidence is placed on the prosecution or district attorney. If no evidence is presented on the allegations included in the petition, then the trial court is required to make a finding that the allegations were not found to be true. Also, as in an adult criminal trial, the juvenile has the right to remain silent.

After the State has presented its case, the counsel for the juvenile may cross-examine witnesses, object to evidence submitted, present its own witnesses and evidence, and present arguments to the court as to why the allegations of misconduct are not true. If the trial judge determines beyond a reasonable doubt that the evidence establishes that the allegations are true, a date is set for the disposition hearing. If the trial judge determines that the allegations have not been established beyond a reasonable doubt, the judge should dismiss the petition.

Judicial Disposition Hearing

Here is a summary of the types of disposition that a juvenile court may take in the disposition of a case:

- **Waived to criminal court:** Cases that were transferred to criminal court as the result of a waiver hearing in juvenile court. As will be discussed in chapter 13, if juvenile jurisdiction is going to be waived and the juvenile is to be referred to adult criminal court, this waiver and transfer must take place before any adjudicatory hearing. As noted in chapter 13, waiver after an adjudicatory hearing probably constitutes a violation of the double jeopardy protection.
- **Placement:** Cases in which youth were placed in a residential facility for delinquents or were otherwise removed from their homes and placed elsewhere.
- **Probation:** Cases in which youth were placed on informal/voluntary or formal/court–ordered probation or supervision. Juvenile probation is discussed in chapter 12.
- **Dismissed:** Cases dismissed (including those warned, counseled, and released) with no further action anticipated. Among cases handled informally, some cases

may be dismissed by the juvenile court because the matter is being handled in another court.

- **Miscellaneous:** A variety of actions not included above. This category includes fines, restitution and community services, referrals outside the court for services with minimal or no further court involvement anticipated, and dispositions coded as "Other" by the reporting courts.

Figure 10.1 is a diagram of juvenile justice proceedings in California which are typical in other US jurisdictions, as well.

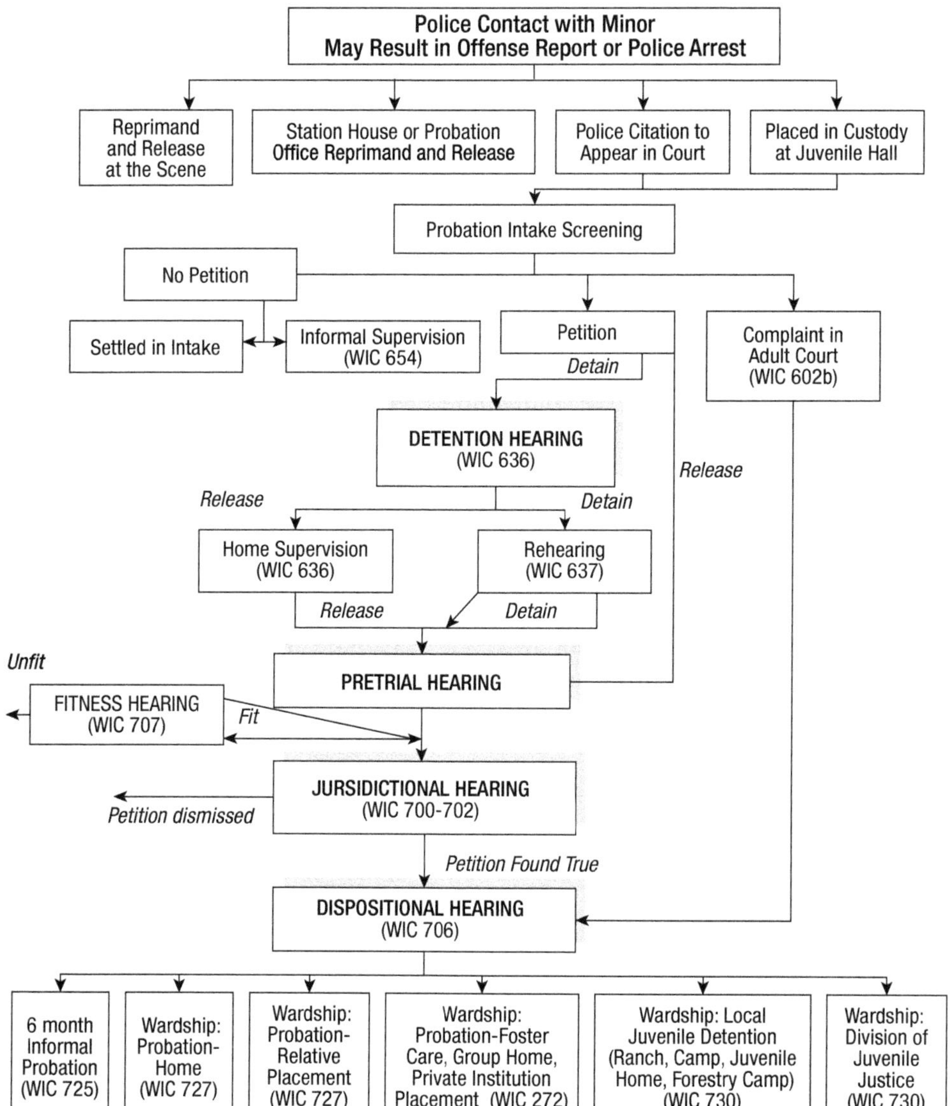

FIG. 10.1 Chart depicting how a minor goes through the juvenile justice system. (*Source*: State of California, Santa Clara Juvenile Justice Website at www.scscourt.org/self_help/juvenile/jjustice/process.shtml, accessed on March 14, 2019.)

Rights at Juvenile Hearings

Right to a Jury Trial

The Sixth Amendment to the US Constitution provides that in all criminal trials, the defendant has the right to a jury. The US Supreme Court through various opinions has held that this right does not completely apply in state courts. In the leading case on this issue, *Duncan v. Louisiana*, the Court held that a defendant in a state criminal case, based on the due process rights contained in the Fourteenth Amendment, has a right to a jury only in serious cases.[4] The *Duncan* rule does not apply to federal courts.

In 1971 in the case of *McKeiver v. Pennsylvania*, the Supreme Court held that juveniles do not have a constitutional right to a jury trial. In the *McKeiver* case, the Court retreated from their previous standard practice of judicial equalization of procedure in adult and juvenile courts. The Court stated that juries are not actually an essential part of juvenile justice due process.[5] The Court's opinion states that imposing a jury trial on the juvenile court system would not remedy the system's defects, and would not greatly strengthen the fact-finding function.

The Court noted that the applicable due process standard in juvenile proceedings is fundamental fairness, as developed by the *In re Gault*[6] and *In re Winship*[7] cases, which emphasized fact-finding procedures. The Court noted, however, that in our legal system, a trial by jury is not a necessary component of accurate fact-finding. The *Winship* case held that the standard of proof in a juvenile case was the same as in an adult criminal case—proof beyond a reasonable doubt.

The *Gault* case held that a juvenile had the following rights in an adjudicatory hearing:

- Fair notice of the charges against him or her.
- The right to be represented by counsel.
- The right to confrontation and cross-examination of the witnesses against the juvenile.
- The privilege against self-incrimination.

Right to a Public Trial

Public trials have long been thought to provide such benefits as alerting witnesses unknown to the parties, educating the public about the legal system, and checking possible judicial abuses through contemporaneous review in the forum of public opinion. The possibility of alerting unknown witnesses can be especially important in situations where their input prevents the unjust infliction of punishment that would otherwise be imposed. Unjustly punishing a juvenile is no more defensible than doing so to an adult. As for the concern with educating the public about the legal system, the public has a deep interest and needs to be educated regarding the juvenile system.

In most states, statutory juvenile laws do not acknowledge an unconditional public right of access to juvenile courts. In many states, juvenile hearings are closed to the public and the press. The concept of the need for confidentiality is used to deny juveniles the right to a public trial.[8] One California appellate court stated "that a First Amendment right of access does not extend to juvenile delinquency hearings."[9]

If the hearing is not open to the public, then who may attend? Legislation restricting access to the juvenile courts is often ambiguous and misleading. Most statutes provide that persons with a direct or proper interest have a right of access to juvenile proceedings but fail to define what is considered a direct or proper interest. This issue raises an interesting question: Which is more important—protecting the privacy of juveniles, or providing juveniles and the public the right to a public trial?

Right to a Speedy Trial

In all US jurisdictions, juveniles are provided the right to a speedy hearing. For example, the State of Illinois statute, IC 31-37-11 (a typical state statute on the issue), provides that when a juvenile is held in detention, the State (prosecuting attorney) must file a delinquency petition within seven days, excluding weekends and holidays, after the juvenile is taken into custody. Failure to do so will result in release of the juvenile. When a juvenile is held in detention and a delinquency petition has been filed, a fact-finding hearing or a waiver hearing must be held within twenty days, excluding weekends and holidays, after the petition is filed. Failure to do so will result in release of the juvenile. When the juvenile is not in detention, a fact-finding hearing or a waiver hearing must be held within sixty days, excluding weekends and holidays, after the petition is filed. These time limitations may be extended if delay is caused by the juvenile, or other extraordinary circumstances.

Right to an Interpreter

This appears to be one aspect of the juvenile justice system that has been decided. In *Lau v. Nichols*, the US Supreme Court interpreted Civil Rights Act, Title VI's prohibition on national origin discrimination to include discrimination based on inability to speak English.[10] The Court therefore included language as an aspect of national origin, and the juvenile has a right to an interpreter if he or she does not understand or speak English.

Right to Bail

An adult criminal defendant has the right to have a bail hearing if he or she is detained prior to trial. There does not appear to be a similar right for juveniles. This is probably based on the concept that normally juveniles should be released to their parents or guardians unless there are justifiable reasons for placing the juvenile in custody. Some states, like Wisconsin, specially provide that juveniles are not eligible for bail.

For example, the Illinois Juvenile Court Act provides no provision for an absolute right of release from custody on bail. According to this Act, if the court finds that it is a matter of immediate and urgent necessity—for the protection of the minor or of the person or property of another—that the minor be detained, or that he is likely to flee the jurisdiction of the court, it may prescribe detention or shelter care and order that the minor be kept in a suitable place designated by the court; otherwise, it shall release the minor from custody. In contrast, the adult criminal defendants have an absolute right of release, and factors similar to those above are important only in determining the amount of bail.

An early Pennsylvania state court noted that a child does not have the right to freedom; a child has a right not to liberty but to custody, and that the child should be in the custody of his or her parents. The court stated:[11]

> The natural parent needs no process to temporarily deprive his child of its liberty by confining it in his own home, to save it and to shield it from the consequences of persistence in a career of waywardness, nor is the state, when compelled, as

parens patriae, to take the place of the father for the same purpose, required to adopt any process as a means of placing its hands upon the child to lead it into one of its courts. When the child gets there and the court, with the power to save it, determines on its salvation, and not its punishment, it is immaterial how it got there.

Appealing a Juvenile Adjudication

The US Supreme Court decision of *In re Gault* has been interpreted to provide a juvenile defendant with the right to appeal an adjudication of delinquency and to have a higher court review this adjudication for possible errors, just as an adult would be able to appeal a conviction.[12] The Court's decision applies to cases which hold that juveniles accused of crimes in a delinquency proceeding must be afforded many of the same due process rights as adults, such as the right to timely notification of the charges; the right to confront witnesses; the right against self-incrimination; and the right to counsel.

Other decisions by the Court, like the *In re Winship*[13] case, have held that juveniles have certain due process rights, including the right to require the government to prove beyond a reasonable doubt that the allegations in the petition are true; and cases like *Breed v. Jones*,[14] involving transfer proceedings, hold that the right of transfer must be provided to the juvenile. As a result, juveniles can clearly appeal on those grounds and on other procedural errors.

Box 10.2 contains excerpts of official court documents questioning the standards to be used by a court where the finding of misconduct by the juvenile was based on the youth's confession. The case involving sixteen-year-old Brendan Ray Dassey was discussed in the popular Netflix documentary series *Making a Murderer*.

Persons Involved in the Hearings

The primary individuals involved in the criminal justice system include counsel, a trial judge, probation officers, and the investigative personnel. Probation officers are discussed in chapter 11. In this section we will discuss the three officials primarily involved in the juvenile hearings: the juvenile defense counsel, the juvenile prosecutor, and the juvenile hearing judge.

Right to Counsel

Juvenile cases can be complex. Accordingly, juveniles who are facing incarceration have a right to a defense attorney who fully understands the rules and laws and can communicate them effectively to the juvenile delinquent. The right to counsel applies to each phase of the juvenile court system process.

In adult criminal cases, the defense attorney must comply with the directions of the defendant as to the important issues: whether to present evidence, testify, plea to enter, etc. The rules are not as clear in juvenile cases. One question that is often debated is whether the counsel works for the juvenile or for the juvenile's parents. There has been no clear-cut court decision on this issue.

According to a statement posted on the North Carolina Office of the Juvenile Defender website, an attorney in a juvenile delinquency proceeding or in an order to show cause proceeding against an undisciplined juvenile shall be the juvenile's voice to the court, representing the expressed interests of the juvenile at every stage of the proceedings. The attorney owes the same duties to the juvenile under the Rules of Professional Conduct, including the duties of loyalty and confidentiality, just as an attorney owes to an adult criminal defendant. Also, the decisions regarding

BOX 10.2 *Brendan Dassey v. Michael A. Dittmann*

860 F3rd 933 (December 8, 2017)
Excerpts from US Court of Appeals, Seventh Circuit's Opinion

Whether Dassey's confession was voluntary or not is measured against a general standard that takes into account the totality of the circumstances. . . . Some factors would tend to support a finding that Dassey's confession was not voluntary: his youth, his limited intellectual ability, some suggestions by the interrogators, their broad assurances to a vulnerable suspect that honesty would produce leniency, and inconsistencies in Dassey's confession. Many other factors, however, point toward a finding that it was voluntary. Dassey spoke with the interrogators freely, after receiving and understanding Miranda warnings, and with his mother's consent. The interrogation took place in a comfortable setting, without any physical coercion or intimidation, without even raised voices, and over a relatively brief time. Dassey provided many of the most damning details himself in response to open-ended questions. On a number of occasions, he resisted the interrogators' strong suggestions on particular details. Also, the investigators made no specific promises of leniency.

A person arguing his confession was involuntary must show that the police engaged in coercive practices. . . . The Supreme Court has made it clear that juvenile confessions call for "special care" in evaluating voluntariness. . . . In juvenile cases, the law is particularly concerned with whether a friendly adult is present for or consents to the interrogation. Concerns about physical exhaustion, naiveté about friendly police in the context of an adversarial police interview, and intellectual disability also take on heightened importance for assessing whether a juvenile's will was overborne. . . . Dassey's case presents different factors pointing in opposite directions. Those most important to our analysis include: his age and intellectual ability; the physical circumstances of the interrogation; the manner and actions of the police in questioning Dassey, including bluffing about what they knew and assuring him of the value of honesty; Dassey's resistance or receptiveness to suggestions by interrogators; and the extent to which he provided the most incriminating information in response to open-ended, non-leading questions.

In *Fare v. Michael C.*, 442 U.S. 707, 727 (1979), the [US Supreme] Court again ruled that a juvenile confession was voluntary. Like Dassey, Michael C. was sixteen years old. He claimed that the police made promises and threats during the interrogation "in the hope of obtaining leniency for his cooperative attitude." Michael C. indicated that his pleas to stop the interrogation were ignored. He also claimed he feared police coercion and pointed out that he "wept during the interrogation." Despite these assertions, the Court determined that Michael C.'s claims of coercion were "without merit."

[The appellate court, overruling the previous opinion of a three-judge panel, held that the finding of the state court that the confession was voluntary was affirmed. As of 2020, Brendan continues to serve his life sentence at the Columbia Correctional Institution in Portage, Wisconsin. He will be eligible for parole in 2048.]

whether to admit to allegations of a petition and whether to testify are those of the juvenile, after consultation with the attorney. Decisions regarding the method and manner of conducting the defense are those of the attorney, after consultation with the juvenile.[15]

According to the National Juvenile Defender Center, the juvenile defender enforces the client's due process rights; presents the legal case and the social case; promotes accuracy in decision-making; provides alternatives for decision-makers; and monitors institutional treatment, aftercare, and reentry.[16]

Prosecutor

Like the adult criminal court prosecutor, the juvenile prosecutor's primary duty is not to prosecute, but to ensure justice. There is, however, a serious issue as to what "justice" means in juvenile proceedings. The prosecutor must protect the interest of the State and/or jurisdiction by creating a more-balanced system, instilling due process of the law. The prosecutor should present the evidence at a juvenile hearing in a fair and impartial manner. The roles and responsibilities of the juvenile prosecutor extend beyond the courtroom. Much of the prosecutor's work can and should be done outside the courtroom. Working collaboratively with other youth-serving agencies in their communities, prosecutors often play a leadership role in these efforts.

Like the duties in adult criminal court proceedings, the prosecutor has a wide spectrum when it comes to discretion and enforcing laws and prevention methods. This discretion can and does directly impact the juvenile delinquent. Juvenile prosecutors may recommend confinement, treatment programs, and/or intervention programs.

Hearing Judge

While co-author Cliff Roberson was a professor of criminology at California State University, Fresno, he also served as judge pro tem (temporary judge when the regularly assigned judge was unavailable) in the superior and municipal courts in Fresno County. After serving in adult criminal court for several years, one day he was assigned as the family law judge for juvenile cases.

His first case involved a petition for the revocation of probation for a fourteen-year-old female who had violated probation. When the case was called at 8:00 a.m., no parent appeared for the juvenile. The appointed public defender stated to the court that he had talked to the mother the day prior to the court date, and the mother had informed him that she normally did not get up that early in the morning. So, she would just forgo her right to be there for her daughter's hearing. The hearing was rescheduled and a subpoena was issued ordering the mother to appear at the hearing. The question in the hearing officer's mind was what kind of home life did the daughter have with a mother who failed to voluntarily appear when her daughter was facing possible incarceration in an institution?

The juvenile court judge or hearing officer is the central actor in the juvenile court system. The role of the judge is complex and requires him or her to meet certain responsibilities that help to ensure a balanced juvenile court system while also protecting the interests of both the juvenile and the community. Duties of the judge include:

- Presiding over prehearing issues, hearings, and appeals;
- Issuing detention location of juvenile before trial;
- Deciding over plea bargains/arrangements;
- Presiding over evidence presented in the case;

- Conducting an orderly hearing in which witnesses are questioned and evidence presented;
- Ascertaining facts alleged in the petition; and
- Providing recommendations for treatment.

Responses and Plea Bargaining

In adult criminal court there are generally three or four pleas that a defendant may enter. In most states, the defendant may plead guilty, not guilty, or the equivalent of no contest. In some states the adult criminal may plead not guilty by reason of insanity. When an adult defendant pleads guilty, the trial judge is required to ensure on the record that the plea is willingly and knowingly entered. Plea bargaining is very prominent in adult criminal court, especially as about 90 percent of concluded cases are based on guilty pleas. In many US jurisdictions there are formal plea agreements that need to be submitted in order for a plea bargain to be accepted, and the trial judge is not bound to accept a plea agreement.

In a juvenile hearing, the juvenile does not plead guilty or not guilty. He or she either admits the allegations in the petition or denies them. In the latter case, a denial is equivalent to a not guilty plea in adult criminal court.

By placing society's interest in "caring for its young" over the individual rights of juveniles, the juvenile justice system has created a situation where the determination of a child's "treatability" has become more important than the determination of whether the allegations in the petition are sustained. In most US jurisdictions, the concept of plea bargaining is not regulated or frequently discussed. It does, however, occur. Frequently during the intake or adjudicatory hearing there will be a discussion as to the disposition of the case if the juvenile admits the allegations contained in the petition. Joseph Sanborn, in his study of juvenile case processing in Philadelphia, concluded that about 20 percent of the cases at adjudicatory hearings were disposed of by informal agreements.[17]

Practicum

You are the juvenile court judge and are hearing a case where Jerry is alleged to have committed the crime of statutory rape (sex with a person under the lawful age to consent, i.e., a child). Jerry's counsel demands a public trial under the US Constitution.

How would you explain to his counsel the reasons that the juvenile does not have a right to a public trial?

Summary

- Juveniles younger than the age of sixteen at the time of referral to court account for about half of all delinquency cases handled by the juvenile courts.
- While a juvenile may be placed in secure detention at various times during case processing, detention is primarily used for temporary holding while youth await adjudication, disposition, or placement elsewhere.
- When a juvenile is adjudicated (judged delinquent), it is like a conviction in criminal court. Generally, juveniles are adjudicated in about 58 percent of petitioned cases.
- After a juvenile has been adjudicated as a delinquent, the court holds disposition hearings to decide what sanctions it should impose and whether the court should place the juvenile under court supervision.

- At intake, authorities decide whether to dismiss the case, handle it informally (without filing a petition), or file a petition to formally request an adjudicatory hearing or waiver hearing.
- In adult criminal court, a guilty or not guilty finding is determined at a trial. In juvenile justice, the equivalent process is called the adjudication hearing, and the terms *guilty* or *not guilty* are replaced with terms that are appropriate to the juvenile justice system.
- A case in the juvenile system generally starts when a law enforcement officer forms the opinion that the youth has committed criminal misconduct.
- In most jurisdictions, the juvenile justice process contains four hearings: temporary custody hearing, jurisdiction or intake hearing, adjudicatory hearing, and disposition hearing.
- The adjudicatory hearing is the fact-finding hearing and determines if the allegations against the juvenile stated in the petition are true. If they are found to be true, then the trial judge sets a disposition hearing, at which time the judge decides what is best for the juvenile's care, treatment, and/or guidance.
- Two rights that an adult criminal defendant has that do not apply to the juvenile adjudicatory hearing are the right to a jury trial and the right to a public trial.
- In US adjudications, juveniles are provided the right to a speedy hearing.
- The US Supreme Court decision in the *In re Gault* case has been interpreted to provide a juvenile defendant with the right to appeal an adjudication of delinquency and to have a higher court review this adjudication for possible errors, just as an adult would be able to appeal a conviction.
- The right to counsel applies to each phase of the juvenile court system process.
- In a juvenile hearing, the juvenile does not plead guilty or not guilty. He or she either admits the allegations in the petition or denies them. In the latter case, a denial is equivalent to a not guilty plea in adult criminal court.

Discussion and Review Questions

1. What is the purpose of the detention hearing?
2. What is required before a juvenile may be detained while waiting for the adjudication hearing?
3. How is plea bargaining involved in the juvenile justice system?
4. What rights does a juvenile have during any hearings in juvenile court?
5. What is the role of defense counsel in juvenile court hearings?
6. Why don't juveniles have a right to bail while awaiting their hearings?
7. Explain how a case is developed in the juvenile system.

Notes

1. Charles Puzzanchera and Crystal Robson, "Delinquency Cases in Juvenile Court, 2010," National Report Series (Washington, DC: US Department of Justice, February 2010).
2. Puzzanchera and Robson, "Delinquency Cases in Juvenile Court, 2010."
3. Leonard Edwards, "Intake Decisions and the Juvenile Court System," *Juvenile and Family Justice Today* (Spring 2011), 17–20.
4. *Duncan v. Louisiana*, 391 U.S. 145 (1968).
5. *McKeiver v. Pennsylvania*, 403 U.S. 528 (1971).
6. *In re Gault*, 387 U.S. 1 (1967).
7. *In re Winship*, 397 U.S. 358 (1970).
8. Susan S. Greenebaum, "Conditional Access to Juvenile Court Proceedings: A Prior Restraint or a Viable Solution?" *Washington University Journal of Urban and*

Contemporary Law, vol. 44 (1993), 135. Available at http://openscholarship.wustl.edu/law_urbanlaw/vol44/iss1/5 (accessed March 14, 2019).

9. *San Bernardino County Department of Public Social Services et al. v. Superior Court of San Bernardino*, 283 Cal. Rptr. 332, 338–39 (Cal. Ct. App. 1991).
10. *Lau v. Nichols*, 414 U.S. 563 (1974).
11. *Commonwealth v. Fisher*, 213 Pa. 48, 53, 62 A. 198, 200 (1905).
12. *In re Gault*, 387 U.S. 1 (1967).
13. *In re Winship*, 397 U.S. 358 (1970).
14. *Breed v. Jones*, 421 U.S. 519 (1975).
15. North Carolina Office of the Juvenile Defender Website at http://ncids.org/JuvenileDefender/Role/Role%20Statement.pdf (accessed March 15, 2019).
16. National Juvenile Defender Center, "National Juvenile Defense Standards," 2012, retrieved from http://njdc.info/wp-content/uploads/2013/09/NationalJuvenileDefenseStandards2013.pdf (accessed March 15, 2019).
17. Joseph Sanborn, "Philosophical, Legal, and Systematic Aspects of Juvenile Court Plea Bargaining," *Crime and Delinquency*, vol. 39 (1993), 509–26.

CHAPTER 11

Juvenile Corrections

CHAPTER OBJECTIVES

After studying this chapter, the reader should be able to:

- Understand why probation is a favorite disposition for delinquents.
- Discuss the various dispositions available to the juvenile court judge.
- Explain the historical development of probation.
- Understand why juvenile justice systems have steadily decreased the use of detention and incarceration of young people.
- Explain the criteria for granting probation.
- Discuss the need for the Interstate Compact for Juveniles.
- Understand the duties and responsibilities of juvenile probation officers.
- Explain how restorative justice works in the juvenile system.

Juvenile Probation

This chapter examines the correctional assistance services available in juvenile corrections. Since probation is the preferred disposition used by juvenile court judges, it is discussed first. Currently, most jurisdictions are deemphasizing secure juvenile detention centers as exemplified by the early shutdown of Massachusetts secure facilities.

Juvenile probation has been termed the "workhorse of the juvenile justice system."[1] Probation appears to be the primary disposition of a juvenile's case when the court considers that community treatment is appropriate. A juvenile who is on probation remains in the community under the supervision of a probation officer. While on probation the juvenile is required to comply with a set of rules and conditions that must be met in order to remain on probation. Before placing a juvenile on probation, the juvenile court judge makes the determination that the juvenile is not a danger to the community, and that supervised community treatment will benefit the delinquent.

Probation does not typically involve prolonged confinement for the juvenile; if any is ordered, at most it will involve only short periods. Under probation, the juvenile court retains authority over the case to supervise, modify the conditions, and resentence the juvenile if the terms of probation are violated. Probation is a legal status created by the juvenile court. While the definition of probation indicates that it does not involve commitment, it is increasingly linked to a short period of commitment at a training school, boot camp, or other local custody facility.

Probation permits the youth to remain in the community under the supervision of the juvenile probation officer. Probation usually involves:

- A judicial finding that the behavior of the child has been such as to bring him or her within the purview of the court. In other words, the juvenile is determined to have committed the alleged offense or offenses.
- Release of the juvenile with the imposition of conditions upon the youth's continued freedom.
- The provisions to help him or her meet these conditions and for determining the degree to which he or she needs them.
- Probation is not just giving the youth another chance; its central thrust is to give the youth assistance in adjusting to the free community.

Nationwide, over 70 percent of all delinquents who appear at a disposition hearing receive probation. Between 2005 and 2016, the number of cases adjudicated delinquent that resulted in an order of probation decreased 53 percent, compared with a 54 percent decrease in the number of cases that resulted in out-of-home placement. See Table 11.1 for a breakdown of the cases.

Probation is a mechanism used by juvenile justice agencies at many different points in the system. It serves as a sanction for juveniles adjudicated in court, and in many cases as a way of diverting status offenders or first-time juvenile offenders from the court system. Some communities may even use probation as a way of informally monitoring at-risk youth and preventing their progression into more-serious

TABLE 11.1 Offense Profile of Juvenile Cases Resulting in Probation

Offenses	2005	2016
Serious offenses	26%	29%
Property crimes	36%	33%
Drug offenses	13%	12%
Public order offenses	26%	26%
Total number resulting in probation	333,700	155,500

Probation remains the most likely sanction imposed by juvenile courts. Probation was the most restrictive disposition used in 62 percent (155,500) of the cases adjudicated delinquent in 2016, compared with 60 percent (333,700) of the adjudicated caseload in 2005.

Between 2005 and 2016, the likelihood of probation for cases adjudicated delinquent was relatively stable for person, property, and public order offense cases, varying by 2 to 4 percentage points, compared with an 8 percentage point range for drug offense cases.

The offense characteristics of cases adjudicated delinquent that resulted in probation changed little between 2005 and 2016, with a slight increase in the proportion of cases involving person offenses and decreases in the proportion of cases involving drug and property offenses. The proportion of public order offense cases remained the same.

Note: Detail may not total 100 percent because of rounding.

Source: Sarah Hockenberry and Charles Puzzanchera, "Juvenile Court Statistics 2016" (Washington, DC: National Center for Juvenile Justice, August 2018).

problem behavior. With such varied uses, there is no doubt that probation touches large numbers of juveniles.

A 2018 study by the Annie E. Casey Foundation noted that in the past twenty years, the nation's juvenile justice systems have steadily decreased the unnecessary use of detention and incarceration of young people. The study points out that the large reduction in confinement has not resulted in significant changes to its primary alternative—probation—which remains deeply flawed both in concept and execution, despite being the most common disposition in juvenile justice.[2]

Historical Development

Although the birth of probation is credited to a Boston shoemaker, John Augustus, there are some English cases in the early 1800s where youths were given a one-day prison sentence. The juveniles were conditionally released after serving the day and agreeing to abide by certain rules and regulations.

From 1841 until his death in 1859, John Augustus appeared in court to receive on probation alcoholics who appeared to be suited for probation. It is estimated that over an eighteen-year period, Augustus supervised about two thousand individuals on probation, most of whom were youths between the ages of sixteen and nineteen. He helped them get jobs and reestablish themselves in the community. Only a few of the individuals under his supervision became involved in subsequent criminal behavior.

Augustus's work inspired the Massachusetts state legislature to authorize the hiring of a paid probation officer for Boston. By 1880, other jurisdictions in the state began to use probation in lieu of imprisonment. By 1890, probation had become a formal part of the state court system in Massachusetts. Missouri and Vermont soon followed suit, and by 1925, the federal government had also established probation services. With the growth of juvenile courts during this same period, probation became an important part of the juvenile court system.

In one of the first cases that Augustus was involved in, the defendant was ordered to appear in court for sentencing in three weeks. At the sentencing hearing, the defendant signed a pledge and promised to become a sober person. The judge was impressed, and fined the defendant one cent.

Probation Practices in Juvenile Justice

Juvenile probation is based on the philosophy that the average delinquent is not a violent or dangerous criminal and is not a danger to the community; rather, he or she is a youth who needs additional guidance in order to conform to society's demands. Probation may involve replacing the youth's commitment to an institution with a conditional release. Probation is essentially a contract between the youth and the juvenile court. If the youth complies with certain orders of the juvenile court (conditions of probation), the court will not require the youth to be committed to a secure facility. If the youth later violates the terms of the contract, the court is no longer restricted by the contract and may commit the youth to a secure facility.

In some states, the youth is informed at the time he or she is placed on probation as to the terms of the commitment being probated. For example, the youth may be committed to a state training school until he or she reaches twenty-one years of age, with the commitment probated for five years. If the youth stays out of trouble for five years, then the commitment is never served. If the youth's probation is revoked, then the youth is committed.

Generally, the youth is placed on probation for a definite period of time. If, however, the probation is revoked, then the youth receives a commitment the length of which is set by the juvenile court judge at a disposition hearing after the probation has been revoked. Generally, states have restrictions on the granting of probation for certain serious crimes. A few states have age limits on the length of the period of probation. In adult criminal cases, it appears that the death penalty may not be probated. This is because the death penalty is limited to those cases where the defendant is beyond rehabilitation. The US Supreme Court has prohibited the use of the death penalty in cases involving juveniles.

The length of the probation period may vary. A five-year period is common for adult felony cases. In fact, the Federal Criminal Code recommends that federal probation periods last for five years. In juvenile cases, the period of probation is usually until the juvenile reaches the age of majority, or the age of twenty-one.

Frequently in adult criminal cases the trial judge will require the defendant to serve a period in jail prior to being placed on probation. For example, one judge, as a matter of policy, does not grant probation in felony cases unless the accused does at least thirty days' time in the local jail. This practice is known as "split sentencing"—something juvenile court judges do not use as a general rule.

Shock Probation

In many adult criminal courts, trial judges will use "shock probation" for youthful offenders who are tried as adults; again, this is typically not used in juvenile courts. In these cases, the judge grants probation only after the accused has sampled prison life. Shock probation is designed to give defendants a "taste of the bars" before placing them on probation.

Evaluations of shock probation have indicated that its rate of effectiveness may be as high as 78 percent. Critics of shock probation claim that even a brief period of incarceration can reduce the effectiveness of probation, which is designed to provide the offender with non-stigmatized community-based treatment.

Criteria for Granting Probation

Listed below are the recommended criteria for granting probation developed by the American Law Institute's Model Penal Code and adapted by the California Penal Code.[3] The criteria are also used in juvenile cases in many jurisdictions.

1. The court shall deal with a person who has been convicted of a crime without imposing sentence of imprisonment unless, having regard to the nature and circumstances of the crime and the history, character, and condition of the defendant, it is of the opinion that his or her imprisonment is necessary for protection of the public because:
   - there is undue risk that during the period of a suspended sentence or probation the defendant will commit another crime;
   - the defendant needs correctional treatment that can be provided most effectively by his or her commitment to an institution; or
   - a lesser sentence will depreciate the seriousness of the defendant's crime.
2. The following grounds, while not controlling the direction of the court, shall be accorded weight in favor of withholding sentence of imprisonment:
   - the defendant's criminal conduct neither caused nor threatened serious harm;
   - the defendant did not contemplate that his or her criminal conduct would cause or threaten serious harm;
   - the defendant acted under a strong provocation;
   - there were substantial grounds tending to excuse or justify the defendant's criminal conduct, though failing to establish a defense;

- the victim of the defendant's criminal conduct induced or facilitated its commission;
- the defendant has compensated or will compensate the victim of his criminal conduct for the damage or injury that he sustained;
- the defendant has no history of prior delinquency or criminal activity or has led a law-abiding life for a substantial period of time before the commission of the present crime;
- the defendant's criminal conduct was the result of circumstances unlikely to recur;
- the character and attitudes of the defendant indicate that he or she is unlikely to commit another crime;
- the defendant is particularly likely to respond affirmatively to probationary treatment;
- the imprisonment of the defendant would entail excessive hardship to the defendant or his or her dependents.

3. When a person has been convicted of a crime and is not sentenced to imprisonment, the court shall place him or her on probation if he or she needs the supervision, guidance, assistance, or direction that the probation service can provide.

Conditions of Probation

Most trial judges believe that a probated disposition is an act of clemency on the part of the court. Accordingly, the court may place conditions that restrict an individual's constitutional rights. For example, a judge may require that the youth voluntarily submit to searches and/or drug testing when requested by the juvenile probation officer. Generally, there are two sets of conditions that are imposed on a probationer: standard conditions that are imposed on every probationer; and special conditions designed specifically for a defendant.

Set forth below are the standard rules or conditions of probation used in the state of North Carolina which are very similar to those used in most states. It is common for states to establish in their criminal procedure codes basic conditions of community supervision for juvenile probationers. Box 11.1 contains excerpts from the Texas handbook of the process that takes place when a juvenile is placed on probation. Most states follow similar procedures.

Conditions of Probation

North Carolina Statute 7B-2510 is typical of the conditions placed on a juvenile when the juvenile is granted probation. This statute provides:

(a) In any case where a juvenile is placed on probation pursuant to G.S. 7B-2506(8), the juvenile court counselor shall have the authority to visit the juvenile where the juvenile resides. The court may impose conditions of probation that are related to the needs of the juvenile and that are reasonably necessary to ensure that the juvenile will lead a law-abiding life, including:
   (1) That the juvenile shall remain on good behavior.
   (2) That the juvenile shall not violate any laws.
   (3) That the juvenile shall not violate any reasonable and lawful rules of a parent, guardian, or custodian.
   (4) That the juvenile attend school regularly.
   (5) That the juvenile maintains passing grades in up to four courses during each grading period and meets with the juvenile court counselor and a representative of the school to make a plan for how to maintain those passing grades.

BOX 11.1 What Happens When a Child Is Placed on Probation?

Excerpts from the Texas Attorney General's Handbook:
2018 Juvenile Justice Handbook

A juvenile court judge may place a child on probation at home, the home of a relative or other suitable person, a foster home, a suitable residential treatment facility, or post-adjudication secure correctional facility other than those operated by TJJD (§54.04(d)(1), F.C.). A juvenile may be removed from the family home if the child cannot be provided the quality of care and level of support and supervision that is needed to successfully complete probation (§54.04(c), F.C.). If a child is placed on probation, the terms of probation must be in writing, and a copy of the court's order must be furnished to the child (§54.04(f), F.C.).

Under court-ordered probation, a child can be required to attend school, abide by curfews, attend counseling, participate in specified programs. and make restitution (ch. 59, F.C.). Community service is a mandatory condition of probation, subject only to limited exceptions (§54.044(a), F.C.). A juvenile may be placed on probation for any term, but in most cases not past his or her eighteenth birthday (§54.04(l), F.C.).

The court must order DPS to suspend a juvenile's driver's license or permit, or deny the issuance of a license or permit, if the juvenile is adjudicated for certain intoxication, controlled substance, or trafficking in persons violations (§54.042, F.C.). The court may also order DPS to suspend or deny a child's license if the juvenile is adjudicated for a graffiti offense or any CINS or delinquent conduct offense for a period not to exceed twelve months. The order must specify a period of suspension or denial not to exceed 365 days (§54.042(b)-(d) and (f), F.C.).

A probation officer is assigned to each juvenile probationer. The probation officer meets with the child on a regular basis to provide supervision and guidance. The probation officer also monitors the child's school attendance and reports to the court if the child is voluntarily absent from school.

If a child breaks any of the probation terms, he or she may be returned to juvenile court for a hearing to modify or revoke the probation. Parents may be expected to participate in their child's probation program—possibly through family counseling, parenting classes, making restitution, or paying all or part of the reasonable costs of treatment programs in which the child is required to participate while on probation (§54.041, F.C.). In some cases, parents may even be ordered to perform community service with their child (§54.044(b), F.C.). If a juvenile court places a child on probation in a determinate sentencing case and transfers supervision on the child's nineteenth birthday to an adult district court for placement on community supervision, the district court must require the payment of any unpaid restitution as a condition of the community supervision. This extends the child's, but not the parent's, responsibility to make restitution after the case is transferred to district court for community supervision (§54.041(h), F.C.).

Note: F.C. (Family Code) and TJJD (Texas Juvenile Justice Department).

Source: Office of Texas Attorney General, 2018 Juvenile Justice Handbook (Austin, TX: Texas Juvenile Justice Department, 2019), available at https://www.texasattorneygeneral.gov/sites/default/files/files/divisions/juvenile-justice/JuvenileJusticeHandbook.pdf (accessed March 11, 2019).

(6) That the juvenile not associate with specified persons or be in specified places.
(7) That the juvenile:
  a. Refrain from use or possession of any controlled substance included in any schedule of Article 5 of Chapter 90 of the General Statutes, the Controlled Substances Act;
  b. Refrain from use or possession of any alcoholic beverage regulated under Chapter 18B of the General Statutes; and
  c. Submit to random drug testing.
(8) That the juvenile abides by a prescribed curfew.
(9) That the juvenile submits to a warrantless search at reasonable times.
(10) That the juvenile possesses no firearm, explosive device, or other deadly weapon.
(11) That the juvenile report to a juvenile court counselor as often as required by the juvenile court counselor.
(12) That the juvenile makes specified financial restitution or pay a fine in accordance with G.S. 7B-2506(4), (5), and (22).
(13) That the juvenile be employed regularly if not attending school.
(14) That the juvenile satisfies any other conditions determined appropriate by the court.

In addition to the regular conditions of probation specified in subsection (a) of this section, the court may, at a dispositional hearing or any subsequent hearing, order the juvenile to comply, if directed to comply by the chief court counselor, with one or more conditions.

Interstate Compact on Juveniles

The Interstate Compact on Juveniles (ICJ) is a multistate agreement that provides the procedural means to regulate the movement across state lines of juveniles who are under court supervision. The ICJ is a legal contract between all fifty states, the District of Columbia, the Virgin Islands, and Guam that provides for the monitoring and/or return of any juvenile who:

- Has run away from home without the consent of a parent or legal guardian.
- Is placed on probation or parole and wants to reside in another state.
- Has absconded from probation or parole or escaped from an institution and is in another state.
- Requires institutional care and specialized services in another state.
- Has a pending court proceeding as an accused delinquent or neglected or dependent juvenile and runs away to another state.

In the early 1950s, *Parade* magazine published a series of articles entitled "Nobody's Children," which depicted the plight of runaways in the United States.

Inspired by these articles, and recognizing that action was needed, a group of organizations sought to develop a uniform set of procedures to facilitate the return of juveniles who had run away to other states, and to create a system in which juvenile offenders could be supervised in other states. Representatives from the Council of State Governments, National Council on Crime and Delinquency (formerly the National Probation and Parole Association), National Council of Juvenile and Family Court Judges, American Public Welfare Association, National Association of Attorneys General, and Adult Parole and Probation Compact Administrators Association drafted the Interstate Compact on Juveniles (ICJ) to meet these needs. The Compact was approved by these organizations in January 1955, and ratified by all fifty states, the District of Columbia, the Virgin Islands, and Guam by 1986.[4]

Juvenile Probation Officers

Juvenile probation officers, also referred to as juvenile correctional treatment specialists, work exclusively with adolescents who have been convicted of a crime and put on probation, rather than being sentenced to jail time. Juvenile probation officers also work with underage individuals who have already served time in jail and are on parole. A college degree in criminal justice or a similar field is typically required, and candidates may also be required to pass a certification exam.

Juvenile probation officers meet with these adolescents and their families to perform assessments and research their family and social history. They are responsible for making regular visits to the youths' homes to make sure that they are complying with terms set by the juvenile court. They also work with the juvenile's family, as well as the court system, to provide counseling for the juvenile and to change or eliminate behavioral issues. If a youth does not comply with his or her court order, the juvenile probation officer must then provide recommendations to the judge for alternate sentencing or treatments.

Restorative Justice

Restorative justice refers to the process of seeking to understand and repair the harm that was done in a given situation, with a focus on restoring the victim and repairing damaged relationships, rather than on punishing the offender. Peacemaking circles, victim–offender mediation, community and family group conferencing, and peer mediation are some of the ways restorative justice can be applied.[5]

The Office of Juvenile Justice and Delinquency Prevention (OJJDP) of the US Department of Justice describes restorative justice this way: "While most approaches to juvenile justice concentrate on punishing or treating delinquent youths, the restorative justice process seeks to repair the harm by involving the entire community in rehabilitating offenders and holding them accountable for their behavior."

According to the Juvenile Justice Initiative website, the current juvenile justice system relies heavily on costly and harmful incarceration and punitive probation, treating black and brown children with disparate, inhumane, and excessively punitive sanctions. This punitive approach has poor outcomes, high recidivism, and little victim satisfaction. The website notes that other nations, including Northern Ireland and South Africa, have set positive examples for healing the wounds of violence and mass incarceration. Unjust sentencing practices have been dramatically altered in Canada and New Zealand, with a shift toward restorative justice aligned with international human rights protections, including proportionality.

The OJJDP has published a national assessment of policy and development for restorative justice.[6] According to the policy, *balanced and restorative justice*

(BARJ) is a framework for juvenile justice reform that seeks to engage citizens and community groups both as clients of juvenile justice services and as resources in a more effective response to youth crime. To do this, the balanced approach mission attempts to ensure that juvenile justice intervention is focused on basic community needs and expectations. Communities expect justice systems to improve public safety, sanction juvenile crime, and habilitate and reintegrate offenders. True balance is achieved when juvenile justice professionals consider all three of these needs and goals in each case, and when a juvenile justice system allocates its resources equally to meeting each need.

Restorative justice is a way of thinking about and responding to crime. It emphasizes one fundamental fact: Crime damages people, communities, and relationships. If crime is about harm, then the justice process should emphasize repairing the harm. As a vision for systemic juvenile justice reform, restorative justice suggests that the response to youth crime must also strike a balance among the needs of victims, offenders, and communities, and that each should be actively involved to the greatest extent possible in the justice process. Restorative justice builds on traditional positive community values and on some of the most effective sanctioning practices, including victim–offender mediation, various community decision-making or conferencing processes (e.g., reparative boards, family group conferencing, and circle sentencing), restorative community service, restitution, victim and community impact statements, and victim awareness panels.

According to the policy, treatment and punishment alone are not capable of meeting the needs of the community, victim, offender, and family. For most of the citizenry, juvenile justice is an esoteric system wrapped in a riddle. Support comes from understanding; understanding, from involvement and participation. Community involvement and active participation in the working of a juvenile court is a reasoned response.

Balanced and Restorative Justice Probation

Some jurisdictions, including Pennsylvania, have adopted the balanced and restorative justice (BARJ) approach to juvenile justice. The BARJ model is a concept developed in part by the OJJDP of the US Department of Justice in order to make the philosophy of restorative justice applicable to the modern US justice system. BARJ uses restorative justice principles to balance the needs of three parties: those identified as offenders or law violators; the crime victims; and the affected community. BARJ is not a program, but rather a philosophy with a coherent set of values and principles to guide the administration of justice.[7] BARJ's goals include:

- **Accountability.** BARJ strategies are designed to provide opportunities for offenders to be accountable to those they have harmed and enable them to repair the harm they caused to the extent possible.
- **Community safety.** BARJ is designed to keep the community safe. Community safety can be accomplished by building relationships and requiring the community to take responsibility for the well-being of its members.
- **Competency development.** BARJ understands the need to increase the pro-social skills of offenders as well as addressing the factors that lead youth to engage in delinquent behavior. It also builds on the strengths evident in each youth to increase their competencies.

BARJ views crime as harmful to both the involved individuals and to the community. Accordingly, crime is not merely a violation of state laws. To accomplish the BARJ approach, the administration of justice should be guided by both the interests of the state and the interests of victims and community members.

It uses the approach that crime may produce a clear victim—an individual who was directly harmed—or victims who were harmed indirectly. For example, drug crimes may appear to have no clear victim, but families and communities are very much affected when one of their members abuses drugs. The involvement of both direct and indirect victims of crime is necessary in the justice process in order for delinquents to gain a better understanding of the harm they have caused, and to increase their empathy for others.

The BARJ philosophy is different from the philosophies of retribution and rehabilitation. The BARJ approach notes that retribution reacts to an offense through punishment, while rehabilitation seeks to improve the individual offender through treatment. In both philosophies, offenders remain relatively passive and are not required to accept responsibility for their crimes. Because of this, retributive and rehabilitative systems may act to encourage offenders to deny responsibility, based in part on the adversarial processes involved in the determination of guilt and appropriate punishment.

According to Jessica Ashley and Phillip Stevenson, who have worked on ways to implement balanced and restorative justice, research has shown that BARJ:

- Offers a more cost-effective means to handle crime over the traditional court system.
- Reduces recidivism rates.
- Increases satisfaction of victims and offenders with the justice system.
- Improves competencies of offenders.
- Increases completion of restitution agreements.
- Lessens the fear felt by victims of crime.
- Increases community involvement.
- Provides individualized attention and services for offenders and their victims.

Part of the BARJ approach is the community justice movement, which aims to increase collaboration with the community to improve the effectiveness of police departments and courts, including prosecutors, defense attorneys, and probation officers. BARJ attempts to involve all parties who have an interest in and are affected by crime.

In Deschutes County, Oregon, probation professionals have embraced the concept of community justice by discontinuing the use of the term "probation department" and renaming it the "community justice department." The county department works closely with citizen groups, schools, faith-based organizations, and businesses in the community. Staffers in the county department are not optimistic about using punishment as a deterrent to crime. They are not convinced the traditional corrections models are very effective in reducing recidivism. Researchers Dennis Maloney and Holcomb Deevy reported that one staff member said:[8]

> We do know that we will never know as much about a community as the community residents themselves do. Our relationship to the community, therefore, is based on the reality that citizens must step forward and become centrally involved, working daily to build community, prevent crime, assist victims, and help offenders make reparation.

According to Maloney and Deevy, community probation holds promise as a vehicle for improving the practices and performance of the juvenile justice system, especially when guided by the BARJ philosophy. The researchers note that while aspects of community probation are consistent with the principles of BARJ, some probation departments continue to rely on punitive measures as the formal response of the justice system.

To implement BARJ, Ashley and Stevenson state that communities should consider the following:

- Offenders should be provided, when appropriate, with meaningful community service options.
- A probation agreement should include specific ways that offenders will complete payment of victim restitution. Since many young offenders find it difficult to pay, the burden of payment often falls on the offender's parents. Offenders can work to repair the harm they caused, ideally in areas that increase their competencies. For example, an offender can work for a business owner from whom he or she stole or repair damage that was the result of vandalism or graffiti.
- Communities can help in finding ways to assist juvenile offenders in paying restitution.
- Victim impact panels should be established to allow crime victims of similar offenses to share their experiences and the impact of crime with offenders.
- Victims who do not want to meet with offenders may provide written statements in lieu of meeting with offenders.
- Offenders who are unable to apologize to victims in person may write letters to their victims or others affected by their offense. The content of these letters should be reviewed before being shared with victims to ensure that they are sincere and will cause no further harm.

Juvenile BARJ-based programs often have several elements in common:

- They are offered to juvenile offenders who are willing to accept full responsibility.
- They are provided with participant referrals at the discretion of the juvenile justice system.
- They are facilitated by a trained individual, who may be an employee of a juvenile justice agency, an allied nonprofit agency, or a volunteer from the community.
- They involve victims and/or community members in the process, but participation is voluntary.
- They keep proceedings confidential.

Revocation of Probation

This section details the legal requirements before a juvenile's probation can be revoked and the juvenile is detained in custody at a residential facility, or other action is taken by a juvenile court.

A juvenile has limited due process rights before his or her probation is revoked. In *Morrissey v. Brewer*,[9] the US Supreme Court established minimal due process requirements for parole revocation proceedings under the Fourteenth Amendment to the US Constitution. As to the revocation of probation, the Court held that "a probationer, like a parolee, is entitled to a preliminary and a final revocation hearing, under the conditions specified in *Morrissey*."[10] Thus, a State "must provide the same process [found in *Morrissey*] when terminating a probationer from probation."[11]

In *Gagnon v. Scarpelli*, 411 U.S. 778 (1973), the US Supreme Court ruled on the rights of individuals in violation of a probation or parole sentence. The Court held that a probationer's sentence can only be revoked after a preliminary revocation hearing and a final revocation hearing.

While *Morrissey* and *Gagnon* holdings make clear that probationers do not retain the full constitutional protections afforded criminal defendants, a probationer has a protected liberty interest in continued probation, and is therefore entitled to due process before probation may be revoked. *Morrissey* and *Gagnon* set forth those minimum due process requirements.

A probation revocation hearing is different from an adjudication or disposition hearing in juvenile court. A probation revocation hearing occurs when a youth is alleged to have violated the terms of the probation agreement. In adult criminal court the probationer has the right to counsel and a hearing. It is assumed that the US Supreme Court would require at least that in a juvenile revocation. In cases involving adults, the burden of proof is not beyond a reasonable doubt, as required in the original criminal trial, but only by a preponderance of the evidence as to whether the terms of the agreement have been violated. A similar holding is expected when determining the burden of establishing that the juvenile's probation agreement has been violated.

In almost all jurisdictions in the United States, and in the federal jurisdictions, the juvenile has a right to:

- Written notice of the violation alleged.
- Notice of the hearing and possible consequences of the outcomes of the hearing.
- Counsel.
- Present evidence at the hearing.
- Appeal the decision of the juvenile judge.

If the juvenile waives the right to counsel or admits the violation, the juvenile judge must make additional inquiries to ensure that the juvenile understands the rights that he or she is waiving.

A typical state statute regarding violations of the terms of a juvenile's probation agreement is Virginia Code 16.1-291: Revocation or modification of probation, protective supervision or parole; proceedings; disposition. Here is a summary of the statute (slightly modified by the authors to enhance clarity):

- A juvenile or person who violates the conditions of his or her probation or parole agreement may be proceeded against for a revocation or modification of such order or parole status.
- A proceeding to revoke or modify probation, protective supervision, or parole shall be commenced by the filing of a petition.
- Except as otherwise provided, such petitions shall be screened, reviewed, and prepared in the same manner and shall contain the same information as provided in §§ 16.1-260 and 16.1-262.
- The petition shall recite the date that the juvenile or person was placed on probation, under protective supervision, or on parole, and shall state the time and manner in which notice of the terms of probation, protective supervision, or parole were given.
- If a juvenile or person is found to have violated the terms of probation or parole, the court may, upon a revocation or modification hearing, modify or extend the terms of the order of probation or parole, including termination of probation or parole.
- However, notwithstanding the contempt power of the court, the court shall be limited in the actions it may take to those that the court may have taken at the time of the court's original disposition.
- In the event that a child in need of supervision is found to have willfully and materially violated an order of the court or the terms of his or her probation, in addition to or in lieu of the dispositions specified in that section, the court may enter any of the following orders of disposition:

- ◦ Order any such child fourteen years of age or older to be (i) placed in a foster home, group home, or other nonsecure residential facility, or, (ii) if the court finds that such placement is not likely to meet the child's needs, that all other treatment options in the community have been exhausted, and that secure placement is necessary in order to meet the child's service needs, detained in a secure facility for a period of time not to exceed ten consecutive days for violation of any order of the court or violation of probation arising out of the same petition.
- ◦ The court shall state in its order for detention the basis for all findings required by this section.
- ◦ When any child is detained in a secure facility pursuant to this section, the court shall direct the agency evaluating the child pursuant to § 16.1-278.5 to reconvene the interdisciplinary team participating in such evaluation, develop further treatment plans as may be appropriate, and submit its report to the court of its determination as to further treatment efforts either during or following the period the child is in secure detention.
- ◦ A child may only be detained pursuant to this section in a detention home or other secure facility in compliance with standards established by the State Board.
- ◦ Any order issued pursuant to this subsection is a final order and is appealable as provided by law.
- ◦ Nothing in this section shall be construed to reclassify a child in need of supervision as a delinquent.

Practicum

A juvenile petition was filed against Joseph alleging that he took an automobile belonging to someone else for a joyride and wrecked the vehicle. At the adjudication hearing the court determined that the allegations were true. It was the second time that a juvenile petition alleging that Joseph had committed criminal misconduct was adjudicated as true.

As juvenile court judge, what are your options regarding the disposition of this case?

Summary

- Juvenile probation has been termed the "workhorse of the juvenile justice system."
- Probation appears to be the primary disposition of a juvenile's case when the court considers that community treatment is appropriate.
- Probation permits the youth to remain in the community under the supervision of the juvenile probation officer.
- John Augustus is considered the originator of the concept of probation.
- In many adult criminal courts, trial judges will use "shock probation" for youthful offenders who are tried as adults. Generally, it is not used in juvenile courts.
- Most trial judges believe that a probated disposition is an act of clemency on the part of the court. Accordingly, the court may place conditions that restrict an individual's constitutional rights.
- The Interstate Compact on Juveniles (ICJ) is a multistate agreement that provides the procedural means to regulate the movement across state lines of juveniles who are under court supervision.

- Juvenile probation officers, also referred to as juvenile correctional treatment specialists, work exclusively with adolescents who have been convicted of a crime and put on probation, rather than being sentenced to jail time.
- Juvenile probation officers also work with underage individuals who have already served time in jail and are on parole.
- *Restorative justice* refers to the process of seeking to understand and repair the harm that was done in a given situation, with a focus on restoring the victim and repairing damaged relationships, rather than on punishing the offender.
- Restorative justice is a way of thinking about and responding to crime. It emphasizes one fundamental fact: Crime damages people, communities, and relationships.
- The harshest sanction that a juvenile court can impose entails the restriction of a juvenile's freedom through placement in a residential facility. Generally, such placement occurs after a youth has been adjudicated delinquent for an offense, but he or she may also be held in detention after arrest or during court proceedings.
- Juvenile parole may be defined as the conditional release of a juvenile from a correctional institution to the community under the supervision of a parole officer. In theory, the juvenile is released from the correctional institution at a time when he or she can best benefit from the release and continued supervision after release.

Discussion and Review Questions

1. Why is the use of probation so popular in juvenile justice?
2. Why do jurisdictions need the Interstate Compact for Juveniles?
3. What is the difference between juvenile probation and juvenile parole?
4. Explain the concepts of restorative justice.
5. What are the primary duties of juvenile probation officers?
6. Why have the rates of secure incarceration of juveniles decreased in the last few years?
7. What are the various dispositions available to the juvenile court judge?
8. What are the criteria for granting probation?

Notes

1. Charles Puzzanchera, "Juveniles on Formal Probation," *Juvenile Justice Statistics Bulletin* (Washington, DC: National Council of Juvenile Justice and Family Court Judges, October 2018).
2. Annie E. Casey Foundation, *Transforming Juvenile Probation: A Vision for Getting It Right* (Baltimore, MD: Annie E. Casey Foundation, 2018). Available at https://www.aecf.org/resources/transforming-juvenile-probation-executive-summary/ (accessed March 10, 2019).
3. Cal Pen Code § 1026.
4. Christopher Holloway, "Interstate Compact on Juveniles" (September 2000), Office of Juvenile Justice and Delinquency Prevention Fact Sheet, posted at https://www.ncjrs.gov/pdffiles1/ojjdp/fs200012.pdf (accessed May 6, 2019).
5. Juvenile Justice Initiative website at https://jjustice.org/about-us (accessed March 10, 2019).
6. Gordon Bazemore and Mark Umbreit, "Restorative Juvenile Justice in the United States: A National Assessment of Policy" (Washington, DC: Office of Juvenile Justice and Delinquency Prevention, October 2000).

7. Jessica Ashley and Phillip Stevenson, "Implementing Balanced and Restorative Justice" (Chicago: Illinois Criminal Justice Information Authority, 2008). Available at https://docplayer.net/677995-Implementing-balanced-and-restorative-justice.html (accessed May 12, 2019).
8. Dennis Maloney and Holcomb Deevy, "In Pursuit of Community Justice: Deschutes County, Oregon," *Youth and Society* vol. 33, no. 2 (2001), 312.
9. 408 U.S. 471, 488–89 (1972).
10. *Gagnon v. Scarpelli,* 411 U.S. 778, 782 (1973).
11. *State v. Rogers*, 144 Idaho 738, 742–43 (2007); *State v. Scraggins*, 153 Idaho 867, 871 (2012).

CHAPTER 12

Juvenile Institutions

CHAPTER OBJECTIVES

After studying this chapter, the reader should be able to:

- Understand the differences between adult and juvenile institutions.
- Discuss the importance of the mission of juvenile institutions.
- Explain the purpose and guidelines for detaining a youth in a detention center.
- Discuss the advisability of placing juveniles in detention.
- Evaluate the success of juvenile boot camps.

Overview

The number of cases involving detention of juveniles decreased between 2005 and 2016 for all offense categories to its lowest level in the analysis period. The largest relative decline since 2005 was for drug offense cases involving detention, down 54 percent, compared with 47 percent for public order offenses, 46 percent for property offenses, and 41 percent for person offenses.[1]

Corrections in the juvenile system are generally classified into two general areas: community corrections and juvenile institutions. The term *community corrections* refers to programs in which the juvenile is "corrected" within his or her community. Probation is the most popular type of community corrections. The term *juvenile institutions* refers to those institutions in which the juvenile is placed in some type of custody, like adult confinement facilities (e.g., jails and correctional institutions). Like adult confinement facilities, juvenile institutions vary according to states and local jurisdictions.

Juvenile institutions continue to be one of the most debated topics involving juvenile justice. There is no general consensus regarding their mission, function, and usefulness, even though they are probably the most important element to be considered. No matter how perfect the police and the courts, if there is a failure in

PHOTO 12.1 Harris County (Houston), Texas, photo of a juvenile justice and detention center. (Photo courtesy of 123rf)

the area of corrections, the overall system will be unsuccessful in reducing crime and rehabilitating juveniles.[2] Photo 12.1 depicts a current-day juvenile institution.

Juveniles who have been adjudicated as delinquent and who are not considered appropriate for probation or who are detained prior to the adjudication hearing are generally placed in a residential facility. (Note: Practices vary in US jurisdictions.)

Detention centers tend to be local facilities; long-term secure facilities tend to be state facilities; and group homes tend to be private facilities. More public facilities are local than state, but state facilities hold more youths. Local facilities (those staffed by county, city, or municipal employees) make up more than half of all public facilities, but fewer than half of all juvenile offenders are held in public facilities. Group homes outnumber all other types of juvenile facilities.

Sexual Violence in Juvenile Institutions

The Prison Rape Elimination Act of 2003 (PREA; P.L. 108-79) requires the Bureau of Justice Statistics (BJS) to carry out, for each calendar year, a comprehensive statistical review and analysis of the incidence and effects of prison rape. PREA further specifies, "The review and analysis . . . shall be based on a random sample, or other scientifically appropriate sample, of not less than 10 percent of all Federal, State, and county prisons, and a representative sample of municipal prisons."

The National Survey of Youth in Custody (NSYC) provides facility-level estimates of youth reporting sexual victimization in juvenile facilities. Interviews of the youth are conducted using audio computer-assisted self-interview (ACASI) technology with a touchscreen-enabled laptop. The first survey (NSYC-1) was conducted from June 2008 to April 2009, and the second (NSYC-2), from February 2012 to September 2012. The NSYC-1 included more than 9,000 youth from 195 juvenile facilities, and the NSYC-2 included 8,700 youth from 326 facilities. These surveys found that juveniles in detention facilities experience higher rates of sexual victimization (9.5% of youths were victimized in 2012) than adults in prisons (4.0% during 2011–2012) and jails (3.2% during 2011–2012).[3]

According to the 2012 survey, the greatest rates of sexual assault in the country's juvenile detention facilities involve the very staff members charged with supervising and counseling the troubled youngsters. About 10 percent of youth in state-owned or -operated juvenile facilities and state contract facilities reported one or more incidents of sexual victimization. Among the 8,700 youth who participated in the 2012 survey, 833 reported experiencing one or more incidents of sexual victimization. Among the high-rate facilities, most reports of sexual victimization involved nonconsensual sexual acts with another youth and sexual acts with facility staff, excluding touching. When rates of sexual victimization were limited to the most serious nonconsensual acts (excluding touching only, kissing on the lips or another body part, and engaging in other less serious acts), the percentages of youth reporting one or more incidents remained high (between 16.2% and 28.8%).[4]

Residential Treatment

The harshest sanction that a juvenile court can impose entails the restriction of a juvenile's freedom through placement in a residential facility. Generally, such placement occurs after a youth has been adjudicated delinquent for an offense. But a youth may also be held in detention after arrest or during court proceedings.

Out-of-home placement results in a burden both on the youths who receive this sanction and on the juvenile justice system itself. The youth experience a disruption in their normal routines, schooling, and family/social relationships. The juvenile justice system must bear the responsibility for mental health care, substance abuse treatment, and education, among other requirements. In 2016, more than 45,000 juvenile offenders were held in residential placement on any given day in the United States.[5]

Houses of Refuge

The development of residential custody centers for juveniles in the United States developed from the "house of refuge" movement. Originally houses of refuge were "training schools" and not prisons. As noted by the Supreme Court of Pennsylvania in the *Ex parte Crouse* case of 1839, the house of refuge was not a prison, but a school.[6] According to the Court:

> Where reformation, and not punishment, is the end, it may indeed be used as a prison for juvenile convicts who would else be committed to a common goal; and in respect to these, the constitutionality of the act which incorporated it, stands clear of controversy. It is only in respect of the application of its discipline to subjects admitted on the order of the court, a magistrate or the managers of the Almshouse, that a doubt is entertained. The object of the charity is reformation, by training its inmates to industry; by imbuing their minds with principles of morality and religion; by furnishing them with means to earn a living; and, above all, by separating them from the corrupting influence of improper associates. To this end may not the natural parents, when unequal to the task of education, or unworthy of it, be superseded by *parens patriae*, or common guardian of the community? It is to be remembered that the public has a paramount interest in the virtue and knowledge of its members, and that of strict right, the business of education belongs to it. That parents are ordinarily entrusted with it is because it can seldom be put into better hands; but where they are incompetent or corrupt, what is there to prevent the public from withdrawing their faculties, held, as they obviously are, at its sufferance?

> The right of parental control is a natural, but not an unalienable one. It is not excepted by the declaration of rights out of the subjects of ordinary legislation; and it consequently remains subject to the ordinary legislative power which, if wantonly or inconveniently used, would soon be constitutionally restricted, but the competency of which, as the government is constituted, cannot be doubted. As to abridgment of indefeasible rights by confinement of the person, it is no more than what is borne, to a greater or less extent, in every school; and we know of no natural right to exemption from restraints which conduce to an infant's welfare. Nor is there a doubt of the propriety of their application in the instance. The infant has been snatched from a course which must have ended in confirmed depravity; and, not only is the restraint of her person lawful, but it would be an act of extreme cruelty to release her from it.

Despite these statements of the Pennsylvania Supreme Court, research reflects that these houses of refuge essentially operated as prisons for youth.

Training Schools

The 1979 *Manual of Standards for Juvenile Training Schools and Services* states that "alternatives to incarceration provide juvenile corrections administrators with the vehicle for and the hope of solving many delinquency problems. However, incarceration of some juveniles for a period is mandatory."[7] Whether incarceration of some juveniles is necessary continues to be an issue in juvenile justice today, with many professionals calling for the elimination of juvenile incarcerations.

While the residential training schools developed from the houses of refuge, they have changed considerably in recent years. The New Jersey Training School (NJTS) is an example of a modern residential training school. The New Jersey Juvenile Justice Commission's largest juvenile facility currently houses approximately two hundred male juveniles. Opened in 1867 as a home for troubled youth, today's NJTS is a secure facility with a state-of-the-art perimeter fence and a twenty-four-hour armed roving patrol. Residents range in age from twelve to twenty-three years of age, with most residents sixteen to eighteen years old. The primary focus of NJTS is to provide care, treatment, and custody for juveniles committed by the courts and to create programs that will rehabilitate young offenders. The NJTS campus includes seven cottages that serve as housing units, a full-service school, a vocational building, recreation facilities, a medical facility, and administrative offices.

The NJTS offers several unique vocational opportunities, including an optical lab program which teaches juveniles to craft eyeglasses. NJTS supplies eyeglasses to all juvenile and adult residents in the state. Through this program, several youths have found jobs with optical employers after their release. The NJTS also offers vocational programs in horticulture, equine science, and communications.[8]

The residential training school for New Jersey females is the Juvenile Female Secure Care and Intake Facility. This facility serves as the intake and secure care unit for all juvenile females sentenced to terms of incarceration in New Jersey. It is the only secure facility in the state that provides education, treatment, and custody for committed juvenile females. It is designed to hold forty-eight females, with eight single rooms that serve as detention cells.[9]

Arizona Detention Services Bureau

The Arizona Detention Services Bureau states that it provides safe and secure living quarters for juveniles who must be temporarily held in secure care to maintain the safety of the community or to ensure that the juveniles appear in court. This service includes health care and assessments, educational services, positive programming activities, and counseling services intended to support their success upon release. While secure care will be necessary for some juveniles, the Bureau believes in maintaining respect and dignity for all.[10]

Arizona requires each county to operate a detention center for juveniles who:

- are likely to commit an offense injurious to self or others;
- need custodial protection for their own interests or the interests of the public;
- may be charged as adults for a serious offense;
- would not appear for a court hearing if they were not detained; or
- must be held for another jurisdiction.

Solitary Confinement of Juveniles

Consider this case: In 2010, a sixteen-year-old Bronx native, known as "Peanut" to his family, was accused of stealing a backpack. Despite police not finding a backpack on him when he was searched, and despite a complaining witness's inconsistent stories, the juvenile was arrested and charged with robbery, grand larceny, and assault, and was sent to Rikers Island, New York City's main jail complex. This arrest was particularly serious for him because he was on probation for a prior "youthful" offense—a crime in which he had played a minor role. Because of the backlog in the New York court system, the juvenile was held at Rikers for three years while awaiting trial. Instead of walking across the stage with his classmates at graduation, he was trapped in the "Bing"—the inmates' name for Rikers Island's solitary confinement unit—for up to ten months at a time.[11]

Jessica Lee noted that a Human Rights Watch report found that "youth offenders often spend significant amounts of their time in US prisons isolated from the general prison population." Juveniles can be placed in solitary confinement for a multitude of reasons, ranging from violence against guards to having "unauthorized amounts of clothing or art supplies." Lee noted that the US Department of Justice found that 47 percent of juvenile detention centers used solitary confinement, and some held juveniles for "up to 23 hours a day with no human interaction."[12] Juveniles are placed in solitary confinement across the country. As of 2016, only seven states have placed any prohibition on juvenile solitary confinement, and even within those seven states, there are exceptions to the rule against using juvenile solitary confinement.[13]

According to Andrew Clark, the placing of incarcerated juveniles into solitary confinement continues to occur in certain US states, despite the accumulating evidence that it may cause substantial psychological damage to the teenagers who must endure it. The practice has been widely condemned by professional and human rights organizations amid a growing appreciation of the immaturity and vulnerability of the adolescent brain.

Although several states and the federal government have been successful in abolishing or dramatically reducing the use of juvenile solitary confinement, it remains common practice in many facilities.[14] As recently as 2019, many states were still placing youths in solitary confinement. There does appear to be a nationwide shift toward abolishing solitary confinement for juveniles, which began to take shape in 2016 after former president Barack Obama banned the practice in federal prisons, with a half-dozen states either prohibiting or strictly limiting its use in their youth facilities.

Private Institutions

Private facilities are operated by private nonprofit or for-profit corporations or organizations; likewise, the staff in these facilities are employees of the private corporation or organization. Private facilities tend to be smaller than public facilities. Although private facilities are more numerous than public facilities nationwide, public facilities hold the largest percentage of juvenile offenders on any given day.

As a rule, private and public facilities hold different populations. Compared with public facilities, private facilities have a greater proportion of court-committed juveniles and a smaller proportion of detained juveniles (those who are awaiting adjudication, disposition, or placement elsewhere). Juveniles in placement voluntarily as part of a diversion agreement are rare, regardless of facility type. Compared with public facilities, private facilities hold a smaller share of delinquents and a larger share of status offenders.[15]

Juvenile Parole

Juvenile parole may be defined as the conditional release of a juvenile from a correctional institution to the community under the supervision of a parole officer. In theory, the juvenile is released from the correctional institution at a time when he or she can best benefit from the release and continued supervision after release.

In actual use, *parole* is a broadly used term that refers to the release of any youth from custody. It differs from probation, which usually requires little or no confinement and is administered by juvenile courts on a county-wide basis.[16] Parole is generally administered by a statewide agency on a statewide basis. Normally, parole is granted only after the juvenile has served a significant portion of the sanctioned confinement. Probation is considered a pre-institutional procedure, while parole is considered a continuation of the correctional process. Release on parole is conditional and may be revoked if the terms of parole are violated. In many states, the term *aftercare* is used in lieu of *parole* for juvenile cases. To many social service providers, the term *juvenile aftercare* is more acceptable than the phrase *juvenile parole*. It appears that about half the states use the term "aftercare" and the remaining use the term "parole."

Juvenile parole can be traced back to the houses of refuge that were established in the latter part of the nineteenth century. Parole is more British and European than American. It was first used by the British to offer a conditional release from prison for those prisoners who agreed to work for a certain period in order to regain their freedom. Parole, unlike probation, was originally motivated by economic rather than humanitarian pressures. Parole provided employers with cheap labor and relieved the British government from having to pay the expenses of imprisonment.

The concept of parole is credited to Alexander Maconochie of England and Sir Walter Crofton of Ireland. Alexander Maconochie was born in Edinburgh, Scotland. After a distinguished career in the British navy, he was appointed the first professor of geography at University College in London. Later, he became involved in studying prison conditions at the Tasmania Island penal colony near Australia. In 1838–1839, he published "Thoughts on Convict Management" and "Supplement to Thoughts on Convict Management." He wrote that the proper object of prison discipline is to prepare men for discharge; the first object of prison is to reform prisoners and prepare them to separate with an advantage both to themselves and to society after their release.

Generally, a juvenile is released from parole after a certain period of time; they may be released earlier depending on the whims of the juvenile judge. For the most part, once the juvenile is released from parole, he or she is left to their own devices and are no longer under supervision by the juvenile justice system. Some jurisdictions provide for parole that is accompanied with extensive supervision.

Types of Juvenile Institutions

Juvenile Detention Centers

A juvenile detention center is a secure twenty-four-hour detention facility for juvenile male and female offenders up to age eighteen who have been arrested and are waiting for court disposition or placement. A detention center is generally considered a secure temporary holding facility. An example of a juvenile detention center is the one operated by Hennepin County in the State of Minnesota.

The Hennepin detention center guidelines provide that admission to the center is determined based on detention criteria and the alleged offense. A detention hearing is held to determine if a juvenile will be released or held for additional hearings. During the first twenty-four hours after admission, parents or legal guardians will be allowed to visit their child anytime for half an hour. Only parents or legal guardians can visit. Due to confidentiality laws, siblings, extended family, and children are not allowed to visit. All visitors must present photo identification. After the first twenty-four hours, visitors must follow this schedule:

- Thursday, Friday, Monday, Tuesday, 8:30 to 9:30 p.m.
- Saturday and Sunday, 10:00 to 11:00 a.m.
- There are no visits on Wednesdays.

In addition to a safe and secure environment, a variety of educational programs and services are provided at the Hennepin facility. A diverse range of activities are provided within the living units and in the recreational areas. Activities include leisure, recreational exercise, life skills, debate, meditation, and many other programs that are beneficial to youth. The center provides high-quality care to juveniles residing at the facility. If a parent or resident feels they would like to object to their experience at the facility, they can submit a grievance procedure form.

Residents eighteen years old and younger who have not graduated from high school or have not earned a GED are enrolled in high school in the center. The school offers:

- High school credits that are transferable to a resident's home school; students can earn .25 credit for every eight hours they work on one subject.
- Classes are taught by teachers from Minneapolis Public Schools.
- Afterschool programming to help residents make up credits and/or improve their academic skills.
- A GED readiness program.

Shelters

In some states, shelters are used rather than detention centers. The State of New Hampshire Department of Health and Human Services regulations provide that shelter care is a probable option for a youth that:

- is not trusted to attend his or her next court hearing;
- cannot return home at the moment of placement, but with focused and steady work with the family, there is an expectation that the youth may be able to return to the family home within sixty days;

- cannot return home and is scheduled to be placed in a more-structured residential home, but needs a temporary structured setting while referrals and interviews occur to finalize the final residential placement;
- needs a temporary intensive residential placement while the juvenile probation and parole officer (JPPO) searches for a new structured placement because the youth was ejected from the previous placement for behavior issues; and
- admission to shelter care facilities is open to both a delinquent child and a child in need of services (CHINS). Shelters cannot accept actively suicidal or physically dangerous youth or youth identified as fire setters.

Juvenile Boot Camps

Juvenile boot camps are frequently used for the adjudicated delinquent who needs residential care but does not need to be in a secure facility. The philosophy behind most boot camps is that if you scream and discipline children enough, they will behave. For example, the boot camps in Mississippi are based on the belief that if defiant teenagers are enrolled in the intense, overpowering, military-like setting of a boot camp, they may actually "fall in line." Unfortunately, this "rehabilitation" appears to be only temporary and based out of fear, and thus does not produce any "lasting" changes in teens.

As noted on the Wingate Wilderness Therapy website, there are no research-based studies that have concluded that the use of boot camps provides long-term rehabilitation for youths, especially when comparing actual results with the boot camps' initial predictions for rehabilitation. After attending a boot camp, the chance of a troubled teen relapsing back into unacceptable behavior is about the same as former prison inmates returning to crime.[17]

Reception and Diagnostic Centers

Reception and diagnostic centers are used in many jurisdictions as the initial residential facility for youths. After spending a short period of time in one of these centers, the juvenile is usually placed in a more-permanent residential placement. In the following section, overviews of two typical reception and diagnostic centers are discussed to provide the reader with an understanding of their approach and functions.

Reception and Diagnostic Center and Juvenile Correctional Centers in Virginia

The Commonwealth of Virginia's Department of Juvenile Justice Handbook describes the Reception and Diagnostic Center and the Department's juvenile correctional centers (JCCs) as places to confine and treat youth who have broken the law.[18]

Staff members work together to:

- Provide a safe, structured environment
- Hold the youth accountable for his or her actions
- Help the youth learn to make good decisions
- Help youth do well when he or she is released
- Give the youth an opportunity to take part in educational and vocational services

The Virginia handbook states that the Resident Orientation Program (ROP) starts as soon as a youth gets to the Reception and Diagnostic Center (RDC). The youth will be given clothes to wear and hygiene items like soap and toothpaste. All the youth's personal belongings will be sent back to his or her family or the placing agency. If the youth is male, he will get a haircut; if the youth is female, she will be instructed on how she may wear her hair. Haircuts and/or hairstyles are not optional. Rules about the youth's hair are in place for security and health reasons.

During the youth's time at the RDC, he or she will be given a medical checkup along with other types of checkups and tests. These are very important and will help the staff learn what type of services the youth will need. According to the handbook, the ROP will teach the youths the rules and explain how they should behave. It will also tell them what will happen if they do not follow the rules. The youths will be taught about their basic rights and the tools available to protect them. The youths will also learn about the right to be free from sexual abuse and harassment and the resources provided through the federal Prison Rape Elimination Act.

The handbook states that during the youth's time at the RDC, the youth will be taught how to work as a team member with other residents and the staff in his or her unit. The handbook warns the youth that the days at the RDC will be very full, and there will be little free time. The youth will be required to attend school, exercise, study, and help with cleaning duties. It takes approximately three weeks for the youth to finish the program at the RDC. After completing the program, the youth will then be assigned and moved to the JCC, where the youth will spend his or her commitment.

Juvenile Reception Center in Wisconsin

The Juvenile Reception Center (JRC) in Madison, Wisconsin, is the point of referral for juveniles alleged to have committed a crime that requires temporary custody; for example, the law enforcement agency apprehending the juvenile is unable to release the juvenile to a parent, guardian, or other responsible adult, and/or in situations in which the law enforcement officer believes the juvenile should be referred for secure custody. The JRC also provides a number of other services related to the physical custody of juveniles, and coordinates the sharing of information with the courts, human services, and law enforcement.

Training Schools

The typical training school provides supervision, programs, and services for juveniles. These facilities are designed and operated to ensure that all entrances and exits are under the exclusive control of facility staff, thereby not allowing a juvenile to leave the facility without authorization. A typical state training school is the New Jersey Training School (NJTS), discussed earlier in this chapter.[19] The primary focus of training schools is to provide care, treatment, and custody for juveniles committed by the courts with a focus on rehabilitation.

Juvenile Probation Camps

Juveniles participate in a structured program at these nonsecure residential camps, focusing on outdoor work, including conservation and related activities. Resident age varies from fifteen to eighteen years.

Ranches

These nonsecure residential programs provide services to youth in rural settings. Typically, the residents participate in a structured program of education, recreation, and facility maintenance, including responsibility for the physical plant, its equipment, and its livestock.

Group Homes

Group homes use either day treatment or local public schools for the education component of their programs. Individual and group counseling, substance abuse treatment, and community service are additional components of group home programs. Generally, youth are placed as geographically close to home as possible.

A group home is a community-based, long-term facility in which juveniles are allowed extensive contact with the community, such as attending school or holding a job. In 1917, Father Flanagan established the well-known Boys Town. After that, group homes became popular as an intervention for juvenile offenders. The definition of what constitutes a group home varies; for example, most people include halfway houses in this category.

Generally, a group home refers to a small residential facility that serves from five to fifteen youths, placed there as result of a court order or through interactions with public welfare agencies. Group homes are less restrictive than juvenile detention centers, but more restrictive than family foster care placements. Group homes are generally staff-secured as opposed to locked facilities, and there are fewer restraints on how youth can interact with the community.

According to the Office of Juvenile Justice and Delinquency Prevention (OJJDP), there are more than 660 facilities nationwide that self-identify as group homes. Group homes constitute 27 percent of all reporting facilities and hold about 10 percent of juvenile offenders.[20]

Group homes generally do not provide academic instruction but allow the youths to continue to attend public schools during their placement. Some group homes may have one set of "house parents," while others may use a rotating staff. Some therapeutic or treatment group homes also employ specially trained staff to assist youth with emotional and behavioral difficulties. Although youth are under supervision by staff twenty-four hours a day, staff members are usually not residents of the home.

There is little research on the overall effectiveness of group homes. Frequently, they are seen as the "last stop" before secure detention, and youths referred to them often suffer from serious mental or behavioral problems that have prevented successful placement in foster care. Many researchers believe that small group settings encourage fraternization among delinquents and may actually promote disruptive and deviant behavior. Association with deviant peers within a group home setting could increase antisocial attitudes and problem behaviors, leading to a variety of negative outcomes for youth throughout adolescence and into adulthood.

Juvenile Residential Reentry Centers

A halfway house is also known as a residential reentry center. The purpose of these facilities is to reintegrate former offenders into society after having been in jail. The intention of these centers is to continue offering support services to former inmates. They are based on the premise that jail is not supposed to break the individual, but to rehabilitate him or her. According to the *Juvenile Justice Guidebook for Legislators*, each year about 100,000 juveniles are released from juvenile detention facilities and other out-of-home placements.

An out-of-home placement can be disruptive for juveniles who have family, school, or community support. Juveniles released from confinement experience other challenges in returning to society.[21] According to the report, approximately two-thirds of incarcerated youth are convicted of nonviolent offenses: approximately 32 percent, a property offense; 10 percent, a drug offense; 10 percent, a public order offense; 10 percent, a technical violation of parole or probation; and 5 percent, a status offense.

The report notes that about 70 percent of juveniles in the system are affected with at least one mental illness. Seventy-one percent of juveniles in residential placement struggle with more than one emotional issue, the most common related to anger management, anxiety, and depression. More than half of incarcerated juveniles report experiencing major depression, and nearly two-thirds report experiencing anxiety. In addition, two-thirds of juvenile offenders report regular drug use, not accounting for any alcohol consumption.

The report points out that juvenile offenders are more likely than their peers to be behind academically. More than half of youth in out-of-home placements have not completed the eighth grade, and in state prisons, 66 percent of juveniles have between a ninth- and an eleventh-grade education. Incarcerated youth are three to five times more likely to have special education disabilities than the general juvenile population. The report estimates that 20 to 50 percent of incarcerated youth have attention deficit hyperactivity disorder and nearly 12 percent are developmentally disabled. Not all juvenile offenders return to school upon release. For instance, New York City reports that two-thirds of juveniles released from formal confinement do not return to school.

Reentry/aftercare programs typically combine two different approaches: surveillance and intervention services. *Surveillance*, or community restraint, practices include contact with parole correctional personnel, urine testing, electronic monitoring, employment verification, intensive supervision, house arrest, and residence in halfway houses. Surveillance methods work to reduce capacity and opportunity to commit future crimes. *Interventions* include counseling, behavioral programs, restitution, probation, and vocational and educational programs. These programs work with individual behavior to prevent future delinquency. Studies suggest that surveillance is more effective when coupled with intervention services.

David Altschuler and Rachel Brash have identified seven domains where juveniles reentering society face both challenges and opportunities:[22]

1. family and living arrangements;
2. peer groups and friends;
3. mental, behavioral, and physical health;
4. substance abuse;
5. education and schooling;
6. vocational training and employment; and
7. leisure, recreation, and vocational interests.

According to Altschuler and Brash, a strong association exists between those who are employed and the absence of criminal behavior. However, as with recently released adult offenders, a juvenile's criminal record presents obstacles to securing employment; thus, it is key that these records can be expunged. Furthermore, if youth are confined during their adolescence, their employment history and academic preparation may be inadequate, which makes it more difficult for them to find jobs.

Career and technical training available in residential placements often does not result in industry certification, or the training might be for industries in which few jobs are available in the juveniles' home communities. In many states, for example, while most incarcerated youth come from urban jurisdictions, many larger correctional facilities are located in more-rural areas. Career training opportunities will often reflect facility locale and staff expertise rather than actual opportunities available in urban settings.

Altschuler and Brash note that it is important for career and technical training offered in facilities to be based on industry-recognized standards so that youth can continue training when they return home after placement. While most delinquent youth will not go past a high school degree in their education pursuits, the likelihood that they will become productive adults is improved if they learn the skills that will lead to employment at family-sustaining wages.

Laurence Steinberg et al. note that a juvenile reentering society will experience many of the same challenges that plague formerly incarcerated adult offenders.[23] In fact, juvenile offenders experience additional obstacles because they are incarcerated during their developmental years. Steinberg and his colleagues state that levels of maturity and development are key to how juveniles will respond to reentry/aftercare services and how well they will cope with the social obstacles of reentering society.

The *Juvenile Justice Guidebook for Legislators* notes that recidivism can be measured in different ways, and that it tends to be unacceptably high. Pathways to Desistance (Pathways), referenced in the guidebook, was a multisite, seven-year project focused exclusively on juvenile offenders.[24] Created by the MacArthur Foundation Research Network on Adolescent Development and Juvenile Justice, Pathways was an attempt to understand desistance—why do some offenders stop offending?—and to study the results of sanctions and services in juvenile justice.

The Pathways project notes that drug treatment services significantly reduced substance use in a six-month period, and when coupled with family involvement, resulted in reduced drug use and reduced reoffending. The project reported that, regardless of the intervention, 91.5 percent of juveniles who commit serious felony offenses have decreased or limited illegal activity within three years. The project also suggests that there is no difference in recidivism rates for incarceration periods ranging between three and thirteen months; in other words, preliminary findings suggest that there is no reduced recidivism with longer incarceration periods.

Pathways reported that six months after release, juveniles who received community supervision and community-based services were more likely to attend school, go to work, and avoid reoffending. In fact, the study found that the longer the duration of supervision, the less likely the juvenile was to reoffend.

Does Detention Make Them Worse?

The current trend appears to indicate that many states are closing their training schools. In a 2009 article in *Time* magazine, Maia Szalavitz stated that juvenile detention makes teens worse; rather than rehabilitating young delinquents, she wrote, juvenile detention—which lumps troubled kids in with other troubled kids—appears to worsen their behavior problems.

Compared with other kids who had a similar history of bad behavior, those who entered the juvenile justice system were nearly seven times more likely to be arrested for crimes as adults. Further, those who ended up being sentenced to juvenile prison were thirty-seven times more likely to be arrested again as adults, compared with similarly misbehaved kids who were either not caught or not put into the system.

The twenty-year-long study, upon which the *Time* article based its conclusions, followed 779 low-income youth in Montreal with annual interviews from ages ten to seventeen, and then tracked their arrest records in adulthood. Researchers also interviewed the teenagers' parents, schoolmates, and teachers. The study accounted for variables such as family income, single-parent-home status, and earlier behavior problems (such as hyperactivity) that are known to affect delinquency risk.

The article noted that the rehabilitation of troubled teens has long been a contentious issue, pitting the individual needs of problem children and families against a system that does not typically give social workers adequate tools or resources to help. Often, the treatment of difficult or drug-using teens occurs en masse—in residential homes, for example—but instead of scaring kids straight, the group experience tends to glamorize delinquency and drug use.[25]

The Massachusetts Experiment

Three types of juvenile institutions were developed in the United States during the Progressive Era: houses of refuge, new reformatories, and separate institutions for juvenile offenders. According to the Office of Juvenile Justice and Delinquency Prevention (OJJDP), in 2016, more than 45,000 juvenile offenders were held in residential placement on any given day in the United States.[26]

Massachusetts created the nation's first juvenile correctional system around 1846. By 1971, however, many juvenile justice professionals considered the Massachusetts juvenile justice system a mess; reform was needed.[27] That year, Jerome Miller, director of Massachusetts Juvenile Justice, and his lead staffer, Tom Jeffers, met in a Boston pub and decided to make drastic changes to the manner in which Massachusetts had handled juvenile justice for more than a century. The two juvenile justice professionals decided to fix the system that was beset by abuse at its training schools. They concluded that the state's large juvenile facilities needed amputations; merely reforming them would not cure the problems.[28]

Massachusetts removed nearly one thousand juveniles from its state training schools, closed the schools, and placed the youths in a diverse array of community programs. State and federal agencies had severely castigated the training schools for abusive and inadequate treatment programs. Legislative hearings revealed major breakdowns in management and operations. The initial response was agency reorganization, and Jerome Miller was hired as commissioner to do the job. Four subsequent commissioners of the Massachusetts Department of Youth Services succeeded in consolidating the dramatic Massachusetts reforms. While several important refinements have been made to the original reforms, most Massachusetts juvenile justice professionals and children's advocates remain committed to the goals and philosophy set forth by Jerome Miller.

Forty years later, the Annie E. Casey Foundation funded an invitation-only symposium focused on "The Massachusetts Experiment." Hosted by the Harrisburg, Pennsylvania–based Youth Advocates Program (YAP) and funded by the Casey Foundation, the symposium commemorated the fortieth anniversary of Miller's rapid closure of Massachusetts training schools. The symposium noted that the Massachusetts system was no longer an experiment due to its decades of successful work with community-based juvenile corrections. The hallmark of Massachusetts programs is their small size; the state also uses secure confinement in a unique and cost-effective manner compared to other corrections systems. The success of Massachusetts programs has influenced juvenile justice reforms in Utah, Missouri, Maryland, and other states.

The findings of the symposium included:

1. Massachusetts was the first state to rely on community-based providers to help serve juveniles. Massachusetts was the first state to commit on a full-scale basis to purchasing services as a methodology.
2. Following the reforms, Massachusetts did not experience a juvenile crime spree. As the state moved most of its juveniles into community or residential programs, half the kids were absolutely crime-free. For the rest of the youth, offending had dropped by 50 percent, with serious crimes dropping even further.

These two factors immediately made Massachusetts a model for similar reforms in Utah and Missouri. Soon, most states had closed at least one large juvenile facility, a trend that swung the other way after the concerns regarding juvenile superpredators in the 1990s. The symposium also marked a starting point for a new push for juvenile de-incarceration. The Youth Advocates Program has grown from a small Pennsylvania operation into one that provides an alternative to incarceration in nineteen states.

As of 2019, public service groups in Massachusetts are working to continue to reform the state's juvenile justice system. Some of the reforms being advocated today in the state deal with racial justice and socioeconomic issues. Reformers are calling for positive youth development to remain a priority in the state.

The decision to close the Massachusetts training schools was unprecedented; as such, the state had no previous example to follow.[29] The training school closures and the transformation of the Department of Youth Services would be accomplished by:

1. Dividing the state into seven semi-autonomous regions
2. Developing a system of community-based treatment
3. Expanding non-institutional options such as forestry programs
4. Relocating detention centers
5. Creating increased placement alternatives
6. Distributing grants-in-aid to cities and towns
7. Developing new secure intensive care units

The process of closing the Massachusetts training school began in January of 1972 when Dr. Miller drove onto the grounds of the Lyman School and announced to the superintendent that they were removing the youth. Each youth was placed in a car and driven to the University of Massachusetts at Amherst, where they were housed for the next thirty days, or until a suitable placement could be located. Thus began one of the most sweeping juvenile justice reforms in history.

The University of Massachusetts organized the transfer of many youths into the community relatively quickly, removing ninety boys and girls from Lyman, Lancaster, and other institutions in the months of January and February 1972. Students at the university served as advocates for the youth while appropriate placement options were located.

Over the next twelve months three more institutions were closed. Once emptied of youth, the institution buildings were torn down, sold, or transferred to other state agencies. Through this process, Miller achieved his goal of ensuring that these abusive institutions would never reopen as training schools. The closing of these institutions forced the state to develop new approaches to serve juvenile justice–involved youth that would not rely on the convenience of institutional confinement.

The reformed system was envisioned to be more community-based, with services provided close to the youths' homes and families. Services were structured through a decentralization and regionalization of the department's resources and administration. A new network of community service programs emerged to serve low- and high-end offenders based on their individual needs. Most services were contracted from private nonprofit agencies. The approach spurred a juvenile justice renaissance in intervention policies and approaches, including the development of new institutions, programs, and treatments; ensuring legal rights to treatment; and addressing aftercare and reentry issues. New programs emerged that were superior to anything offered by the previous institutional system.

Practicum

Assume that you have been appointed as the director of juvenile corrections in your home state.

What steps would you take to reduce the number of juveniles in residential correctional facilities?

Summary

- The number of cases involving detention decreased between 2005 and 2016 for all offense categories to its lowest level in the analysis period.
- Corrections in the juvenile system are generally classified into two general areas: community corrections and institutions.
- Community corrections refer to those programs in which the juvenile is "corrected" within his or her community.
- Probation is the most popular type of community corrections.
- Juveniles who have been adjudicated as delinquent and are not considered appropriate for probation or who are detained prior to the adjudication hearing generally are placed in a residential facility.
- The harshest sanction that a juvenile court can impose entails the restriction of a juvenile's freedom through placement in a residential facility.
- The development of residential custody centers for juveniles in the United States developed from the "house of refuge" movement.
- Whether incarceration of some juveniles is necessary continues to be an issue in juvenile justice, with many professionals calling for the elimination of juvenile incarcerations.
- While residential training schools developed from houses of refuge, they have changed considerably in the past few years.
- The placing of incarcerated juveniles into solitary confinement continues to occur in certain US states, despite accumulating evidence that shows it may cause substantial psychological damage to the teenagers who must endure it.
- Juvenile parole may be defined as the conditional release of a juvenile from a correctional institution to the community under the supervision of a parole officer.
- A juvenile detention center is a secure twenty-four-hour detention facility for juvenile male and female offenders up to age eighteen who have been arrested and are waiting for court disposition or placement.
- In some states, shelters are used rather than detention centers.
- The philosophy behind most boot camps is that if you scream and discipline children enough, they will behave.

- The typical training school provides supervision, programs, and services for juveniles.
- Group homes use either day treatment or local public schools for the education component of their programs.
- A halfway house is also known as a residential reentry center. The purpose of these facilities is to reintegrate former offenders into society after having been in jail. It intends to continue offering support services to former inmates.
- The current trend appears to indicate that many states are closing their training schools.
- In 1971 Massachusetts removed nearly one thousand juveniles from state training schools, closed the schools, and placed the youths in a diverse array of community programs.

Discussion and Review Questions

1. Explain the role of houses of refuge in the development of the current juvenile justice system.
2. Why are many individuals opposed to the solitary confinement of juveniles?
3. Explain the "Massachusetts Experiment."
4. Why are jurisdictions decreasing the number of youths in residential centers?
5. How effective are juvenile boot camps?
6. When should a juvenile court judge use a residential center as a correctional treatment for the youth?
7. Does retention in a juvenile residential facility increase the likelihood that the juvenile will later be involved in new criminal misconduct? Explain your answer.

Notes

1. Sarah Hockenberry and Charles Puzzanchera, "Juvenile Court Statistics 2016," National Center for Juvenile Justice (Washington, DC: US Department of Justice, August 2016).
2. Howard N. Snyder and Melissa Strickland, "Juvenile Offenders and Victims: 2006 National Report," Office of Justice Programs (Washington, DC: US Department of Justice, March 2006).
3. Office of Justice Programs, Bureau of Justice Statistics, "Data-Collection Profile," NCJ 252833 (Washington, DC: US Department of Justice, June 2019).
4. Allen J. Beck, David Cantor, John Hartge, and Tim Smith, "Sexual Victimization in Juvenile Facilities Reported by Youth, 2012," NCJ 241708 (Washington, DC: US Department of Justice, June 2013). Available at https://www.bjs.gov/content/pub/pdf/svjfry12.pdf (accessed June 27, 2019).
5. OJJDP website at https://www.ojjdp.gov/ojstatbb/publications/statbb.asp?ID=T3 (accessed March 12, 2019).
6. *Ex parte Crouse*, 4 Whart. 9, 11-12 (Pa. 1839).
7. Commission on Accreditation for Corrections, "Manual of Standards for Juvenile Training Schools and Services" (Rockville, MD: Commission on Accreditation for Corrections, March 1979), ix.
8. New Jersey Office of the Attorney General, "New Jersey Training School" website at https://www.state.nj.us/lps/jjc/secure_njts.htm (accessed March 12, 2019).
9. "New Jersey Training School" website.
10. As posted on Arizona's Juvenile Detention website at https://superiorcourt.maricopa.gov/juvenile-probation/detention-services/ (accessed March 12, 2019).
11. As reported by Jessica Lee, "Lonely Too Long: Redefining and Reforming Juvenile Solitary Confinement," *Fordham Law Review*, vol. 85, no. 2 (2016), 845–76.

12. Lee, "Lonely Too Long," 849.
13. Lee, "Lonely Too Long," 854.
14. Andrew B. Clark, "Juvenile Solitary Confinement as a Form of Child Abuse," *Journal of the American Academy of Psychiatry and the Law*, vol. 45, no. 3 (September 2017), 350–57.
15. Howard N. Snyder and Melissa Sickmund, "Juvenile Offenders and Victims: 2006 National Report," Office of Juvenile Justice and Delinquency Prevention (Washington, DC: US Department of Justice, 2007).
16. Max Grunhut, *Penal Reform: A Comparative Study* (Oxford, UK: Oxford University Press, 1948).
17. Wingate Wilderness Therapy website located at https://www.wingatewildernesstherapy.com/Boot-Camps-For-Troubled-Teens/Mississippi-MS/ (accessed March 17, 2019).
18. Commonwealth of Virginia Department of Juvenile Justice, "Residential Handbook" (November 2013), posted at http://www.djj.virginia.gov/pdf/residential/Resident-Handbook.pdf (accessed May 8, 2019).
19. New Jersey Juvenile Justice Commission website at https://www.state.nj.us/lps/jjc/secure_njts.htm (accessed May 8, 2019).
20. Development Services Group, Inc., "Group Homes," Literature Review (Washington, DC: Office of Juvenile Justice and Delinquency Prevention, 2008), posted at https://www.ojjdp.gov/mpg/litreviews/Group_Homes.pdf (accessed May 9, 2019).
21. National Conference of State Legislatures, *Juvenile Justice Guidebook for Legislators: Reentry & Aftercare* (Denver, CO: National Conference of State Legislatures, 2011), posted at https://www.ncsl.org/documents/cj/jjguidebook-reentry.pdf (accessed May 11, 2019).
22. David M. Altschuler and Rachel Brash, "Adolescent and Teenage Offenders Confronting the Challenges and Opportunities of Reentry," *Youth Violence and Juvenile Justice*, vol. 2, no. 1 (January 2004), 72–87, posted at https://doi.org/10.1177/1541204003260048 (accessed May 11, 2019).
23. Laurence Steinberg, He Len Chung, and Michelle Little, "Reentry of Young Offenders from the Justice System: A Developmental Perspective," *Youth Violence and Juvenile Justice*, vol. 2, no. 1 (January 2004), 21–38, posted at https://doi.org/10.1177/1541204003260045 (accessed May 11, 2019).
24. MacArthur Foundation Research Network on Adolescent Development and Juvenile Justice, *Issue Brief #2: Creating Turning Points for Serious Adolescent Offenders: Research in Pathways to Desistance* (Philadelphia: MFRN, 2006).
25. Maia Szalavitz, "Why Juvenile Detention Makes Teens Worse," *Time*, August 7, 2009, posted at http://content.time.com/time/health/article/0,8599,1914837,00.html (accessed May 9, 2019).
26. "OJJDP: Juvenile Residential Facility Census" (Washington, DC: US Department of Justice, 2018), available at OJJDP website at https://www.ojjdp.gov/research/JRFC.html (accessed March 16, 2019).
27. John Kelly, "Learning from Massachusetts' Juvenile Justice Experiment," *Youth Today*, December 19, 2011, posted at https://youthtoday.org/2011/12/learning-from-massachusetts-juvenile-justice-experiment/ (accessed March 10, 2019).
28. Barry Krisberg and James Austin, "What Works with Juvenile Offenders: The Massachusetts Experiment," in *Reforming Juvenile Justice: Reasons and Strategies for the 21st Century*, edited by Dan Macallair and Vincent Schiraldi (Dubuque, IA: Kendall/Hunt Publishing, 1998), 173–96.
29. Center on Juvenile and Criminal Justice, "Juvenile Corrections Reform in Massachusetts" (no date), posted at www.cjcj.org/Education1/Massachusetts-Training-Schools.html (accessed May 13, 2019).

CHAPTER 13

Transfers to Adult Criminal Court

CHAPTER OBJECTIVES

After studying this chapter, the reader should be able to:

- Understand the due process requirements for discretionary transfers.
- Discuss the power of a prosecutor in deciding whether to direct file in adult criminal court.
- Discuss the importance of the *Kent* and *Breed* cases.
- Analyze the issues involved in transfer cases.

Overview

In this chapter we will explore transfers from juvenile court to adult criminal court and direct filing in adult criminal court. A juvenile may end up in adult criminal court by the juvenile court waiving jurisdiction or by direct filing in adult criminal court. Generally, most jurisdictions' statutes provide that the prosecuting attorney may directly file the case in adult criminal court under special circumstances.[1]

As noted by Richard Redding, starting in the 1980s, many states passed legal reforms that were designed to get tough on juvenile crime.[2] One important reform was the revision of transfer (also called waiver or certification) laws to expand the types of offenses and offenders eligible for transfer from the juvenile court to the adult criminal justice system for trial and sentencing.

In many situations the reforms lowered the minimum age for transfer, increased the number of transfer-eligible offenses, or expanded prosecutorial discretion and reduced judicial discretion in transfer decision-making. Redding notes that in 1979, fourteen states had automatic transfer statutes requiring that certain juvenile offenders be tried as adults; by 1995, twenty-one states had such laws, and by 2003, thirty-one states.

Another change was that the age at which juvenile court jurisdiction ends was lowered to fifteen or sixteen in many states. Redding also notes that recently, some states have reduced the scope of transfer laws, and one state has raised the age at which juvenile court jurisdiction ends, from sixteen to eighteen years of age. Redding also notes that transferred juveniles, particularly those convicted of violent offenses, typically receive longer sentences than those sentenced in the juvenile court for similar crimes.

All states have transfer laws that allow or require criminal prosecution of some young offenders, even though they fall on the juvenile side of the jurisdictional age line.[3] Transfer laws are not new, but legislative changes in recent decades have greatly expanded their scope. The transfer "exception" has become a more prominent feature in response to youthful offending.

States have multiple transfer mechanisms and transfer laws vary considerably from state to state, but all fall into three basic categories:

- Judicial waiver laws allow juvenile courts to waive jurisdiction on a case-by-case basis, opening the way for criminal prosecution. A case that is subject to waiver is filed originally in juvenile court but may be transferred with a judge's approval, based on articulated standards, following a formal hearing. Even though all states set minimum thresholds and prescribe standards for waiver, the waiver decision is usually at the discretion of the judge. However, some states make a waiver presumptive in certain classes of cases, and some even specify circumstances under which a waiver is mandatory.
- Prosecutorial discretion or concurrent jurisdiction laws define a class of cases that may be brought in either juvenile or adult criminal court. No hearing is necessary to determine which court is appropriate, and there may be no formal standards for deciding between them. The decision is entrusted entirely to the prosecutor.
- Statutory exclusion laws grant adult criminal courts exclusive jurisdiction over certain classes of cases involving juvenile-age offenders. If a case falls within a statutory exclusion category, it must be filed originally in criminal court.

All states have at least one of the above kinds of transfer law. In addition, many have one or more of the following:

- "Once adult/always adult" laws are a special form of exclusion requiring criminal prosecution of any juvenile who has been criminally prosecuted in the past—usually without regard to the seriousness of the current offense.
- Reverse waiver laws allow juveniles whose cases are in criminal court to petition to have them transferred to juvenile court.
- Blended sentencing laws may either provide juvenile courts with criminal sentencing options (juvenile blended sentencing) or allow criminal courts to impose juvenile dispositions (criminal blended sentencing).

Nearly all states give juvenile courts discretion to waive jurisdiction over individual cases. Most states have laws designating some category of cases in which waiver of jurisdiction may be considered, generally on the prosecutor's motion, and granted on a discretionary basis. This is the oldest and still the most common form of transfer law, although most states have other, less-traditional forms as well.

Discretionary waiver statutes prescribe broad standards to be applied, factors to be considered, and procedures to be followed in waiver decision-making, and require that prosecutors bear the burden of proving that waiver is appropriate. Although waiver standards and evidentiary factors vary from state to state, most consider both the nature of the alleged crime and the individual youth's age, maturity, history, and rehabilitative prospects.

In addition, most states set a minimum threshold for waiver eligibility: generally, a minimum age and a specified type or level of offense, and sometimes a sufficiently serious record of previous delinquency. Waiver thresholds are often quite low, however. In a few states—such as Alaska, Kansas, and Washington—prosecutors may ask the court to waive virtually any juvenile delinquency case. As a practical matter, however, even in these states, waivers are likely to be the exception.

Statistics on Waivers

For every 1,000 petitioned delinquency cases where discretionary waiver is appropriate, only about 9 are judicially waived to criminal court. The number of judicially waived cases hit a historic peak in 1994—when about 13,100 cases were waived—and has fallen 35 percent since that year. There are two causes that might account for this trend:

- Juvenile arrests for most crimes, and particularly for Violent Index offenses, have fallen almost every year since 1994.
- The nationwide proliferation and expansion of nontraditional transfer mechanisms also may have contributed to the reduction in waivers. In states with prosecutorial discretion or statutory exclusion laws cases, when the prosecutor directly files the case in adult criminal court, the case is not included in juvenile court statistics.

The likelihood of judicial waiver among petitioned delinquency cases was lower in 2007 than in 1994 for all offense categories and demographic groups. National information on juveniles whose cases were filed directly in adult criminal court is fragmentary, since there are no national data sets that track cases which bypass juvenile courts.

Many states do not track and account for all of their juvenile transfer cases regardless of the type of waiver or transfer. Only thirteen states are identified as publicly reporting even the total number of their transfers, including cases of juveniles who reach adult criminal courts as a result of statutory exclusions or prosecutors' discretionary choices, as well as judicial waiver decisions. States that publish information on the offense profiles or demographic characteristics of these youth, or provide details regarding their processing or sentencing, are even rarer.[4] In addition, there are wide variations in the ways that states document juvenile transfers.

Waiver of Jurisdiction

The US Supreme Court in *Kent v. United States* in 1966 placed limitations on a juvenile court's exercise of its statutory power to relinquish its jurisdiction so that certain minors may be tried as adult criminals.[5] Prior to the *Kent* case, the appellate courts had paid little attention to the transfer proceedings.[6]

Kent v. United States

Morris A. Kent Jr. first came under the authority of the juvenile court of the District of Columbia in 1959. He was then aged fourteen. He was apprehended as a result of several housebreakings and an attempted purse snatching. He was placed on probation, in the custody of his mother, who had been separated from her husband since Kent was two years old. Juvenile court officials interviewed Kent from time to time during the probation period and accumulated a "social services" file.

On September 2, 1961, an intruder entered the apartment of a woman in the District of Columbia. He took her wallet. He raped her. The police found in the apartment latent fingerprints, which were developed and processed. They matched the fingerprints of Morris Kent, taken when he was fourteen years old and under the jurisdiction of the juvenile court. At about 3:00 p.m. on September 5, 1961, Kent was taken into custody by the police. Kent was then sixteen, and therefore subject to the initial jurisdiction of the juvenile court. He was still on probation to the juvenile court as a result of the 1959 court proceedings.

Upon being apprehended, Kent was taken to police headquarters where he was interrogated by police officers. It appears that he admitted his involvement in the offense, which led to his apprehension, and he also volunteered information as to similar offenses involving housebreaking, robbery, and rape. His interrogation lasted from about 3:00 p.m. to 10:00 p.m. the same evening. Sometime after 10:00 p.m. Kent was taken to the Receiving Home for Children. The next morning, he was released to the police for further interrogation at police headquarters, which lasted until 5:00 p.m. that day.

The record does not show when his mother became aware that the boy was in custody, but shortly after 2:00 p.m. on September 6, 1961, the day following the petitioner's apprehension, she retained counsel. Counsel, together with the petitioner's mother, promptly conferred with the social services director of the juvenile court. In a brief interview, they discussed the possibility that the juvenile court might waive jurisdiction and remit Kent to trial by the district court. Counsel made known his intention to oppose a waiver. Kent was detained at the Receiving Home for almost a week. There was no arraignment during this time, and no determination by a judicial officer of probable cause for the petitioner's apprehension.

The decision by the Court in this case was a 5-4 decision, which indicates that it was a highly debated issue. The Court determined there was not enough investigation prior to the juvenile court waiver of jurisdiction. The Court in the majority opinion noted that Kent did not receive a hearing, access to counsel, or access to his record prior to the waiver. The Court remanded the case to the district court to determine whether the waiver was proper. Because Kent was twenty-one years old at the time of this decision, the juvenile court no longer had jurisdiction if the waiver was proper.

The Supreme Court noted that the juvenile court judge held no hearing before waiving jurisdiction. The judge did not confer with Kent, his parents, or his counsel. The judge entered an order reciting that after a full investigation, he waived jurisdiction of Kent and directed that Kent be held for trial for the alleged offenses under the regular procedure of the US District Court for the District of Columbia (adult criminal court).

The juvenile court judge made no findings. He did not recite any reason for the waiver. He made no reference to the motions filed by Kent's counsel. The Court stated that it must assume that the juvenile judge denied, *sub silentio*, the motions for a hearing, the recommendation for hospitalization for psychiatric observation, the request for access to the social services file, and the offer to prove that Kent was a fit subject for rehabilitation under the juvenile court's jurisdiction.

The Supreme Court stated that it presumed that prior to entry of the juvenile court judge's order, the judge received and considered recommendations of the juvenile court staff, the social services file relating to Kent, and a report dated September 8, 1961 (three days following the petitioner's apprehension), submitted to the judge by the juvenile probation section. The social services file and the September 8 report were later sent to the district court, and it appears that both referred to Kent's mental condition. The September 8 report spoke of a rapid deterioration of Kent's personality structure and the possibility of mental illness. Neither this report nor the social services file was made available to Kent's counsel.

The Supreme Court noted that the provision of the Juvenile Court Act governing waivers expressly provides only for a full investigation. It states the circumstances in which jurisdiction may be waived and the child held for trial under adult procedures, but it does not state standards to govern the juvenile court's decision as to waiver.

At the time of the offense, the statutory provision of the District of Columbia Code read as follows:

> If a child sixteen years of age or older is charged with an offense which would amount to a felony in the case of an adult, or any child charged with an offense which if committed by an adult is punishable by death or life imprisonment, the judge may, after full investigation, waive jurisdiction and order such child held for trial under the regular procedure of the court which would have jurisdiction of such offense if committed by an adult; or such other court may exercise the powers conferred upon the juvenile court in this subchapter in conducting and disposing of such case.[7]

The Supreme Court agreed with the court of appeals that the statute contemplates that the juvenile court should have considerable latitude within which to determine whether it should retain jurisdiction over a child, or—subject to the statutory delimitation—whether it should waive jurisdiction. The Supreme Court, however, noted that this latitude is not complete. At the outset, it assumes procedural regularity sufficient in the particular circumstances to satisfy the basic requirements of due process and fairness, as well as compliance with the statutory requirement of a full investigation.

The Supreme Court held that the statute gives the juvenile court a substantial degree of discretion as to the factual considerations to be evaluated, the weight to be given them, and the conclusion to be reached. It does not confer upon the juvenile court a license for arbitrary procedure. The statute does not permit the juvenile court to determine in isolation and without the participation or any representation of the child the critically important question of whether a child can be deprived of the special protections and provisions of the Juvenile Court Act. It does not authorize the juvenile court, in total disregard of a motion for hearing filed by counsel, and without any hearing or statement or reasons, to decide—as in this case—that the child will be taken from the Receiving Home for Children and transferred to jail along with adults, and that he will be exposed to the possibility of a death sentence instead of maximum treatment for a juvenile, in Kent's case, of five years, or until he is twenty-one.

The Supreme Court concluded that it did not consider whether, on the merits, Kent should have been transferred; but there is no place in our system of law for reaching a result of such tremendous consequences without ceremony, without hearing, without effective assistance of counsel, without a statement of reasons. It is inconceivable that a court of justice dealing with adults, with respect to a similar issue, would proceed in this manner. The Supreme Court stated that it would be extraordinary if society's special concern for children, as reflected in the District of Columbia's Juvenile Court Act, permitted this procedure. The Supreme Court held that it does not.

The Court noted that the theory of the District's Juvenile Court Act, like that of other jurisdictions, is rooted in social welfare philosophy rather than in the *corpus juris*. Its proceedings are designated as civil rather than criminal. The juvenile court is theoretically engaged in determining the needs of the child and of society rather than adjudicating criminal conduct. The objectives are to provide measures of guidance and rehabilitation for the child and protection for society, not to fix criminal responsibility, guilt, and punishment. The State is *parens patriae* rather than prosecuting attorney and judge. But the admonition to function in a parental relationship is not an invitation to procedural arbitrariness.

The Supreme Court opined that because the State is supposed to proceed in respect of the child as *parens patriae* and not as adversary, courts have relied on the premise that the proceedings are civil in nature and not criminal, and have asserted that the child cannot complain of the deprivation of important rights available in criminal cases. It has been asserted that he can claim only the fundamental due process right to fair treatment.

The Supreme Court held that meaningful review requires that the reviewing court should review. It should not be remitted to assumptions. It must have before it a statement of the reasons motivating the waiver, including, of course, a statement of the relevant facts. It may not assume that there are adequate reasons, nor may it merely assume that full investigation has been made.

The Supreme Court stated that it is incumbent upon the juvenile court to accompany its waiver order with a statement of the reasons or considerations therefor. The Supreme Court noted that it did not read the statute as requiring that this statement must be formal or that it should necessarily include conventional findings of fact. But the statement should be sufficient to demonstrate that the statutory requirement of full investigation has been met; and that the question has received the careful consideration of the juvenile court; and it must set forth the basis for the order with sufficient specificity to permit meaningful review.

The Supreme Court noted that it did not mean to indicate that the hearing to be held must conform with all of the requirements of a criminal trial, or even of the usual administrative hearing; but the hearing must measure up to the essentials of due process and fair treatment.

Double Jeopardy and the Waiver Decision

Another US Supreme Court decision involving the transfer of juveniles to adult criminal court was the *Breed v. Jones* case.[8] The issue in this case was whether the prosecution of the respondent as an adult—following juvenile court proceedings, which resulted in a finding that the respondent had violated a criminal statute, and a subsequent finding that he was unfit for treatment as a juvenile—violated the Fifth and Fourteenth Amendments to the United States Constitution.

Prior to *Breed v. Jones*, in most jurisdictions the juvenile court would hold a hearing to determine if the allegations in the petition were true, and if true, then decide whether the juvenile court would take corrective action or would transfer the case to the adult criminal court. Jones's counsel contended that this procedure violated the constitutional provisions against double jeopardy since the juvenile would be tried twice for the same delinquency.

Breed v. Jones

In the *Breed v. Jones* case, a petition was filed in the Superior Court of California, County of Los Angeles, Juvenile Court, alleging that the respondent (Jones), then seventeen years of age, was a person described by California Welfare & Institutions Code § 602 (1966), in that, on or about February 8, while armed with a deadly weapon, he had committed acts which, if committed by an adult, would constitute the crime of robbery. The following day, a detention hearing was held, at the conclusion of which the respondent was ordered detained pending a hearing on the petition.[9]

At the adjudicatory hearing on March 1, the juvenile court found that the allegations in the petition were true and that the respondent was a person described by § 602, and it sustained the petition. The proceedings were continued for a dispositional hearing, pending which the court ordered that the respondent remain detained.

At the dispositional hearing conducted on March 15, the juvenile court indicated its intention to find the respondent not amenable to the care, treatment, and training program available through the facilities of the juvenile court. Jones's counsel orally moved to continue the matter on the ground of surprise, contending that Jones was not informed that it was going to be a fitness hearing. The court continued the matter for one week, at which time, having considered the report of the probation officer assigned to the case and having heard her testimony, it declared the respondent unfit for treatment as a juvenile, and ordered that he be prosecuted as an adult.

The counsel for Jones filed a petition for a writ of habeas corpus in juvenile court, raising the double jeopardy claim. Upon the denial of that petition, Jones sought habeas corpus relief in the California Court of Appeal, Second Appellate District. Although it initially stayed the criminal prosecution pending against respondent, that court denied the petition.

After a preliminary hearing Jones was ordered held for trial in superior court, where information was subsequently filed accusing him of having committed robbery while armed with a deadly weapon. Jones entered a plea of not guilty, and he also pleaded that he had already been placed once in jeopardy and convicted of the offense charged, by the judgment of the juvenile court. The adult criminal court found Jones guilty of robbery in the first degree and ordered that he be committed to the California Youth Authority.

In December 1971, Jones, through his mother as guardian *ad litem,* filed the instant petition for a writ of habeas corpus in the United States District Court for the Central District of California. In his petition he alleged that his transfer to adult court and subsequent trial there placed him in double jeopardy. The district court denied the petition, rejecting his contention that jeopardy attached at his adjudicatory hearing. It concluded that the distinctions between the preliminary procedures and hearings provided by California law for juveniles and a criminal trial are many and apparent, and the effort of Jones to relate them was unconvincing, and that even assuming jeopardy attached during the preliminary juvenile proceedings, it was clear that no new jeopardy arose by the juvenile proceeding sending the case to the adult criminal court.

The US Supreme Court finally decided the issue. The Supreme Court noted that the parties agreed that, following his transfer from juvenile court, and as a defendant to a felony information, the respondent (Jones) was entitled to the full protection of the double jeopardy clause of the Fifth Amendment, as applied to the states through the Fourteenth Amendment.

The Court also noted that in addition, the parties agreed that the respondent was put in jeopardy by the proceedings on that information, which resulted in an adjudication that he was guilty of robbery in the first degree and in a sentence of commitment. Finally, there was no dispute that the petition filed in juvenile court and the information filed in superior court related to the "same offense" within the meaning of the constitutional prohibition. The Court stated that the point of disagreement between the parties, and the question for their decision, was whether, by reason of the proceedings in juvenile court, respondent was "twice put in jeopardy."

The Supreme Court stated that jeopardy denotes risk. In the constitutional sense, jeopardy describes the risk that is traditionally associated with a criminal prosecution. The Court pointed out that although the constitutional language, "jeopardy of life or limb," suggests proceedings in which only the most serious penalties can be imposed, the clause has long been construed to mean something far broader than its literal language.

The Supreme Court noted that at the same time, however, it has held that the risk to which the clause refers is not present in proceedings that are not "essentially criminal." The Court opined that although the juvenile court system had its genesis in the desire to provide a distinctive procedure and setting to deal with the problems of youth, including those manifested by antisocial conduct, their decisions in recent years have recognized that there is a gap between the originally benign conception of the system and its realities. And that with the exception of *McKeiver* v. *Pennsylvania*, the Court's response to that perception has been to make applicable in juvenile proceedings constitutional guarantees associated with traditional criminal prosecutions.[10]

The Supreme Court noted that in some of its decisions the Court has evinced awareness of the threat which such a process represents to the efforts of the juvenile court system, functioning in a unique manner, to ameliorate the harshness of criminal justice when applied to youthful offenders. The fact that the system has fallen short of the high expectations of its sponsors in no way detracts from the broad social benefits sought or from those benefits that can survive constitutional scrutiny. The Court held that it was simply too late in the day to conclude, as did the district court in this case, that a juvenile is not put in jeopardy at a proceeding whose object is to determine whether he has committed acts that violate a criminal law and whose potential consequences include both the stigma inherent in such a determination and the deprivation of liberty for many years.

As a result of the US Supreme Court decision in *Breed v. Jones*, jurisdictions had to change their procedures for cases being transferred to the adult criminal courts. Accordingly, if there is a question that the juvenile court may want to waive jurisdiction and refer the case to the adult system, there must be a hearing on the fitness of the juvenile to be treated in the juvenile justice system before the hearing to determine if the allegations of misconduct in the petition are true. Accordingly, the transfer decision must be made before any determination as to the truth of the allegations in the petition.

The *Breed* case holds:

- Due process prohibits trying a juvenile in adult court after there has been a prior adjudicatory juvenile hearing involving the same misconduct.
- A finding of probable cause to hold the youth may be established at the transfer hearing without violating the double jeopardy protection if the child is transferred to adult criminal court.
- Since the same evidence is often used in both the transfer hearing and the subsequent trial in either adult or juvenile court, a different judge is required at trial from the judge that was involved in the transfer hearing.

Transfer Requirements for Discretionary Waivers

If the juvenile court waives its jurisdiction it is required to enter a transfer order that specifically states the reason for its decision and certifies why it has reached that conclusion. The majority of jurisdictions require that a transfer order contain certain elements. The juvenile court is not required to make specific findings of fact for each of the requirements, but is only required to consider them in making the decision whether to transfer.

For example, the State of Texas requires that:

- the child is alleged to have committed a felony;
- the child was fourteen or older at the time a capital felony, an aggravated controlled substance felony, or a first-degree felony was committed;
- the child was fifteen or older at the time any other type of felony was committed;
- there has not been an adjudication hearing concerning the offense;
- there is probable cause to believe that the child committed the offense; and due to the seriousness of the offense or background of the child, it is best for the welfare of the community to pursue criminal proceedings; and
- if the juvenile is eighteen years of age or older, the Family Code requires the court to make additional findings of due diligence.[11]

Right to Appeal Waiver

A juvenile does not have a constitutional right to be tried in juvenile court in the majority of jurisdictions.[12] An appeal about the lawfulness of a transfer proceeding is generally only permitted after conviction or deferred adjudication in adult criminal court of the actions that arose from the transferred conduct, in which case, the juvenile appeals the criminal conviction and alleges that the case was not properly tried before an adult criminal court.[13]

Direct Filing in Adult Criminal Court

Mandatory Waiver

Many states require juvenile courts to waive jurisdiction over cases that meet specified age/offense or prior record criteria. Cases subject to mandatory waiver are initiated in juvenile court, but the court has no other role than to confirm that the statutory requirements for mandatory waiver are met.

Functionally, a mandatory waiver law resembles a statutory exclusion, removing a designated category of cases from juvenile court jurisdiction. However, the juvenile court may retain power to make necessary orders relating to appointment of counsel, detention, and other preliminary matters. Under certain circumstances, the statutes of the jurisdiction may require that the juvenile be transferred to adult criminal court. A common requirement for a mandatory transfer is if the juvenile has previously been transferred to adult criminal court through certification and has allegedly committed a felony. The exceptions to this mandatory transfer requirement generally include: if the juvenile was not indicted by the grand jury; the juvenile was found not guilty; the case transferred was dismissed with prejudice; or the juvenile was convicted in the case transferred, but the conviction was reversed on a final appeal.

A mandatory transfer proceeding does not require the diagnostic study, investigation, or social evaluation of the juvenile prior to hearing. The requirement that the summons state the purpose of the hearing is to consider discretionary transfer to adult criminal court does not apply to a mandatory certification proceeding. It is sufficient on a mandatory certification proceeding that the purpose of the hearing is to consider whether mandatory transfer is applicable.[14]

Direct Filing

In addition to the mandatory requirement transfers, in most jurisdictions the prosecutor may directly file a case in adult criminal court if certain requirements exist. A criticism of the direct filing is that it gives the prosecutor too much power. For example, from 2008 to 2012, the State of Florida's prosecutors transferred juveniles into adult court at a higher rate than any other state in the nation. During that time period, over 12,000 Florida children—some as young as twelve years old—were transferred into adult courts. Florida law authorized three mechanisms for a juvenile to be transferred: grand jury indictment, waiver, or direct file.[15]

According to Kevin Huguelet, while there are three mechanisms available to Florida prosecutors, about 98 percent of juvenile transfers to adult court are via the direct file method. *Direct file* is a statutory provision that allows prosecutors to choose whether a case will be adjudicated in juvenile or adult court. In Florida, direct file is either *mandatory*—if the juvenile meets certain statutorily enumerated criteria—or *discretionary*—"when in the state attorney's judgment and discretion the public interest requires that adult sanctions be considered or imposed."

The decision by a state attorney to use discretion to direct file a child cannot be appealed or reviewed by a judge; the case will simply be filed in adult court, and there is nothing the juvenile can do to protest. According to Huguelet, this process of unfettered prosecutorial power violates the basic tenets of the American adversarial system. Many jurisdictions have similar statutes for direct filing in adult criminal court when the youth is of a certain age and the crime is a serious felony.

Presumptive Waiver

In some states, presumptive waiver laws define a category of cases in which waiver from juvenile to adult criminal court is presumed appropriate. Statutes in these states leave the decision in the hands of a judge, but weight it in favor of transfer. A juvenile who meets age, offense, or other statutory thresholds for presumptive waiver must present evidence rebutting the presumption, or the court will grant the waiver and the case will be tried in adult criminal court.

Practicum

Assume you are a juvenile court judge in a state that allows the discretionary waiver of a juvenile case when the juvenile is over the age of fifteen and the crime alleged is a felony. Before you is a youth who is sixteen years old. It is alleged in the petition that he stole a neighbor's car and while driving it caused a serious wreck of another car, and seriously injured the other driver. The police at the scene took a test of the youth's blood alcohol level and it was above the level set forth in the state's DWI statute for adults.

What considerations and actions should you take before waiving juvenile court jurisdiction and allowing the transfer of the case to adult criminal court?

Summary

- A juvenile may end up in adult criminal court by the juvenile court waiving jurisdiction or by direct filing in adult criminal court.
- All states have transfer laws that allow or require criminal prosecution of some young offenders, even though they fall on the juvenile side of the jurisdictional age line.
- Transfer laws vary considerably from state to state, but all fall into two basic categories:
  - Judicial waiver laws allow juvenile courts to waive jurisdiction on a case-by-case basis.

  - Prosecutorial discretion or concurrent jurisdiction laws define a class of cases that may be brought in either juvenile or criminal court.
- Nearly all states give courts discretion to waive jurisdiction over individual cases.
- For every one thousand petitioned delinquency cases where discretionary waiver is permitted, only about nine are judicially waived to adult criminal court.
- Most states do not track and account for all their juvenile transfer cases regardless of the type of waiver or transfer.
- The US Supreme Court in *Kent v. United States* in 1966 placed limitations on a juvenile court's exercise of its statutory power to relinquish its jurisdiction so that certain minors may be tried as adult criminals.
- In the *Kent* case, the Supreme Court held that at a waiver hearing, the juvenile has a right to due process.
- In the *Breed* case, the Court held:
  - Due process prohibits trying a juvenile in adult court after there has been a prior adjudicatory juvenile hearing involving the same misconduct.
  - A finding of probable cause to hold the youth may be established at the transfer hearing without violating the double jeopardy protection if the child is transferred to adult criminal court.
  - Since the same evidence is often used in both the transfer hearing and the subsequent trial in either adult or juvenile court, a different judge is required at trial from the judge that was involved in the transfer hearing.
- A juvenile does not have a constitutional right to be tried in juvenile court in the majority of jurisdictions.
- Some states require juvenile courts to waive jurisdiction over cases that meet specified age/offense or prior record criteria.
- In many jurisdictions the prosecutor may directly file a case in adult criminal court if certain requirements exist.

Discussion and Review Questions

1. What is the importance of the Supreme Court decision in *Kent v. United States*?
2. What is required before a juvenile court judge may waive jurisdiction and transfer a case to adult criminal court?
3. What requirements did the Court place on juvenile court judges in the *Breed v. Jones* case when the judge is considering transferring a youth to adult criminal court?
4. What are the issues involved when a prosecutor has the authority to file a case involving a juvenile directly in adult criminal court?
5. What are the three general types of transfer approaches that may be used to transfer a juvenile to adult criminal court?

Notes

1. Cliff Roberson, *Juvenile Justice: Theory and Practice*, 2nd ed. (Boca Raton, FL: CRC Press, 2010).
2. Richard E. Redding, "Juvenile Laws: An Effective Deterrent to Delinquency," *Juvenile Justice Bulletin* (Washington, DC: Office of Juvenile Justice and Delinquency Prevention, June 2010), 1–3.
3. Patrick Griffin, Sean Addie, Benjamin Adams, and Kathy Firestine, "Trying Juveniles as Adults: An Analysis of State Transfer Laws and Reporting," Office of Juvenile Justice

and Delinquency Prevention National Report Series (September 2011), posted at http://www.ncjj.org/pdf/Transfer_232434.pdf (accessed May 14, 2019).

4. Griffin et al., "Trying Juveniles as Adults."
5. *Kent v. United States*, 383 U.S. 541 (1966).
6. F. Thomas Schornhorst, "The Waiver of Juvenile Court Jurisdiction: Kent Revisited," *Indiana Law Journal*, vol. 43, no. 3 (Spring 1968), 583–613. Available at http://www.repository.law.indiana.edu/ilj/vol43/iss3/4 (accessed March 26, 2019).
7. D.C. Code § 11-914 (1961), now § 11-1553 (Supp. IV, 1965).
8. *Breed v. Jones*, 421 U.S. 519 (1975).
9. Section 602: Except as provided in Section 707, any person who is under eighteen years of age when he or she violates any law of this state or of the United States or any ordinance of any city or county of this state defining crime, other than an ordinance establishing a curfew based solely on age, is within the jurisdiction of the juvenile court, which may adjudge such person to be a ward of the court.
10. *McKeiver* v. *Pennsylvania,* 403 U.S. 528 (1971), which denied the juvenile the right to a jury trial.
11. Tex. Fam. Code §54.02(j)(4).
12. *In Matter of P.B.C.*, 538 S.W.2d 448 (Tex. Civ. App.—El Paso, 1976).
13. *Rodriguez v. State*, 191 S.W.3d 909 (Tex. App.—Dallas, 2006).
14. Jill Long and Mata Jenna Reblin, "Juvenile Court Waiver of Jurisdiction and Discretionary Transfer to Criminal Court" (February 2013), posted at https://juvenilelaw.org/wp-content/uploads/2017/06/Juvenile-court-Waiver-of-Jurisdiction.pdf (accessed May 14, 2019).
15. Kevin Huguelet, "Florida's Direct File Law: How State Attorneys Hold Too Much Power," University of Miami website (May 2014), posted at https://lawreview.law.miami.edu/floridas-direct-file-law-state-attorneys-hold-power/ (accessed May 14, 2019).

CHAPTER 14

Enhancing Juvenile Protection

CHAPTER OBJECTIVES

After studying this chapter, the reader should be able to:

- Understand the processes involved in the termination of parental rights.
- Discuss the importance and need for child protective orders.
- Debate the need to keep certain juvenile information from becoming public.
- Analyze the processes involved in expungement of juvenile records.
- Explain the issues involved when youths are involved in the dual system.
- Explain the functions of a juvenile drug court.
- Discuss the benefits and disadvantages of a juvenile drug court program.
- Explain the use of teen courts and why they are popular.
- Explain the issues involved in status offenses.

Overview

This chapter will explore several different issues that affect the protection of the child. The topics include termination of parental rights, child protective orders, disclosure restrictions on juvenile information, expungement of juvenile records, dual system youths, and specialized courts. Expungement of juvenile records involves the removing of juvenile justice or adult criminal court records. The term *dual system youths* refers to the high number of youths involved in the juvenile justice system that are also on public welfare or other welfare rolls. While these topics may not appear to be related, they are all designed to help protect youths.

Termination of Parental Rights

Numerous research studies have indicated that youths from an unstable home environment are more likely to be involved in the juvenile justice system than youths from a stable home environment. Parental rights over a child may be involuntarily terminated when a child cannot be returned safely home because of risk of harm by the parent or the inability of the parent to provide for the child's basic needs. The specific circumstances under which these rights can be terminated vary for each state. In this section, the general rules of involuntary termination will be explored. The overall consideration of the termination statutes is the safety and welfare of the child. The most common grounds for determining the need to terminate parental rights include the following:[1]

- There is a high probability that if the child is returned to the parents, the child will be severely abused or neglected.
- There is a possibility that the child will be subject to sexual abuse.
- Other children in the household have been abused or neglected.
- The child may be abandoned.
- The parents are unable to safely provide for the child because of long-term mental illness or deficiency of one or both parents.
- One or both parents have alcohol- or drug-induced incapacity.
- Failure to support or maintain contact with the child.
- There has been an involuntary termination of the rights of the parent to another child.

Generally, the above factors are grounds for terminating parental rights, especially where the parent has been advised of the situation and has failed to correct the conditions. Other grounds include parental behaviors that led to state intervention and the parent(s) is unable to provide a safe home for the child, despite reasonable efforts by a state agency to provide services to prevent out-of-home placement or to achieve family reunification after out-of-home placement. (For more information on the reasonable efforts' requirement, see Child Welfare Information Gateway's Reasonable Efforts to Preserve or Reunify Families and Achieve Permanency for Children at https://www.childwelfare.gov/topics/systemwide/laws-policies/statutes/reunify/.)

According to the Child Welfare Information website, in approximately thirty states and Puerto Rico, a parent's rights can be terminated if he or she has been convicted of committing sexual abuse or another sexual offense. In fourteen states and Puerto Rico, a parent's rights can be terminated upon conviction for child sexual exploitation (including prostitution or child pornography). A conviction for human trafficking or sex trafficking of a minor can result in the termination of a parent's rights in six states. In twenty-one states, a man's parental rights can be terminated if he has committed rape or sexual assault of the child's mother and the child was conceived as a result. Being required to register as a sex offender constitutes grounds for termination in nine states.

The Child Welfare Information website also notes that a felony conviction of the parent(s) for a crime of violence against the child or another family member is grounds for termination in every state, the District of Columbia, Puerto Rico, and the Virgin Islands. In twenty-seven states, a conviction for any felony that results in long-term incarceration and requires the child to enter foster care because of a lack of alternatives may also constitute grounds for termination of parental rights. All states recognize abandonment of a child as grounds for termination, while twelve states specifically include cases in which a newborn infant has been relinquished to a safe haven provider.

Protective Orders

The court that can issue child or juvenile protective orders varies in different states. In most states they are issued by the family or domestic court. For the most part these orders are issued to protect the child or juvenile. For example, in the Commonwealth of Virginia a court may issue a *protective order* (sometimes known as a restraining order) if there are incident(s) of family abuse. The court can order a person to have no contact, or limited contact, with the victim or victim's children, or to leave the home and stay away for a certain period of time. If a person does not follow the rules and violates the protective order, that person can be arrested.

A juvenile restraining order is a court order to protect a person suffering unlawful violence or credible threats of violence. The court can order a person not to harass, attack, strike, threaten, assault, hit, follow, stalk, molest, destroy personal property of, or disturb the peace.

The Virginia law, like those in most jurisdictions, states that family abuse is an act involving violence, force, or threat, including any forceful detention which results in physical injury or places one in reasonable fear of death, sexual assault, or bodily injury, and is committed by a person against a family or household member.

The general steps in obtaining a personal protection order (PPO) are as follows:

1. Request in writing a preliminary PPO with the proper court. This PPO when granted will be good for a short period of time (e.g., fifteen days).
2. The judge will then set a date for a hearing on whether a permanent PPO should be granted, or the request denied.

(Note: A PPO is not effective until the person that it has been filed against is served with a copy of the PPO.)

Disclosure of Juvenile Information

According to the Juvenile Law Center, approximately 95 percent of the youth in the juvenile justice system have committed nonviolent offenses. The Center states that because adolescence is a transitional and volatile stage in life, most young people naturally mature into adulthood without any additional contact with the law.[2]

According to researchers Riya Saha Shah and Jean Strout, records are created for each youth involved in the juvenile justice system the moment the child comes into contact with the system. Many of these records are easily accessible to individuals both inside and outside the system. Records serve an important informational function to aid the court in disposition and case planning, but over time their utility diminishes. Children's juvenile court records tell the story of what they once did—not the story of who they are. These records interfere with children's opportunities to move ahead in life and demonstrate their ability to make better choices.[3]

The Juvenile Law Center offers the following guidelines as the ideal way to handle juvenile records:

- The youth's law enforcement and court records are not widely available and are never available online.
- The sealed records are completely closed to the general public.
- Sanctions are imposed on individuals and agencies that unlawfully share confidential or expunged juvenile record information or fail to comply with the expungement of records.

The Juvenile Law Center contends that states must do more to protect juvenile records in a manner that does not negatively affect a young person's future. The Center conducted the first comprehensive evaluation of how juvenile records are handled across the fifty states and the District of Columbia. The purpose of the evaluation was to see how individual states fared in two key areas: confidentiality of records during and after juvenile court proceedings; and the availability of records and process for sealing or expungement. The Center concluded that no state system was perfect, and that the protection of juvenile records and information must be given a higher priority. To learn how your state fared in this evaluation, visit www.jlc.org/juvenilerecords.

Most states allow courts, youth-serving agencies, and law enforcement personnel to access juvenile records. There are some states that also give broad access to juvenile record information to the media, employers, schools, government agencies, and victims. Some of these states require a court to hold a hearing to determine whether a record may be accessed. A few states circumvent their own protections by exempting categories of records from the confidentiality regulations based on age of the child and the type or seriousness of the offense.

Juvenile records generally include arrest reports, school records, medical or behavioral health records, prior juvenile court history and involvement, family placement, social history, and any records of aftercare.

Court Cases

In most states, court cases involving juvenile defendants do not use the juvenile's complete name in the case name nor in the decision. For example, one of the leading cases on the rights of youth decided by the US Supreme Court is *In re Gault.* Another case is *New Jersey v. T.L.O.* In some states, however, if the juvenile reaches the age of eighteen before the case is concluded, the court may identify the youth by name.

Co-author Cliff Roberson in a text on family violence cited a North Carolina Appellate Court ruling on child abuse by the juvenile's mother. When the case reached the state appellate court, the juvenile was over the age of eighteen. The state court styled the case as *In the Matter of* (at this point the juvenile's name was included). A textbook on family violence included the complete name of the court case, which was a matter of public record. Several years later, the former juvenile—by this time, a college student in a New York college—took a course in which this textbook was used. The student was shocked and embarrassed to learn that her mother had abused her, and that the matter had been litigated in the North Carolina courts.[4]

Expungement of Juvenile Records

Often the sealing of records may be ineffective because even if they are technically sealed, the record still exists, and is physically still accessible. In most states that seal juvenile records, a court judge may order the records unsealed. Some states limit which records may be sealed or expunged based on the age of the youth or the seriousness of the crime.

What Is Expungement?

Expungement is a court proceeding in which an offender of a prior criminal conviction seeks to have his or her records of that conviction removed from state or federal repositories. If successful, the records are said to be "expunged."

The Juvenile Law Center defines *expungement* as the physical and complete erasure of a juvenile record, as if it never existed. The Center notes that many state statutes on the subject use the word more broadly, often interchangeably with the word *sealed.*

If a criminal conviction or juvenile record has been expunged, the individual—when asked—may reply that he or she has not been convicted of that crime. A typical state statute on expungement provides that a petitioner whose record has been expunged does not have to disclose that fact on an application for employment or credit, or any other type of application. However, the petitioner whose record has been expunged shall have the duty to disclose the fact of the record and any matter relating thereto to any government regulatory or licensing agency, any utility and its agents and affiliates, or any bank or other financial institution. Several states, like Alabama, provide that an expungement order shall not entitle an individual to ship, transport, possess, or receive a firearm.

Expungement Process

Many states require the youth to file a petition to seal or expunge a record. After the youth's attorney submits a petition, there is a court hearing and finally a ruling on the question as to the sealing or expungement of the record. This can be a lengthy and costly process. Some states have implemented an automatic sealing procedure. In a few states the process of expungement or sealing may be initiated by a third party or an agency. At least one state, Virginia, only allows for expungement of minor offenses, granting public access to juvenile records prior to expungement. Virginia does have provisions for automatic expungement of juvenile records involving minor offenses.

Almost all states provide for sanctions when sealing or expungement regulations are violated. Generally, the sanctions include a fine and/or short periods of jail time. In many states violating these regulations is considered a misdemeanor crime.

Sealing

The Juvenile Law Center defines *sealing* as the mechanism for limiting access to juvenile records. In most jurisdictions, according to the Center, this means that the record is unavailable to the public, but remains accessible to select individuals and agencies, such as law enforcement personnel. The Center notes that state laws vary on who has access to sealed records and whether a court order is needed to access them.

Dual System Youths

Dual system youths are those who are involved in both the child welfare system and in the juvenile justice system. According to researchers Denise Herz and Carly Dierkhising, youths who are involved in both systems are a vulnerable population who are often unrecognized because of challenges in information-sharing and cross-system collaboration.[5] These challenges currently prevent the possibility of accurately estimating the number of dual system youth nationwide, and limit the understanding of best practices used by jurisdictions who are trying to implement integrated systems models.

The researchers note that several recent research reports involving dual system youths indicate that a dual system youth is most likely to:

- Be a male
- Be an African American
- Be involved with child welfare on average between four to five months
- Be charged with an offense against a person

- Have a detention rate of approximately 20 percent
- Have a recidivism rate of 15 to 30 percent at the end of one year

The researchers concluded that many youths in the juvenile justice system have been involved with the child welfare system in some way prior to their involvement in delinquency. They concluded that approximately half of youth petitioned to the juvenile delinquency court have touched the child welfare system.

Juvenile Competency Procedures

In this section, the procedures for determining the competency of juveniles in juvenile court proceeding will be explored. Most jurisdictions have either statutes, court rules, or case law outlining the procedures under which competency to stand a juvenile adjudication hearing is decided.[6] One state, Oklahoma, has specific case law from the state court of criminal appeals explaining that since juvenile proceedings are not criminal but rehabilitative, it was the intent of the legislature not to have the competency statutes apply to juveniles.[7]

The Dusky Standard

Generally, both adult and juvenile competency standards are based on the US Supreme Court case of *Dusky v. United States*.[8] In that case, the Supreme Court held that the test must be whether the person has a reasonable degree of understanding as well as factual understanding of the proceedings against him or her. Several states have added to the test. For example, the Wyoming Supreme Court held that those standards should be applied in light of juvenile norms.[9] Georgia's definition of juvenile incompetency states: "Incompetent to proceed means lacking sufficient present ability to understand the nature and object of the proceedings, to comprehend his or her own situation in relation to the proceedings, and to assist his or her attorney in the preparation and presentation of the case in all adjudication, disposition, or transfer hearings." Arkansas holds that the juvenile is incompetent if he or she does not have sufficient present ability to consult with his or her attorney with a reasonable degree of rational and factual understanding of the proceedings against the youth.

Factors Used to Evaluate the Dusky Standard

States use a variety of factors to determine if a juvenile meets the Dusky standard. For example, in Maine, the state forensic service examiner's report must address the juvenile's capacity and ability to appreciate the range of possible dispositions that may be imposed on him or her; appreciate the impact of his or her actions on others; and disclose to counsel facts pertinent to the proceeding at issue, including the ability to articulate emotions, and the ability to accurately and reliably relate a sequence of events. The juvenile being tested must also display logical and autonomous decision-making; display appropriate courtroom behavior; testify relevantly at proceedings; and demonstrate any other capacity or ability either separately sought by the juvenile court or determined by the examiner to be relevant to the juvenile court's determination.

In some states, the juvenile's age may be used as a factor in determining competency. For example, the age or immaturity of the juvenile may be used as a basis for determining competency in Georgia, Idaho, Maine, Maryland, and Vermont.

Some states use the term *chronological immaturity* when referring to a condition based on the juvenile's age and significant lack of development skills when the youth has no significant mental illness or intellectual disability. In some states, however, age alone does not render a person incompetent.

In some states, a juvenile who does not meet the Dusky standard of required competency may not be certified to be tried as an adult. In other states, the juvenile may be transferred to adult criminal court and the adult criminal court will proceed under the guidelines used in that jurisdiction for persons lacking mental competency.

Juvenile Drug Courts

This section will examine the specialized courts that handle juveniles who have specific problems; the United Nations Standards for Juveniles; and status offenses.

The first specialized court examined will be the juvenile drug courts. The first adult drug court started in Miami-Dade County, Florida, in 1989 as a response to the growing crack cocaine problem. Presently all fifty states have drug courts. As of June 2015, the estimated number of drug courts operating in the United States was over three thousand. The majority target adults, including DWI (driving while intoxicated) offenders and a growing number of veterans; others address juvenile, child welfare, and other types of cases.[10] The first juvenile drug court program started in Key West, Florida, in October 1993. By June 2015, there were 409 juvenile drug courts operating in the United States.[11]

In the US Department of Justice, juvenile drug courts are intensive treatment programs established within and supervised by juvenile courts to provide specialized services for eligible drug-involved youth and their families. According to the Juvenile Accountability Incentive Block Grants Program, cases are assigned to a juvenile drug court docket based on criteria set by local officials to carry out the goals of the drug court program. Juvenile drug courts provide:

- Intensive and continuous judicial supervision over delinquency and status offense cases that involve substance-abusing juveniles; and
- Coordinated and supervised delivery of an array of support services necessary to address the problems that contribute to juvenile involvement in the justice system.

Service areas include substance abuse treatment, mental health care, primary care, family support services, and education.[12] The different types of drug courts include adult drug court, juvenile drug court, family drug court, veterans' treatment court, and reentry courts. In this text we will discuss only juvenile drug courts.

Indicators of Need for a Juvenile Drug Court

According to the US Department of Justice, the potential benefits of developing a juvenile drug court program in a particular community are as follows:

- The program will help to increase understanding regarding the extent to which delinquency is associated with drug and alcohol use in the community;
- The juvenile justice system has an existing ability to address drug use issues through substance abuse treatment, supervision, and other core adolescent and family services (e.g., family therapy, mentoring, vocational training); and
- The juvenile drug court program will promote a degree of accountability for both juvenile offenders and service providers.

Once the extent of juvenile substance use is determined, local officials should decide whether existing resources—including the judicial system, school system, treatment services, and other community organizations and services—can adequately address the needs of juveniles in a timely and effective manner. Local officials should develop an inventory of community resources that addresses the needs of juvenile offenders who use or are at risk of using drugs and alcohol. This inventory should include both treatment-specific resources and other core services, including education, mental health and public health services, family therapy, literacy skill building, mentoring, prosocial activities, vocational training, and other family support services.

The first step in planning and implementing a juvenile drug court is to identify the nature and extent of problems that the program must address, goals that the program must achieve, and indicators that will reveal the degree to which these goals are met. In most instances, this process is initiated by a juvenile court judge, who is frequently joined by representatives from the prosecutor's office, the public defender's office, and juvenile intake and probation staff. If a review of caseload and case disposition characteristics suggests that a juvenile drug court would be useful, this initial planning group should invite representatives from social service agencies, treatment agencies, and other youth service agencies.

Juvenile Drug Court Goals

According to the National Institute of Justice, the goals of the juvenile drug court should include the following:

- Provide immediate intervention, treatment, and structure in the lives of juveniles using drugs through the ongoing, active oversight and monitoring by the drug court judge.
- Improve juveniles' level of functioning in their environment, address problems that may be contributing to their use of drugs, and develop/strengthen their ability to lead crime- and drug-free lives.
- Provide juveniles with skills that will aid them in leading productive substance-free and crime-free lives, including skills relating to their educational development, sense of self-worth, and capacity to develop positive relationships in the community.
- Strengthen the families of drug-involved youth by improving their capacity to provide structure and guidance to their children.
- Improve system capacity to promote accountability for both juvenile offenders and the services they are provided.

Development of Juvenile Drug Courts

To stem the street drug dealing and the crime and violence associated with illegal drug use, arrests and prosecutions of drug offenders have escalated dramatically, and penalties for the possession and sale of illegal drugs have been toughened. As a result of this nationwide war on drugs, unprecedented numbers of drug offenders were arrested, charged with felonies, prosecuted, convicted, and incarcerated.[13] Many researchers contend that the war on drugs was really a war on the hippie movement. Currently many jurisdictions are rethinking the costly war on drugs and the harsh penalties that were imposed on drug offenses. For example, in the 1960s, a football player from a major university was convicted of possession of several grams of marijuana and received an eight-year prison term. Today in many jurisdictions, this would be a minor crime, and in others, it wouldn't be a crime at all.

The influx of drug offenders into the justice system severely strained the courts, forcing some to the brink of collapse. To address growing caseloads, courts employed delay-reduction strategies, including specialized court dockets to expedite drug-case processing. However, these strategies did not address the complex issues underlying substance abuse—including family and mental health problems—and did little to stem the tide of drug offenders flowing into the system; habilitate drug offenders already in the system; or reduce recidivism among released offenders. The result was a revolving door syndrome that cycled drug offenders in and out of the justice system for years.

According to the Bureau of Justice Assistance (BJA), frustration with this syndrome propelled a philosophical shift in the field toward therapeutic jurisprudence. The basic tenets of therapeutic jurisprudence are that the law is a therapeutic agent; positive therapeutic outcomes are important judicial goals; and that the design of the program influences therapeutic outcomes. Some innovative jurisdictions began to reexamine the relationship between criminal justice processing and services for those who use alcohol and other drugs. They determined that treatment and justice practitioners share essential goals—stopping the illicit use and abuse of all addictive substances, and curtailing related involvement with the criminal justice system. Each one possesses unique capabilities and resources that complement and enhance the effectiveness of the other.

From these findings, a partnership emerged, and the concept of treatment-oriented drug courts developed. Courts began working closely with a wide range of stakeholders within a problem-solving framework, with therapeutic outcomes as a goal. As one of several criminal justice initiatives that started at the grassroots level and spread throughout the nation, drug courts joined a growing number of specialized community courts, all designed to reflect community concerns and priorities, access community resources, include community organizations in policy-making decisions, and seek general community participation and support.

Therapeutic jurisprudence, formerly just an academic theory, was being applied every day in drug courts. With the success of adult drug courts in reducing recidivism, the application of drug court principles to populations in the juvenile court was a logical step, and some juvenile court judges drew on the experience of an adult court in their locale to begin a juvenile drug court. However, the circumstances and needs of youth and their families are different from those of adult criminal offenders. It quickly became apparent that applying drug court principles to youth populations would not be as simple as replicating the adult model, and that a drug court for youth would look very different from one aimed at adults.

The increase in drug and alcohol use among juveniles peaked later than in the adult population. By 2000 the Centers for Disease Control and Prevention reported that rates of smoking, drinking, and other illicit drug use among students had increased in the early 1990s and remained alarmingly high. Half of all students reported alcohol use, and nearly one-third were binge-drinking. More than one-fourth of high school students were marijuana users; 9.5 percent had used cocaine by the end of high school; and 14.6 percent had used inhalants. The number of juvenile drug offense cases processed during 1995 was 145 percent greater than in 1991.

As this trend continued, juvenile court judges experienced many of the same frustrations the adult courts had faced. They found that dealing with substance-abusing juveniles within the traditional juvenile court often meant long treatment waiting lists, disjointed service delivery, lack of family engagement, and no input into the nature or extent of treatment. Consequently, a number of innovative juvenile courts started drug treatment programs that focused on the problem of substance abuse.

Juvenile courts had a significant advantage over adult courts in applying the therapeutic jurisprudence theory. Because the original orientation of juvenile courts was rehabilitation, the use of therapeutic interventions was not new in this setting.

As noted in chapters 1 and 2, the juvenile court's mission is to correct and rehabilitate children who have violated the law, to protect the community from their delinquent behavior, and to strengthen the family. Accordingly, juvenile drug courts did not represent a dramatic philosophical shift from past and current juvenile justice considerations and objectives.

The basic concepts of juvenile drug courts remained consistent with the principles of traditional juvenile court practice. Accordingly, juvenile courts found that drug treatment programs could be successfully operated within the existing framework of ethical, legal, and professional standards.

How Juvenile Drug Courts Function

A juvenile drug court is a docket within a juvenile court to which selected delinquency cases—and, in some instances, status offenders—are referred for handling by a designated judge. The youth referred to this docket are identified as having problems with alcohol and/or other drugs. The juvenile drug court judge maintains close oversight of each case through frequent (often weekly) status hearings with the parties involved. The judge both leads and works as a member of a team that comprises representatives from treatment, juvenile justice, social services, school and vocational training programs, law enforcement, probation, the prosecution, and the defense. Together, the team determines how best to address the substance abuse and related problems of the youth and his or her family that have brought the youth into contact with the justice system.

Most communities that establish juvenile drug courts initiate these programs to provide intensive judicial intervention and supervision of juveniles and families involved in substance abuse—a level of intervention not generally available through the traditional juvenile court process. The juvenile drug court is a unique, community-based approach that builds strong community partnerships and enhances the capacity of these partners to assist in the habilitation of substance-abusing youth.

Juvenile Drug Treatment Programs

Since the early start-up of juvenile drug courts, the professionals in the field have learned that programs for youth must incorporate individually tailored and developmentally appropriate, comprehensive treatments that draw on the strengths and address the needs of participants and their families. They have also learned that the engagement of the neighborhood and broader community is important to long-term success with the juvenile substance-abusing offender.

Effective juvenile drug courts provide collateral programs that enhance social and life skills for participants. Some examples are:

- Literacy programs that develop and improve reading, writing, and interpersonal communication skills.
- Vocational and job training.
- Recreational activities.
- Mentoring.
- Community service.
- Health-care screenings and referrals.

Maine Juvenile Drug Court Program

The state of Maine has a typical juvenile drug treatment court system, including court-supervised, post-plea (but pre–final disposition) drug diversion programs that provide comprehensive community-based treatment services to juvenile offenders and their families. The Maine system shares the primary goal of all juvenile drug court programs: to reduce substance abuse and the likelihood of arrest among participants.[14]

According to its website, Maine is one of the few states to successfully implement a statewide system of juvenile drug courts. Currently six juvenile drug courts are in operation, which serve seven counties. The first program in Maine was the Bangor Juvenile Drug Court which became operational on January 26, 2000. The program functions through a collaboration among the Maine District Court, the Maine Department of Behavioral and Developmental Services/Office of Substance Abuse, and the Maine Department of Corrections/Juvenile Services. The juvenile drug courts target youth who:

1. demonstrate a medium to high risk of criminal recidivism;
2. demonstrate a substantial substance abuse problem;
3. have an ability to participate in substance abuse treatment; and
4. have a parent or other adult figure that is willing to participate or play an active role in the youth's participation in the program.

Referrals can come from a variety of sources, including the district attorney, juvenile community corrections officer (JCCO), defense counsel, school official, or other interested person.

The juvenile drug court programs run about fifty-two weeks and are divided into four phases, each with distinct treatment goals and specified completion times:

- First phase: focuses on assessment and planning; lasts approximately eight weeks.
- Second phase: designed to build support and teach participants about new skills; lasts approximately twenty weeks.
- Third phase: intended to strengthen skills and solidify support; lasts approximately twelve weeks.
- Fourth/final phase: monitoring phase; lasts about ten weeks.

Juvenile drug court participants can receive a variety of treatment services, including individual therapy, group therapy, family counseling, intensive outpatient services, and residential services. In addition to treatment for substance abuse, other types of services are offered as well, such as educational programming, job training, mental health services, and recreational planning.

Maine's juvenile drug courts use rewards and sanctions to ensure compliance to program goals and objectives, but there is no structured sanctions protocol in place. Rather, rewards and sanctions are determined on a case-by-case basis. The decision to reward or sanction a youth is usually decided during a review of participant progress at weekly staffing sessions. The drug court team arrives at a consensus about the particular course of action to take with youth. The presiding judge imposes the sanction or reward during the weekly status hearing. Types of sanctions include detention, community service, house arrest, increased reporting, or a written assignment. Types of rewards include curfew extension, advancement to the next phase, or praise/applause for the youth.

Teen Courts

As the juvenile justice system evolves, many jurisdictions have created special courts and programs to address special issues involving juveniles. Not all jurisdictions have adopted these courts and programs, and there may be additional special courts and programs that are not discussed in this section.

One of the more popular special courts is teen court. As noted by the Office of Juvenile Justice and Delinquency Prevention (OJJDP), there are several basic criminological theories supporting the use of young people in the teen court process. One theory is that, in court, youth will respond better to prosocial peers than to adult authority figures. This peer justice approach assumes that just as association with delinquent peers is highly correlated with the onset of delinquent behavior, peer pressure from prosocial peers may push youth toward prosocial behavior. Another theoretical perspective views teen courts through the lens of procedural justice. Teen courts can make an impact on juvenile offenders by increasing their knowledge of the criminal justice system and influencing their perceived fairness of the system.[15]

Teen courts, also known as *youth courts* or *peer courts*, are designed to serve as problem-solving courts within the juvenile justice system. Teens charged with certain types of offenses can be sentenced by a jury of similar-aged peers. The purpose is to provide an alternative disposition for youths who have committed a delinquent act and are otherwise eligible for diversion. Depending on their training, community support, and agreements with traditional court systems, most teen or youth courts are recognized as valid, legal venues for the process of hearing cases, sentencing, and sentence completions. A typical teen court is the one in Santa Fe County, New Mexico, discussed in box 14.1.

BOX 14.1 Teen Court for Santa Fe County, New Mexico

Teen Court is a first-time offender's program with alternative sentencing that is run for teens, by teens, and has been serving teens and families in our community since 1994.

Teen Court is a nationally recognized early intervention and restorative justice program for juveniles (ages twelve to seventeen), giving the offender a second chance while holding them accountable for their actions. The Teen Court program serves as a community-based intervention/diversion program designed to provide an alternative response for the juvenile justice system. The teen accepts responsibility for their offense, appears before a judge and their peers, and is sentenced.

The goal of the Teen Court program is to interrupt developing patterns of criminal behavior by promoting feelings of self-esteem, motivation for self-improvement, and a healthy attitude toward authority. Teen Court challenges the offenders, as well as the volunteer teens, to perform at their highest level of ability. Teen Courts give appropriate offenders a second chance, yet holds them accountable for their actions. The courts use positive peer pressure to ensure that young people who commit even minor offenses give back to the community and avoid further contact with the justice system.

The sanctions are determined by the Teen Court jury, and include community service, jury duty, and letters of apology. Other possible sanctions can include behavior modification classes, essays, counseling, educational programs, gender-specific programs, and substance abuse prevention workshops.

Source: Santa Fe County Community Service website at https://www.santafecountynm.gov/community_services/teen_court (accessed March 26, 2019).

According to the Global Youth Justice website, there are more than 1,800 volunteer-driven and youth-led youth justice and juvenile justice diversion programs called variously teen court, youth court, student court, peer court, and peer jury. These programs are located on five continents, making it the most replicated juvenile justice and youth justice program around the globe. Adults and youth from hundreds of additional communities around the world are in various stages of implementing one of these rapidly expanding affordable and scalable diversion programs. For more information on the teen courts in your jurisdiction, visit the Global Youth Justice website at https://www.globalyouthjustice.org/our-work/youth-teen-student-peer-court/.

Status Offenses

According to the Vera Institute, one in eleven formally processed juvenile court cases in 2014 was for a status offense. The Institute's Status Offense Reform Center noted that status offenses are not crimes, but rather behaviors prohibited under law because of a youth's status as a minor. The Center notes that the five most common behaviors that are designated as status offenses are skipping school, acting out, running away, underage drinking, and violating curfew. Turning to the juvenile justice system to handle these cases can have negative consequences on the juvenile, the family, and the community.[16] The result, according to the Center, is that kids charged with status offenses may be arrested and can end up in locked facilities, which further exacerbates the circumstances that drive their behaviors. This approach is not only costly in terms of justice system expenses, but also serves to further criminalize underserved kids who are often subject to harsh biases and discipline, including girls, kids in poor communities, kids of color, and LGBTQ/gender-nonconforming youth.

Vera Institute concludes that many jurisdictions are presently recognizing the value of rethinking their approach to status offenses. These forward-thinking communities have adopted the goal of keeping these youth out of their juvenile justice systems entirely, instead using community-based approaches. These approaches have led to reduced court caseloads, lower government costs, and more meaningful and lasting support to children and families in their communities.

Starting in the late 1960s and 1970s, there was a move toward deinstitutionalizing status offenses. The movement was encouraged by the 1974 Federal Juvenile Delinquency Act. *Deinstitutionalization* refers to situations where the juveniles who committed status offenses are diverted from the juvenile justice system to other social agencies outside the juvenile court's jurisdiction. Under most state systems, the county or district attorney is given the authority to divert an offender, and this decision is generally made before a juvenile court petition is filed.

Who Commits Status Offenses

In 2004, juvenile courts in the United States formally processed an estimated 159,400 status offense cases.[17] Only a juvenile court can adjudicate status offenses (acts that are considered illegal only when juveniles commit them). Once a status offense case has been referred for juvenile court intake, the court must decide whether to process the case by filing a petition, or to refer the youth away from the juvenile justice system to other juvenile service agencies. Table 14.1 provides an offense profile of petitioned status offense cases for 1995 and 2004.

Between 1995 and 2004, the petitioned status offense caseload for girls increased 42 percent, compared with a 37 percent increase in caseload for boys.

TABLE 14.1 **Offense Profile of Petitioned Status Offense Cases, 1995 and 2004**

Most Serious Offense	1995	2004
Running Away	17%	13%
Truancy	29%	35%
Curfew violations	10%	10%
Ungovernability	14%	14%
Liquor law violations	23%	19%
Miscellaneous offenses	7%	9%

Source: Anne L. Stahl, "Petitioned Status Offense Cases in Juvenile Courts, 2004," OJJPD Fact Sheet (February 2008), posted at https://www.ncjrs.gov/pdffiles1/ojjdp/fs200802.pdf (accessed May 16, 2019).

In 2004, boys accounted for 56 percent of the total petitioned status offense caseload—63 percent liquor law violation cases, 65 percent curfew violation cases, 54 percent truancy cases, and 55 percent of ungovernability cases. Girls accounted for most petitioned runaway cases, at 62 percent, the only status offense category in 2004 in which girls represented a larger proportion of the caseload than boys.

Adjudication and Disposition

Adjudicatory hearings establish responsibility for an alleged act; courts hold disposition hearings to decide what sanctions they should impose on a juvenile who has been adjudicated. The likelihood of adjudication for petitioned status offense cases was 63 percent in 2004, compared with 50 percent in 1995. For year 2015, 62.6 percent of the juveniles adjudicated as status offenders and placed in residential facilities were male and 37.4 percent were female.[18]

Among the status offense categories in 2004, adjudication was least likely in petitioned runaway cases (43%) and most likely in cases involving liquor law violations (78%). The likelihood of adjudication for petitioned curfew violation cases in 2004 (73%) was higher than that for both truancy (58%) and ungovernability cases (57%). In 2004, truancy cases were the largest share of the adjudicated status offense caseload that resulted in out-of-home placement.

Except for cases involving truancy and liquor law violations, the likelihood that an adjudicated status offense case would result in out-of-home placement decreased for each of the major status offense categories between 1995 and 2004. Probation was the most restrictive disposition used in 52 percent of the petitioned status offense cases in 2004. Courts ordered probation in 70 percent of adjudicated ungovernability cases, 64 percent of runaway cases, 61 percent of cases involving truancy, 48 percent of cases involving liquor law violations, and 20 percent of curfew violation cases. In 2004, the juvenile was not adjudicated a status offender in 37 percent of formally handled cases; the court dismissed 87 percent of these cases, 3 percent resulted in informal probation, and in 10 percent of these cases, the youth voluntarily agreed to other informal dispositions such as community service.

Detention

In 2004, juveniles were securely detained in 7 percent of petitioned status offense cases, about the same proportion as in 1995 (6%). Before 1997, runaway cases comprised the largest proportion of the detained status offense caseload. Since that time, however, cases involving liquor law violations have accounted for the largest share of detentions—28 percent in 2004.

Diversion

Diversion was implemented for status offenders because many legislators and the general public objected to status offenders being treated like delinquents. They also felt that status offenses were minor in terms of criminal nature, and juveniles were better off having their families or some other agency deal with the matter than being formally processed by the justice system. Formal processing of status offenses was thought to lead to labeling and further delinquent acts, thus negating the whole purpose of rehabilitation.

Currently, status offenses still exist in all states, and many juveniles are still confined for such offenses. Juveniles who are adjudicated for status offenses are generally classified as children in need of supervision (CHINS), persons in need of supervision (PINS), and minors in need of supervision (MINS).

Curfew Laws

In recent years many cities have eliminated their juvenile curfew laws based on the simple fact that research has shown that they do little to deter crime or reduce juvenile victimization. In addition, the juvenile curfew laws disproportionately punish minorities and black youth. For example, in Austin, Texas, black youths made up only 8 percent of the juvenile population in 2016, but black youths received 17 percent of all juvenile curfew tickets by the police.[19] Box 14.2 contains excerpts on a curfew law for juveniles.

BOX 14.2 *Qutb v. Strauss*

11 F.3d 488 (5th Cir. 1993)

(Excerpts from the opinion of Circuit Judge E. Grady Jolly)

This appeal presents a challenge to the constitutionality of a nocturnal juvenile curfew ordinance enacted by Dallas, Texas. The ordinance makes it a misdemeanor for persons under the age of seventeen to use the city streets or to be present at other public places within the city between certain hours. Several plaintiffs sued the city to strike down the ordinance. The district court ruled for the plaintiffs, holding that the ordinance violated both the United States and the Texas Constitutions, and permanently enjoined enforcement of the ordinance. The city appeals. Because we conclude that this ordinance does not violate the United States or Texas Constitutions, we reverse the district court.

. . . Although the ordinance restricts the hours when minors are allowed in public areas, the ordinance also contains several exceptions, or defenses. A person under the age of seventeen in a public place during curfew hours does not violate the ordinance if he or she is accompanied by a parent or guardian, or is on an errand for a parent or guardian. Likewise, minors would be allowed in public places if they are in a motor vehicle traveling to or from a place of employment, or if they are involved in employment-related activities. . . .

A minor violates the curfew if he or she remains in any public place or on the premises of any establishment during curfew hours, and if the minor's activities are not exempted from coverage. If a minor is apparently violating the ordinance, the ordinance requires police officers to ask the age of the apparent offender, and to inquire into the reasons for being in a public place during curfew hours before taking any enforcement action. An officer may issue a citation or arrest the apparent offender only if the officer reasonably believes that the person has violated the ordinance and that no defenses apply. If convicted, an offending party is subject to a fine not to exceed $500.00 for each separate offense.

. . . The district court held that the curfew impermissibly restricted minors' First Amendment right to associate, and that it created classifications that could not withstand constitutional scrutiny. Accordingly, the district court permanently enjoined enforcement of the curfew, and the city now appeals.

The plaintiffs argue that the curfew ordinance violates the Equal Protection Clause of the Fourteenth Amendment. The Equal Protection Clause is essentially a direction that all persons similarly situated should be treated alike. Only if the challenged government action classifies or distinguishes between two or more relevant groups must we conduct an equal protection inquiry. Here, it is clear that the curfew ordinance distinguishes between classes of individuals on the basis of age, treating those persons under the age of seventeen differently from those persons age seventeen and older. Because the curfew ordinance distinguishes between two groups, we must analyze the curfew ordinance under the Equal Protection Clause.

Under the Equal Protection analysis, we apply different standards of review depending upon the right or classification involved. If a classification disadvantages a "suspect class" or impinges upon a "fundamental right," the ordinance is subject to strict scrutiny.

In this case, no one has argued, and correctly so, that a classification based on age is a suspect classification. The minor plaintiffs, however, have argued that the curfew ordinance impinges upon their "fundamental right" to move about freely in public. For purposes of our analysis, we assume without deciding that the right to move about freely is a fundamental right. We are mindful, however, that this ordinance is directed solely at the activities of juveniles and, under certain circumstances, minors may be treated differently from adults.

In conclusion, we find that the state has demonstrated that the curfew ordinance furthers a compelling state interest, i.e., protecting juveniles from crime on the streets. We further conclude that the ordinance is narrowly tailored to achieve this compelling state interest. Accordingly, we hold that the nocturnal juvenile curfew ordinance enacted by the city of Dallas is constitutional. The judgment of the district court is therefore REVERSED.

Truancy

Truancy is generally considered any unexcused or unverified absence from school. Since states enact their own school attendance laws, the legal definition of truancy may vary from state to state. Truancy has been linked to poor academic performance and school dropouts, and increases the likelihood that youth will engage in drug and alcohol use, fighting, theft, and more-serious forms of delinquency. Over the long term, adults who were chronically truant as adolescents are more likely to have poorer health outcomes, lower-paying jobs, and a greater chance of being incarcerated during their lifetime.[20]

Males are more likely to skip school than females. The frequency and severity of truant behavior increases as young people get older. Researchers have found that truancy increases with age, peaking among sixteen-year-olds. Youth who associate with peers engaged in problem behaviors are more likely to skip school than those who associate with peers engaged in prosocial activities. Low levels of parental control and monitoring have been associated with truancy. However, parental involvement (i.e., discussions with children about school, assisting with homework, participation in parent-teacher organizations) has positive effects on school performance and reduces the likelihood of future truancy.

Practicum

Assume that you are a concerned citizen located in a state that uses teen and juvenile drug courts. The governor requests that you give her your opinion on the creation of a juvenile status offense court to reduce the use of regular juvenile courts handling cases involving status offenses.

What would be your thoughts on the subject, and how should the program work?

Summary

- Protective orders are those issued by a court for the primary purpose of protecting a child from future possible violence.
- Termination of parental rights is frequently necessary to protect the child.
- Juvenile drug courts are intensive treatment programs established within and supervised by juvenile courts to provide specialized services for eligible drug-involved youth and their families.
- Cases are assigned to a juvenile drug court docket based on criteria set by local officials to carry out the goals of the drug court program.
- The goals of the juvenile drug court should include:
  - Providing immediate intervention, treatment, and structure in the lives of juveniles using drugs through ongoing, active oversight and monitoring by the drug court judge.
  - Improving juveniles' level of functioning in their environment, addressing problems that may be contributing to their use of drugs, and developing/strengthening their ability to lead crime- and drug-free lives.
  - Providing juveniles with skills that will aid them in leading productive substance-free and crime-free lives, including skills relating to their educational development, sense of self-worth, and capacity to develop positive relationships in the community.

  - Strengthening the families of drug-involved youth by improving the capacity of families to provide structure and guidance to their children.
  - Improving system capacity to promote accountability for both juvenile offenders and the services they are provided.
- As a result of this nationwide war on drugs, unprecedented numbers of drug offenders were arrested, charged with felonies, prosecuted, convicted, and incarcerated.
- To address growing caseloads, courts employed delay-reduction strategies, including specialized court dockets to expedite drug-case processing.
- One of the more popular special courts is teen court.
- Teen courts, also known as youth courts or peer courts, are designed as problem-solving courts within the juvenile justice system.
- Teens charged with certain types of offenses can be sentenced by a jury of similar-aged peers. The purpose is to provide an alternative disposition for youths who have committed a delinquent act and are otherwise eligible for diversion.
- According to the Vera Institute, one in eleven formally processed juvenile court cases in 2014 was for a status offense.
- The five most common behaviors that are designated as status offenses are skipping school, acting out, running away, underage drinking, and violating curfew.
- Turning to the juvenile justice system to handle these cases can have negative consequences on the juvenile, the family, and the community.

Discussion and Review Questions

1. What are the purposes of protective orders?
2. What are some of the reasons that a court would terminate parental rights?
3. How do juvenile drug courts function?
4. What are the goals of juvenile drug courts?
5. How do juvenile drug courts differ from teen courts?
6. What are the goals of teen courts?
7. What are status offenses?

Notes

1. Child Welfare Information Gateway website at https://www.childwelfare.gov/topics/systemwide/laws-policies/statutes/groundtermin/ (accessed May 27, 2019).
2. Juvenile Law Center website at https://juvenilerecords.jlc.org/juvenilerecords/#!/map (accessed May 28, 2019).
3. Riya Saha Shah and Jean Strout, "Future Interrupted: The Collateral Damage Caused by Proliferation of Juvenile Records," Juvenile Law Center (February 2016), posted at https://juvenilerecords.jlc.org/juvenilerecords/#!/map (accessed May 28, 2019).
4. Paul Harvey Wallace and Cliff Roberson, *Family Violence: Legal, Medical, and Social Perspectives*, 8th ed. (New York: Routledge, 2017).
5. Denise C. Herz and Carly B. Dierkhising, "Dual System Youth Design Study: Summary of Findings and Recommendations for Pursuing a National Estimate of Dual System Youth," Office of Juvenile Justice and Delinquency Prevention (Washington, DC: US Department of Justice, March 2019).
6. Linda A. Szymanski, "Juvenile Competency Procedures" (October 2013), posted at Juvenile Justice Geography, Policy, Practice & Statistics website at www.ncjj.org/pdf/JJGPS%20StateScan/JJGPS_StateScan_JuvenileCompetencyProcedures_2013_1.pdf (accessed May 29, 2019).

7. *G.J.I. v. State*, 778 P.2d 485 (1989).
8. *Dusky v. United States*, 362 U.S. 402 (1960).
9. *In the Interest of SWM v. State*, 299 P.3rd. 673 (2013).
10. National Institute of Justice, "Practice Profile: Juvenile Drug Courts" (no date), posted on NIJ website at https://www.crimesolutions.gov/PracticeDetails.aspx?ID=14 (accessed May 15, 2019).
11. National Institute of Justice, "Drug Courts" (August 2018), posted at https://www.nij.gov/topics/courts/drug-courts/Pages/welcome.aspx (accessed May 19, 2019).
12. Caroline S. Cooper, "Juvenile Drug Court Programs," *JAIBG Bulletin* (May 2001) (Washington, DC: US Department of Justice).
13. Bureau of Justice Assistance Report, "Juvenile Drug Courts: Strategies in Practice," NCJ 197866 (Washington, DC: US Department of Justice, March 2003).
14. National Institute of Justice, "Program Profile: Maine Juvenile Drug Treatment" (November 2013), posted on NIJ website at https://www.crimesolutions.gov/ProgramDetails.aspx?ID=339 (accessed May 15, 2019).
15. Development Services Group, "Teen Youth Court," Literature review (Washington, DC: Office of Juvenile Justice and Delinquency Prevention, 2010), posted on OJJPD website at https://www.ojjdp.gov/mpg/litreviews/Teen_Youth_Court.pdf (accessed March 25, 2019).
16. Vera Institute of Justice website at https://www.vera.org/projects/status-offense-reform-center/learn-more (accessed May 16, 2019).
17. Anne L. Stahl, "Petitioned Status Offense Cases in Juvenile Courts, 2004," OJJPD Fact Sheet, (February 2008), posted at https://www.ncjrs.gov/pdffiles1/ojjdp/fs200802.pdf (accessed May 16, 2019).
18. M. Sickmund, T. J. Sladky, W. Kang, and C. Puzzanchera, "Easy Access to the Census of Juveniles in Residential Placement," 2019. Available at https://www.ojjdp.gov/ojstatbb/ezacjrp/ (accessed May 16, 2019).
19. Statement of Troy Gray, assistant chief of police of the Austin Police Department, as reported in a *Houston Chronicle* editorial, July 10, 2019, E-1.
20. Sydney McKinney, "Truancy: A Research Brief," December 2013, Status Offense Reform Center (Pittsburgh, PA: National Center for Juvenile Justice, 2013).

CHAPTER 15

Comparative Review of Juvenile Justice and Delinquency

CHAPTER OBJECTIVES

After studying this chapter, the reader should be able to:

- Discuss and analyze the United Nations efforts to protect juveniles.
- Analyze how different nations have attempted to reduce juvenile delinquency.
- Compare the philosophy and treatment of juveniles by the United States and selected countries.
- Understand the worldwide effort to reduce juvenile delinquency and correct those who have committed delinquent acts as juveniles.

Overview

This chapter will explore the United Nations' activities to protect juveniles and address juvenile justice and delinquency in selected countries, to provide the readers with a comparative view of the issues. Each country has its own traditions and customs regarding how children should be raised. What is perfectly acceptable in one country may be seen as misconduct in another. As societies increasingly become more global and less homogenized, understanding and accepting cultural differences in child rearing becomes more important.[1] It is interesting to note that most nations did not develop a juvenile justice system until the 1900s, and that there are many similarities among the nations in the handling of juvenile delinquents.

United Nations Standards on Juvenile Justice

Since its creation in 1948, the United Nations has been concerned with the rights, safety, and dignity of children around the world. One of the missions of the UN is to protect children living in war-torn countries. In the last part of the twentieth century, the UN began to focus on protecting children who are involved with justice systems.[2] In 1983, the UN passed the General Assembly Resolution 40/33. When it was determined that this resolution was not specific or direct enough, the United

Nations Standard Minimum Rules for the Administration of Juvenile Delinquency was passed in 1990.

The UN Standards are commonly referred to as "The Beijing Rules." The UN General Assembly called upon member states (nations) to adapt, wherever this is necessary, their national legislation, policies, and practices, particularly in training juvenile justice personnel, to the Beijing Rules, and to bring the Rules to the attention of relevant authorities and the public.

The following is only a summary; the complete Standards, along with discussions on each, may be found at https://www.ohchr.org/Documents/ProfessionalInterest/beijingrules.pdf. The Standards include:

- Nations should endeavor to develop conditions that will ensure the juvenile a meaningful life in the community, which, during that period in life when she or he is most susceptible to deviant behaviour, will foster a process of personal development and education that is as free from crime and delinquency as possible.
- In those legal systems recognizing the concept of the age of criminal responsibility for juveniles, the beginning of that age shall not be fixed at too low an age level, bearing in mind the facts of emotional, mental, and intellectual maturity.
- The juvenile justice system shall emphasize the well-being of the juvenile and shall ensure that any reaction to juvenile offenders shall always be in proportion to the circumstances of both the offenders and the offense.
- Basic procedural safeguards, such as the presumption of innocence, the right to be notified of the charges, the right to remain silent, the right to counsel, the right to the presence of a parent or guardian, the right to confront and cross-examine witnesses, and the right to appeal to a higher authority shall be guaranteed at all stages of the proceedings.
- Upon the apprehension of a juvenile, her or his parents or guardian shall be immediately notified of such apprehension, and, where such immediate notification is not possible, the parents or guardian shall be notified within the shortest possible time thereafter.
- In order to best fulfill their functions, police officers who frequently or exclusively deal with juveniles or who are primarily engaged in the prevention of juvenile crime shall be specially instructed and trained. In large cities, special police units should be established for that purpose.
- Detention pending trial shall be used only as a measure of last resort and for the shortest possible period.

United Nations World Youth Report

The United Nations also publishes a World Youth Report on various subjects involving children. Its 2003 report included a chapter on juvenile delinquency.[3] The report contained some interesting conclusions regarding juvenile delinquency in various world countries. The conclusions are interesting, and indicate that there are similar issues in almost all countries regarding delinquent activity by youths. The report's conclusions are summarized as follows:

- Countries in transition have witnessed a dramatic increase in juvenile delinquency rates.
- Many of the criminal offenses committed by youth are related to drug abuse and excessive alcohol use.
- The problems and issues in juvenile delinquency are becoming more complicated and universal, and crime prevention programs are either unequipped to deal with the present realities or do not exist.

- Many developing countries have done little or nothing to deal with the changing complexity of juvenile delinquency. While developed countries are engaged in activities aimed at juvenile delinquency prevention, the overall effect of these programs is weak because the mechanisms in place are often inadequate to address the existing situations.
- On the whole, current efforts to fight juvenile delinquency are characterized by the lack of systematic action and the absence of task-oriented and effective social work with both offenders and victims, whether real or potential.

Basic Assumptions of Delinquent Behavior

The World Youth Report 2003 made some basic assumptions about the behavior of delinquents. The assumptions included:

- It is impossible to develop effective prevention programs without understanding the reasons behind juvenile involvement in criminal activity.
- Different approaches are used in scientific and practical literature on juvenile crime and violence to define and explain delinquent behavior by young people.
- Criminologists view juvenile delinquency as encompassing all public wrongs committed by young people between the ages of twelve and twenty.
- Sociologists view the concept more broadly, believing it covers a multitude of different violations of legal and social norms, from minor offenses to serious crimes committed by juveniles, including status offenses.
- Antisocial behavior may be a normal part of growing up or the beginning of a long-term pattern of criminal activity.
- Statistical data in many countries show that juvenile delinquency is largely a group phenomenon, and that between two-thirds and three-quarters of all juvenile offenses are committed by members of various groups. Even those juveniles who commit offenses alone are likely to be members of various gangs.
- Data from the Russian Federation indicate that the rate of criminal activity among juveniles in groups is about three or four times higher than that of adult offenders.
- Juvenile group crime is most prevalent among fourteen-year-olds and least prevalent among seventeen-year-olds.

Causes of and Conditions for the Formation of Delinquent Trajectories

According to the World Youth Report 2003, the causes and conditions that encourage the formation of delinquent trajectories include the following:

- There is evidence of a universal increase in juvenile crime taking place concurrently with economic decline.
- In many cases, street children later become young offenders after having already encountered violence in their immediate social environment as either witnesses or victims of violent crime.
- Socioeconomic instability is often linked to persistent unemployment and low incomes among the young, which can increase the likelihood of their involvement in criminal activity.
- Delinquent behavior often occurs in social settings in which the norms for acceptable behavior have broken down.
- Geographical analysis suggests that countries with more-urbanized populations have higher registered crime rates than do those countries with strong rural lifestyles.

- The ongoing process of urbanization in developing countries is contributing to juvenile involvement in criminal behavior.
- Worldwide studies show that children who receive adequate parental supervision are less likely to engage in criminal activity.
- The growing gap between rich and poor has led to the emergence of unwanted others. The exclusion of some people is gradually increasing with the accumulation of obstacles, including ruptured social ties, unemployment, and identity crises, all of which have contributed to the development of a "new poor" and increased delinquent behavior.
- Peer influence is a strong factor in contributing to delinquent behavior.

Regional Aspects of Delinquency

Some of the conclusions of the World Youth Report 2003 regarding the regional aspects of delinquency include:

- In Africa, juvenile delinquency tends to be attributed to hunger, poverty, malnutrition, and unemployment, which are linked to the marginalization of juveniles in the already severely disadvantaged segments of society.
- In Asian countries, juvenile crime and delinquency are largely urban phenomena. The most significant trends in the region include the rise in the number of violent crimes committed by young people.
- In Latin America, the young have been hit the hardest by the economic problems linked to the debt crisis in the region, which has increased unemployment and homelessness among the youth. This situation has led to an increase in violent crime by the young.
- In the Arab world, the problems associated with juvenile delinquency vary from one country to another. Some countries have experienced socioeconomic difficulties while others have become prosperous.
- In industrialized countries, the increased prosperity and availability of a growing range of consumer goods have led to increased opportunities for youth crime, especially in the crimes of theft, vandalism, and destruction of property.
- In many countries in Eastern Europe and the former Soviet Union, the number of mothers and fathers deprived of their parental rights is increasing every year. The youth, alienated from society, often become involved in delinquent groups.

Preventing Juvenile Delinquency

The World Youth Report encourages early intervention as the best approach to preventing juvenile delinquency. Prevention requires individual, group, and organizational efforts aimed at preventing juveniles from committing delinquency. The report also recommends that countries implement the United Nations Standard Minimum Rules for the Administration of Justice (Beijing Rules), discussed earlier in this chapter.

The report recommends that greater attention be given to the role and responsibility of communities in dealing with juvenile delinquency. Communities can reduce the level of juvenile delinquency by changing the urban environment through providing opportunities to engage young people's interest. The report concludes that stopping recurrent crime is best achieved through "restorative justice," which should be regarded as an alternate mode of juvenile justice. One of the key elements of restorative justice is reconciliation between the victim and the offender, a process necessary not only for the correction of the offender, but also for the restoration of justice for the victim.

Comparative Study of Youth Crime

Solomon Ehiemua in a comparative research report states that an important issue for communities and society is whether a child or teenager will develop into a socially adequate member of society, or, instead, take a path that leads to antisocial behavior and juvenile delinquency.[4] Ehiemua notes that scholars have focused for decades on the causes of juvenile delinquency. He also notes that the role of child rearing and its relevance for juvenile delinquency has been evaluated and interpreted differently. Ehiemua indicates that a 1927 study by Banham Bridges pointed out that the factors which operate to turn a child's behavior in one direction rather than another may be very obscure and beyond the detection of expert sociologists.

Ehiemua, in his comparative study of different nations, notes that scholars have determined and described different types of poor parenting that are likely to impair the child-rearing process and contribute to juvenile delinquency. According to Ehiemua, the types of poor parenting include:

- **Uninvolved parenting.** Uninvolved parents provide little emotional support and a low level of monitoring. They place few requirements on their children, and generally do not give sufficient feedback.
- **Permissive parenting.** While permissive parents have more contact with their children, their parenting is characterized by a low level of monitoring.
- **Authoritarian parenting.** Authoritarian parents have tight control of their children and are very demanding on them. There are strict rules and high standards of behavior. The parents accept very little input from their children and resort to corporal punishment for rules violations.

As a result of his study, Ehiemua formed some general conclusions regarding child-rearing practices in selected countries. Those generalized conclusions are as follows:

- The ideals of proper parenting for a great many people in the United States are based on middle-class European behaviors.
- The positive attitude toward education in England and Wales has been shown to be a factor in reducing the probability of those children participating in offenses.
- Parents in African countries are often unaware of the impact their child-rearing practices have on their children's cognitive and social behavior.
- Parental practices in Brazil show that the mother's involvement in child rearing is greater than the father's involvement. When dealing with children who are difficult to manage, Brazilian mothers showed a significantly higher level of physical punishment and coercive actions toward them.
- Ehiemua concludes that the relevance of the statement "to spare the rod is to spoil the child" may depend on the cultural values within each society.
- Ehiemua also notes that in a group-oriented society, it takes a community to raise a child, and in an individualistic society, it takes a parent to raise a child.

Australia

According to the Australian Law Reform Committee (ALRC), children's first contact with the formal juvenile justice system often occurs when they are arrested, summonsed, or have other contact with police as a person suspected or accused of a crime. Most states and territories provide some, although differently defined, statistics on children's involvement at this entry point into the juvenile justice system. Since there are different definitions of police involvement in Australian states and territories, the statistics do not accurately represent the number of children involved with police due to juvenile crime allegations. While the figures are not strictly comparable across jurisdictions, they do provide an indication of the number of children involved with police.[5]

Definition of Child

By law in Australia, a person is legally an adult at the age of eighteen. Under the age of eighteen, the youth is considered a juvenile. Eighteen is the age at which a person can vote, marry without prior consent of the court, enter into contracts, initiate and defend civil litigation on his or her own behalf, and exercise a host of other adult legal rights and responsibilities.

In Australia, the term *young people* is commonly used in relation to people between the ages of twelve and twenty-five. For clarity, in this section the term *juvenile* will be used to designate youths under the chronological age of eighteen years old.

In Australia, the family has primary responsibility for caring for children and preparing them for adulthood. A juvenile's development throughout childhood is a responsibility jointly shared with the state. This joint effort between families and the state is designed to encourage the development of an individual capable of participating in and contributing to society.

Legal Process

The traditional view in Australia has been that juveniles are objects of concern to the legal system; while they are subjects of the law and of the legal process, they are not participants in the legal process. This reflected the assumption that children do not—and should not—have the capacity themselves to participate in legal processes to enforce their rights, and that they could and should rely on the exclusive protection and participation of adults in the legal process to ensure the exercise of their rights. However, this view of juveniles and the legal process is changing in Australia.

Canada

According to a survey, 37 percent of Canada's youth reported that they engaged in one or more delinquent behaviors in their lifetime, either acts of violence, acts against property, or the sale of drugs.[6] The survey indicated that boys (30%) were twice as likely as girls (15%) to have engaged in violent behavior. Boys were also slightly more likely than girls to admit that they had committed acts against property (30% vs. 26%). Foreign-born youths reported lower rates of delinquent acts compared to youths born in Canada (15% to 23%), but there was no significant difference in the prevalence of delinquency between youths with Canadian-born parents and youths with foreign-born parents.

Sixty percent of the youths found guilty in youth courts in 2008–2009 were sentenced to probation either alone or in conjunction with community service or fines. About 15 percent were sentenced to a custodial sentence, with an average sentence of thirty-six days. While aboriginal youths represented only 6 percent of all youth population, 27 percent were remanded to youth court. About 60 percent of the victims of youth crime were under the age of eighteen years.

The Youth Criminal Justice Act enacted in 2003 and amended in 2007 establishes the national age of criminal responsibility at twelve years old, and states that youths can only be prosecuted if they break a law of the Criminal Code (previously, youths could be prosecuted or punished solely on the grounds that it was in the youth's best interests). The Act stated that the Canadian Charter of Rights and Freedoms also applies to youths. Youths sixteen years old or older may be tried as adults in certain cases.

In Canada, there is a separate youth justice system for young people from the ages of twelve to seventeen that are accused of committing a crime.[7] At a hearing before the youth court, the youth has a right to bail if certain conditions are met; he or she also has the right to an attorney, the right to call witnesses, and the right to appeal to a higher court.

The Youth Criminal Justice Act places restrictions on who can see and use a youth record and in what circumstances. People that may have access to a youth court record include:

- The youth and his or her attorney, parents, or other adults that the court has recognized as assisting the youth;
- The Crown prosecutor;
- The judge;
- Police officers investigating the offense;
- The victim of the offense;
- Social workers; and
- Agencies involved in preparing reports or developing extrajudicial measures or sanctions.

China

According to researchers Ren Ling and Hongwei Zhang, China has made great strides in the treatment of juvenile offenders since the 1980s under the fundamental principle of "giving priority to education and supplementing it with punishment." China has abolished capital punishment for juveniles, established conditional non-prosecution, due process rights for juvenile suspects, and sealing of juvenile criminal records.

Until the 1980s, Chinese youthful offenders were handled either by grassroots organizations such as neighborhood committees or by the police, using administrative rules with no judicial oversight. In 1984, a juvenile court was established in Shanghai. Many researchers consider this the symbolic first step toward building a legalistic juvenile justice system nationwide in China.[8] By 2001, there were more than three thousand juvenile courts in China, with more than fifteen thousand judges.

Currently China's juvenile justice system is governed by the Juvenile Delinquency Prevention Law of the People's Republic of China.[9] According to the law, juveniles are defined as Chinese citizens who are younger than eighteen years old. Among the legal rights are the right to receive the nine-year compulsory education, to not be discriminated against in terms of gender or disability, to not receive corporal punishment in school, to not be employed when younger than sixteen, to not have personal information disclosed to the public, and to not be exposed to pornographic materials. The law also stipulates that no organization or individual may conceal, destroy, or discard mail of any juvenile.

The Act defines education as a main measure and punishment as a subsidiary measure. Under this principle, juveniles are placed separately from adults when in custody, and juvenile offenders are housed separately from adults for punishment; juvenile trials are not open to the public; information from juvenile cases may not be disclosed to the public; juvenile offenders are not to be discriminated against for their right of inheritance; and juvenile offenders are not to be discriminated against for their education or employment on their release.

According to the researchers, Chinese tradition maintains that crime must be nipped in the bud; it is necessary to implement early prevention and intervention techniques before violations develop into full-scale crimes. For juveniles who are involved in serious offenses, the law stipulates that both informal and formal rehabilitation measures may be used. The major informal measure is a collaborative effort between parents and schools to enforce serious education, discipline, and supervision. The main formal measure is to send juveniles to work-study schools upon the request of parents and schools, with approval from governmental departments of education. Dealing with delinquents remains an administrative rather than a judicial measure in China. These work-study schools are designed to offer special programs of education for troubled juveniles, and their main principle is rehabilitation through education and strict discipline.

France

France defines juveniles who are criminally liable for their acts as youths under the age of eighteen. Accordingly, under French law a youth may not be tried in adult criminal court unless he or she is eighteen years old or older. France has specialized juvenile courts that work with the public prosecutor and the Youth Judicial Protection Service to handle youths who are involved in criminal misconduct. Since 2005, the French juvenile courts have authority to hear and determine offense cases involving minors and to enforce penalties on minors.[10]

The French juvenile courts are presided over by one juvenile court judge and two law judges. For serious or violent offenses, there are juvenile assize courts which have jurisdiction for offenses committed by youths aged sixteen to eighteen. The juvenile assize courts have three professional judges and a jury made up of nine randomly chosen citizens.

Before a minor may be sentenced, he or she must be deemed criminally responsible, which is generally defined as capable of understanding. Punishment may not be imposed on youths under the age of ten because they are not considered responsible. Only measures of protection, assistance, supervision, and education may be imposed on them. For children ages ten to thirteen, educational penalties can be taken. If the child does not comply with the penalty, he or she may be placed with foster care providers or in a specialized center for juvenile offenders.

Children between the ages of thirteen to sixteen years old may be sentenced to imprisonment at an institution for minors, but they are liable to only half the sentence prescribed for adults. They cannot be remanded to custody unless they have committed a violent or serious offense.

Children between the ages of sixteen to eighteen can be remanded in custody, depending upon the kind of offense they committed. The special provisions for dealing with minors may be modified by the judge.

France has two different mechanisms for protecting youths who are in danger. There is *administrative protection*, which is supervised by the Child and Maternal Health Services, part of the Child Welfare Authority, and judicial protection. Administrative protection plays a role of prevention for families in difficulty and comes into play when a minor is at risk of being in danger. Protective measures can be taken for the minor with the consent of his/her parents.

Judicial protection occurs when a minor's health, safety, or morality is at risk, or if the conditions for the minor's education are seriously jeopardized.

The judicial system intervenes mostly when prevention proves inadequate in protecting the minor, or when child welfare has failed. There are two possible types of intervention:

- An educational action in open custody: The family's consent is needed when the educator makes a decision concerning a minor. Whenever possible, the judge allows the minor to live in his usual living environment and asks an educator to assist and advise the minor and his parents.
- A care order: This can be made by the juvenile court judge when it is proven necessary to remove the minor from his or her home.

Great Britain

Early common law in England made no provisions for children who committed criminal offenses if the children were over the minimum age for criminal responsibility, which was originally at the age of seven. The Children Act in 1908 created a special justice system for youthful offenders. The juvenile court, which handled both criminal and noncriminal cases, was renamed the youth court in 1991. The court had jurisdiction for offenders ages ten to sixteen. Juveniles under the age of fourteen are classified as children, and those between the ages of fourteen and under seventeen are classified as young persons. Youths seventeen and older are handled in adult courts, but there are special sentencing provisions for offenders under the age of twenty-one.[11] Nearly all offenses committed by children are tried in youth court. On serious offenses, like murder, young persons are more likely to be tried as an adult. If a young person is tried in an adult court, he or she will normally be returned to a youth court for sentencing.

Youth courts also handle children under the age of seventeen in "care proceedings," which means that the juvenile may be in need of court-ordered care, protection, or control because of a number of factors, such as unstable home care or neglect. A care order is one of the sanctions available to a youth court. The court may also place the youth under the supervision of a social worker by use of a supervision order. The court may also prohibit the youth from certain activities, such as a night restriction, requiring the youth to obey curfews.

In 1994, the Criminal Justice and Public Order Act increased the permissible punishments that a youth court may impose. In 2000, the Criminal Justice and Court Services Act gave the youth courts the authority to use community service as a punishment option.

India

According to Max Schlenker, juvenile justice in India started in 1850, when specific laws were passed that protected young children by focusing on an apprenticeship program. If a youth committed a nonviolent and nonserious crime, the youth was placed into an apprenticeship program with a professional like a tailor, blacksmith, farmer, etc. and was taught a professional skill to use once the youth had completed his or her rehabilitation. The government's philosophy was that apprenticeship was superior to direct punishment or confinement because it would deter future offenses and provide the young criminals with the ability to find employment when they finished their apprenticeship.[12]

However, juvenile delinquency rose drastically, according to the data, after the laws were enacted. To remedy the situation, India passed the Whipping Act of 1864. At the time, India was under British control, and Great Britain decided to replace physical punishment like whipping with a jail system more like the American process. In doing so, each region of India, over the course of many years, developed different and conflicting legal proceedings for young criminals.

In 1960, India enacted the Children Act, which created a uniform process for juvenile courts to follow. In 2000, India redesigned their court system with the Juvenile Justice (Care and Protection of Children) Act. This law, amended in 2006, reintroduced the idea of vocational programs and apprenticeships that were more adapted to the modern world. Since 2006, volunteer organizations have been allowed to work with young criminals to provide them with work opportunities, job experience, and education. In 2015, the law was amended to permit sixteen- to eighteen-year-olds to be tried as adults if accused of a serious crime like murder or armed robbery.

Japan

According to the Juvenile Law of Japan, persons under twenty years of age are classified as juveniles and subject to special procedures. There is a strong public movement to change the maximum age for juvenile jurisdiction to eighteen years. A juvenile criminal is defined under Japanese law as a person who is fourteen to twenty years old who committed a crime.[13] A law-breaking juvenile is a person under the age of fourteen involved in the violation of criminal laws.

For many years the Japanese Juvenile Law was basically unchanged. In a 1997 case, a fourteen-year-old boy killed two elementary school children and injured three others in Kobe. After that the call for harsher punishment on minors spurred various amendments to legislation. In 2000, the law was amended to lower the age of minors who could be tried as an adult, from sixteen to fourteen. In 2007, the age of minors who can be sent to juvenile correctional facilities was lowered from fourteen and older to "around twelve" after an elementary school girl stabbed her classmate to death with a utility knife. In 2014, the revision went further and raised the maximum prison term from fifteen to twenty years for minors who commit a serious crime before they turn eighteen.[14]

In Japan, the juvenile law is designed to help youth become productive members of society through educational support. Cases of juvenile offenders, except when grounds for suspicion are insufficient, are sent to a family court where examiners trained in psychology and education investigate the offender's personal history, family background, relationships with friends, and so on. Offenders deemed at risk of fleeing before the family court procedure starts are sent to juvenile classification facilities for examination by experts there. The family court decides what custodial measures should be taken. Offenders sent to a juvenile reformatory are subject to education and guidance programs for rehabilitation. Those placed on probation or provisionally released from the reformatory receive counseling from probation officers.

The Japanese Juvenile Law provides that sentences given to juvenile criminals who have not reached the age of eighteen at the time the crime was committed shall be made lighter than those that would be given to criminals who are eighteen years of age or older when the crime is committed.

Practicum

The governor of your state has asked you to brief her on the juvenile justice systems in Canada, Great Britain, and France.

List the items that you would cover in the briefing.

Summary

- Each country has its own traditions and customs regarding how children should be raised. What is perfectly acceptable in one country may be seen as misconduct in another.
- As societies increasingly become more global and less homogenized, it becomes more important to understand and accept cultural differences in child rearing.
- Since its creation in 1948, the United Nations has been concerned with the rights, safety, and dignity of children around the world.
- One of the missions of the UN is to protect children living in war-torn countries.
- The UN Standards are commonly referred to as "The Beijing Rules." The UN General Assembly called upon member states (nations) to adapt, wherever necessary, their national legislation, policies, and practices, particularly in training juvenile justice personnel, to the Beijing Rules and to bring these rules to the attention of relevant authorities and the public.
- The United Nations publishes a World Youth Report on various subjects involving children. Its 2003 report included a chapter on juvenile delinquency.
- The report contained some interesting conclusions regarding juvenile delinquency in various countries.
- According to researcher Solomon Ehiemua, the types of poor parenting include:
  - **Uninvolved parenting.** Uninvolved parents provide little emotional support and a low level of monitoring. They place few requirements on their children, and generally do not give sufficient feedback.
  - **Permissive parenting.** While permissive parents have more contact with their children, their parenting is characterized by a low level of monitoring.
  - **Authoritarian parenting.** Authoritarian parents have tight control of their children and are very demanding on them. There are strict rules and high standards of behavior. The parents accept very little input from their children and resort to corporal punishment for rules violations.
- In Australia, the family has primary responsibility for caring for children and preparing them for adulthood. A juvenile's development throughout childhood is a responsibility jointly shared with the state.
- The Canadian Youth Criminal Justice Act enacted in 2003 and amended in 2007 establishes the national age of criminal responsibility at twelve years old, and states that youths can only be prosecuted if they break a law of the Criminal Code (previously, youths could be prosecuted or punished solely on the grounds that it was in the youth's best interests). The Act stated that the Canadian Charter of Rights and Freedoms also applies to youths.
- Until the 1980s, Chinese youthful offenders were handled either by grassroots organizations such as neighborhood committees or by the police using administrative rules with no judicial oversight. In 1984, the first juvenile court was established in Shanghai.
- France defines juveniles who are criminally liable for their acts as youths under the age of eighteen. Accordingly, under French law a youth may not be tried in adult criminal court unless he or she is eighteen years old or older.
- Early common law in England made no provisions for children who committed criminal offenses if the children were over the minimum age for criminal responsibility, which was originally seven years old. The Children Act in 1908 created a special justice system for youthful offenders.
- Juvenile justice in India started in 1850 when specific laws were passed that protected young children by focusing on an apprenticeship program. If a youth committed a nonviolent and nonserious crime, the youth was placed into an apprenticeship program with a professional.

- According to the Juvenile Law of Japan, persons under twenty years of age are classified as juveniles and subject to special procedures. There is a strong public movement to change the maximum age for juvenile jurisdiction to eighteen years.

Discussion and Review Questions

1. Explain the purpose of the United Nations Standards on Juvenile Justice.
2. What is the philosophy of the Chinese justice system?
3. How does the Japanese juvenile justice system differ from the Canadian system?
4. What are the key features of the French juvenile justice system?
5. Of the nations studied in this chapter, which nation has the best approach to solving juvenile justice issues, and why?

Notes

1. Solomon Ehiemua, "Juvenile Delinquency: Comparative Study Between Child Rearing Practices in Developed and Developing Countries," *European Journal of Research in Social Science*, vol. 2, no. 4 (2014), 59–65.
2. Max Schlenker, "SOCHUM II: Juvenile Delinquency Around the World" (2017), posted on Shorthand Social webpage at https://social.shorthand.com/ymuntaiwan/3yJT67aWhT/sochum-ii-juvenile-delinquency-around-the-world (accessed June 1, 2019).
3. United Nations, Department of Economic and Social Affairs, "World Youth Report 2003: The Global Situation of Young People" (New York: United Nations Reproduction Section, 2004), 189–211, posted at https://www.un.org/esa/socdev/unyin/documents/worldyouthreport.pdf (accessed May 31, 2019).
4. Ehiemua, "Juvenile Delinquency: Comparative Study."
5. "A Statistical Picture of Australia's Children," Australian Law Reform Commission, https://www.alrc.gov.au/publications/2-statistical-picture-australias-children/juvenile-justice (accessed May 29, 2019).
6. Josée Savoie, Canadian Centre for Justice Statistics, Statistics Canada, "Youth Self-Reported Delinquency, Toronto—2006," *Juristat*, vol. 27, no. 6 (2007), 32–45.
7. "Youth," Areas of Law, Provincial Court of Alberta (2018), posted on Alberta Courts website at https://www.albertacourts.ca/pc/areas-of-law/youth (accessed June 2, 2019).
8. Ren Ling and Hongwei Zhang, "Introduction: Advancing Empirical Research on China's Juvenile Delinquency and Juvenile Justice: Continuity and Expansion," *Journal of Contemporary Justice*, vol. 34, no. 2 (May 2018), 120–27, https://doi.org/10.1177/1043986218769793 (accessed June 3, 2019).
9. Lening Zhang and Jianhong Liu (November 2007) "China's Juvenile Delinquency Prevention Law: The Law and the Philosophy," *International Journal of Offender Therapy and Comparative Criminology*, vol. 51, no. 5 (November 2007), 541–54, https://journals.sagepub.com/doi/10.1177/0306624X06292675 (accessed June 17, 2019).
10. "The French Legal System" (2012), Ministry of Justice website, http://www.justice.gouv.fr/art_pix/french_legal_system.pdf (accessed June 1, 2019).
11. Donald J. Shoemaker, and Cary Jensen, "Juvenile Justice," Britannica (2018), posted at https://www.britannica.com/topic/juvenile-justice (accessed June 2, 2019).
12. Schlenker, "SOCHUM II."
13. Japanese Juvenile Law, article 3, paragraph 1, item 1 (2000).
14. Masami Ito (May 23, 2015) "Shifting the Scales of Juvenile Justice," *Japan Times* website at https://www.japantimes.co.jp/news/2015/05/23/national/social-issues/shifting-scales-juvenile-justice/#.XPLS1HdFxnQ (accessed June 1, 2019).

GLOSSARY

Adjudicated This is the juvenile equivalent of the adult criminal finding of *guilty*.

Adjudicatory hearing is the fact-finding hearing and determines if the allegations against the juvenile stated in the petition are true. Adjudicatory hearings establish responsibility for an alleged act.

Adversary system Our concept of justice, in which one side represents the plaintiff or state and the other side represents the defendant, while the judge acts as the independent referee.

Age–crime curve is related to the Pathways to Desistance program, based on the concept that the prevalence of delinquency tends to increase from late childhood, peak in the teenage years (from fifteen to nineteen), and then decline in the early twenties.

Age of Enlightenment, for most of the eighteenth century, promoted optimism, certainty, reason, tolerance, humanitarianism, the belief that all problems could be solved, and a belief in human progress.

Age of Reason represented a genesis in the way humans viewed themselves, and was based on the need for the pursuit of knowledge, and understanding the universe.

Aggravation or circumstances in aggravation Facts which tend to justify the imposition of a more-severe punishment.

Anomie is defined as "a state of lawlessness." Durkheim used the term to describe a condition of normlessness. Thus, norms have lost their meaning and have become inoperative for a large portion of society.

Antisocial behaviors generally include various forms of oppositional rule violation and aggression, such as theft, physical fighting, and vandalism.

Antisocial personality disorder This term is so broad that it might be applied to almost any criminal. In the *Diagnostic and Statistical Manual of Mental Disorders (DSM-5)*, the American Psychiatric Association has replaced the terms *psychopath* and *sociopathic* with the term *antisocial personality disorder*.

Arrest The seizure of a person to answer for a criminal charge.

Asthenic body type The asthenic person has a thin and narrow build with long arms, and is delicate in bone structure and appearance.

Augustus, John A Boston shoemaker who is credited with the creation of probation in the United States.

Balanced and restorative justice (BARJ) A framework for juvenile justice reform that seeks to engage citizens and community groups both as clients of juvenile justice services and as resources in a more-effective response to youth crime.

Beijing Rules See the United Nations Standards on Juvenile Justice.

Biological theories are based on the concept that certain individuals are predisposed to commit crime because the juvenile has inherited biochemical and/or genetic factors.

Birth order as a cause of delinquency is a concept that the order of one's birth has an effect on one's decision to become involved in criminal behavior.

Boot camps Juvenile boot camps are frequently used for the adjudicated delinquent who needs residential care but does not need to be in a secure facility.

Breed v. Jones In this case, the US Supreme Court provided additional answers to questions involving transfer proceedings and held that the double jeopardy clause applied to juvenile proceedings. The Court also held that due process prohibits trying a juvenile in adult court after there has been a prior adjudicatory juvenile hearing involving the same misconduct.

Broken Windows Theory The broken windows theory of delinquency causation uses broken windows as a metaphor for disorder in the community. Broken windows in a community indicate that the community is in disorder and unsafe.

BUILD Program The BUILD, Inc. program is based in Chicago. Since 1969, they have helped thousands of kids stay out of gangs by creating programs to keep them off the streets. The program provides restorative justice programs and helps to build stronger community ties with at-risk youth with the help of former gang members, the police, and neighbors.

Bullying A repeated aggressive behavior where one person (or group of people) in a position of power deliberately intimidates, abuses, or coerces another individual with the intention to hurt that person physically or emotionally.

Chicago School started when members of the department of sociology at the University of Chicago in 1920 conducted the first large-scale study of crime in the United States. The study produced a large mass of data and many observations about crime. The school viewed the urban environment as the appropriate landscape for studying human nature.

Children's Bureau created by 1912 Act of Congress. The Act directed the Children's Bureau to investigate and report on all matters pertaining to the welfare of children and child life among all classes of people and shall especially investigate the questions of infant mortality, the birth rate, orphanages, juvenile courts, desertion, dangerous occupations, accidents and diseases of children, employment, and legislation affecting children in the several states and territories.

Classical school of criminology The first recognized school of criminology based on the proposition that individuals have "free will," and that any criminal act they commit is because they chose to commit the crime.

Cognitive development theories are based on the works of Jean Piaget. Piaget's theory of cognitive development is a comprehensive theory about the nature and development of human intelligence.

Collective efficacy This concept was developed following the broken windows theory. Collective efficacy is the glue that binds neighborhoods together. Researchers contend that it helps explain why some communities fight crime and disorder and others do not.

Community-based services are treatment modalities delivered to clients in the community, usually on conditional liberty status (parole).

Community corrections refer to those programs in which the juvenile is "corrected" within his or her community.

Competency looks at the mental state of the juvenile or defendant at the time of the trial to determine if the person has a reasonable degree of understanding as well as factual understanding of the court proceedings against him or her. A defendant must be able to assist his or her counsel in defending the case.

Conflict theorists contend that criminal law is a direct expression of the ruling class; it is concerned with the protection of their property and the consolidation of their political power. According to these theorists, the "real" function of policing is political rather than the control of crime per se.

Containment Theory holds that people have several social controls, containments, or protective barriers which push them to resist pressures to commit criminal misbehavior. We all have different pushes and pulls toward crime.

Contempt of cop A phrase coined by former Los Angeles police officer and later novelist Joseph Wambaugh when he wrote the novel *The Blue Knight* in 1972. According to the novel, when citizens don't give police officers a "Yes, sir!" and obey their requests, the cops gets mad. Presently, this is used as a slang phrase when an individual, often a youth, does not act with "proper" respect when stopped by an officer.

Contraband Any item possessed by a confined juvenile offender or found within a facility that is illegal by law or expressly prohibited by those legally charged with the administration and operation of the secure facility.

Control balance theory states that a person lives his or her life in one of three states: control surplus, control equilibrium, or control deficit.

Corrections in the juvenile system are generally classified into two general areas: community corrections and institutions.

Critical criminologists claim that mainstream theorists are being misguided in their efforts to explain and prevent violations of criminal law, and that these violations are not an accurate representation of social harm to all society members. Critical theorists note that criminal law tends to overlook the harmful actions of the powerful.

Culturally prescribed goals are described by Merton as the values in a society, and socially structured means are the norms for attaining the prescribed goals.

Curfews Laws which require juveniles to stay out of public places and the streets during certain hours. The use of curfews as a mechanism of social control is not new. Curfews may be traced back more than 1,100 years to the rule of Alfred the Great (849–899) in England. During that era, an evening bell was rung to signal to residents of Oxford that they should douse their fires and return to their homes for the night.

Cybercrime is a broad category of offenses that involve the use of computers and computer networks.

Delinquency refers to criminal misconduct without regard to the age of the offender.

Delinquency and drift theories hold that a delinquent youth has no commitment to societal norms or to criminal norms.

Delinquent subculture theory was developed by Albert Cohen. Like strain theory, this theory places emphasis on low-income youths' difficulty in obtaining conventional markers of success.

Dependency proceedings are based on the doctrine of *parens patriae*—in essence, the right of a state or federal government to take action to protect children. Developed in early English common law, *parens patriae* refers to the right of the ruler to protect the people. In the United States, the doctrine refers to the government's responsibility as the supreme guardian of children, mentally ill adults, and people who are unable to protect themselves.

Detention is primarily used for temporary holding while youths await adjudication, disposition, or placement elsewhere. Many states also use detention for sanctioning purposes; juveniles may be committed to a detention facility as part of a disposition order or as a sanction for a probation violation.

Detention center A detention center for juveniles is a secure twenty-four-hour facility for male and female offenders up to the age of eighteen who have been arrested and are waiting for court disposition or placement. A detention center is generally considered a secure temporary holding facility.

Detention hearing A hearing held to determine if the juvenile should continue in temporary custody until the adjudicatory or dispositional hearing is held. At the detention hearing, the judge reviews the initial detention decision, considers what is in the best interests of the community and/or the youth, and decides whether to continue the youth's detention.

Development theories, unlike traditional theories of delinquency causation, are focused on explaining the differences in offending rates of delinquents over a period of time.

Difference and defectiveness theories are based on the concept that criminals are biochemically different from noncriminals.

Differential association theory is based on the concepts that criminal behavior is learned and not a necessary outcome of a socially disorganized society, or because the offender is different from the noncriminal and criminal behavior is learned with other persons in the process of communication. Simply being in a criminogenic environment does not cause criminal behavior.

Direct filing in adult criminal court In most jurisdictions the prosecutor may directly file a juvenile case in adult criminal court if certain requirements exist. Generally the direct filing statutes are limited to cases involving serious felonies.

Discretionary jurisdiction waiver statutes These statutes prescribe broad standards to be applied, factors to be considered, and procedures to be followed in waiver decision-making and require that the prosecutors bear the burden of proving that waiver is appropriate. Although waiver standards and evidentiary factors vary from state to state, most consider both the nature of the alleged crime and the individual youth's age, maturity, history, and rehabilitative prospects.

Dismissed Cases dismissed (including those warned, counseled, and released) with no further action anticipated.
Disposition hearing is the one in which the judge decides what is best for the juvenile's care, treatment, and/or guidance; similar to the sentencing hearing in adult criminal court.
Drug courts are intensive treatment programs established within and supervised by juvenile courts to provide specialized services for eligible drug-involved youth and their families. Cases are assigned to a juvenile drug court docket based on criteria set by local officials to carry out the goals of the drug court program.
Dual system youths are those involved in both the child welfare system and the juvenile justice system.
Due process Procedures that effectively guarantee individual rights in the face of criminal prosecution and that are fundamental rules for fair and orderly legal proceedings.
Dusky standard Generally, both adult and juvenile competency standards are based on the US Supreme Court case of *Dusky v. United States*. In this case, the Court held that the competency test must be based on whether the person has a reasonable degree of understanding as well as factual understanding of the proceedings against him or her.
Dysplastic body type The dysplastic type person has a body type that is part pyknic and part asthenic.
Early childhood disruptive behavior Many studies indicate that one of the best predictors of future behavior is past behavior. Children showing persistent disruptive behavior are likely to become child delinquents and, in turn, child delinquents are likely to become serious, violent, or chronic juvenile offenders.
Ecological theories developed from the work of the "Chicago School" on gangs. These theories use ecological reasons to explain delinquency.
Ecology is currently linked to the idea of protecting the environment. In its original meaning, ecology was considered as a branch of biology in which plants and animals are studied in their relationship to each other and to their habitat.
Ectomorph body type A person who is thin, small, and bony with a small face, sharp nose, fine hair, and relatively little body mass and relatively great surface area.
Emotional problem theories assume that delinquency is caused by the inability to cope with everyday problems; the delinquent is responding to very subtle psychological factors that prevent the delinquent from functioning normally.
Endomorph body type A person who is fat, round, and fleshy with short tapering limbs and small bones.
Exclusionary rule The rule used to exclude evidence that was obtained by the violation of a constitutional right, such as an illegal search.
Exonerated A finding that the alleged act occurred, but was justified, lawful, and proper.
Expungement of criminal conviction or records An expungement hearing is a court proceeding in which an offender with a prior criminal conviction seeks to have the records of that conviction removed from state or federal repositories. If successful, the records are said to be "expunged." Another definition of "expungement of record" is the process by which the record of a criminal conviction is destroyed.
Family Inclusive of the wide variety of primary caregiving units in our culture. Family is a biological, adoptive, or self-created unit of people residing together consisting of adult(s) and child(ren), with the adult performing duties of parenthood for the child(ren). Persons within this unit share bonds, culture, practices, and significant relationships.
Family structure and juvenile court Does family stability influence the juvenile judge in making the decision to incarcerate the juvenile delinquent? Researchers conclude that juvenile court decisions are influenced by perceptions of juveniles' family backgrounds, which include family structure, quality of care, and economic resources.
FERPA Family Educational Rights and Privacy Act; i.e., the federal laws regarding parents' rights to inspect their children's school records.
Formal norms are norms or standards of behavior that are officially imposed on us by a higher authority, such as the state. A statute prohibiting certain acts would be a formal norm.
Free will The concept that human behavior is the product of free choice and that

the individual chooses to commit crime. According to this concept, humans, including juveniles, can make a rational choice to commit or refrain from committing criminal misconduct.

Functional family therapy (FFT) is a family-based prevention and intervention program that has been applied successfully in a variety of contexts to treat a range of high-risk youth and their families.

Gagnon v. Scarpelli A case in which the US Supreme Court established minimal due process requirements for probation revocation proceedings under the Fourteenth Amendment to the US Constitution.

Gang The federal definition of a gang is an association of three or more individuals whose members collectively identify themselves by adopting a group identity which they use to create an atmosphere of fear or intimidation, frequently by employing one or more of the following: a common name, slogan, identifying sign, symbol, tattoo or other physical marking, style or color of clothing, hairstyle, hand sign, or graffiti. A gang's purpose in part is to engage in criminal activity, and they use violence or intimidation to further their criminal objectives.

Gang Rescue and Support (GRASP) Project A program for youth who are at risk of gang involvement. The program has achieved success and is run by ex–gang members.

Gang Resistance Education and Training (G.R.E.A.T.) Program An evidence-based, national and international gang and violence prevention program that has been building trust between law enforcement and communities.

Graham v. Florida In this case, the US Supreme Court held that sentencing a juvenile defendant to life imprisonment without the possibility of parole violated the Eighth Amendment of the US Constitution.

Group homes tend to be private facilities that are used in lieu of institutions for juveniles. A group home is a community-based, long-term facility in which juveniles are allowed extensive contact with the community, such as attending school or holding a job.

Homeboy Industries is an organization that offers a variety of services to people who are no longer involved in gangs.

Houses of refuge Houses of refuge were very similar to adult penitentiaries. They were large, fortress-like, congregate-style institutions located in urban areas for youth who were designated as abandoned, delinquent or incorrigible. The early houses of refuge in the United States were designed to house poor, destitute, and vagrant youth deemed by authorities to be on the path toward delinquency.

Hyperactivity as a cause of delinquency is based on the concept that children who are restless, squirmy, and fidgety are more likely to be involved in later delinquent behavior.

In re Gault The US Supreme Court's decision in this case held that juveniles accused of crimes in a delinquency proceeding must be afforded many of the same due process rights as adults, such as the right to timely notification of the charges, the right to confront witnesses, the right against self-incrimination, and the right to counsel.

In re Winship This US Supreme Court case held that juveniles have certain due process rights, including the right to require the government to prove beyond a reasonable doubt that the allegations in the petition are true.

In the Matter of S.W. An appellate court decision on searches made by a school resource officer (SRO). Are they, when conducting a search, a school official or a police officer? The US Supreme Court has not ruled on this issue as of this date. Several state courts have ruled, reaching decisions like the one reached in *In the Matter of S.W.*, which held that the *T.L.O. v. New Jersey* standard governs searches conducted by school resource officers working in conjunction with school officials, where these officers are primarily responsible to the school district rather than the local police department.

Informal norms are generally created out of face-to-face interactions with others. Informal norms are generally not written down and are considered as appropriate conduct that a person should follow in society. An example of violating an informal norm is cutting in line at a store.

Insanity defense is based on the classical belief that humans have "free will" to choose between good and bad behavior. Sometimes, however, a person, because of mental health issues, lacks the ability to make a rational choice. Insanity defense is based on the status of the defendant or juvenile at the time the criminal act was committed.

Institutional anomie theory (IAT) is based on Merton's strain theory and Durkheim's conceptualization of anomie. Those researching this theory aimed to explain crime rates at the aggregate level.
Intake hearing See *jurisdiction hearing*.
Integrated cognitive antisocial potential theory (ICAP) is based on the concept that an individual's antisocial propensity (AP) determines whether the juvenile will commit criminal misconduct. The AP refers to a person's risk or propensity to engage in crime and the decision-making process that turns the potential process into the actual process. The key construct is antisocial propensity, which tends to persist over time and has a wide variety of behavioral manifestations.
Integrated theories are a group of theories that expand upon the arguments of other theories to provide more-complete explanations of delinquent misconduct. These theories involve the linking and synthesizing of different theories of delinquent causation to explain why individuals commit criminal misconduct.
Interdepartmental Committee on Children and Youth was established in 1948 by the federal government. Its purpose was to develop closer relationships among federal agencies concerned with children and youth.
Interstate Compact on Juveniles (ICJ) A multistate agreement that provides the procedural means to regulate the movement across state lines of juveniles who are under court supervision.
J.D.B. v. North Carolina In this case, the US Supreme Court noted that any police interview of an individual suspected of a crime has "coercive aspects to it." Those interrogations that occur while a suspect is in police custody heighten the risk that statements obtained are not the product of the suspect's free choice.
Jurisdiction hearing The hearing that takes place as soon as reasonably possible if the juvenile is in temporary custody. At the jurisdiction or intake hearing, the judge advises the juvenile of the facts and the misconduct alleged in the petition and what can happen at the hearing.
Juvenile A young person below the age of majority as defined by the local jurisdiction.
Juvenile delinquency Misconduct committed by an individual who is considered a juvenile in the jurisdiction involved. In determining if a delinquent is a juvenile, the courts use the chronological age, not the mental age.
Juvenile institutions Refers to those institutions in which the juvenile is placed in some type of custody similar to adult confinement institutions.
Juvenile justice process In most jurisdictions this process includes four hearings: temporary custody hearing, jurisdiction or intake hearing, adjudicatory hearing, and disposition hearing.
Juvenile police officer Many large police departments have officers assigned as juvenile police officers. A juvenile police officer is different from a school resource officer (SRO) because the juvenile police officer performs his or her duties under the supervision of the law enforcement agency and not the school administration.
Juvenile probation camps Nonsecure residential programs where juveniles participate in a structured outdoor work program including conservation and related activities. Resident age varies from fifteen to eighteen years.
Juvenile probation officers Court officers who work exclusively with adolescents who have been convicted of a crime and put on probation, rather than being sentenced to jail time; also referred to as juvenile correctional treatment specialists.
Juvenile reentry centers A halfway house is also known as a residential reentry center. The purpose of these facilities is to reintegrate former offenders into society after having been in jail and to continue offering support services to former inmates.
Kent v. United States This US Supreme Court case was decided in 1966. The case opinion established the procedural guidelines to be used in the waiver of a juvenile delinquent from juvenile to adult court jurisdiction.
Labeling theory contends that people come to identify and behave in ways that reflect how others label them.
Lau v. Nichols In this case the US Supreme Court interpreted Civil Rights Act, Title VI's prohibition on national origin discrimination to include discrimination based on the inability to speak English.
Law enforcement officer Any person vested by law with a duty to maintain public order or to make arrests for offenses.
Lay witness A nonexpert witness.

Magistrate A judicial officer with the power to issue a warrant, including magistrates, district judges, superior court judges, and any other judicial officer authorized by law to conduct a preliminary examination of a person accused of a crime or issue a warrant.

Making a Murderer A popular Netflix documentary series involving the interrogations of a juvenile who appeared to have mental health issues.

Mandatory waiver of jurisdiction Many states require juvenile courts to waive jurisdiction over cases that meet specified age/offense or prior record criteria. Cases subject to mandatory waiver are initiated in juvenile court, but the court has no role other than to confirm that the statutory requirements for mandatory waiver are met. Functionally, a mandatory waiver law resembles a statutory exclusion, removing a designated category of cases from juvenile court jurisdiction.

Massachusetts Experiment In 1971, the Commonwealth of Massachusetts removed nearly one thousand juveniles from state training schools, closed the schools, and placed the youths in a diverse array of community programs. The Massachusetts system is no longer considered an experiment due to its years of successful results with community-based juvenile corrections. The hallmark of Massachusetts programs is their small size; Massachusetts also uses secure confinement in a unique and cost-effective manner compared to other corrections systems. The success of the Massachusetts Experiment has influenced juvenile justice reforms in Utah, Missouri, Maryland, and other states.

McKeiver v. Pennsylvania In this case, decided in 1971, the US Supreme Court not only denied juveniles the constitutional right to a jury trial, but also retreated from the previously standard practice of judicial equalization of procedure in adult and juvenile courts.

Mental disorder A substantial disorder of an individual's emotional processes, thought processes, cognition, or memory.

Mental disorder theories attempt to classify delinquent behavior using certain mental disorders such as psychosis, neurosis, and/or impulse disorders.

Mentally incompetent Refers to an accused who lacks sufficient present ability to assist in his or her defense by consulting with counsel with a reasonable degree of rational understanding of the facts and the legal proceedings against the defendant.

Mesomorph body type A person who is big-boned and muscular and tends to have a large trunk, heavy chest, and large wrists and hands.

Midcentury White House Conference on Children and Youth met in Washington, DC, in 1950. The conference considered methods to strengthen juvenile courts and develop juvenile police services, and studied prevention and treatment services of social agencies, police, courts, institutions, and aftercare agencies.

***Miranda* warning** Warnings required before officers can interrogate a suspect who is in detention.

Mitigation or circumstances in mitigation Facts that tend to justify the imposition of a lesser punishment.

Morrissey v. Brewer A case in which the US Supreme Court established minimal due process requirements for parole revocation proceedings under the Fourteenth Amendment to the US Constitution.

Motion to suppress evidence A motion presented prior to trial to determine the admissibility of certain items of evidence.

Multiple-factor approach in criminology grew out of discrepancies in the single-factor approach. Theorists argue that crime should be understood in terms of varied contributions made by a variety of factors. Their basic assumption is that crime is the product of many factors—biological, psychological, economic, and social—and that different crimes will result from different combinations of factors.

National Crime Victimization Survey (NCVS) This survey is an annual data collection conducted by the US Census Bureau for the Bureau of Justice Statistics (BJS). Each year, data are obtained from a nationally representative sample of about 240,000 interviews on criminal victimization, involving 160,000 unique persons in about 95,000 households.

National Youth Gang Center (NYGC) assists state and local jurisdictions in the collection, analysis, and exchange of information on gang-related demographics, legislation, literature, research, and promising program strategies. NYGC coordinates activities of the OJJDP Gang Consortium, a group of federal agencies, gang program representatives, and service providers that works to coordinate gang information and programs. NYGC also provides training and technical assistance for OJJDP's Rural Gang, Gang-Free Schools, and Gang-Free Communities Initiatives.

Negotiated plea A plea that has been agreed upon by the defendant and the state; a plea bargain.

Neoclassical school Like the classical school, this school of thought is based on the concept of free will and the idea that people are guided by reason. The neoclassical school differs from the classical school in that it recognizes differences in criminal circumstances, and that some people, like juveniles and persons with unstable mental conditions, may not be able to act "reasonably," or they have a limited ability to reason.

Neurosis is a type of disorder that was first used to cover a group of diseases that affected the nervous system.

New Jersey v. T.L.O. In this case, the US Supreme Court held that the assistant vice principal's search of a student's purse in his office did not violate the Fourth Amendment.

OJJDP Comprehensive Gang Model An evidence-based framework for the coordination of multiple data-driven, anti-gang, and violence-reduction strategies to address serious, violent, and entrenched youth street gang problems.

OJJDP Statistical Briefing Book Offers access to a wealth of information about juvenile crime and victimization and about youth involved in the juvenile justice system.

Omnibus Crime Control and Safe Streets Act of 1968 Enacted in 1968, this Act provided block grants to states in order to improve and strengthen law enforcement. While not specifically mentioning juvenile delinquency, this Act's broad crime control and prevention mandate authorized funding of delinquency control and prevention programs.

Parens patriae Developed in early English common law, *parens patriae* refers to the right of the ruler to protect the people.

Parenting style can affect everything from how much a child weighs to how he or she feels about him- or herself. Sociologists contend that it is important to ensure that the parenting style is supporting healthy growth and development, because the way the parent interacts with a child and how the parent disciplines the child will influence him or her for the rest of the child's life.

Parole Juvenile parole may be defined as the conditional release of a juvenile from a correctional institution to the community under supervision of a parole officer.

Parole revocation Revocation of a juvenile's conditional liberty made at a due process hearing by the youth hearing officer due to a probable cause determination of violation of the conditions of release.

Pathways to Desistance This longitudinal study of serious adolescent offenders was a large collaborative, multidisciplinary project that followed 1,354 serious juvenile offenders ages fourteen to eighteen and included 184 females and 1,170 females for seven years after their adjudication.

Physical custody The exercise of physical custody and control over a committed juvenile, excluding those occasions in which the juvenile has been released by furlough, out to court, etc.

Placement Cases in which youth were placed in a residential facility for delinquents or were otherwise removed from their homes and placed elsewhere.

Plea In a juvenile hearing, the juvenile does not plead guilty or not guilty. He or she either admits the allegations in the petition or denies them. In the latter case, a denial is equivalent to a not guilty plea in adult criminal court.

Positivist theorists take the position that human behavior is not the result of free choice; juvenile crime is determined by internal and external influences. The juvenile does not choose between right and wrong, but rather his or her conduct is determined by biological, psychological, or sociological influences.

Prescriptive norms are norms that tell us what we can or should do (e.g., we should give up our seat on the bus to a disabled person).

Presumptive waiver of jurisdiction laws Many states' statutes define a category of cases in which waiver from juvenile to criminal court is presumed appropriate. Statutes in these states leave the decision in the hands of a judge, but weight it in favor of transfer. A juvenile who meets age, offense, or other statutory thresholds for presumptive waiver must present evidence rebutting the presumption, or the court will grant waiver and the case will be tried in adult criminal court.

Principle of utilitarianism This principle is based on the concept that an act is not to be judged by an irrational system of absolutes but by a supposedly verifiable principle of the greatest happiness for the greatest number of people.
Private institutions Private facilities are operated by private nonprofit or for-profit corporations or organizations. The staff in these facilities are employees of the private corporation or organization. Private facilities tend to be smaller than public facilities.
Privilege against compulsory self-incrimination Based on the Fifth Amendment to the US Constitution, a person cannot be compelled to incriminate him- or herself.
Privileged communications refer to those between individuals that are protected from discovery or use in a trial. Generally, communications between a party and his or her attorney are privileged.
Probable cause exists when the facts and circumstances within the officer's knowledge, and of which he or she has reasonably trustworthy information, are enough to cause a reasonably cautious person to believe that an offense has been or is being committed.
Probation Cases in which youth are placed on informal/voluntary or formal/court-ordered probation or supervision. A disposition that imposes conditions not involving prolonged confinement, or, if any, at most involving only short periods of confinement.
Project Safe Neighborhoods (PSN) is designed to create and foster safer neighborhoods through a sustained reduction in violent crime, including (but not limited to) addressing criminal youth gangs and the felonious possession and use of firearms.
Proscriptive norms are norms that forbid certain actions (e.g., you should not commit murder).
Prosecutor Like the adult criminal court prosecutor, the juvenile prosecutor's primary duty is not to prosecute, but to ensure justice. There is, however, a serious issue as to what "justice" means in juvenile proceedings. The prosecutor must protect the interest of the state and/or jurisdiction by creating a more-balanced system, instilling due process of the law, and should present evidence at a juvenile hearing in a fair and impartial manner.
Protective orders The court that can issue a child or juvenile protective order (also known as a restraining order) varies in different states. In most states they are issued by the family or domestic court, primarily to protect the child or juvenile. The court can order a person to have no contact, or limited contact, with the victim or victim's children, or to leave the home and stay away for a certain period. If a person violates the protective order, that person can be arrested.
Psychoanalytic theory is based on Sigmund Freud's concepts and social learning theories.
Psychological approaches to delinquency causation contend that criminal misconduct originates primarily in the personalities of the delinquent.
Psychopath is a term used by psychiatrists—along with *sociopath* and *antisocial personality*—to describe individuals who exhibit a certain group of behaviors and attitudes.
Public defender An attorney who works for the state and has the duty of defending indigent defendants.
Pyknic body type The pyknic type person has a round body and is fat and fleshy.
Radical criminology is based on the economic determinism theses of Karl Marx. Both Marx and Friedrich Engels contended that delinquency and economic conditions were linked. Marx based his delinquent causation theory on the conflict between the material forces of production and the social relations to production.
Ranches These nonsecure residential programs provide services to youth in rural settings. Typically, the residents participate in a structured program of education, recreation, and facility maintenance, including responsibility for the physical plant and its equipment and livestock.
Rape Penetration, no matter how slight, of the vagina or anus with any body part or object, or oral penetration by a sex organ of another person, without the consent of the victim.
Rational choice theory states that criminal behavior is no different from noncriminal behavior in that it is conduct that persons intentionally choose to undertake (i.e., they are not compelled or forced to commit a crime). The rational choice theory is a modified and updated version of the classical school of thought.
Reasonable doubt The burden of proof that is required before a defendant may

be convicted of a crime. The burden is on the prosecution to prove a fact with a high degree of certainty.

Reasonable suspicion A suspicion based on facts or circumstances which by themselves do not give rise to the probable cause requisite to justify a lawful arrest, but which give rise to more than a bare suspicion—that is, a suspicion that is reasonable as opposed to imaginary or purely conjectural—a suspicion based on facts that would cause a reasonable person to conclude that criminal activity is ongoing or has occurred.

Rebuttal evidence Evidence to rebut or negate evidence presented by the other party.

Reception/diagnostic centers These centers are used in many jurisdictions as the initial residential facility for youths. After spending a short period of time in one of these centers, the juvenile is usually moved to a more-permanent residential placement.

Redirect examination The examination by the party who called the witness to cover matters that were covered in the cross-examination.

Rehabilitated The conclusion that a defendant has reformed.

Release on own recognizance Release of a defendant without bail upon his or her promise to appear at all appropriate times, sometimes referred to as "personal recognizance."

Residential contract programs Any residential placement contracted by the department for services to committed juvenile. Programs include (but are not limited to) group homes, group care agencies, and foster care homes.

Restitution A court order to repay the victim of a crime.

Restorative justice is a process that seeks to repair the harm caused by crime by involving the entire community in rehabilitating offenders and holding them accountable for their behavior.

Revocation (of parole) The youth hearing officer's administrative decision (after a due process hearing) to revoke the juvenile's conditional liberty due to a probable cause determination that he/she has violated the conditions of release.

Right to bail An adult criminal defendant has the right to have a bail hearing if he or she is detained prior to trial. There does not appear to be a similar right for juveniles.

Right to speedy trial In all US jurisdictions, juveniles are provided the right to a speedy hearing.

Roper v. Simmons This case, decided by the US Supreme Court in 2005, held that the death penalty could not be imposed on individuals who were under the age of eighteen when the crime was committed.

School resource officers (SROs) Uniformed, armed police officers who are assigned to work directly in schools. The SRO's duties involve a combination of law enforcement, teaching, and mentoring. Their law enforcement duties include investigating criminal complaints and ensuring the safety of the school by patrolling the school grounds.

School-to-prison pipeline Based on the concept that students who are disciplined in their schools are also more likely to end up in the juvenile justice system. The term is often used to describe a path through the education system for mostly racial minority and at-risk students.

Sealing of juvenile records The records of a juvenile are generally sealed from the public. The Juvenile Law Center defines "sealing" as the mechanism for limiting access to juvenile records. In most states a court judge may order the records unsealed. Some states limit which records may be sealed or expunged based on the age of the youth or the seriousness of the crime.

Search A governmental intrusion into an area where a person has a reasonable expectation of privacy.

Search warrant A written order, in the name of the state or municipality, signed by a judge or magistrate authorized by law to issue search warrants, directed to any law enforcement officer, commanding him or her to search for personal property, and, if found, to bring it before the issuing judge or magistrate.

Seattle Youth Violence Prevention Initiative (SYVPI) was launched in 2009 as a partnership between the City of Seattle and several community-based organizations designed to reduce youth violence in Seattle, keep young people out of trouble, and get them back in school. SYVPI focuses on youths ages twelve to seventeen who are at the highest risk of committing or being victimized by violence.

Seizure Taking any person or thing or obtaining information by an officer pursuant to a search or under other color of authority.

Sex offender A juvenile whose primary or secondary conviction is for a sexual offense or who has a history of sex offenses.

Shock probation In many adult criminal courts, the trial judges will use "shock probation" for youthful offenders who are tried as adults. Generally, it is not used in juvenile courts. In these cases, the judge grants probation only after the accused has sampled prison life. Shock probation is designed to give defendants a "taste of the bars" before placing them on probation.

Social bond theories Travis Hirschi is given credit for developing the social bond theory of delinquency. He concluded that delinquent behavior was caused by a lack of social attachments. He later modified his ideas and renamed his theory the self-control theory of crime, which holds that misconduct is committed because of the available opportunity and lack of self-control on the part of the delinquent.

Social contract theory of governmental power Social contract theorists contend that the state or royalty receive their authority to govern based on an implied contract that the people of a given area agree to live by. In this implied contract the citizens agree upon rules or laws to live by in return for the state's protection.

Social control theories These are also described as socialization theories. According to social control theorists, the process of socialization is the dominant method by which groups control individuals. Social control theorists hold that people's relationships, commitments, values, norms, and beliefs encourage them not to break the law. Accordingly, if a person's moral codes are internalized and the individual has accepted them, and he or she has a stake in the wider community, he or she will voluntarily limit the propensity to commit deviant acts.

Social development model is a general theory of antisocial behavior developed by researchers attempting to explain key elements of a career in criminal misconduct by studying its onset and persistence.

Social disorganization theory developed from the Chicago School, and concluded that delinquency is closely related to the process of invasion, dominance, and succession. According to the theory, when a neighborhood is invaded by new residents, established relationships that bonded people together are destroyed and the natural organization of the neighborhood is severely impaired. This condition creates a state of social disorganization. Because the neighborhood is in transition, the residents no longer identify with it and thus do not care as much about its appearance or reputation.

Social learning theory is based on the concept that new behaviors can be acquired by observing and imitating others. According to the theory, learning is a cognitive process that takes place in a social context and can occur purely through observation or by direct instruction, even in the absence of motor reproduction or direct reinforcement.

Social norm A basic sociological concept that is used to explain human behavior. Norms have also been referred to as "rules of conduct." They are also seen as blueprints for behavior.

Social structural perspective is the idea that human behavior is more than a matter of choice or personal characteristics.

Social structural theorists believe that you need to look at the dynamics of social status, relationships, and institutions, such as the economy, polity, family, and education in order to understand the concentration of crime in disadvantaged urban communities.

Socialization refers to the learning process by which a person becomes part of a social group and learns the group's norms.

Status offender is a juvenile who has committed at least one activity that is deemed offensive when committed by juveniles, because of their age at the time of the activity. The offensive act would not be a crime if committed by an adult. Common status offenses include truancy, possession and consumption of alcohol, curfew violations, failure to attend school, and purchase of cigarettes.

Status offenses involve misconduct by a juvenile that would generally not be considered an offense if the offender was an adult.

Statutory rape laws criminalize adults for having sex with underage minors.

Stop and frisk is the act of stopping a person for investigative purposes and frisking him or her for the presence of a weapon.

Strain theories are based on the principle that when an individual does not conform to society's norms and laws it is because there are excessive pressures or strains placed on the individual which cause the misconduct.

Subcultural theories developed from the Chicago School and symbolic interaction theories. Subcultural theorists contend that certain groups or subcultures in society have values and attitudes that are conducive to crime and violence.

Subpoena Order issued by the clerk of the court in which a criminal proceeding is pending at any time for witnesses required by any party for attendance at trial and at hearings, for taking depositions, or for any other lawful purpose.

Subpoena duces tecum A subpoena of a witness that also orders the witness to bring certain documents to court.

Summons An order issued by a judicial officer or, pursuant to the authorization of a judicial officer, by the clerk of a court, requiring a person against whom a criminal charge has been filed to appear in a designated court at a specified date and time.

Symbolic interaction (SI) was coined by George Herbert Bloomer in 1937. Bloomer focused on situations and interactions with society that lead up to the delinquent behavior rather than the differences or defectiveness of the delinquent. The basic positions of SI are that people act toward things based on the meanings that things have for them, and the meanings that things have are derived from social interaction with others.

Symbolic interaction (SI) theories of delinquent causation examine the influence of an individual's associations with peers, family, and other social units on the individual.

Teen courts make use of peer juries to decide nonserious delinquency cases.

Temporary detention A brief investigative detention.

Termination of parental rights The parental rights over a child may be involuntarily terminated when specific circumstances are present under which the child cannot be returned safely home because of risk of harm by the parent or the inability of the parent to provide for the child's basic needs. The specific circumstances vary for each state.

Terrible twos Mothers will tell you that two-year-old children are very unruly. While this is probably correct, most children outgrow early problem behaviors. The ones who do not outgrow such behaviors are of concern because of the increased risk that they may become child delinquents.

***Terry*-type stop** A detention that will ordinarily be for a short duration and that will be no longer than necessary to effectuate the purpose of the detention; an investigative stop by an officer to determine if criminal activity is ongoing.

Thinking pattern theories are psychological theories focused on the delinquent's cognitive processes. The two most popular thinking pattern theories are cognitive development theories and the criminal personality.

Tinker v. Des Moines Independent Community School A US Supreme Court decision stating that students have freedom of speech unless it disrupts the operation of the school.

Training schools The general focus of training schools is to provide care, treatment, and custody for juveniles committed by the courts and to create programs that will rehabilitate young offenders.

Trait theory holds that youths engage in delinquent or criminal behavior due to aberrant physical or psychological traits that govern their behavioral choices; delinquent actions are impulsive or instinctual rather than rational choices.

Transfer hearings occur prior to the adjudicatory hearing to determine whether juvenile court should retain jurisdiction or if juvenile should be waived and transferred to adult criminal court.

Truancy is generally considered any unexcused or unverified absence from school. Since states enact their own school attendance laws, the legal definition of truancy may vary from state to state.

United Nations Standards on Juvenile Justice These standards are commonly referred to as "The Beijing Rules." The UN General Assembly called upon member states (nations) to adapt, wherever this is necessary, their national legislation, policies, and practices, particularly in training juvenile justice personnel, to the Beijing Rules, and to bring them to the attention of relevant authorities and the public.

United Nations World Youth Report The United Nations publishes a World Youth Report on various subjects involving children.

Venue The geographic location of a court.

Verdict A judgment by the court; in a criminal court, it refers to the finding of guilty or not guilty.

Vernonia School District 47J v. Acton In this case, the US Supreme Court upheld the constitutionality of a random drug-testing regimen implemented by the local public schools in Vernonia, Oregon.

Victim A person against whom a criminal offense has allegedly been committed, or the spouse, parent, lawful representative, or child of someone killed or incapacitated by the alleged criminal offense, except where the spouse, parent, lawful representative, or child is also the accused.

Victim impact statements Statements which victims or victim representatives are permitted to submit for court consideration at sentencing time.

Waived to adult criminal court Cases that are transferred from a juvenile court to an adult criminal court as the result of a waiver hearing in juvenile court.

Waiver of juvenile court jurisdiction In all jurisdictions, juvenile court judges may waive juvenile court jurisdiction in certain cases and transfer jurisdiction to adult criminal court so the juvenile can be tried as an adult.

Writ of habeas corpus A writ issued by a court requesting that the person detaining another person produce the prisoner and establish that the confinement is legal.

Youth gangs The phrase *youth gangs* is ambiguous and without a clear-cut distinction; a general reference to gangs often implies youth gangs (also called street gangs). In some cases, youth gangs are distinguished from other types of gangs.

Youth hearing officer A staff member of the due process proceedings office who has received special instruction to ensure continual safeguarding of the due process rights of juveniles during hearings; e.g., conditional liberty (parole) suspension, conditional liberty (parole) revocation, and conditional liberty (parole) reinstatement.

Zero-tolerance policy means that a school has zero tolerance for any kind of misbehavior or violation of school rules, no matter how minor, unintentional, or subjectively defined it may be.

Index

www.ingramcontent.com/pod-product-compliance
Ingram Content Group UK Ltd.
Pitfield, Milton Keynes, MK11 3LW, UK
UKHW051417150926
475561UK00005B/215